Periods of European Literature

EDITED BY
PROFESSOR SAINTSBURY

XII.

THE LATER NINETEENTH CENTURY

PERIODS OF EUROPEAN LITERATURE.

EDITED BY PROFESSOR SAINTSBURY.

A COMPLETE AND CONTINUOUS HISTORY OF THE SUBJECT.

In 12 Crown 8vo Volumes.   Price 5s. net each.

---

*" The criticism which alone can much help us for the future
is a criticism which regards Europe as being, for intellectual
and spiritual purposes, one great confederation, bound to a joint
action and working to a common result."*

—Matthew Arnold.

WILLIAM BLACKWOOD & SONS, Edinburgh and London.

THE
LATER NINETEENTH CENTURY

BY

GEORGE SAINTSBURY, M.A.

PROFESSOR OF RHETORIC AND ENGLISH LITERATURE IN THE
UNIVERSITY OF EDINBURGH

WILLIAM BLACKWOOD AND SONS
EDINBURGH AND LONDON
MCMVII

800

PREFACE.

In arranging the last volume of this *History of European Literature*, it may not be improper to supply that part of a possible *general* preface which, for more reasons than one, could not be given in the first as it actually appeared. I have seen, during the earlier course of the publication, remarks—perhaps natural, if not entirely reasonable—expressing dissatisfaction with the irregular order of the appearance of the volumes, and the jagged outline—as of tallies with one-half wanting—which was in some cases presented. A little thought might, I think, have shown the critics that this, if not unavoidable, was by far the least of two or more evils; and a slight sketch of the history of the undertaking may make it clearer.

About a dozen years ago, circumstances having made my hands, which had been very busy, comparatively idle for some time before my appointment to the Chair I now hold, Mr Blackwood kindly asked me whether I had any literary schemes. Accordingly I laid before him two of those which I had long

cherished, but which were practically out of the
question in the constantly broken leisure, and the
never-for-any-long-time-interrupted occupations, of
journalism. These were the interconnected projects
of a *History of [Modern] European Literature* and
a *History of Criticism*, both Ancient and Modern,
the two being in my own design intended to work
together, and to supply treatises, one of which practically did not exist at all, while the other only
existed in the excellent but necessarily incomplete,
and in some respects really antiquated, work of
Hallam. Mr Blackwood expressed approval of both
schemes; and after some discussion it was agreed
that I should execute the *History of Criticism* "off
my own bat," the *History of Literature* in the co-
operative or collaborative manner, but according to
a general scheme devised by myself, and so as to
make it not merely a series but a book.

I knew that the labour saved in appearance by
this latter proceeding would, according to the general
principle of compensation, have to be paid for with
other coin than that of the realm; and that part of
the payment would be misconception and disappointment at the apparent irregularity above referred to.
I was, however, perfectly certain that to attempt to
get the whole "copy" of the book in hand, before
issuing any of it, would only lead to far worse disappointment; and that to count on contributors being
ready to step into their places, at a regular interval
of no matter what length, was altogether to miscalcu-
late the nature of literary man. Had I done the

first, it is probable that not a volume would have yet appeared; and had I done the second, that I should myself be in a madhouse or in my grave,—*sic melius situs* perhaps, but that is another question. Moreover, though it was clear that the last volume ought to appear last, it was by no means so clear that the first ought to appear first, or (to me at least) that any other need necessarily come in its numerical place. If the periods had been at first carelessly or too generally divided, or if the contributors had been invited to go, or had insisted on going, as they pleased, disaster might have resulted. But I had sketched the "tallyings" of the whole jointed-map pretty accurately from the first, and I cannot too heartily express my thanks to my friends for the amiability with which they have followed my lines and leadership. Even some Continental and American critics have been good enough to recognise in the result an attempt, original and meritorious if not wholly successful, to exhibit European literature from the comparative point of view. And I am sure that if, as I should have liked to do, I had begun the work at thirty instead of at fifty, and had been able to devote the whole of my time to it, I never could have carried out my own plan more satisfactorily even to myself than these friends have carried it out for me; while for others the satisfaction is no doubt much greater. Indeed, the slight differences of appreciation and point of view, subordinated as they are to a general scheme, are a distinct gain.

The repartition was originally designed with all the

care that I could muster; and it has at least justified
itself by not proving absolutely unworkable. My first
principle was to cut the slices so as to include distinct
compartments with real contents. Few will question
this as regards the Dark Ages; the great Mediæval
period; the Renaissance; the Augustan Ages (though
one reviewer did ask plaintively whether the Age
of Shakespeare was not an Augustan Age?); the
Romantic Revolt and Triumph,—while the subject of
the present volume prescribed itself in time. And
though some have objected to "The Transition" as
a *rifiuto*, I do not think they were always the persons best acquainted with the subject. The "First
Half of the Seventeenth Century" and "The Mid-
Eighteenth Century" may look more accidental. But
they are not really so, for the dying of the Renaissance dolphin with its hectic colours, and the substitution of Thought the raven for Hope the swallow,
are too characteristic of the first, as is "the reign of
prose and sense" in the second, not to supply sufficient differences.

But having divided, I had to unite, where it was
possible and necessary, by as it were *mortising* certain
periods; and this seemed specially desirable in regard
to the mediæval drama, and to the palmy days of
Spanish and of Dutch literature. So far from this
arrangement being a drawback, it seems to me to
have positive advantages. As to the minor fittings—
innumerable as they are—I need not trouble the
reader; nor as to the pains that they imposed on
me as editor. But I must again express my grati-

tude to the contributors for the invariable kindness
with which they have met my requests for dove-
tailing and keying - on. At any rate, the whole,
whatever may be its faults, has been planned as a
whole from the beginning, and executed as a whole
to the end. In so vast a scheme there must be
flaws and dropped stitches. I know some individual
writers whom I myself miss; and I am prepared for
the charge that we have been unjust to the minor
countries—to Portugal perhaps most of all. But it
is difficult to do everything; and we have done what
we could. If we have not dealt (as some would have
had us deal) with everything that literature is about,
as well as with literature, I do not think we are much
the worse for it.

The volume which follows necessarily differs, in
more than a single point, from most, if not all, of its
predecessors. There is, in the first place, the onerous
obligation, not merely as in the former cases to sum
up with a "Pisgah-sight" of literature in the different
countries for the period, but to out-Pisgah Pisgah and
re-"survey with" more "extensive view" the survey
of those periods themselves. It may well seem to
some that this is too ambitious an enterprise—that it
wants the means, and tempts the fate, not merely of
Moses but of Icarus. But it seems to me that the
scheme would be incomplete without it—nay, that a
person who was afraid of it had no business to under-
take that scheme at all. And so, with all invocation
of the Muses and all deprecation to Nemesis, I shall
yet dare the attempt.

Another condition of difficulty is the further increase of a general disability, which has rested in
increasing measure upon every writer in the successive volumes of the book. We have contracted
our range from more than half a millennium in the
first volume to little more than half a century in
the last; and yet this contraction, as everybody can
apprehend at once, has not kept pace, and could not
possibly keep pace, with the growth of material. In
all the later volumes, and in this more than any
of them, it has been necessary to omit much, to
take much by representation and in sample, to deal
summarily even with consummate examples. And
in this, as in the volume immediately preceding it,[1]
this necessity is made more awkward by an increasing familiarity on the part of the reader both with
the subjects that are and the subjects that are not
dealt with. I cannot hope to enjoy many readers
who will be so sweetly reasonable as to take my
estimate of the room allottable to this country, this
department, this writer, as the right one. I can
only say that I have used the best of my judgment
in the matter—bad as that best may be, or at least
seem.

The revival of some literatures which had made
little show for a time, and the actual entrance of
some which had hardly before been admitted, as
Hoffähig in European literature, made another aggra-

---

[1] Which, partly owing to the accidents of the subject, but also by
design, to give more room here for the Conclusion, contains not a
little work belonging to us.

vation of the difficulty; but there was only one
rational way of overcoming this. In the earlier
volumes of this series which I have myself written,
as well as in all other works of literary history in
which I have been engaged, I have sedulously
eschewed translations. Here, in the case of Russian,
of Norwegian, and of some other divisions, I have
not hesitated to use them as the foundation—with
this due warning—of even a critical judgment. And
I do this with the less hesitation, inasmuch as it is
perfectly notorious that the extremest Ibsenomania or
Tolstoyolatry is compatible with an inability, at least
as complete as mine, to read a single sentence of
Russian, or to do more than spell out Norse. What
I have said of translation I may also say of second-
hand knowledge, not derived even from translation
itself. There is not very much of this in the book;
but there is necessarily some.

One anomaly may (or must) strike careful readers;
and I shall confess it as such at once. The objection
to mentioning living persons in a general history of
literature, or of anything else, is with me most sincere
and most strong. But it applies chiefly to our own
countrymen; and with less and less force to foreign
countries which have more and more distant intercourse with ours. The distinction is not an idle
one; it is simply the other good old rule of "present
company" transposed into a new set of conditions.
Moreover, it so happens that in some literatures of
Europe, owing to causes political and miscellaneous
as well as purely literary, a very distinct fresh start

was made in the fourth quarter of the century, after
something of a stationary state in the third.   In
Germany, for instance, the limitation, though it would
have given us Nietzsche, would have left us hardly
anybody else who had not been already mentioned
in Mr Omond's volume; and so elsewhere.   While
to pass from places to influences, it would have been
impossible to complete the quartette or quadrilateral
of Zola-Ibsen-Nietzsche-Tolstoi, which is so remarkable, with its most agreeable and not its least important angle; or to show how the influences themselves have worked abroad, where a very large part
of the actual literary product is due to them, while
with us it has been very much smaller, and in real
importance less even in proportion to its bulk.   It
will be found, therefore, that in English only one
or two living persons, and those of the highest and
longest standing, are so much as named; in French
few, but only a few, more; while in the other
countries the etiquette has not been allowed to effect
exclusion of anybody who seemed to the writer proper
to be mentioned for the purpose concerned.   And if
this inconsistency offends any one I shall be sorry;
but I cannot pretend to be very penitent.

In conclusion, I hope it may not be impertinent
or nauseating to say a very few more words about
the general purpose of this *History of European
Literature*—which will, I trust, some day drop the
" Periods " necessitated by the scheme of its appearance and challenge its proper position as that " New
Hallam " which was announced in its prospectus.

Some have described these volumes as "school-books," and others have been good enough to call them a "popular series." We certainly must have attained a pretty high state of culture as a nation if they are either one or the other. It was, indeed, the editor's hope in planning the book originally, and is still now as he takes leave of it, that it may be of the greatest value to students, whether in the highest forms of schools, in universities, or in subsequent and private pursuit of knowledge. He would also have much liked to think that people might take the volumes home from the library instead of novels or travels. But what they were chiefly planned to do was to supply intelligent possessors of larger and smaller collections of literature with something like an atlas or dictionary of the subject, aiming rather at the connection and *ensemble* of the atlas than at the scrappiness and broken lights of the dictionary. In so far as they do this, they will have achieved their main object: it would be a pity to think it an object out of, or above, practical book-politics.[1]

[1] Most of the contributors to the earlier volumes have been good enough to give me some assistance in this by proof-reading. And outside our own circle I owe special thanks to Mr Edgar Prestage for the contribution inserted and acknowledged in its proper place, as well as to Dr K. Breul and one or two others for help of various kinds.

EDINBURGH, *Midsummer Day*, 1907.

CONTENTS.

CHAPTER I.

ENGLISH AND FRENCH POETRY.

CHAPTER II.

ENGLISH AND FRENCH—THE DOMINATION OF THE NOVEL.

CHAPTER III.

ENGLISH AND FRENCH—PERIODICAL LITERATURE—CRITICISM AND ESSAY-WRITING.

CHAPTER IV.

ENGLISH AND FRENCH—THE OLDER PROSE KINDS—DRAMA.

CHAPTER V.

GERMAN LITERATURE.

CHAPTER VI.

THE SOUTHERN LITERATURES.

CHAPTER VII.

THE NEW CANDIDATES.

CONCLUSION.

I.

OF THE PRESENT VOLUME.

II.

OF THE WHOLE MATTER.

THE LATER NINETEENTH CENTURY.

CHAPTER I.

ENGLISH AND FRENCH POETRY.

THE SUBJECT GROUPED ROUND TENNYSON AND HUGO—TENNYSON IN
1850—CHARACTERISTICS OF ENGLISH NINETEENTH-CENTURY POETRY
AS SHOWN IN HIM—HIS WORK IN THE PERIOD—"MAUD"—THE
"IDYLLS"—THE "BALLADS"—ADDITIONAL CHARACTERISTICS OF
THESE AND OTHERS—BROWNING—HIS PARTICULAR LINE OF
DEVELOPMENT—ITS MANIFESTATIONS—'MEN AND WOMEN'—THE
1863 COLLECTION—'DRAMATIS PERSONÆ'—'THE RING AND THE
BOOK,' AND ITS FOLLOWERS—MRS BROWNING—APPARENT DIVERG-
ENCIES—THE SPASMODICS—MATTHEW ARNOLD—"PRE-RAPHAELITE"
POETRY—ROSSETTI, MORRIS, AND SWINBURNE—THEIR CHARACTER-
ISTICS, ESPECIALLY METRICAL—THEIR SCHOOL AS YET UNSUCCEEDED
—OTHER PRINCIPAL FIGURES—CHRISTINA ROSSETTI, THOMSON,
O'SHAUGHNESSY—OTHERS: MINOR AND NOT SO MINOR—LIGHTER
POETRY—FRENCH POETRY: HUGO—THE SHOCK OF CIRCUMSTANCE—
ITS RESULT IN THE 'CHÂTIMENTS,' THE 'CONTEMPLATIONS,' AND
THE 'LÉGENDE'—THE MAGIC OF HUGO'S STYLE—OTHER AND LATER
WORK—HIS VIRTUE—THE "COMPANIONS": VIGNY, MUSSET, LAMAR-
TINE, GAUTIER—GÉRARD DE NERVAL—LAPRADE—LECONTE DE LISLE
—BANVILLE—BAUDELAIRE—THE "PARNASSIENS" AND THEIR RAMI-
FICATIONS—THE SECOND 'PARNASSE'—THE THIRD—VERLAINE—
INNOVATIONS IN PROSODY—NOTE ON PROVENÇAL REVIVAL.

THE familiar, and in a certain lower sense convenient, practice of labelling periods in literary

A

history by the names of great literary practitioners

The subject grouped round Tennyson and Hugo. has some sufficiently obvious drawbacks. But there is rather exceptional justification for it in the case of the subjects of this chapter,[1] though exactly the contrary may be not uncommonly found affirmed. There is no age of poetry—not even that of Pope, hardly even that of Chaucer's latest days and posthumous supremacy— which is the Age of X or of Y with such critical accuracy of title as the later nineteenth century is the Age of Tennyson in England, the Age of Victor Hugo in France. The angry or contemptuous rejoinder that

---

[1] The literature of monographs, which the necessary foreshortening of this volume makes more specially useful, is of course enormous in reference to this and the next chapters as far as individual writers or batches of them are concerned. But I do not know many general treatments besides those of Professor Hugh Walker in *The Age of Tennyson* (London, 1897) and my own *Nineteenth Century Literature* (London, 1896, third edition 1901), as far as English is concerned. For the French part, the portions appurtenant may be taken out of recent histories of French literature, especially those of M. Lanson, of the great collaborative History edited by M. Petit de Julleville, and the works of M. Emile Faguet, with which anybody may, if he chooses, compare the present writer's *Short History of French Literature* (sixth edition, Oxford, 1901) in its enlarged dealing with the special period. Professor Dowden's later work on the subject unfortunately stops at 1850, though of course it has some *prospection.* Those, however, who are really interested in this latter subject should not fail to consult, and may be strongly advised to possess themselves of, M. Catulle Mendès' *Le Mouvement Poétique Français de* 1867-1900 (Paris, 1903), which, besides a brilliant report on the special period and a preface going back to the origins of French poetry, contains an elaborate *Dictionary* of French poets for the whole nineteenth century. The very names of the French and English writers who have written books or essays bearing on the subject would occupy pages, and the shortest critical account of their criticisms a volume.

the one is a fogey to the young bloods of English verse, and the other a fossil to those of French, will leave the student of comparative and perpetual literary history entirely unruffled. He knows how these temporary occultations arise, how they begin, how they continue, and how, with an ineluctableness as great as that of their other stages, or greater, they end. And having in each case sufficient distance, focus, range found, to enable him to make those positive pronouncements from which he will wisely abstain in reference to things yet more nearly contemporary, he is able to lay it down that, while both poets had important and not to be slighted competitors of sometimes very different tendencies, the characters of English poetry which most generally and typically distinguish it from 1850 to 1900 are those most representatively found in Tennyson, and the corresponding characters of French poetry those found in Hugo. In arranging the contents of this chapter, therefore, we shall give most space to these leaders— for the space so given will actually save space in regard to most, if not all, of the others.[1]

At the point where we left Tennyson,[2] exactly at the division of the century, with the publication of

Tennyson in 1850. *In Memoriam,* it was open to others besides affectionate grumblers like Edward Fitz-Gerald to say that his work was in a sense done. It is even still possible to say so, emphasising the "in a sense." That is to say, nothing that he was to pro-

---

[1] See note on opposite page.
[2] V. *The Romantic Triumph,* chap. i.

duce, in the remaining forty-two years of his life, though by far the greater part of that production was to add immensely to the sum of poetic delight which he provided, was to give an entirely novel *kind* of delight. The very highest qualities of the *Idylls* were already manifested in the magnificent fragment of the *Morte d'Arthur*, which he had published years before. The best thing in *Maud*[1] had already seen the light. The experiments in dialect to come were mere curiosities. The Dramas, though it might be excessive to wish that he had never written them, neither obtained for him the position of a great dramatist, nor added to his reputation as a great poet. Nay—in consequence of his unhasting, unresting habit of composition, and his entire freedom, not merely from the necessity of throwing things raw upon the world, but from any inclination to do so—not a few of the most exquisite pieces that were to follow, *Tithonus*, *The Voyage*, many others, were already written. He was constantly adding to the volume, and in a certain sense to the variety, of his poetical achievements. The ambitious and imposing structure of the *Idylls*, the curious experiment of *Maud*, the fresh arrangement of the old mixed kinds in *Enoch Arden* (1864), the *Ballads* (1880), *Tiresias* (1885), *Demeter* (1889), and the posthumous *Death of Œnone* itself (1892), no sensible lover of poetry would dispense with, even in their weaker parts; while in their greater, to the very last, they could hold their own with all but the sprightliest runnings, the "Crême

---

[1] "Oh! that 'twere possible!"

de Tête," of the earlier vintages. Nor, in almost any case, are they mere recasts. No poet is less open than Tennyson to the charge of simply turning out plaster from a mould; in none is the touch of the actual chisel, the result of the fresh eye and hand, more perceptible.

But by 1850, though he had not yet made himself popular, the style and school of poetry which *Characteristics* he had thus fully exemplified, and the *of English nine-* enjoyment of which he had taught first *teenth-century* to few, then to many, was the style *poetry as shown* *in him.* and school of nineteenth century poetry proper in England. The rudiments, the scattered principles and precepts, of this style and school had of course been contributed, as is always the case, much earlier. Coleridge had upheld, illustrated, caused, the "poetic suspension of disbelief" as to matter, and had more than heralded that great return to the glorious syllabic liberty of true English prosody, Tennyson's own further extension of which he was in his later days to misunderstand after a fashion so human, if so melancholy. Wordsworth had unlocked the vast "cabinet of quintessence" which contains the nepenthe of Nature. Southey, Scott, Byron, had directed the seeker for Subjects to elder times and foreign countries. Above all, acting chiefly on the Coleridgean inspiration, direct or indirect, Shelley and Keats in their different ways had revived, had almost re-created, the taste for poetry as poetry,—for poetry in which the treatment altogether overpowered the subject. And Keats, the youngest of the great Seven, the nearest in birth to the actual nineteenth century itself, though the first to die in it, had given further grouping, arrangement, tactic, to the forces of nineteenth century poetry itself, by the intensity and concentration of his appeal to visual sensation on the one hand, and to verbal music on the other.

The first point as characteristic of the new poetry could, of course, escape no one. It was noticed, in regard to one of the very earliest utterances of that poetry, by no less a person than William Pitt, in the naïf but important observation that in *The Lay of the Last Minstrel* he saw effects which would not have surprised him in painting, but which he never could have expected in poetry. In other words, Johnson's edict, fifty years earlier, that the poet is not "to paint the streaks of the tulip," has been antiquated already, and is, in such poems as *The Eve of St Agnes*, to be antiquated still further.

The second process—the substitution, for the comparatively rudimentary sound-studies of eighteenth century and even of older poetry, of an elaborate *accompaniment* of vowel- and consonant-music, almost dispensing with a regular setting of notes—was rather more slowly achieved by the poets, and very much more slowly understood by the readers. The mere ear had been so dulled and brutalised by the rasp and rattle of the couplet, that men could not at once apprehend more intricate and poetical music; while the theory of fixed pause and syllabic uniformity still had many adherents. On the very eve of the be-

ginning of our half-century, in the year 1849, a most
courteous, unusually intelligent, and in part admiring
reviewer of Tennyson's own poems up to that date,
expressed horror at the "cacophony" of the exquisite
song—

"A spirit haunts the year's last hours,"

and of many other of the poet's early experiments in
true English prosody.

In the work of our period proper, Tennyson had
no new instruments, of equal importance with these,
His work in to bring into play; nor did he very
the period. materially alter the general system of
employing them in poems rather short than long,
and when long, for the most part broken up,—devoted to subjects chosen from the widest possible
range of literature, history, geography, manners,
thought, emotion,—flouting, as it were, the old distribution of poetry into Kinds — and being epic,
elegiac, lyric, didactic, descriptive, and what not,
all by turns and all at once. But he had to illustrate his methods and exhibit his instruments anew;
and by the new exhibitions and illustrations to introduce fresh neophytes to the already instituted
mysteries. His first considerable work as Laureate
—for the "Wellington" Ode (1852), good as it is,
is not extensive — caused great searchings of heart
at the time. There was always in Tennyson—though
he never condescended to the silliness about poetry
"dropping the exhausted past" which Mr Arnold
was smiting just at this very moment—an attention
and sensitiveness to current thought and taste rather

remarkable in a poet who, in some ways, was very much of a recluse. He never really shut himself in a *tour d'ivoire* like Vigny — in fact, some of his admirers may think that he might have done so with advantage occasionally. *Maud* (1855) is full, and at first was even fuller, of very local and temporary things—the megrims and mopings of the "discouraged generation of 1850," the progress- and perfectibility-mania which so oddly accompanied these, the excitement of the Crimean War and of the earlier Continental revolutions—nay, something of the actual "spasmodic" measles itself. An attempt, too, to introduce, if only sketchily, modern manners and types into the characters of his half-told story was not happy, nor were some of the metrical experiments—especially, as ill-luck would have it, those of the opening. Yet the best things in the poem are so numerous and so consummately exquisite that no one, except the singular persons who would refuse apples of gold unless they were presented in pictures of silver, could resist them. And then (1859) came the *Idylls*.

Maud.

To say that the *Idylls* made Tennyson popular, would be to say a true thing in an inaccurate way. To say that the *Idylls* came just at the time when the popular taste had been educated (as far as it could be) up to the poet's level, and that the book set his work in an accessible and inviting condition for the general, would be quite accurate. And it is not inaccurate to say that the connection thus established, not merely between

The Idylls.

popular taste and Tennyson, but between Tennyson and the general historical current of English poetry, has never been broken. The very revolters and re-vilers to this moment show symptoms of his influence; while all who are not revolters and revilers give de-velopments—sometimes with much that is original and additional—of his forms, his diction, his metre, and his general poetic method. Of that method

The Ballads. itself the *Ballads* of 1880 gave probably the most remarkable single example as a book among his later work; but no non-dramatic piece, and no large part even of the dramas, was in any proper sense inferior. Almost any volume would suffice to give an intelligent student a notion of what Tennyson's poetry was, and what—to the great extent in which it was representative thereof—was the poetry of the English nineteenth century.

To what has been said above as to the two chief means of appeal of this poetry to the mind's eye,

Additional characteristics of these and others. and directly to the ear, with suggestion through it to the mind, there can be no necessity to add much here.[1] But on some other points a little more may be said, much

---

[1] Quotation and example are, as a rule, impossible. But there are two lines of the famous swan-song, *Crossing the Bar*, which illustrate this double appeal too triumphantly to be omitted—

" With such a tide as moving seems asleep,
    Too full for sound or foam "—

where *both* senses are hit, with perfect ease and effect, though with a minimum of effort and in a bare baker's dozen of words, after a fashion which would be difficult for the painter and all but impossible for the musician to equal.

of which will apply to French and, indeed, to other
European poetry during the time. The coming
forward of the Novel has relieved the poet of the
necessity of telling a story—of the bondage of the
Matter—and has allowed him to concentrate himself
on the treatment; while the immense and ever-increasing *curiosity*, as to the past and the foreign in time
and place, has provided him with increasingly various
subjects in so far as he requires them. But perhaps
none of these three alteratives, powerful as the effect
of each is, is more remarkable than the fourth, provided by the removal of the bondage of the Kind.
Except Catullus, it is difficult to think of any ancient
poet the miscellaneous character of whose work cor-
responds to that which we are accustomed to see;
and though from the Renaissance onward "Miscellanies" became more and more frequent, they
never, even to the extreme end of the eighteenth
century, became the rule. Even as they tended to
become so, you had titles of plain confession, "Miscellany Poems" or the like, "Poems on Several
Occasions" and the like again. That you need not
lodge the *in forma pauperis* plea of "Miscellany"—
that there need be no "Occasion" beyond your own
inclination, reading, or what not—had been a position
never openly admitted, and one which, if formally
advanced, would have pretty certainly met with the
staunchest and sternest critical opposition from neo-
classic stalwarts. That in the intervals of your
tragedies, your epics, your volumes of odes and the
like, you might sheaf incidental oddments, could be

granted as a licence; but you had to earn it by regular service in a recognised regiment unless you wished to be regarded as a mere irregular.

This etiquette, which had been obsolescent even before his time, Tennyson wholly ignored. The three collections which represented his poetic appeal for nearly twenty years were simply "Poems," though the first betrays a consciousness of the older custom in the addition "chiefly Lyrical." It would be scarcely too much to say that they were *all* lyrical, in that wider and better sense of the word which regards lyric as an expression, first of all, of the writer's emotion, interest, impression, thought, rather than as an attempt to convey a definite story, a formal argument, or any other such matter to the reader. The growth of this phase or aspect of poetry had indeed been remarkable, and for hundreds of years almost regular. It had shown itself in the breaking down of the romances into ballads; it had received an enormous impetus from the invention and diffusion of the romance in the other sense, the sonnet, and above all the French artificial forms. But it had only now definitely got the upper hand. Even in those of Tennyson's later books, which affected more unity and more adherence to Kind, the affectation was greater than the reality. *The Princess* has the most unity of all; but even in *The Princess,* not very strongly knit at first, the author found the necessity of unknitting it still more, and improving it most of all, by the inserted lyrics. *In Memoriam,* deep and pervading as may be its unity of mood, has none of action; and a great number of its most beautiful sections could be, and in thought very often are, dissociated from their context without the slightest loss. Almost as much might be said of *Maud ;* the title-piece in *Enoch Arden*, and the other constituent of length and " subject "—*Aylmer's Field* —are far inferior to such smaller pieces as *The Voyage* and *In the Valley of Cauterets*. And while the *Idylls* certainly did not gain as a whole by the attempt to make them into an epic of Arthur, they have, even in their entirety, scarcely more than the faintest epic character. Even that *epyllic* condition which Professor Lushington would have kindly imparted to them, though it may help their popular, by no means equally helps their poetic, interest. That this multiple, atomic, *myrioramic* style of poetry is intrinsically superior to the old substantive or structural kind, it is not necessary here to argue. It has the advantage, according to what has been called the " doctrine of the Poetic Moment." But how great an exponent Tennyson was of it, how numerous are his moments, how exquisite is their pleasure, how various, how inexhaustible, this hardly requires argument at all.

The curve of the record of Tennyson's greatest English craftsfellow during the period was less dissimilar in fact than in appearance. With *Browning.* him also it was quite possible to say that just as Tennyson only varied and repeated his claims after *In Memoriam*, so did Browning after *Christmas Eve and Easter Day* (1850), which appeared in the same year. *Paracelsus* had shown these claims more decidedly than *Pauline*. *Strafford* and *Sordello* had emphasised them rather doubtfully. *Bells and Pomegranates*, in its various divisions, had made them plain for any who would—though very few did will—to see. And now the longer single poem exhibited them in the particular application which was to take up most of the rest of the poet's nearly forty years of remaining life—the curious, intensely idiosyncratic, but by degrees more and more popular, "boxing about" of some subject, character, incident, thought, from a succession of different points of view.

In the larger poetical classification Browning, as critics seem to be at last beginning to see, is less *His particular* opposite to Tennyson than complementary *line of develop-* of him. There is really very little to *ment.* choose between the two in the three great points above defined—the appeal to the mind's eye, the appeal to the actual ear, and the promiscuous preference (if the paradox be allowable) of a vast number of subjects drawn from all literature and history, and of forms adapted at the moment rather than taken from a registered pattern-book. It is quite true that Browning frequently—not always—prefers discord to elaborate harmony as a means of arresting the ear; that his pictures are strongly outlined, high-lighted, and filled with separate and almost splashy detail, instead of being finished like the illuminations of a manuscript; that in choosing subjects he pays greater attention to striking historic incident, problematic clash of character and motive,

to variety, vividness, bustle. But these are only
" diversities of operations." The general spirit in
these three great functions is just the same as Tennyson's, and just as different from that common to poets
of any preceding century.

His general appeal, however, though certain, when
answered at all, to be answered with a heat and hurry
Its manifest- of sudden enthusiasm, was made in far less
ations. generally intelligible language than Tennyson's; and the actual reply was postponed for some
twenty years longer. Indeed, for a time the poet
seemed rather to slacken his efforts to make himself
heard. Whether first the happiness of his marriage,
and secondly the unhappiness of his widowerhood,
had anything to do with this silence and its breach,
is a question not for us; but as a matter of fact he
published nothing of importance between *Christmas
Eve* itself in 1850 and *Dramatis Personæ* in 1864
except *Men and Women* (1855). An examination of
Men and this exception itself, however, should have
Women. shown any one, and probably did show a
good many people, that there was no case of a burnt-
out volcano here. Perhaps, as has been said, *Men and
Women* does not show anything absolutely new in
gift after *Bells and Pomegranates*, after *Christmas Eve*.
But it shows the old gifts combined, intensified, re-
directed. The rearrangement of the *Works* in the
last collected edition has rather obscured the fact that
the original two volumes contained perhaps an actual
majority of his greatest things—" Love among the
Ruins," "A Toccata of Galuppi's," "Mesmerism,"

"Childe Roland," "The Last Ride Together"—a dozen others.

Such things could not but sink into any receptive mind; but the poet gave them plenty of time to produce their effect, and then, before issuing any new book, collected his by this time copious verse into the three-volume edition of 1863, and followed it *The* 1863 up immediately with the new *Dramatis Collection.* *Personæ* in the next year. If this arrangement was a piece of skilful calculation, he deserves credit as a man of business. If it was the result of a happy accident, Fors Fortuna is not such a spiteful goddess as some will have her to be. The collected works brought home to thousands of readers who had only dimly heard of Browning the richness of a new poetical inheritance; and they had no sooner begun to ask why he who had given so much gave no more than the "more" came, after a fashion unusually acceptable and triumphant. It is not improbable that the final criticism, which has not yet been reached, will pronounce *Dramatis Personæ* the last book of Dramatis Browning's greatest period. It is not a Personæ. big book, but in it he exemplifies at the very best that "Miscellany" method of the century which has been dwelt upon. Among nearly a score of pieces there is hardly one—"May and Death," the possible exception, would be a great thing for some poets — which is not masterly. The opening piece, "James Lee" (which was afterwards rather unfortunately altered in title to "James Lee's Wife"), "Too Late," "Abt Vogler," "Rabbi Ben Ezra," "Caliban upon

Setebos," "Confessions," "A Likeness," and "The Epilogue," are all consummate in their special kinds. In some, notably "A Likeness" and "Mr Sludge," the poet gives his fancy for audacious *bravura* in conceit, diction, rhyme, the fullest play; but he never (as he did afterwards) caricatures himself. And throughout the book we have the infinitely comfortable spectacle of an expression that can give utterance to anything that it wishes to express, fed by a thought which never leaves it at a loss for something worth expressing. Those who were capable of understanding and relishing English poetry between 1858 and 1870 had such chances as no dozen years in the history even of that poetry have ever much bettered. But even in these years no greater book appeared than *Dramatis Personæ*. And not the least attractive point in it is that it is almost the last book in which the author gave free play to that extraordinary metrical faculty which was long mistaken, which he certainly allowed to play a kind of high-jinks with itself at times, but in which he has had few superiors. In the books which succeeded, during the last twenty years of his life, he used—not quite exclusively but mainly—the extremely free blank verse which he had indeed practised from the first, and which is, of course, the easiest, and perhaps the most suitable, vehicle for the kind of utterance which he was chiefly to affect.

It was undoubtedly the first of these, *The Ring and the Book* (1868), which actually made him popular, though not very many students in the future, who came across it without knowing the context of time and

circumstance, would ever believe in its popularity.
It is, in fact, an experiment, on a scale
almost gigantic, in that process of "boxing
it about" which has been described above.
An actual old Italian story of domestic crime is presented, after the poet's fashion of dramatic mono-
logue, by most of the actors and persons concerned in
or with it, and by the poet himself, each practically
telling the whole story over again from his or her own
point of view. This—in less or more complication,
though never again in such complication as here, and
applied sometimes to individual characters or incidents, and sometimes to groups—was the staple of
Browning's production for the rest of his life, during
which he was regarded with an ever-increasing fanaticism, fostered by Browning Societies and private
coterie readings, and encouraged by the poet himself
in a fashion rather unusual with Englishmen. He
undoubtedly tended during part of the period, and in
not a few of the books, towards self-caricature, and
towards a tedious multiplication of unimportant
matter. But he never wholly lost his power; and
in his very last book, *Asolando* (1889), in which (as
in one or two others he had partly done) he returned
to the better "miscellany" style, he is not so very far
below even *Dramatis Personæ*, even *Men and Women*.

The less valuable part of this very voluminous later
production has made his entire work top-heavy to an
extent which, on the analogy of similar cases in the
past, may seem rather dangerous; and it is certain
that a reader, beginning on *Prince Hohenstiel-*

The Ring and the Book, and its followers.

B

Schwangau (1871), or *Redcotton Night-cap Country* (1873), or *The Inn Album* (1875) in another century, or perhaps another decade or two, would be very likely to decide that this poet was not for him. But the root of the matter is so strong in Browning, and the flowers which it sent up all through his career so numerous, so various, so brightly and variously coloured and shaped, and at their best so rare and exquisitely scented, that he can never miss very much of his deserts.

If his production rather lessened during the time of his marriage, his wife's increased. At least four important volumes — *Casa Guidi Windows*

Mrs Browning.

(1851), *Aurora Leigh* (1856-57), *Poems before Congress* (1860), and the posthumous *Poems*, which were issued a year after her death in 1861—belong to our period. They are, however, rather important for her special discourser than for the general literary historian. The first and third contain a great deal of crude *Italomania*—an amiable but tedious disease, the extinction of which has been a mercy. *Aurora Leigh* is a verse-novel,—a kind which was rather largely practised in the middle of the century, and the last notable example of which was the *Glenaveril* (1885) of the second Lord Lytton, but not a good kind, inasmuch as the practitioner generally seeks relief from the necessities of the novelist in the licence of the poet, and *vice versa*. The posthumous poems contain some good things, especially the beautiful "Great God Pan"; and the whole production is noticeable for the evident influence of the husband in restraining or

reforming the worst faults of his wife's maiden work,
—her appalling false rhymes (which good nature in
vain endeavours to defend as assonances, since they are
rather worse as assonances than as rhymes), her gush,
her mislocutions. For Browning's locutions, like his
rhymes, are often violent, but never false. On the
whole, however, ample justice has been done to this
"great poetess and almost great poet" (as she was once
described) in the last volume. She is not really a
representative of the later nineteenth century in any
way, but only of the decadence of the earlier. One
might regard her work with greater affection if it had
not helped to fix a stigma on Romanticism, and to
encourage an entirely wrong idea of the Romantic
tradition and its fate. Although by no means always,
Mrs Browning too often showed traces of that Romanticism which early went acid or rancid: the true
variety has kept and mellowed to the present day.

It is no surrender but a support of the position that
Tennyson—or rather the tendency in poetry which
Apparent Tennyson represents—marks the dominant
divergencies. of English nineteenth century poetry
throughout, to admit, or rather cheerfully to lay down,
that tendencies partly divergent, and in some cases
intentionally if not really contrary, showed themselves
almost before his was thoroughly and generally recognised—at least as soon as it was. For this is the
rule rather than the exception, especially in rather
artificial and very "literary" periods. The first noteworthy appearances of these a little anticipated or
almost immediately followed 1850, and were repre-

sented by the first poems of Matthew Arnold (1822-1888) on the one hand, and by the so-called "Spas-modics"—Sydney Dobell (1824-1874), Alexander Smith (1830-1867), the late Mr P. J. Bailey (1816-1905), and minors scarcely worth noticing, to some extent.   Nor need this latter school itself re-ceive much attention.   Sydney Dobell (*The Roman*, 1850; *Balder*, 1854; *England in Time of War*, 1856; and other things) had, in a loose, incalculable, un-satisfactory fashion, nearly as much poetic quality as his greatest panegyrists have assigned to him, though his possession of it was far more uncertain than they would admit; the author of *A Life Drama* (1852), ridiculously praised at first, has been unintelligently undervalued since; and *Festus* (1836) had at least its day of popularity.   But all three, and all the rest, are emphatically *crude*.   It has been said that Tennyson, with that universal sensitiveness to the current which helped him to his representative character, is a Spas-modic, though never a mere Spasmodic, in *Maud;* and the worst parts of that remarkable book show the kind at its best.   It is a kind of which, for once, ridicule *is* a test; and it was well and duly killed by the *Firmilian* (1854) of Aytoun (1813-1865).   It was yeasty and frothy; its victims ran the risk of being what one of themselves frankly calls "ginger-beer bottles burst"; it seldom yielded liquor much stronger, more generous, with more of the divineness of vinosity, than ginger-beer itself.   But wherever there is fermentation, there is at least the possibility of spirit.   Meanwhile, its members were as often close

The Spasmodics.

to Tennyson as they were far from him: they were
even sometimes accused of plagiarism. And, to keep
up the metaphor, they might have been described in
a good old word as "stummed" Tennyson—wine that
had gone flat and stale, and was trying to refresh
itself by heady new must of a coarser vintage.

There is nothing coarse or heady about Mr Arnold's
poetry (*The Strayed Reveller*, 1849; *Empedocles*, 1852;

Matthew Arnold. Poems, 1853, 1855, 1867); and there can
be no question that he set himself, with
more or less deliberation, against the manner and
method of Tennyson, of whom, though he was
decently reticent in public, his private judgments
were always uncomplimentary and unappreciative.
Yet all his work, and especially the earliest, is full
of Tennysonian reminiscences; and even where there
is most divergence we always feel dimly the suck of
the current out of which our boatman is trying to pull
us. Further, Mr Arnold is frankly in that current in
respect of his adoption of what we have called the
"Miscellany" style. His theories of poetry would
seem likely to have pointed him directly to the "long
poem"—the considerable, though carefully concentrated, action of the ancients and the seventeenth
century; yet he never attempted it. His anti- or
extra-Tennysonianism shows itself, however, strongly
in regard to the two appeals so often mentioned in
this context, and still more obviously, though as a
matter of consequence, in metre and diction and
rhyme. He does not—he cannot with Keats and
Tennyson himself behind him—entirely neglect

the increased appeals to eye and ear; but he seldom
lays himself out for them, and in particular hardly
ever indulges in that pure poetry of sound which, if
it is not independent of meaning altogether, permits
and half encourages the reader to let the meaning go
its own way and to go *his* own with the music.

He seems positively to dislike rhyme—a dislike
which, from the cases of Campion, and Milton, and
Collins, we cannot necessarily attribute to a sense of
his inability to master it, but which in his case was
not quite unconnected therewith. And he is not satisfied with blank verse, or with Campion's or Collins's
unrhymed stanzas, or with the unrhymed Pindarics of
Sayers and Southey. He tries (probably after Heine,
who had not himself invented it, but who did it consummately) the plan—to which German lends itself
not ill, but of which English is very impatient—
of breaking up blank verse itself into short fragments,
the breakages being purposely made so as to develop
trochaic rather than iambic rhythm. Anapæsts he
very rarely affects, and hardly ever with success, his
tendency being in the same way to break them up
into that (in English) most dangerous and difficult
foot, the amphibrach. His blank verse itself is
always good, and at its very best admirable; but
it is an extremely sober and ascetic sample of the
metre, rejecting the varied pause and free syllabic
equivalence by which Tennyson was refashioning the
medium. But it is in his diction, perhaps, that the
revolt from Tennyson (save when he adopts a phrase
unintentionally) and the falling back on Wordsworth

are most perceptible. He either cannot attain or will
not attempt the many-coloured gorgeousness or delicacy, the many-voiced harmonies in major and minor
keys of Keats, and Shelley, and Tennyson himself.
In one of his less short poems (a great favourite with
some critics), *Balder Dead*, he affects a sort of savage
simplicity; in some of his shorter pieces a Words-
worthian commonness. Whether in all cases he very
strictly carries out his own critical principles (*v. infra*,
chap. iii.) as to the importance of the worthy action
and the like, may not be quite so certain. But he
does evidently endeavour throughout to infuse, and
succeeds not ill in infusing, a peculiar serious under-
tone, a running "criticism of life," which is melancholy without being exactly despairing. And very
often, probably most often, without any reference to
any theory at all, he writes admirable and delightful
poetry, whereof we would fain have much more than
we possess. After the publication of his first book in
1849 he lived nearly forty years; but almost all his
poetry was written in the first twenty, and the larger
and better part of this in the first ten.

The Spasmodics were but a failure of a school; and
though Mr Arnold expresses a distinct tendency, or
group of tendencies, and has exercised
"Pre-Raphaelite" influence up to the present day, he can
poetry. hardly be said to have founded one. But,
in a decade more, a real school, an actual stage
further—though only a stage further—than Tennyson, came into being. In the words of the loveliest
of all carols, it came "all so still as dew in April, that

falleth on grass and spray and flower." Hardly anybody paid the least attention to *The Defence of Guene-*
vere and Other Poems, by William Morris
Rossetti,
Morris, and
Swinburne.
(1834 - 1896), when it appeared in the
year 1858, dedicated to Dante Gabriel
Rossetti (1828-1882), a name known only to the
comparatively few who did know it as one of the
most characteristic of the little band of "pre-
Raphaelite" painters who had for some time been
ruffling the decencies and dulnesses of English art.
A year or so later (1860) came a couple of most un-
theatrical dramas, *The Queen Mother* and *Rosamond*,
by Algernon Charles Swinburne (*b.* 1837), dedicated
to the same person. Of this the "irresponsible,
indolent reviewers" of the time took even less notice
than of the other. Yet, if any had had eyes to see,
there was here, especially in the first-named book,
something sightworthy ; and, what is more, something
which ought rather to have impressed the sight as more
novel and original than it actually was, than to have
passed as trivial and negligible. The selection of subjects was in the first book intensely and exclusively
mediæval ; in the second, mediæval with a dash of
sixteenth century ; and the diction of both was a
very remarkable archaised English, rather fifteenth
century than anything else, and presenting the closest
relation to Malory's *Morte d'Arthur*, but handled (with
individual differences in each case) in a fashion which
made it nothing so little as *pastiche*. But more remarkable than subject or mere diction was the general
style, and, so to speak, *facture*, of the poetry. This

aimed rather at giving things and thoughts mediæval
as they recreated themselves under the influence of
nineteenth-century thought than at strict antiquarian
revival. It combined itself with a very strong infusion
of Elizabethan "conceit," with a singular mystical
passion found before in English only in some seventeenth-century writers, and with at least *quantum suff.*
of originality, both individual and *scholastic*, to complete the mixture. These characteristics had been
illustrated earlier in two not widely circulated periodicals—*The Germ*, which appeared in our very year
1850, and *The Oxford and Cambridge Magazine* a little
later. In both of these men would have found work
by the dedicatee himself, and in *The Germ* his famous
"Blessed Damozel"—the proclamation, as it were, of
the new school, which, not merely from the position of
its eldest member in painting, but from a real analogy
and kinship between this *pictura* and this *poesis*, has
received the name of "pre-Raphaelite."

A still further inquiry, supposing there to have
been any one competent to perform it,—but Mr
Arnold would not have cared, and Mr Pater and
others were too young,—would have shown that the
originality, though very considerable, was relative,
and that the new singers were quite legitimate and
representative descendants of Keats through Tennyson. Still, they had really started a new stage of this
descent; and, in another decade or a little more, Mr
Swinburne had far excelled his early venture by the
successive publication, during the three years 1864-66,
of *Atalanta in Calydon, Chastelard,* and the *Poems and*

Ballads. Mr Morris had, if not excelled — he never
did excel—the best things in *The Defence,* varied his
appeal into longer strains and more popular tone in
The Life and Death of Jason (1866), and *The Earthly
Paradise* (1868-70). And at last, the inspirer, after
a fashion, of both, and the man who fished this new
murex up, had broken his long silence in the *Poems,*
by Dante Gabriel Rossetti, of 1870, which were followed ten years later by another volume; while Mr
Morris made additions to *his* list in *Love is Enough*
(1872), *Sigurd the Volsung* (1876), and *Poems by the Way*
(1891). Very seldom have three poets helped each
other in such a singular fashion by exhibiting the same
general conception of poetry, applied with the utmost
individuality of taste and quality. Mr Morris, after
his first predilection for Froissart and Malory, turned
to Scandinavian, classical, and other literature, and
developed a faculty of verse-narrative unsurpassed
since Scott, producing also, latterly, a kind of saga-
romance in prose. Mr Swinburne, the most cosmopolitan of the three, was by preference, if anything,
Greek and French; Rossetti [1] was the first English
poet since the seventeenth century to give the real
Italian sentiment of his Italian blood in the language
of his English country. We must not dwell on the
individual documents of their craftsmanship, more's
the pity. But from "The Blessed Damozel" herself

[1] Rossetti was, like Sainte-Beuve, a quarter-Englishman. The
devotees of the race and *milieu* theory might employ themselves
worse than in comparing the result of three-quarter French blood
born and brought up in France, and three-quarter Italian born
and brought up in England.

to "Rose Mary," and from "Rapunzel" to "Meeting in Winter," not to mention that most plenteous harvest which is not yet gathered in, there is nothing but pleasure for the lover of poetry.

The very strong pictorial element in all three, and in all their followers (who for some years crammed the *Their characteristics, especially metrical.* courts of minor poetry to suffocation, and still are not unfrequent there), has been of course set down to Rossetti's professsion, and to the fact that Morris himself was a painter *manqué,* and a decorator born. It would be absurd to deny all influence to these facts; but the characteristic was in all probability in much larger degree merely an intensifying of the tendencies described above, and already shown by their father Tennyson and their grandfather Keats. For the musical appeal developed equally; and none of the three (so far as is known to the present writer) had any professional connection with music. But this last was helped by the special metrical gifts of all. Mr Morris, at first a master of singularly weird and haunting melody, dropped these Æolian strains later for metres always excellently modelled but more suitable for narrative than the eery notes of *The Wind* and *The Blue Closet.* Rossetti, supreme in the sonnet, is hardly less supreme in any slow measure that he chooses to adopt, and very seldom tries fast ones. As for Mr Swinburne, prosody has no difficulties that he cannot master. He can be excellent in slow measures, though his extreme fluency is rather a danger to him there. But at high velocities he has no rival. If the simile of the conjurer were not supposed (why, one does not quite know) to be degrading, no other could be so suitable for his absolute command of metres of any intricacy, velocity, variety, moment, and length.

There are those who would represent this movement in poetry as exhausted, just as there were those who

Their school as yet un-succeeded. represented Tennyson's as exhausted thirty or forty years ago. This is probably, as that was certainly, a mistake. One of the halts, or apparent refluxes, which so often occur in literature has indeed been observable in the verse of the last ten or fifteen years of the nineteenth century and later. Restless or ambitious persons have in some instances—not entirely without success—endeavoured to struggle against both, very much after the manner in which Mr Arnold struggled against the first. They have gone back to Mr Arnold himself, or, farther, to his master, Wordsworth, for a sort of poetical quietism; they have decried, as much as they could, the poetry of tapestry and painted window, the poetry of inarticulate music accompanying the articulate. Others have even revived, after himself or his other master Heine, the Arnoldian rhymelessness; others again have cultivated—with very considerable success at times—looser, more popular, less elaborately artistic strains, depending largely on adjustment to events of the moment or moods of the hour. We have had "Celtic Renascences"—anticipated, by the way, and given for far more than they are worth any-where else, by Tennyson himself in *The Voyage of Maeldune;* "Decadences"; sentimentalities and anti-sentimentalities; all sorts of "'nesses and 'tudes and 'ties," to borrow Hobbes's scornful phrase, differentiated occasionally by those popular triumphs of what is not poetical at all, of which the safe example in our period and the period before ours is Martin F. Tupper (1810-1889), but of which it would be possible to give instances much more recent and far more hopeless. But there has been no real new school of poetry since the pre-Raphaelite, and it is scarcely rash to doubt whether there soon will be any. There is no room for new schools of poetry in an age where every one reads, until some very new and very vigorous schoolmaster makes his appearance.

In the whole of such a book as this, but in these later volumes more especially, it becomes, as one has *Other principal* to remind the reader, impossible, and what *figures.* is more undesirable, to give a mere *compterendu* of the second-, much more of the third- and tenth-rate writers of the time. We have sketched in broad lines the main course of the river of poetry in England from 1850 to 1900. We shall endeavour in the conclusion to sketch the relations of these lines to the earlier meanderings. It only remains here to mention, with brief characterisations, some individuals remarkable for performance not of the second-rate kind. They were not numerous at the beginning,— the generation of 1850 scarcely won its way through the slough of "discouragement," even in the case of Mr Arnold; that slough caught and clutched and kept men like Arthur Hugh Clough (1819-1861), clogged the wings of men like the second Lord Lytton (1831-1891), tempted the Spasmodics into their forcible-feeble efforts to get clear of it. The pre-

Raphaelite movement had a healthier, or at least a less foiled and baffled, fringe. The exquisite genius of Christina Georgina Rossetti (1830-1894) gave us our greatest English poetess (for the rough and scanty essays of Emily Brontë and the sentimental slovenliness, half redeemed by better things, of Mrs Browning, cannot really stand in the comparison) with *Goblin Market* (1862) and *The Prince's Progress* (1866), and a hundred delightful things, from "Sleep at Sea" to "Heaven overarches sea and land." With less of the Paradise and more of the Purgatory, Arthur O'Shaughnessy (1844 - 1881) (*An Epic of Women* (1870), *Music and Moonlight* (1874)), and James Thomson the Second (1834-1882) (*The City of Dreadful Night* (1880)), displayed that strange faculty of producing great poetry without being exactly great poets which is almost a note of the nineteenth century, and had been struck first long before them by Beddoes. Probably some Sainte-Beuve of the future will group these three with at least one living poet to show what a real, though what a curiously constituted, spirit of poetry was abroad at the time, and what exquisite lyric at any rate it could utter.

At no other, perhaps, could this group (which as to the three named poets we can characterise without *Christina* difficulty) have existed; certainly at none *Rossetti,* *Thomson,* (unless we can suppose a pair of Pagan *O'Shaughnessy.* singers contemporary with Prudentius and exhibiting his characteristics, with the Pagan difference) is it easy to imagine one displaying such identity in diversity and such uniformity in variance. Miss Rossetti, a lady of ardent piety and delicate imagination, not devoid of passion and a sense of humour, and of wide interests in art and letters; Thomson, a plebeian, educated rather above his station, of recalcitrant and revolutionary temperament, combined with a strong aspiration for pleasure, of an eager and active, though not exactly wide or supple, intelligence, pessimist and nihilist to the core, it may be partly in consequence of untoward fortune and mischievous influences of companionship; O'Shaughnessy, equally unorthodox or not much less so, but not anarchic, vaguely optimistic till he too was attacked by misfortune, physical and mental, which he was not strong enough to bear, a Pagan of the " æsthetic " persuasion, a man of science by profession and of letters only by choice, with the facile music of his country elevated and ennobled by study and poetic ardour.   Yet all three come very close at times, and none ever goes very far apart from the others except under the influence of mere opinion and subject.   All in their different degrees—though Thomson probably had not by nature, and certainly did not acquire, the exquisite lyrical gift of Miss Rossetti and Mr O'Shaughnessy—were by nature what we have called lyric poets in the wide sense, affecting no elaborate structures of work, or succeeding little in them.   All in their several ways paint and play, on and in words, as much as they write, and that they may write.   All are full of the echoes of the past, if actuated by the temper of the present; " literary " to the tips of the fingers; affected for good or for ill irremediably by the printed book ; in no sense plagiaries or unoriginal, but reminiscent in their very original movements, and relative in their most absolute *aseity*.

For the reasons given in the Preface, and obvious enough if they had not been given at all, it seems *Others—minor and not so minor.* better not to attempt lists of minorities, even when the minority is strong enough to take the sting out of the injurious application of the word. Reference to monographs will easily supply the want, and these monographs themselves, even taken together, will not supply what this book at least attempts to give. The streaks of the minor tulips we must neglect with an almost neo-classic rigidity. Besides Clough and "Owen Meredith," the second Lord Lytton, above mentioned, the summits of these lower ranges are : Kingsley (1819-1875), not a copious poet, but a much better one than he usually receives credit for being ; Coventry Patmore (1823-1896), who, by an alteration of the same phrase, may be pronounced a much better poet than those who have been disgusted with the over-praise he has received from a coterie, may be inclined to believe ; Lord De Tabley (Mr Leicester Warren), 1835-95, to whom, after long and incomprehensible denial of recognition to a talent which had never "quite got itself free," some recognition came just before his death—are, perhaps, the best worth noticing.[1]   But if

[1] Since the passage above was first written the majority has gained, and England and his friends have lost, a very remarkable figure in Mr W. E. Henley (1849-1903). He published little, and did not (for

the "new Chalmers" (much sighed for by lovers of poetry [1] who are also regular students of literature) ever comes into existence, its later nineteenth century volumes will have something more than voluminousness to show and to urge. In diffusion of poetic talent this period probably exceeds any other except the so-called (and longer) Elizabethan, from 1580 to 1660; in the accumulation and crystallisation of that talent into genius by individuals, it only comes short of the same time certainly, and perhaps of its own predecessor from 1798 to 1850. In elaborate and various application of the Art of Poetry it is second to none, and indeed is not very likely to be soon supplanted.

One of its most interesting lower or applied varieties may perhaps deserve an appendix-paragraph of special mention. In the older and regular *Lighter poetry.* satire the period has not been very prolific or at all happy in its efforts; indeed the kind

a man who was a journalist half his life-time) perhaps even write very much. But the unique *In Hospital* of 1873-75 was followed by a sufficient number of pieces (*A Book of Verses*, 1888; *The Song of the Sword*, 1892; *Hawthorn and Lavender*, &c.) to establish his reputation in verse, and *Views and Reviews* gave at least samples of his critical powers; while his influence as editor and literary "class-leader" was extraordinary. Great physical (and some other) affliction, as well as the demands of journalism, undoubtedly affected his productiveness. But with those who knew him he will always keep the impression which he made of a "vein of genius,"—phrase cast about so often recklessly and falsely, but in his case fit to be used with the utmost critical exactitude.

[1] No ill succedaneum for it exists in Mr A. H. Miles's *Poets and Poetry of the* [19th] *Century*,—10 vols., London, *n.d.*,—which gives extracts only, but very full and instructive ones.

has generally been eschewed in English for nearly a
hundred years, and no one of our greater poets has
shown the aptitude for it which, for instance, Victor
Hugo, if he could have kept his temper and borrowed
a sense of humour, might have achieved, and by mere
rhetoric sometimes very nearly did achieve, in the
heavier kinds; or for the same kind of the lighter in
which Heine was a master. Tennyson had little
humour, and was ill at the weapon of wit. Browning,
with plenty of the first and not a little of the second,
was rather untrustworthy with the one, and, like
"Van, want*ed* grace" in the other; and so with the
rest. But in the kind or kinds of poetry which are
satirical without being exactly satire, or humorous
without any satirical tendency at all, except in so far
as the *ludicrum humani sæculi* is never far from the
writer or the reader, the age has been far from ill-
provided. Here, as elsewhere, it is still "literary";
it still owes a good deal—in the liberal sense which
involves no necessary payment but a due acknowledgment of the debt — not merely to the ancients
and to the foreigner, but to Prior and Praed, to the
Anti-Jacobin and *Rejected Addresses* and the *Two-
penny Postbag*. But once more, in accordance with its
own usual way, it has improved what it has borrowed
very fairly. Parody, that dubious, but at its best
extremely amusing and surely not reprehensible, deg-
radation of art, has been specially invited by some of
the manners and by almost all the mannerisms of the
time. Not *Rejected Addresses* themselves surpass, or
perhaps quite equal, the best exercises of parody by

more than one hand or dozen hands on Tennyson and Browning and Mr Swinburne. Mr Morris is not parodiable, though he can be caricatured; and only the "demon" in Mr H. D. Traill (1842 - 1900), as Matthew Arnold called it,[1] attempted Rossetti with much (and then with not very much) success. But the *Bon Gaultier Ballads* of Aytoun and Sir Theodore Martin (b. 1816), when our special period was still young (1855), were the forerunners of many merry and far from unwise things, which it may be hoped will continue to be produced, for "the land without a laugh" is a dismal place. Rather early two remarkably different writers, Edward Lear (1812-1888) and Charles Lutwidge Dodgson (1832-1898), took the bold step of obeying Hazlitt's wise glorification of "pure nonsense" by reintroducing it into literature, in much better guise than it had last worn in the French *Amphigouri* of the mid - eighteenth century. Mr Lear's *Nonsense Rhymes*, 1861, and other nonsense books, were comparatively simple. Mr Dodgson, "Lewis Carroll," a mathematician of eccentric genius, cast more widely and aimed higher, both in prose (*Alice in Wonderland*, 1865) and verse, and seems really likely to have attained the position of classic in his kind.

Notable work has also been done by the revival of what is called "verse of society." This, written by Prior with a consummateness never surpassed by

---

[1] By mistake, too, in the particular case, for I happen to know, both from Mr Traill himself and from the real author, that he did *not* parody Mr Arnold's "Poor Mathias" as its writer thought.

any Frenchman, and with touches of something that Frenchmen did not often, between the mid-seventeenth century and the early nineteenth, put into poetry, had been occasionally continued during the English eighteenth; but no poet had specially devoted himself to it. At the beginning of the nineteenth Praed paid particular attention to it, and after a certain interval the torch was held up by the late Mr Locker Lampson (1821-1895), and handed on to the living Mr Austin Dobson. He must be silence for us: but the kind invites a word of speech. It is not, at its best, mere *bric-à-brac;* it has a touch, a background, a finish (as the wine merchants say) of "high seriousness" behind its front, and face, and first flavour of pleasant trifling; and it gives particular opportunity to the elaboration of poetic medium, which has been specially characteristic of this century both in England and in France. Nor must we here omit Charles Stuart Calverley (1831-1884) (*Verses and Translations*, 1862, *Fly Leaves*, 1872), who worked up the old scholarly traditions of English public school and university education, after a fashion foreshadowed to some extent by the unequal and ill-starred Maginn, into pleasant union with burlesque; and James Kenneth Stephen (1859-1892) (*Lapsus Calami*, 1891), for whom could have been spared many of his survivors.[1]

[1] Two writers—one of them but very recently admitted to our majority—may find best place here together in a note, because, with some strong differences, there were numerous and remarkable points of resemblance between them. Both were Scotsmen ; both exhibited

Never, perhaps, was there a more curious contrast between the nearly contemporary careers of the two *French poetry —Hugo.* greatest poets of two neighbouring countries than that which our period saw between those of Tennyson and of Hugo. Both were still to be very long; both were to be unceasingly glorious. But whereas, as we have said, Tennyson had in 1850 practically lodged all the main diploma-pieces of his genius, and was thenceforward merely to increase the

that uncertainty between the two forms of *Dichtung*—novel-writing and poetry—which is more common in Germany than with us ; both had a somewhat unco-ordinated Romantic ambition, which never in the one instance, rarely in the other, found satisfactory organ or expression, and which was again German, rather than English, in the forms of expression which it took. Of these, Robert Buchanan (1841-97), the younger by a good many years, but the less gifted and the first to die, created a very strong prejudice against himself, alike by the substance and the manner of his attack on what he was pleased to call *The Fleshly School of Poetry* in 1871, and was always a sort of Ishmael in letters. He was critic (in the Ishmaelite fashion) as well as poet and novelist, dramatist (not so unsuccessfully) as well as critic ; but all his work was crude,—it never, save in a few pieces like the *Coruiskin Sonnets* and one or two others, reached anything like the true point of "projection." Of much greater genius, and with no blot on his reputation, but also the author of much imperfect to little perfect work, was George Macdonald (1824-1905). His numerous novels (from *David Elginbrod*, 1862, onward) display no small power ; but his literary fame rests, and probably always will rest, on two books—*Phantastes* (1858) and *The Portent* (1864). The latter is a prose story of the semi-supernatural kind, wonderfully impressive, and complete in its incompleteness. The former, much more unequal, but rising higher still, is a prose *märchen* with abundant verse insets, including the immortal lines—

"Alas ! how easily things go wrong"—

and others not less beautiful. It should have been pruned, or rather lopped and topped unmercifully ; but its opening part is unique in English.

volume and variety of its manifestations, if Victor
Hugo had died in that year, and nothing of his but
what he had published had been known, only the
affectionate exaggeration of partisans could even have
divined—and the sober judgment of criticism could
certainly not have endorsed the divination—how great
a poet he really was. Not only had his Muse for
some ten years been nearly silent, but it is impossible to say that even in the finest things of the
earlier books, from the *Odes et Ballades* to *Les Rayons
et les Ombres*, except, perhaps, in "Gastibelza," and
less certainly in

     "Mais tu ne prendras pas Demain à l'Eternel !"

the full virtue of the Hugonic style — the most
rhetorical of all styles that are poetry, the most
poetical of all styles that are rhetoric — had been
revealed.

     The revelation at last was due to one of those
soul-catastrophes which ruin the faculties as often
The shock of as they stimulate them; but of which the
circumstance. stimulation, when the shock takes that
form, far surpasses any other. It is impossible
here—for it may be still necessary to remind some
readers that this *Literary History of Europe* does
not pretend to be a history of European politics or
of European philosophy, or a biographical dictionary
of the lives of celebrated men — to recount or to
moralise on the possible nature and the curious
history of the shock itself; but the fact of it—
when Hugo found himself an exile at the founda-

tion of the Second Empire—is beyond dispute. The
first literary result, the pamphlet of *Napoléon le
Petit* (1852), was not reassuring; and there was
much in Hugo's first return to poetry, the *Châtiments*
of 1853, which was entirely lacking in dignity, and
deserved the description of mere splenetic raving
and foaming at the mouth.

But there was also much else; and no one, unless
as much blinded by political or personal frenzy as
Its result in the Hugo himself, could fail to perceive it in
Châtiments, the the little book which appeared, not quite
Contempla-
tions, and the complete, in Brussels, and unmutilated
Légende. with "Genève et New York" on the title-
page, but printed at Jersey, shortly afterwards. Even
those who like Bonapartism as little as Republican-
ism, and who are quite sure that both, bad or
good, make themselves worse by gnashing and yell-
ing in place of argument, must yet see everywhere
here the evidence of the poet's old luxuriance of
expression having returned to him, informed by an
infinitely higher poetical intensity. Sometimes the
pure poetic treatment, the divine inspiration of the
Muse, masters the lower intention, the "common
subject," altogether; and then we get "Le Chant de
Ceux qui vont sur la Mer" and the "Chasseur
Noir." The astounding thing about this latter—the
thing that makes it one of the greatest poems of
the century — is that the mere partisan fury, the
questionable opinion, is actually there, but is trans-
figured, "vanished," burnt up by the fire from the
altar, so that even those who would willingly see

all the republics in the world perish rather than that one hair should fall from the head of a legitimate king, may feel every fibre in heart and soul thrill like the wood-leaves themselves under the breath of this incomparable spirit of poetry. But even where this wind is not strong enough to chase the political miasma before it,—even where the fire cannot quite burn the rubbish and ordure of partisanship,—both wind and fire are almost always present, always *in potentia* if not *in essentia*, unmistakable to those who know such things when they feel them.

The promise was more than fulfilled by the *Contemplations* (1856) and by the first part of the *Légende des Siècles* (1859), when the poet's wrath, though still supplying energy, had settled from its first chaotic ferment and tempestuous bluster. Both are collections of the miscellaneous kind which has been characterised at some length above in the notice of Tennyson, their titles indicating with sufficient accuracy that the one is more introspective, the other more descriptive and external. The *Légende*, in fact, ranks with the very greatest books in French verse, and not far below the greatest in the verse of any country. The variety and brilliancy of its successive pictures cannot be too highly praised; and it perhaps, as a whole, presents Hugo's peculiar poetic style at its most accomplished and best *The magic of* sustained point. The power of this style *Hugo's style.* is extraordinary, and almost as hard to analyse as the power of other intoxicating agents.

For Hugo's effect is directly and distinctly *intoxicating*. It touches the reason hardly at all; its appeal to the imagination proper, though existent, is rather vague and elemental. But as a stimulant of poetical emotion the very greatest styles are not its superiors. It is not always, though it very often is, a rushing mighty wind: it is nearly as often quite a still small voice. There are few things more different than Gastibelza's

> "Le vent qui vient de la montagne
>   Me rendra fou";

and the refrain of the *Chasseur Noir*—

> "Les feuilles du bois, du vent remuées,
>   Sifflent : on dirait
> Qu'un sabbat nocturne emplit de huées
>   Toute la forêt ;
> Dans une clairière au sein des nuées
>   La lune apparaît";

and that couplet of the far later *Quatre Vents de l'Ésprit* (1882), which I remember citing[1] as absolutely characteristic when it first appeared, and to which certain excellent judges have given their votes since,—the couplet in the great Cavalcade of the Statues—

> "Et la Seine fuyait avec un triste bruit
> Sous ce grand chevalier du gouffre et de la nuit."

But different as they are, they all have that immediate and magical effect on the senses of the mind — that direct touch of the poetic nerve—

---

[1] In the *Fortnightly Review* for 1882.

which is perhaps the best, if it be not the only, criterion of pure poetry.[1]

Hugo's return upon prose fiction (see next chapter) was probably one of those signs, often given by *Other and later work.* nature, of a climacteric change. He wrote much more poetry,—indeed he wrote it to the last, and never with any distinct "dotage,"—but except in the best things of *Les Quatre Vents de l'Esprit,* he never quite recovered the trumpet-tones of his three great books in the 'fifties. In *Les Chansons des Rues et des Bois* (1865) he endeavoured to be in the main light and good-humoured (scarcely with very marked success), and the fresh shock which prompted the *Année Terrible* (1872) had an effect very different from that of the first, eighteen years

---

[1] Perhaps the Hugonic quality is nowhere better shown than in the great posthumous miscellany, *Toute la Lyre* (1888). One might think this likely to be a mere rubbish-heap in the case of a man who had reached almost the utmost limits of life, who had published dozens of volumes of verse, and who, to speak frankly, was quite man of business enough to turn over his poetical capital as soon and as often as he could. Yet in these more than 750 pages and nearly 30,000 lines,—written at all ages from twenty to eighty,—though they may contain nothing of the author's very greatest, his characteristic *quality*, his unfailing power of poetical stimulus, is omnipresent. He may be as questionable as elsewhere,—in one place he calls Mérimée *flat*, a platitude being about as possible to the author of *Colomba* as a bad verse to the author of the *Châtiments*. He may be more often trivial. But we can never read more than a few lines without the inevitable result. *Accipimus solitam flammam;* and we are once more at the mercy of the Muse. And there is another thing, which is indeed common to him with most of the great poets, but eminently present. When you read Victor Hugo after, say, twenty years, it is at once as if you were reading him for the first time, and as if you had read him yesterday.

earlier.   With one or two fine pieces, and several
fine passages, the book is as a whole quite unworthy
of him,—egotistic to senility if not anility, out of all
focus and proportion, bombastic, scolding.   Of its
followers during the fifteen years in which, returning
to Paris from those Channel Islands which had been
at once his Patmos and his Parnassus, he became a
sort of living idol till his death in 1885, only one,
twice mentioned already, fully redeems the declension.   But there are some magnificent things here;
and there are magnificent things also of a quasi-
poetic kind in a prose fruit of his sojourn in "the
little isle"—the characteristic and curious book on
William Shakespeare (1864).   Victor Hugo never
would learn, perhaps never could have learnt, enough
English to appreciate Shakespeare's poetry thoroughly,
and much of the book is rhapsody of a kind as often
silly as it is grandiose.   But he had obtained *tant
bien que mal* a very fair idea of those sides of Shakespeare's greatness which slope nearest to his own.
And that real grandeur—not mere grandiosity—of
expression which, let them say what they will, accompanies him unweariedly, and very often throws
its mantle over all sorts of smallnesses, finds not
unfrequent opportunity under the benign influence
of the Angel of the Sea.   It is rather curious that
Hugo, when he was at his best, was almost always
writing by the sea; and that when he wrote in Paris
or Brussels he was very frequently at his worst.

But at worst, as at best, Hugo never lacks greatness—which indeed those who have for the last two

decades depreciated, or affected to depreciate, him also
do not lack, though in another category.[1]

His virtue.

He is not only by far the greatest poet
of France, but he is the first poet who, in his own
words, gave France *toute la lyre*. Before him, at
least since the sixteenth century, there had been
a constant and an increasing tendency to shirk
singing for the sake of saying, — a tendency the
natural result of which was that the singing voice
was lost. With Hugo it once more became vocal.
That he strained it, that he threw it into falsetto,
that he set to it things ignoble, trivial, bombastic,
prosaic in themselves; that in his revolt from Boileau
he forbade Boileau's idol of good sense not only to
stand in the place where it should not, but also to
occupy its legitimate and desirable haunts, may be
and is perfectly true. But if he had intended—as
he certainly did not—to confirm by this his practice,
his theory that "nothing depends on the subject,"[2]
he could not have done more happily. He is always
a poet, even where not merely sense and truth, but
taste, good feeling, every good quality almost that
can be named except poetry, have left him. But
Poetry never leaves him. We may sometimes —
nay, very often — wonder why she stays, how she
can endure the bad company, and, in later days, the
sometimes dull company, that she is forced to endure.

[1] I do not refer to those who, like Planche, object to poetry which
appeals less to the mind's mind than to the mind's senses. I think
them wrong, but not despicable.

[2] See the Preface of *Les Orientales*.

But there is, perhaps, no poet of the greater clans who is such a useful study for the purpose of separating poetry from other things commonly found with her, and often thought to be inseparable from her. Nay, there have been some who said, and very sincerely thought, that this Ruth not merely went with him wherever he went, but, as far as France was concerned, died and was buried with him when and where he died. This may be too pessimistic: according to all literary history it is—for poetry, if ever there was one, is a Phœnix. But with whom in France the "sole Arabian bird" has once more set up housekeeping, there are some who do not know.

The older and greater contemporaries of Hugo were dealt with in the last volume; and though some of *The "Companions"— Vigny, Musset, Lamartine, Gautier.* them lived almost as long as he did, or at any rate far into our own period, they hardly altered their position as poets. The last seven years of Musset's life (which for once cannot be called too short) were silent, and matter only for silence. Vigny, who survived for another seven, allowed a pessimistic quietism to benumb him almost as much, — though some few fine notes were occasionally heard from the jealously closed *tour d'ivoire*, and have gained him, from those who do not consider poetry as poetry, additional fame. Lamartine lived till 1869, that eve of the catastrophe which, with its successor the Terrible Year itself, saw (by a strange coincidence, if such things there be) the extinction of so many of the great lights of the first period. Sainte - Beuve (1869), Mérimée (1870), Dumas (1870), had long been dead to poetry. Only Gautier (*d.* 1872), whose finest poetic volume—*Émaux et Camées* (1852, more fully 1858 and later)—appeared actually after the beginning of our half century, occasionally though rarely relieved his "tale of bricks"—bricks more durable than some marble—of prose, with verse never inferior; but for the most part did other and lower work, always with that inviolable conscience of art which would redeem not merely peccadillos such as his, but sins such as his were never. He waits, putting aside altogether the ludicrous belittling which the generation of dwarfs who have followed him in his own country have sometimes indulged in, for his due reward of fame, till the day of "Comparative Literature"[1] has at last reached more than its dawn. But an intermediate generation, sometimes very remarkable, had already made some beginnings—to a large extent under the inspiration of Gautier himself, —and with still younger men who came a little before the dwarf period, were to form the last definite school, corresponding to our own pre - Raphaelites, that French poetry has yet known. For Symbolists, Decadents, and the rest of the still later tickets, are mere names like our own earlier Spasmodics. They signify in reality nothing of any lasting power at any time, and nothing that counts for all time at all.

[1] The phrase is ugly, and in fact not English ; but "Comparative *Study of* Literature," the proper one, is rather long.

Some names which were dealt with very briefly in the last volume under the head of minor poetry *Gérard de Nerval.* fall to be noticed again here,—partly because their owners saw something of the latter part of the century, partly also because they were not poets merely, or even perhaps mainly. The greatest of them from the literary point of view was Gérard de Nerval, whose short and troubled life was ended in 1855 by a mysterious death—generally called suicide, but asserted by those who knew him best to be more probably the work of the human wild beasts who haunt all great cities at night, and who more particularly infested Paris till the Commune a few years later first attracted their support, and then performed the involuntary service to humanity of getting rid of them for the time.

Interesting as Gérard's verse is, his prose-poetry is more interesting. His *Voyage en Orient* (1848-50) —one of the many written at no great distance of time by men of talent and genius—has its own special place among these,—making up by its dreamy poetry and strange pathos without mere sentimentality for the absence of the rhetoric of Chateaubriand and Lamartine, the metallic brilliancy of Kinglake, the curiously natural vividness of Eliot Warburton, and the humorous many-sidedness of Thackeray. This dream-quality is more evident still in his *Filles du Feu*—at least, in the better of them. *Aurélia*, his last book, written partly in madness and interrupted by violent death, is one of the most pathetic books of

the world for fit readers, though not for the general
in any way; while in *La Bohême Galante* and *Les
Faux Saulniers* the dream-character takes a more
cheerful quality.   Gérard is never merely grotesque.[1]

Most of these descend from Hugo or from Gautier,
not without a considerable touch of Musset.   But one
Laprade. of the eldest represents Lamartine very
strongly, and one of the youngest Vigny.
The former of these, M. Victor de Laprade (1812-1887),
was not more than a decade younger than Hugo
himself, and only a year younger than Gautier.   He
might even have been mentioned in the last volume,
for he began to publish idealist, and often directly
religious, poetry as early as 1839 with *Les Parfums
de Madeleine;* while *Psyche,* only two years later, is
perhaps his most frequently quoted single thing.   His
election to the Academy, in the room of Alfred de
Musset, had something of irony in it, as these elections
so often have; but even those (never wanting in
France) who do not warmly welcome "the lilies and
languors of virtue" could not, if they were in any
way critical, deny that M. de Laprade was a poet.

Verse like his, however, has never been either staple
or representative in his country; and the three poets
Leconte de Lisle. whom we shall mention next were his very
opposites in different directions.   The eld-
est of them, Leconte de Lisle (1818-1894), was also the
eldest who can be said to belong wholly to our period;

---

[1] The resemblance to his of the books with which, towards the close
of his life, the late Mr Du Maurier set off his brilliant performance in
the Art of Design is most interesting, and can hardly be fortuitous.

for though he was born, according to some, as early as 1818, he published nothing, or nothing noteworthy, till 1853, when his *Poèmes Antiques*, followed two years later by *Poèmes et Poésies*, and seven years later again by *Poésies Barbares*, developed the earlier Romantic lines in the special direction of that exotic tendency which had always distinguished them. M. Leconte de Lisle spelt his Greek names with abundant *k*'s and *h*'s and diphthongs and accents; he went to uttermost isles and icebergs of North and West, farthest sands and forests of South and East, for his subjects. Proper and even common names from Celtic and Hindostani, from Rune and Ogham, stimulated the taste or bewildered the brains of the surprised Parisian in his verse. Later, he undertook a whole series of elaborate translations of classical (principally Greek) poets, and he distinguished himself—at all times more or less, but in ever-increasing measure—by violent iconoclasm and anti-Christianity. So far, the description must be scarcely fascinating to those who do not know his work; but that work, especially the earlier part of it, to no small extent redeems the follies and the pedantries which it pleased the author to enshrine in it. Even his most outlandish and *baroque* pieces often have a fine rhetorical colour, and a resonant clangour which is rather more than rhetorical. And not seldom, especially in the extraordinarily beautiful "Requies" which serves as epilogue to *Poèmes et Poésies*, he can quit all pedantry, and nearly all partisanship, and give us true and pure, though always melancholy, poetry.

D

Melancholy, save very rarely, and just as often as is necessary to save a poet from the reproach of "regarding life through a horse-collar," abstained *Banville.* from touching the *lyra jocosa* (and yet not merely *jocosa*) of Théodore de Banville (1823-1891). M. de Banville began before he was twenty with a volume entitled *Les Cariatides,* and followed it up four years later, in 1846, with one called *Les Stalactites.* These at once showed a singular devotion to the poetry of form—to which Hugo had been allowed by his stormy temperament to pay only divided attention, but which had been carried very far already by Gautier—and a most unusual and admirable faculty of handling it. Not merely in practice, but also in theory (for he wrote a *Petit Traité* (1872) on the subject which is a standard authority), M. de Banville showed himself an absolute master of French versification in all the most intricate forms, old and new, thirteenth century and eighteenth, which have been from time to time invented to beguile or disguise the admitted want of quantity in the language, and its tendency towards mere declamation. He was an excellent dramatist and an admirable writer of prose stories, as well as a poet; but he returned to serious verse with *Les Odelettes* in 1856, and next year produced the best book of comic verse in French which had appeared for generations in *Les Odes Funambulesques* (continuation in 1869). And thenceforward, during the Second Empire and the Third Republic, he wrote constantly and always well — especially in lighter vein. There have been complaints that his

Muse lacked sincerity, severity, and seriousness. But there are more Muses than one, and M. de Banville was a favoured servant of more than one or two of the Nine.

The most remarkable of the group, however, and perhaps of the French poets specially of our time, has *Baudelaire.* yet to be noticed. For long years the name of Charles Baudelaire (1821-1866) was an apple of discord with critics; and to this day current criticism of the orthodox kind may be said rather to have accepted him with a grumble, than to have frankly given him his proper place as the greatest *influence* in French poetry of the last fifty years. Yet there were some who recognised him as soon as they saw him,—or at least his work,—and who have never had a doubt about the matter. His days were rather few, and, if not exactly evil, not very good. Born in 1821 of a good middle-class family, and well educated, possessing some little—though very little—means, and absolutely set against any profession, he "commenced man of letters" as soon as he was of age, spent another period of the same length in the excited and not particularly wholesome literary life of Paris, went to Belgium in 1864, became affected by general paralysis, and died in Paris two years later. He had contributed to many periodicals, and done work always of mark; but he actually published only one book of poems— the famous volume called *Fleurs du Mal*, in 1857. The government of Napoleon III. — which, though those who most violently attacked it were but as the

Pharisees in a certain famous indictment, was as little
morally immaculate as any government mentioned in
history — had at different times curious spasms of
hypocritical and hypercritical morality. And just at
this time it selected Baudelaire and Flaubert—the
most gifted men of the actual generation in prose and
verse respectively, and both of them, though fond of
"inconvenient" subjects, incapable of treating them
in a way really immoral—for prosecution; and Baudelaire had not merely to undergo condemnation, but
to leave out of his book a few poems which he might
just as well never have put into it. The first edition
being thus suppressed, a second, omitting the condemned pieces, but with rather considerable additions, appeared in 1861. But Baudelaire's whole
work—and then not quite the whole of it—was never
collected till after his death, when it appeared, with
an admirable introduction by Théophile Gautier, in
four volumes, comprising the Poems, a collection of
Petits Poèmes en Prose (imitated to some extent from
a remarkable book by Louis Bertrand of Dijon,
Gaspard de la Nuit), some stories, and a good many
criticisms,—the whole imbued with a singular uniformity of spirit.

A paradoxer of severe morality—a part as yet not
often, if ever, played, but presenting opportunities—
might maintain that if the government could have
suppressed this spirit, or even if they had suppressed
all the work which so evenly displayed it here, there
might have been some excuse for them. For there is
no doubt that, though the expression is almost invari-

ably of high, and sometimes of the highest, literary
value, the spirit itself is morbid, and, in weak natures
exposed to its contagion, dangerous in the highest
degree. The "Romantic despair" which Chateaubriand
had first made public, which Byron had vulgarised,
which Lamartine, Hugo, Musset had preached in their
different ways, reached in Baudelaire a point which,
though forty years have passed since his death, nearly
fifty since the publication of his poems, and all but
two generations since the writing of some of them,
has never been really surpassed, though it may have
been exaggerated and caricatured. But we have here
more to do with the real literary value and novelty of
the expression itself and its all powerful influence on
successors. In temper this influence has been more
powerful than one could wish; in form it could hardly
have been improved. Baudelaire was not as careful
in strict prosody as his friends Gautier and Banville,
and he did not even attempt to rival the latter in
elaborate rhythmical effects. But he carried further
than any poet before him in French the English
poetic method of investing the usual poetic diction
and form with a sort of impalpable overcoat of
suggestion — the employment of visual image and
audible word-play, so as to illustrate and accompany
the direct action and conduct of the subject. Another
poet to be mentioned, Paul Verlaine, directly carried
this a little farther; but he would certainly not
have carried it so far as he did but for Baudelaire's
initiative, and, with some additional charm, he is not
Baudelaire's equal in force.

The poets just mentioned had already made their appearances, in all cases for some, in most for many, *The* years, when in 1866 there was issued a *Parnassiens* remarkable collection of verse which gave *and their* *ramifications.* title to a new—to the last considerable— school of French poetry. This, as it were, gathered up and registered Romanticism in its latest form. It was entitled *Le Parnasse Contemporain*, was published by Alphonse Lemerre, and was succeeded during the next decade (1869-70 and 1876) by two other collections of the same title. These in most cases introduced to the public poets some of whom are still alive, and among whom are to be found all the best poets and almost all the true poets that France has produced to the present day. Planned by two quite young men, MM. Catulle Mendès and Xavier de Ricard, it contained no preface or prose manifesto; but its character and design were sufficiently indicated to the expert, even in those days, by the fact that its first six pages were occupied by verses from the pen of Théophile Gautier. Banville followed him; Leconte de Lisle gave sixteen pages of his most characteristic if not quite of his best work, bristling with *kh*'s and capital *C*'s duly cedillaed; there were as many of Baudelaire, including two of his last and finest things, —the wonderful hymn, "A la très chère, à la très belle" and " La Rançon." The veteran Emile Deschamps, with a few others of the First and Middle Romantic schools, appeared—among them Philoxène Boyer (1827-1867), the hero of Banville's delightful parody, " Dans les salons de Philoxène Nous étions quatre-vingt rim-

eurs," and Auguste Vacquerie (1819-1895), brother of
the ill-fated husband of Léopoldine Hugo. Vacquerie
was a kind of aide-de-camp of Hugo himself, and
wrote much verse, which might have been fine poetry
if it had quite succeeded in being poetry at all, notably
a curious Hugonic *charge* in dramatic form entitled
Tragaldabas (1874). This all Hugonians have endeavoured to admire, and some have succeeded in
thinking that they admired it. But the attraction of
the *Parnasse* for lovers of poetry consisted mainly in
the large number of unknown, or almost unknown,
novices who, under aspirations a little though not
very different, but all with a serious and obstinate
attachment to the art of poetry as forty years had
made it at last possible in France, contributed each
his sonnet or poem, his batch of sonnets or poems,
to the general enterprise.

Here were the first, or almost the first, verses of
François Coppée (*b.* 1842), a man then not much
over twenty, but displaying quite clearly already,
under or beside the "impassibility" which was supposed to be characteristic of the school of "Art, first
of all," that tendency to sentiment and domesticity
which he afterwards developed; of Catulle Mendès
(*b.* 1840), who became in this same year Gautier's son-
in-law, a writer of more than usual talent who has
unfortunately succumbed both then and later to the
temptation of dealing with inconvenient things, but
who on this occasion was quite void of offence in
this particular respect; of Sully Prudhomme (*b.* 1839),
a poet approaching his thirtieth year, who was to

become the favourite versifier of those who love "thoughtful" poetry in France. Here, obviously of the school of Baudelaire, but paying more attention than Baudelaire had done to form, and already aiming at something not yet known to French prosody, was a poet who some twenty years later, after strange and invidious adventures, reappeared—appearing as for the first time to the short-memoried or the ignorant —and became for a time the most indubitable poet that France in one of her vacant interlunar periods has possessed—Paul Verlaine (1844-1896). Here was another who (also later) was to be elevated for a time by a sort of literary *blague* or *claque* to the same position as chief of yet another school, the "Symbolists" —Stéphane Mallarmé (1842-1898). Here (indeed he should have been mentioned earlier, for he came between Banville and Leconte de Lisle) was another creole poet, José Maria de Hérédia (*d.* 1905), whose name would have been a poetical fortune in 1830, and who succeeded in obtaining considerable repute, now and afterwards, by sonnets of admirable workmanship, but perhaps with not very much else. And here were others, Léon Dierx (*b.* 1838), Henri Cazalis, Emmanuel des Essarts, Villiers de L'Isle Adam (1838-1889), whom it was interesting for the lover of poetry to look up or to follow in the slender volumes of Parnassian verse which they or some of them from time to time put forth, following the liturgy of Lemerre, as their predecessors thirty years earlier had "followed the ritual of Renduel."

There was nothing aggressive or partisan in the

title of *Parnasse*, which was merely a revival of an
The second   old French seventeenth-century label ; but
Parnasse.   the book, in any case a remarkable one,
and coming after Sainte-Beuve's series of articles on
" La Poésie Française " in 1865, might be thought to
show, and did in fact show, a rally of poetical energy
in France.   As the names above given will indicate at
once, especially to those who know their later work,
writers of the most different character were in fact
included among the nearly forty contributors to the
book.   But, as very often if not usually happens, a
definite confession of faith was made up for them :
and by degrees " Impassible," the caricature-epithet
referred to above, was invented as a synonym for
" Parnassien."   They were supposed all to have sworn
allegiance to the doctrine of "Art for Art's sake ";
to have forsworn " the subject," and so forth.   As a
matter of fact there was little community, and certainly no definite and aggressive purpose,— only a
devotion in different degrees to the three great principles of nineteenth-century poetry so often formulated
—appeal to the eye, appeal to the ear, and the preference of short lyrical or semi-lyrical pieces, having
strong connections of suggestion with art and literature or philosophy, to large narrative canvasses.   There
was, in addition, something of the Romantic devotion
to new metres and elaborate harmonies, instead of the
inevitable Alexandrine solid, or Alexandrine cut into
lengths, of eighteenth and late seventeenth century
poetry that was not confessedly light.

The reception of the book was scarcely enthusiastic ;

but it pleased its contributors well enough to induce
them to repeat the experiment. And in 1869 there
appeared (in parts, the reception of which by sub-
scribers was interrupted by the war of 1870, and
not finally terminated till after peace was concluded)
a new volume with the same title, but bulkier by a
hundred pages, and sweeping still more of the poets
of the day into its net. Gautier no longer led off,
though he appears later; the post of honour was
given to a poem of some size on "Kain," by Leconte
de Lisle (who would doubtless have deserted the
fellowship if they had spelt it with a C), and Banville
followed with (among other things) ten charming
Ballades Joyeuses, part of a larger batch which he
afterwards (1875) published separately. Even Sainte-
Beuve, who died this year, contributed; and though
Baudelaire was gone, the two Deschamps, Auguste
Barbier, a survivor of 1830 itself, and others of the
old guard, rallied again round the new standard.
Victor de Laprade, who had not been enlisted for
the earlier volume, here gave a pleasing piece of
verse; and among older and younger recruits were to
be found Albert Glatigny (1839-1873), an ill-starred
child of the better Bohemia; Anatole France (*b.* 1844),
to become later one of the most delightful critics and
tale-tellers of France; Joséphin Soulary (1815-1891),
a poet almost as old as Gautier and a most skilful
sonneteer; André Theuriet, another novelist to be;
Armand Silvestre (1839-1900), whom something of
the same evil angel attended as that which haunted
M. Catulle Mendès, but a master of *gauloiserie* in

his prose, and of ethereal fancy in his verse; Louisa
Siefert (1845-1877), a poetess keeping up the *éploré*
character of French poetesses; and the jeweller-
bibliophile-poet Claudius Popelin (1825-1892), one of
the frequenters of the Princess Mathilde's literary and
artistic *salon*. Possibly—I do not remember—a fine
sonnet of Gautier's in this volume, entitled "L'Impassible," helped some one to invent the nickname above
noted, though there is no coincidence of meaning.

The third *Parnasse*, seven years later, had again
enlarged itself to accommodate fresh recruits of
older and younger generations,—Madame
The third. Ackermann (1813-1890), another pensive
and, in this case, philosophic poetess; Emile Bergerat,
the husband to be of Gautier's younger daughter;
the veteran Marseillais poet and dramatist, Autran
(1813-1877); Paul Bourget, famous since in prose;
the painter, Jules Breton (?-1906); the eccentric
but powerful author of *Les Va-nu-Pieds*, Léon Cladel
(1835-1892); and some much younger men, among
whom one, Maurice Rollinat, made a certain stir for a
time with independent volumes of verse. Gautier
was now dead, and excepting Hugo himself—who
was too much of a divinity to appear in a collection
except by absence—there really was hardly a poet in
France who had not at one time or another made
appearance on this Parnassus. The *cometic* and deceptive apparition of a Richepin, the pseudo-Tyrtæan
outpourings of a Deroulède, and some other things
require little more than allusions; and we shall
content ourselves with repeating that "Symbolists,"

"Decadents," and the like, much more "Naturists," "Simplists," and other tickets which have followed, are mere foam-balls in the river of poetry, worth casting an eye at perhaps, certainly not worth elaborately recording. Only one poet indeed of the last twenty years of the nineteenth century in France (be it said with no discourtesy to some ingenious and agreeable writers whom we have not mentioned or have mentioned but slightly [1]) deserves record, and he has been mentioned as having appeared at a date nearly forty years distant from the present time.

The incalculable and no doubt slightly "unhinged" eccentricity of Paul Verlaine meddled *Verlaine.* with the Commune, saved itself by exile in England, and on returning merged itself for some time in *cloaques* (as the French appropriately call them) of vice, which there is no need for us to explore.[2] But Verlaine was the very paragon of that doubleness which, incident to humanity at all times, has never been more apparent, unless it be in the times of the Roman Empire, than during the nineteenth century. In the later 'eighties he emerged from his sloughs of debauchery, and, by his bad points and his good at once, obtained a position which was by no means the reward of charlatanism and effrontery

---

[1] The reformation of form, however (despite *vers libres* and the like), has maintained itself, and in the latest of many periodical miscellanies, *Vers et Prose* (1905), better quality has been shown than in anything of the kind since the last *Parnasse* itself.

It has been complained that Verlaine has been made the victim of a "legend." There is some truth in this. But unluckily a good deal of the skeleton of the legend is simple fact.

only, though there was in it something due to both.
In half a dozen most remarkable little books of verse
Poèmes Saturniens (1890 ; these are mostly older, some
as old as 1867), *Sagesse* (1881), *Amour* (1888), *Fêtes
Galantes* (1869), *Bonheur* (1891), *Parallèlement* (1889)
he rivalled Baudelaire in the audacity, the eccen
tricity, and the constant melancholy even in passion
though not in the originality of his tone. And he
went a long way beyond him in endeavouring to
supple and complicate the rebel prosody of French,
so as to enable it to give voice to the faint and
mystical melody which he wished to produce.

In fact, the importance of the closing years of
the nineteenth century for French poetry consists
Innovations largely and almost wholly in these metrical
in prosody. experiments, which are, to at least some
extent, not violations of the real principles of the
language, but partly recurrences (after the same
fashion which has proved so beneficial in other countries) to its earlier cadences and harmonies, partly
formal adoptions by serious poetry of the hints
which had long been given by such things as the
syncopes and slurs and reduplications of lighter
French verse. These last licences the *chansonniers*
had always given themselves ; but they had put
an air of " patter " and jargon on the language.
Verlaine and others — some of whom have been
probably helped in the process, or instigated to it,
by being not wholly of French blood—followed up
the *enjambement*, and other freedoms which had so
fearfully scandalised extreme classics in the verse

of 1830, by attempting to escape from the bondage
of three centuries in the matter of alternate masculine and feminine rhymes; from the hard and
fast cæsura, the neglect of which had nearly a
hundred years earlier been one of the great means
of emancipating English; and from the preference
of, if not the sole reliance on, verses of an even
number of syllables. To the greatest and final
secret, that of syllabic equivalence, no French poet
has yet thoroughly attained; and the extraordinary
deficiency of the language in natural accent no
doubt makes it very hard to do so. Possibly some
great poet, when he appears, will succeed even in
this. At any rate, when he does appear, he will
find at his disposal a prosody at least experiment-
ally enlarged, suppled, freed to a very remarkable
degree from purely arbitrary restriction.[1] He will
find opportunities of clothing his verse with an
accompaniment of haunting, suggestive melody connected with, but not limited to, the actual meaning
of the words, to which even Hugo attained rather
in spite of difficulties than in consequence of facilities
in his material and methods. It is, however, quite
possible that the traditional tendencies will be too

[1] What has been said above of the "vers libre" in its more sober
developments must not be considered as extending to the further
attempt at abolishing metre altogether, which has been made by
some writers.   In English, owing to the characteristics of the
language, verse and prose, though perhaps always distinguishable,
can be blended so as to be hard to distinguish.   The non-quantita-
tive, and even atonic, character of French makes it necessary to keep
a strong barricade between them, though the rules of behaviour on
the poetic side need not be so meticulous as Malherbe thought.

strong. Even if they are, they will remain, with
what Hugo could do, what even a far inferior
artist, Baudelaire, could do, what Verlaine himself
did, as a remarkable gain,— as a new province
acquired to the France of poetry, which might
almost console her for the loss of Alsace-Lorraine
to the France of politics. For if they have lost
their German lands, the French have at last mastered something like those cords of the German
lyre which, by one of the strange workings of
the Law of Compensation, the Germans themselves
have been almost powerless to wake since the
death, in Paris, of Heinrich Heine.[1]

[1] A note is also probably the best place for a few words on the
revival of Provençal as a literary language. This was represented
by two stages. The work of the barber-poet Jacques
Jasmin (who was born at Agen in 1798, and died in
1864) was very popular in the second quarter of the
century—Longfellow translated *The Blind Girl of Castel-Cuillé* (1835).
This was more or less genuine dialect work in the Gascon form of the
Langue d'Oc. But it no doubt inspired to some extent the more
deliberate and "literary" attempts which followed to reconstitute
Provençal by means of deliberate work consciously intended. Even
the famous *Miréio* (1858) of Frédéric Mistral (*b.* 1830), though presenting a rather less popular form of the language, anticipated the
formation of the *Felibrige* or society for carrying out this purpose, of
which Mistral himself, Aubanel, Roumanille, and others were members.
In this, as in other similar attempts to galvanise literary corpses
from Greek to Irish, partisans have taken enthusiastic interest. But
it has yet to be proved whether any one of them—Norwegian is not
quite a member of the class—has been, or will be, completely
successful. Even *Miréio* itself (though it has been translated into
all the languages of Europe, and though its author has been the
subject of a *Bibliographie Mistralienne* of respectable bulk) has perhaps a stronger appeal to the prevailing taste for local and provincial
colour than to that for pure poetry or pure literature.

*Note on Proven-
çal Revival.*

CHAPTER II.

ENGLISH AND FRENCH—THE DOMINATION OF
THE NOVEL.

THE NOVEL ABOUT 1850—CHANGE IN THE FRENCH DIVISION—HUGO'S
LATER ROMANCES—FROM INCIDENT TO MANNERS AND ANALYSIS—
FLAUBERT : HIS THEORY OF STYLE AND PRACTICE OF FICTION—
'MADAME BOVARY'—THE OTHERS—'LA TENTATION DE SAINT-
ANTOINE' — IMPORTANCE AND EXCELLENCE — FEUILLET — THE
"NATURALISTS"—THE GONCOURTS—DAUDET—ZOLA—THE 'ROUGON-
MACQUART' SERIES — THE FAULTS OF NATURALISM — AND THE
REVENGE OF ART — THE LAST BOOKS — THE SCHOOL OF ZOLA —
MAUPASSANT — THE REST — THE ENGLISH NOVEL IN 1850 —
BULWER—DICKENS—THACKERAY : 'ESMOND,' ETC.—THE 'ROUND-
ABOUT PAPERS'—SOME GENERAL REMARKS ON THESE—THE NEW-
COMERS — KINGSLEY — "GEORGE ELIOT" — THE TEMPTATION OF
DEMAND AND SUPPLY — CHARLES READE — ANTHONY TROLLOPE —
MISS YONGE — MRS GASKELL — THE NEW ROMANCE — MORRIS —
STEVENSON.

IT will probably be necessary for a longer space
of time to pass than is at present available, before
The novel about 1850. we can establish the more recent literature of the nineteenth century in a firm
perspective, before we can be quite certain how far
the late and rapid growth of prose fiction has
culminated, and whether it has begun to decline.

What is, however, certain is that the novel itself has been much more the dominant in literature during this half century than at any previous time. Up to the eighteenth it cannot claim dominance at all—it can hardly claim admission save on sufferance. In the earlier nineteenth, thanks to Scott, it attains dominance, but does not universally hold it. With the later there is no further doubt. From every point of view, low and high, serious and satiric, this Cinderella of literature has become the favourite Princess. It is a novel, not a tragedy, that the aspirant to letters wraps up in his baggage when he comes to Paris or London. It is with novels that the professional man or woman of letters makes his plentiful or her scanty income. The novel gives the reviewer his daily dreadful occupation, and finds the hands of the idle reader their something to do. The changes of mere outward literary fashion—from unlimited volumes to three, with excursions in the direction of periodical, illustrated, and other presentation,—from three volumes again to one—concern the novel. It is with the novel finally that the young or young-old generations knock at the door,—that the Tolstois, and the Björnsons, and even the Ibsens (whose works are really novels *par personnages* as much as dramas), apply for admission, and that the old distanced literatures, with their Valeras and their d'Annunzios, reapply for it.

It is perhaps rather difficult to establish a calculus which will enable us satisfactorily to differentiate between the progress or the decadence—to be absol-

E

utely impartial in terminology—of the various nations
in this respect. But the predominance of the kind
is as unquestionable in the three other great older
literary languages—Italian, Spanish, and German—
as in French and English; while as for the newer
competitors, they have (with the partial exception
noted) but little else to show.

There are reasons other than merely polite ones
for beginning here with France, as we began with
England in the last chapter. In or about 1850 the
French novel, from causes easily discoverable in its
earlier history, was in a relatively more advanced
position than the English—and it has undergone far
less development since. One of these reasons is of
that purely and almost brutally historic kind which
seems to annoy some readers as if it were a personal insult. France had felt the influence of Scott
almost, if not quite, as much as England had; and
the great French novelists of the century had chosen
to be born, or to take to writing, earlier than those
of England. By 1850, or a little later, there had
appeared (and consequently in the preceding volume
there has been noticed) almost all the work of
Balzac, Charles de Bernard, and Nodier, the best of
that of Dumas, a large and definitely constitutive
part of that of Hugo, Mérimée, Gautier, George Sand,
Sue, Sandeau. Of the names of the first class, only
Flaubert's and (if he may be admitted to this class)
Feuillet's had yet to be registered; and no school
of real importance but the "Naturalist" was to
make its appearance. In England it was very

different. Except the disappointing and never consummate talent of Bulwer, and the eccentric genius of Dickens, nothing at all decisive had appeared since the death of Scott until the years immediately preceding 1850, when Thackeray's too long-delayed and too short-lived period began; while within a few years from 1850 itself, remarkable new developments in more than one direction showed themselves in the English novel, and were illustrated and sustained by persons some of whom are not dead or silent yet. With France, then, let us begin.

About the time at which we do begin, a distinct change passed over both French and English novel-*Change in the* writing, though in the former case it was *French division.* not so much of a new birth as in the latter. For the past quarter of a century the chief, though by no means the whole, bent of the French novel, putting aside the work of Balzac and a few others, had been historical, or at any rate in the direction of the romance of incident. From Hugo and Dumas down to Féval and Amédée Achard, through Sue and Soulié, the most popular as well as the greatest writers of prose fiction had, with the mighty exception noted, addicted themselves to the following, as they understood it, of Scott. The short life of Soulié had already come to an end, and that of Eugène Sue was not to be far prolonged; but Hugo returned to the style during his exile with something of his poetry and much of his grandiose rhetoric, and Dumas and the minors continued it as long as they lived. It is, however, noticeable that the best work of all but

Hugo in the kind was done.   Nothing of Dumas after 1850 has really helped those critics who, in the last fifteen or twenty years, have succeeded in establishing his fame on a pretty durable basis. Achard's charming *Belle-Rose* is of 1847.   Paul Féval's equally charming *Fée des Grèves* is not much later. The one triumph of the style produced long after the middle of the century, Gautier's *Capitaine Fracasse*, was, as all "Theophilists" know, a book planned and partly written thirty years earlier.   In the enormous demand for the *roman-feuilleton,* imitations of its most popular kind were sure to be constantly multiplied ; but its palmy days were over, and have not, in France, returned.   Not merely the romance of adventure, but the historical romance generally of the last decades there, has been either a merely "book-made" thing or an antiquarian and scholastic study, or something delightful in itself like M. France's *Rôtisserie de la Reine Pédauque*, but with the maladies both of thought and of style, and even of conceit, on it,—not the artful, artless chronicle of "cape and sword" that charmed all in our fathers' days and many in our own, and will charm some, let us hope, for ever.

The Hugonic romance is a matter sufficiently curious, even in itself, to deserve a separate paragraph.

Hugo's later romances.   It does not seem to have been, as in the case of some other poets, notably Scott and Mr Morris, an effect of the impulse to produce fictitious narrative surviving the purely poetic *nisus* (for Hugo produced vast quantities of verse, some of it consummate, after he returned to prose fiction), but rather a variation of the same great new birth of creative energy which the shock of 1850-52, and the inspiring effect of the scenery of the Channel Islands, begot in him. From 1862 to 1874 he published four such romances—the first, *Les Misérables*, of enormous length; the second, and by far the best, *Les Travailleurs de la Mer* (1866), much shorter; with, later, *L'Homme qui Rit* (1869) and *Quatre-Vingt-Treize* (1874). In all, the qualities of the novel proper, and even of the romance "it-by-itself-it," have very little place. The story is ill-constructed, without verisimilitude, sometimes hardly existent; the characters are huge, cloudy sketches rather than men or women ; and both are subjected to, and whelmed in, floods of gorgeous but sometimes almost frigidly bombastic declamation, description, apocalyptic preaching, and prophesying of all sorts. As the appetite for Hugo was now in full force, and as modern man distinctly prefers reading prose to reading verse, it is probable that these romances (at any rate the two first) very largely extended his popularity ; but their faults, especially those of the two last, have as probably contributed to that popularity's very unjust occultation. For though there are magnificent or exquisite passages almost everywhere, and though *Les Travailleurs de la Mer* showers these with such steadiness that it holds the reader throughout, this is not the case with the others. And the author's faults — his colossal lack (the adjective means much) of humour, reason, and taste ; his contempt of construction, proportion, and

even the most liberally interpreted verisimilitude; his
fatiguing verbosity, his childish egotism, his equally
childish ignorance and prejudice—force themselves
on the attention as they seldom or never do when
it is fascinated and enchained by the unequalled in-
toxication — the " little brain-fever," as it was well
called—of his poetry.

The seed of Beyle and Balzac germinated more
slowly, but it came fairly true, as the gardeners say,
From incident and the crossings of its products even gave
to manners some very interesting varieties. The novel,
and analysis. like the drama, of character plays an ever-
lasting and sometimes rather bewildering *chassé-croisé*
with the novel as with the drama of manners—indeed,
manners and character are so close that in the Greek
critics we never quite know which word to choose for
use in translation. And it so happened that a comparatively greater, or at any rate a more rapid, change
came upon French manners than that which displayed
itself in any other country of Europe. The Revolution, reinforced by the Code Napoléon, had made
surer work than men thought, as well as more root-
and-branch work than they had ever feared or hoped.
During the Restoration, and even during the July
Monarchy to some extent, the prestige of the ancient
aristocracy continued, but that aristocracy was neither
restored to its old possessions—let alone powers—nor
true to itself. The new *bourgeoisie* had accordingly
a fairer chance in France than anywhere else; and
it was specially favoured by the Second Empire.
Manners grew sensibly worse, and morals, to say

the least, did not improve. That there was much room for a serious decadence in this last respect students of the eighteenth century will no doubt decline to admit; but even such students must allow that the disappearance of the *older* French *bourgeoisie* (which had much of the moral strictness of the English middle class until recent times) and of the smaller country gentry (who neither desired nor could afford the licence of the Court and the towns) did threaten some extension, if no positive deepening, of immorality. Compare Marivaux and Feuillet, writers both intentionally on the side of morality; compare Crébillon and, let us say, Feydeau or M. Armand Silvestre, writers openly neglectful of "the young person." The result may in some cases not be so very unflattering to the later nineteenth century in point of talent; it will scarcely be so satisfactory in the point of what may be called moral healthiness.

Of the greatest French novelist of our special time it is apparently still a moot-point—not, indeed, for the present writer, but for some critics— whether he is to be called a novelist or a romancer. Gustave Flaubert was born as early as 1821, and it was partly accident which prevented him from making a mark in literature earlier than he did. As it was, he had already, in 1848, published in the *Artiste*, under Gautier's editorship, some fragments of what was afterwards to be *La Tentation de Saint-Antoine*. He was a man of some means, adopted no profession, and early began a series of travels which had a great influence on his future work. How far

Flaubert.

the theory, put forth after his death by his friend and
travelling companion Maxime Du Camp, that an illness about this time materially and radically affected
Flaubert's physical and mental constitution, and determined afresh the course of his whole literary life,
is a fact, and how far a fancy, will probably always
be matter of opinion. What seems certain is that in
Flaubert, as in Rossetti, there was a singular combination or contrast of extravagant hilarity and boyish-
ness with saturnine and morbid intensity, and that the
latter tendency increased, as it usually does, with age.
It was not likely to be relieved or heightened by a
theory of literary composition which became more
and more a practice, and which Flaubert, besides
exemplifying in his work, has championed unflinchingly in his correspondence. This is itself an extension and exaggeration of the more general and more
popular theory of "Art-for-Art's-sake," which, discern-
ible in all but the earliest and most ancient times, has
reappeared, and will doubtless reappear continually,
but which is a special note of the period under consideration.

This famous doctrine—partly a reaction from the
excessive subject - worship which, equally old and
commoner in old times, is no doubt in the ordinary
constitution of humanity assured of equal duration,
and partly a revolt against the commercial and materialist tendencies of the mid-nineteenth century—may
have been learnt from Théophile Gautier, as Gautier
no doubt learnt it from Hugo's preface to the *Orientales*. But in Gautier himself, sweetness of dispos-

ition, variety of interests, atmosphere and circumstance, and not least, perhaps, the sometimes partly
benign necessity of working for a living with no
degrading compromise (Gautier was the staunchest of
men to his friends and his principles), but at the same
time with no fantastic eccentricity or will-worship,
had kept the theory within reasonable bounds. Flau-

His theory of ·bert, able to indulge his fancies, living
style and prac- much alone, possessed of no relieving or
tice of fiction. varying tastes, and not possessed of the
spontaneously "impeccable" style of his editor, friend,
and master, early began and pursued, with increasing
concentration almost to the point of monomania, a
laborious *cultus* of style which literally reached the
old "Ciceronian" pitch of devoting a night to a clause,
if not to a word. Exaggerating, and almost caricaturing, the Romantic doctrine of the *mot propre*, he reached
the proposition laid down *totidem verbis* in Guy de
Maupassant's most interesting preface to the *Correspondence*, and constantly endorsed in the text thereto,
that there is only *one* word or *one* phrase that can
fully or adequately express a writer's idea, and that
"naught's had, all's spent," unless this one word, this
one phrase, is reached. His practice matched his
theory; and perhaps it may be admitted that the
result in his case—as by no means in some others that
we shall come to—justified both. With Flaubert we
rarely feel — as we do in others, both French and
English, of the same school — a sense of excessive
"art" in the phrase itself,—a suspicion that, as a
most naïf, but in this instance most just, critic once

observed, "Oh, the fellow merely wrote that in the natural way first, you know, and changed it afterwards to make it seem unusual!" But what the phrase escapes, the stories, the situations, the atmosphere generally of the books too commonly pay for. There is everywhere as regards the moral, and everywhere (except in *Madame Bovary* perhaps) as regards the artistic "nervous impression," a sense of the not quite natural, the not quite inevitable,—of a lack of freshness, spontaneity, clear air, and open sky. Flaubert is rather too constantly in the hospital and the museum, among preparations, employing instruments. He is never at a loss; and yet the last thing that judicious admirers could say of him would be Dryden's words of Chaucer, "Here is God's plenty!"

Yet he is so great as to be almost of the greatest, and his influence has been felt all over Europe throughout the last quarter of the nine-

Madame Bovary.

teenth century, and in France ever since *Madame Bovary*. This, undoubtedly his most considerable and characteristic book, appeared in 1859. The scene, the scheme, almost the whole substance and treatment alike of the book, might have struck a hasty judge as Balzacian; but, for a careful one, the difference must always emerge before fifty pages have been read. In Balzac the old French domination of the type, though largely individualised and differentiated, is always present. Emma Bovary is not a type, she is a person; and so are all the characters of the book persons—not of the intense and living but fantastic style of Balzac and Dickens, but of the individualised

kind of Fielding and Thackeray. The difference is
more striking still in the style and in all those parts
of the novel — description especially — where style
reigns paramount. Flaubert has no rhetoric in the
ordinary sense: he has the very essence of it in the
older and better. His phrase convinces: we know it
to be the right one; it not merely carries the author's
meaning wholly and clearly with it, but with no
lavish expense—indeed, with a certain parsimony of
words—sets that meaning, with all light and shade,
all background and foreground and distance and fram-
ing, full in the reader's sight. Delightful in the
ordinary sense it can hardly be called: the sordid and
almost passionless immorality and selfishness of the
heroine, the crass stupidity of her hapless husband,
the ignoble notes of the minor characters, transport
us only with admiration; but they do transport us
with that. One may wish that the author had chosen
to do something else: but what he chose to do he has
done consummately. The strenuous and delicate observation of ordinary and modern things which Flaubert had here shown was changed in his next work
to an observation equally strenuous, no little research,
and a far greater dose of imagination, as to things
very far from modern and ordinary. *Salammbô* (1862)
is a Carthaginian novel, a gorgeous ghastly dream-
panorama of blood, and gold, and orgie, and dim
tumultuous horror. It has never been, and perhaps
can never be, genuinely popular; it is, in fact, a sort
of novel-nightmare. But once granting the subject,
the sincerity and solidity of the workmanship grow

on one at every reading, and it is difficult for an

The others. impartial judge to put it below *Madame Bovary.* Not quite so much can be said for *L'Education Sentimentale*, the next (1869), the longest, and the least popular of all. The unfavourable criticisms on it have perhaps been not wholly fair; but it is a book which conspicuously underlies the objection of colourlessness and want of action. As the most imposing multiplier makes nothing of a multiplicand which is zero, so even the most diabolically clever workmanship will lose itself over mere nullity. Yet the details escape this censure; and there is a certain ironic "criticism of life" in the whole which is not without value.

No more striking contrast could be found than the next volume — a rehandling and completion of the

La Tentation de fragments which had appeared many years *Saint-Antoine.* in the *Artiste* into a complete book. The alternation of reality and dream already noticed betrays itself strikingly here; and the *Tentation*, without the repulsiveness of *Salammbô*, excels even that book in imaginative and descriptive power. There are many, no doubt, who do not like, and more perhaps who do not either like or understand, its kind; but for those who appreciate "the fairy way of writing," as Dryden says, *La Tentation de Saint-Antoine* (1874) is one of the great books of the century. Flaubert's last finished volume was a leash of short stories (1877) illustrating his different manners: *Un Cœur Simple*, a wonderful quiet picture of a Norman peasant; *Herodias*, where the reader's know-

ledge of the story makes him anticipate a *Salammbô*
in little, and where he finds it; and *La Légende de
Saint-Julien l'Hospitalier*, a triumph in the manner
of the *Tentation*. After his death in 1881, and unfinished, appeared *Bouvard et Pécuchet*, something in
the style of *L'Education*,—a curious satire on the
vanity of human pursuits, wrought up with astonishing
pains, but only saved from failure by its incompleteness, and perhaps fortunate to be saved in this way.
A play of no merit—*Le Candidat*,—a very few travel
sketches, and the abundant and extraordinarily interesting correspondence above referred to with George
Sand and others, complete Flaubert's work.

That work deserves to be dwelt on here at what
may at first seem disproportionate length, because it
Importance and is by far the most important work in novel
excellence. which belongs wholly (putting aside the
insignificant anticipations of the *Tentation*) to the
latter half of the century. It is great in itself : with
that of Dickens and Thackeray and Balzac, who belong, the last wholly to the earlier half, the other two
very mainly, it seems to the present writer to deserve
a rank which can be shared by no other novelists
after Scott, and Miss Austen, and perhaps Dumas.
In certain aspects—in its "realism," in its almost
despairing and all but Laocoontic struggle with style
("all but"—for it triumphs), in its cult of the ugly
occasionally, in its divorce from faith and morals, in
a dozen other ways, good and bad—it is typical of all
later work, on one side of literature, to the present
day. Our optimists have not dispelled—our pessim-

ists have not outgrown or out-travelled—the Flaubertian gloom : though the former have recoiled from the point to which he led, and the latter have tried to outdo him, not merely in gloom but in grime.

He is, however, most interesting of all, as it may seem to some, because it is possible to discover in him not merely something redeeming when he is compared with the Zolas and the Goncourts, but the reason and the source of this redemption. Flaubert was a pessimist; he was a Realist, if never a Naturalist; it would be impossible to go much beyond him in perceiving and rendering the dismal-ironic side of life. But, like Heine and like Thackeray, he had never "put off the old man"—in this case the good old man—of Romanticism. He kept it out nowhere completely, except in *Bouvard et Pécuchet*, his one approach to failure; there are flashes of it even in *Madame Bovary* and in the *Education*; for good or for evil it dominates *Salammbô* and the *Trois Contes*, and the *Tentation* most of all. Idle to urge, as has been urged, that this last is anti-religious or anti-theistic! Even if the purpose be granted, the execution foils it. The book is shot, saturated, bursting, with the sense of wonder, the sense of the supernatural, the sense of the inexplicable; and where these are, Religion is safe, and God, however "far withdrawn," is "making Himself the awful rose of dawn," sooner or later, without fear or fail. As for *Saint-Julien l'Hospitalier*, it is undisguisedly Christian,—of the best period of Christianity. And even where Flaubert's religious sense

seems absent, his poetic — at least his romantic—
sense remains; while in respect to his literary expression it is difficult to speak too highly. He may
be unnecessarily erudite, he may have encouraged his
imitators to "get up" the slang of the engineer's
shop, and the dissecting - room, and the Stock Exchange, and worse places still. But he always (with
the usual exception) passes his erudition duly through
the limbeck. It does not annoy us; it does not press
unduly on us; we do not want to say to it, "Get
thee to the wastepaper-basket." He does not "keep
a milk-walk for babes"; he walks himself too much
in the shadow and not enough in the sun; he followed
bad examples, and, from his imitators, men have
imagined that he set worse. But it was not really
so. He bears no token of the sabler streams which
he has touched, and in which the Goncourts and the
Zolas wallow after him, saturating hide and soul.
One thinks, in connection with him, of the mediæval
tales—fellows of those he rendered so well—in which
kind Saints rescue the sinner, and bring him or her
safe at last. Perhaps some one some day will write
"The Miracles of the Muses," and then Flaubert will
find a place beside Sister Beatrice.

If there seem to any reader too much enthusiasm
here, "it shall not occur again." There is indeed, in
Feuillet. the remaining tale of the French novel
during the nineteenth century, very much
to amuse, and not a little to delight, but little
indeed to transport, except on a very small scale.
The nearest, and therefore the greatest, miss of such

transport was probably made by Octave Feuillet
(1821-1890), whose very great powers have for some
time been unduly depreciated, first by mere political
spite, and secondly by the objection which has occupied the "warm young men" of the last two
decades to sentiment, prettiness, and, perhaps, one
must add, "good form." Feuillet's *Memoirs*, not published till some time after his death, are among the
most amusing of a kind in which France, as in other
kinds, is not quite so rich as once she was; but they
do not tell much of his early life. The son of an
official in Normandy, where he afterwards lived, and
the scenery of which supplies the best descriptive
parts of his novels, he was long credited with having,
among other literary tentatives, served as one of the
"young men" who devilled for Dumas in his busiest
days; but this has been denied. At any rate, he
found a place on the *Revue des Deux Mondes* as early as
1848, was a very popular dramatist as well as novelist
for many years, shared in the unjust, and not a little
ignoble, unpopularity which came upon favourites of
the Empire after the Empire's collapse, but was not
in the least daunted or depressed by it, and in his
latest days produced in *La Morte* one of the strongest
of all his books. Others worth mentioning are the
attempts, in styles not his own, *Onesta* and *Bellah*,
which belong to the period of our last volume; the
pathetic *La Petite Comtesse* (1856), one of his best,
and the first which showed him as novelist *en titre*
to Imperialist society; *Le Roman d'un Jeune Homme
Pauvre* (1858), his most popular and most unex-

cceptionable book, though certainly *not* his best;
Histoire de Sibylle (1862), a book which made
freethinkers very angry, for Feuillet was always
orthodox in religion; *Monsieur de Camors* (1867),
which perhaps shares in the general opinion the
chief place with the *Jeune Homme Pauvre*, though its
moral complexion is very different; *Julia de Trécœur*
(1872), the most powerful and passionate of all, but
lacking in variety and breadth, and injured by an end
as close to melodrama as to tragedy, and very disagreeable—with others, down to the above-mentioned
La Morte (1886). In this the author is still, in his
own peculiar way, on the side of virtue, and in it
he has drawn a masterly portrait of a woman who has
been " philosophised " into complete indifference to all
moral laws, and not merely to that which the French
novelist usually razes from his code. Even in regard
to this excepted commandment M. Feuillet, though at
least on a level with his fellows in taking its breach
almost as a matter of course, cannot be said to be
exactly tolerant of, or even complacent to, the errors
he describes. His fault, from the reasonably moral
point of view, is that he depicts laxity in characters
whose other traits are incongruous with it. For the
rest, his manners-painting is exceedingly clever, his
character-drawing only short of the first, his plots
ingenious if not quite attaching enough, his freedom
from mere repetition and self-copying remarkable,
and his writing, if not of surpassing excellence like
Flaubert's, still an excellent specimen of that standard
French which once had hardly a rival as a current

F

literary language.   Although the men were very different, and their subjects likewise, Feuillet occupies in French a position not very different from that of Anthony Trollope in English ; and the return of favour which seems to be coming to the, for a time, unjustly neglected Englishman will probably come to the Frenchman likewise.[1]

The most remarkable development of the Second Empire in the way of producing a school of novel-writing partook to a certain extent of the characteristics of both these two great Normans. But it was personally nearer to Flaubert than to Feuillet, though it lacked the poetry of the first as much as it lacked the polish of the second. As in many similar cases in the history of Literature, personal comradeship has been rather freely translated into literary resemblance.   There was formed in these years a sort of *cénacle* or coterie, in which Flaubert appeared when he was at Paris, and which more ordinarily consisted of the brothers (Jules, 1830-1870 ; Emile, 1822-1896) de Goncourt, the Russian novelist Tourguenief, and two younger writers, one a southern Frenchman, Alphonse Daudet (1840-1898), and the

The "Naturalists."

---

[1] There was a time when popular (and even some critical) judgment would have put with Flaubert and Feuillet their contemporary Ernest Feydeau (1821-1873), whose *Fanny* (1858) attracted Sainte-Beuve by its unusual motive — the intense jealousy, not of the husband towards the lover, but of the lover towards the husband. But Feydeau had little real talent, his appeals became more and more to the merely scandalous, and he was beaten even there by the coarser daring of the Naturalist school.   His best thing, though perhaps his least known, is a really pleasing story entitled *Sylvie*, rather in the style of Gautier's *Jeune-France.*

other a Marseillais of Italian extraction, Emile Zola
(1840-1903). The Russian will dwell among his
own people; of the others and of the yet younger
Guy de Maupassant, who was closely and directly
connected with Flaubert himself, some notice must
be taken here. The voluminous and disgusting
though not quite dull memoirs of M. Émile de Goncourt have, together with his and his brother's work,
made the pair (or at least the survivor) very easy for
any person of ordinary intelligence and some literary

The Goncourts. experience to appraise. They were really
learned and accomplished students of the
history, the manners, and, above all, the art of the
eighteenth century, and in the decade of 1850-
1860 they published a large number of monographs
on subjects coming under these heads. About the
later date they began to produce, still (until the
death of the younger—certainly the more amiable and
perhaps the more gifted of the pair) in collaboration,
another series of novels, on new or supposed new
principles of treatment and style (*Sœur Philomène*,
1861; *Renée Mauperin*, 1864; *Germinie Lacerteux*,
1865; and others); while after his brother's death
Emile continued the series, caricaturing the earlier
examples in *La Fille Elisa*, *Chérie*, &c.

The epithets and tickets " Realism," " Naturalism,"
" the document," " the personal epithet," &c., which
have accumulated round these writers and their
friends, perhaps rather darken than lighten counsel.[1]
In the Goncourts' own case, the selection and

[1] For more on these, see Conclusion

treatment of subject are determined by something like the following considerations. Story in the ordinary sense is not to be expected. The older "classical" requirements of a certain rank of pre-eminence in heroes and heroines are entirely done away with. Morality of any kind ceases to come into play, though immorality of almost any kind is allowed to take its place. The above-mentioned *Germinie Lacerteux*, for instance, is the history of a domestic servant, no better than she should be, but also no prettier, and no more interesting;[1] *Chérie*, to go to the other work, is that of a weakly pet daughter of a man of affluence. Every possible source of ordinary attraction in literature is studiously kept out of the way; and a photographic reproduction of ordinary things (with a preference for the disagreeable and uninteresting) is the sole spring, if spring it can be called, that is set working. In regard to style, the same studious care is used to avoid anything that is in the least *obvious*. Late in his own life, and after Flaubert's death, Emile de Goncourt had the amazing indiscretion to take the author of *Madame Bovary* and *La Tentation* to task because his epithets and expressions were not "personal" enough — because they were, though "admirably good," only those *de tout le monde*. His own and his brother's, he said, were *personnelles*. The fatuity of

[1] Additional light is thrown on the method by the fact that the original of Germinie was the authors' own *bonne*, with whom they had played as children, who had served them twenty-five years with affectionate devotion, and whose misdeeds they only discovered after her death.

this is characteristic of the whole school or batch of
schools which have succeeded in different countries.
But the distinction is not quite so new as M. de
Goncourt seemed to think. It occurs between the
epithet of Shakespeare and the epithet of Stanyhurst;
it is found of old between the epithet of Plato and
the epithet of Aristides; it was hit off once for all by
Julius Florus in Quintilian's story when he asked his
ambitious nephew " whether he wanted to write better
than he could ? " The only distinction of the moderns
is that with them sometimes, if not always, degrada-
tion of subject has been associated with preciousness
of expression.[1]

In M. de Goncourt, senior, if not in *les deux
Goncourt* (to dismiss them with a phrase reconciling
Daudet. because of its extraction from a charming
poem of Gautier's), the most amiable criticism that is competent can discover few good literary
qualities save erudition and industry. The critical
state of their friends M. Daudet and M. Zola need
not be quite so ungracious. The gifts of the first-
named were indeed extraordinary : it is very difficult
to say precisely what evil fairy can have interfered
to deprive him of the position of a supreme man of
letters. That he began too early ; that he had no
proper training; that he was thrown into an utterly
unhealthy state of society, and especially of literary

---

[1] Sainte-Beuve seems to have declared that one of their books
(*Madame Gervaisais*) was *fatiguant*. He did not review it, but his
abstinence from puffing it drew down on him some of the most disgusting effusions of the Goncourtian bile. "Fatiguing" is the exact
word for their whole work in novel.

society,—these are rather excuses than anything
better. He was born at Nîmes in 1840; and his
experiences of his compatriots in southern France
later inspired what, if not the highest, has been
beyond all doubt the most popularly amusing record
of his talent—the successive sketches of *Tartarin de
Tarascon.* But he left the South as a mere boy, and
at seventeen became an under private secretary to
the notorious Duc de Morny. He wrote and published
poems very early; and plays when he was scarcely
of age, not unsuccessfully. But prose fiction was his
real vocation; and it may be regretted that he ever
left the direction of his first three books of importance—*Le Petit Chose* (1868), *Lettres de Mon Moulin*
(1869), and *Contes du Lundi* (1873). All these
showed a charming blend of pathos and humour,
and the last two (the first is a record of his own
experiences and struggles slightly travestied) delightful satiric and imaginative power as well.

It was not, however, till well after the downfall of
the Empire that he launched novels in form, and they
at once acquired great popularity. *Fromont Jeune et
Risler Aîné* (1874), *Jack* (1876), *Le Nabab* (1878), *Les
Rois en Exil, Sapho, Numa Roumestan, L'Immortel,
L'Evangéliste,* followed each other with fair rapidity,
though not at the headlong speed of the ordinary
romancier - feuilletoniste. Unfortunately, though the
pathos and the humour continued, the poetic imagination or even fancy declined or disappeared. In its
place appeared certain ugly features which, popular
for a time, and with the literary populace serving no

doubt as attractions, gradually disgusted those who are not the vulgar with M. Daudet. The worst of these was not the curious touch of something which even those who dislike the charge of plagiarism, and regard it as often, if not always, absurd, can hardly call by any other name as regards Thackeray in *Fromont Jeune* and Dickens in *Jack*. It was the constant and growing tendency to drag in real persons, and especially real persons in scandalous aspects. Morny himself, and other not too immaculate members of the Imperial entourage, appeared in *Le Nabab;* the characters of *Les Rois en Exil* were as obviously divers ill-starred, and not always well-behaved refugees, from the King and Queen of Naples downwards. "Numa Roumestan" was Gambetta almost without concealment; the sordid hero and heroine of *L'Immortel* were fully identified with an Academic personage of a former generation and his wife. It is noteworthy in literary history that this practice of introducing into literature the matter and the methods of the baser journalism never fails to stamp the person guilty of it with increasing vulgarity, at the same time that it cramps and sears his inventive powers; and these results were only too clearly seen in M. Daudet. Something perhaps may in charity be set down to increasing ill-health, which carried him off comparatively early; but hardly any of his later books are good as wholes, though he never quite lost the faculty of short tale-writing. The best, if the "grimiest," of his later work is the powerful *demi-monde* novel of *Sapho*, in which the old pathos

and passion not seldom return to him, though the
nature of the subject, while shocking the mere moralist, can only remind the literary student of the
far greater pathos and power shown in *Manon Lescaut*.
It seems probable that future judgment will class
M. Daudet as the most lamentable failure of a great
novelist that the later nineteenth century produced.

No similar verdict is likely to be pronounced by
any one on Emile Zola, even though a large variety

Zola.

of critical judgments is to be expected
on him. Whatever M. Zola was, he was
not a failure—though the quality of his success is
quite another matter. Very few, if any, writers can
ever have set more decidedly before them a definite
object, or have chosen the means to the attainment of
that object with greater shrewdness, or have laboured
with the means towards the end in a more untiring
and straightforward fashion. He became a clerk in
the famous bookselling house of Hachette, taking
also vigorously to journalism, and, before very long,
to novel - writing. His earliest efforts were, like
Balzac's, of a melodramatic and sensational kind,
though pretty early—at the age of twenty-four—he
published a volume of short stories (*Contes à Ninon*)
which, like Daudet's, show a better vein than he
chose later to cultivate. He was, however, grop-
ing for this vein, which he himself desired to find;
and he struck it not much later in two or three
books, of which *Thérèse Raquin* (1867) has been
much praised by some. Here the new tendencies
of "naturalism" and "physiology"—of attaching

the novel-interest to studies of vice and crime executed with minute fidelity to at least supposed fact,
and of rigidly obeying so-called scientific principles
—are very apparent.

It was not, however, till after the catastrophe
of 1870 and the re-establishment of order that—
The Rougon-   again in resemblance, and this time no
Macquart   doubt designed resemblance, to Balzac—
series.   M. Zola undertook the scheme of a
great novel-cycle which, both as whole and in its
parts, was to illustrate these principles. The common
title, *Les Rougon-Macquart : histoire naturelle et sociale
d'une famille sous le second Empire*, tells its own
story quite clearly and honestly. Imagining a family
—or rather two families—which in legitimate and
illegitimate branches finds representatives in every
class of society from all but the highest to the
very lowest, and, relying on the now popular principles of heredity and the *milieu*, as well perhaps
as on the older one of the "ruling passion," M. Zola
proceeded to select for the various books of the series
frameworks and backgrounds, including and presenting *quicquid agunt homines*—politics,[1] business,[2] art,[3]
ecclesiastical life ;[4] the Stock Exchange,[5] the markets,[6]
the taverns,[7] the places less generally described by
their names in modern polite society ;[8] the manners
and customs of shops,[2] railways,[9] public offices ;[1] the
fortunes of love (as he understood it) and of war ;[10]

[1] *Passim.*   [2] *Au Bonheur des Dames.*   [3] *L'Œuvre.*   [4] *Le Rêve.*
[5] *L'Argent.*   [6] *Le Ventre de Paris.*   [7] *L'Assommoir.*   [8] *Nana.*
[9] *La Bête Humaine.*   [10] *La Débâcle.*

the actual practice of medicine, commerce, and the rest. To carry out his idea completely, he not only furnished himself with "documents" by observing, or getting his friends (who, it is to be feared, sometimes played him tricks) to observe, the conduct of human persons in human affairs, but betook himself to a gigantic and (in its own mistaken way) almost admirable study of books and manuals. Horticulture and obstetrics; the precise method of administering extreme unction, and the precise manner of bidding or breaking on the Stock Exchange; peasant farming;[1] the management or mismanagement of a locomotive,[2] and the art and mystery of coal-mining,[3]— he mastered, or appeared to master, them all, and embodied the results in his books with an utter indifference to possibly inartistic effect, or rather with a conviction, now calm, now furious, that such embodiment *is* art, and the be - all and end - all of art.

Of this enormous panorama, which was eked out later by books less definitely belonging to the *The faults of Naturalism.* series, though often connected with it more or less, it is both much less difficult and much less presumptuous than it may appear to give summary criticism. In what is loosely called "power" M. Zola is by no means wanting. But his theory is hopelessly wrong; and the inevitable consequence (seen also in other cases, but conspicuous here) is that the more directly he applies this power on his chosen lines, the farther he goes from

[1] *La Terre.*   [2] *La Bête Humaine.*   [3] *Germinal.*

the true end. In the first place, he has neglected the truth that the end of Art is delight, and has returned (though with a new "reading") to the old "heresy of instruction." In the second, the predominance of merely technical detail is so clear an error that it is hardly necessary to waste any words upon it. In the third, the subordination of Art itself to certain scientific or pseudo-scientific hypotheses is yet again an obvious confusion of kinds which needs no argument. And lastly, the heaviest charge in the indictment against Naturalism is that it is *not* natural,—that the concentration of attention on the lower, the more animal, the more disgusting sides of nature is at least as much a fault, both from the point of view of science and from that of logic, as the concentration of it in an optimist direction is, while from the point of view of Art it is much worse.

It is, however, curious (or rather not curious at all) that such an author was unable wholly to keep *And the revenge* out the romantic and ideal element, and *of Art.* that wherever the fork was not vigilant enough to prevent the recurrence of this, really fine things occur, though partially, as it were, and by accident. On the one occasion where M. Zola seems to have wished to be totally "unobjectionable," in *Le Rêve*, he was too much out of his element with cathedrals and chastity. When he gives himself up wholly to whatsoever is foul, whatsoever is ignoble, whatsoever is of evil report,—as in *Pot-Bouille*, *Germinal*, *La Terre*, *L'Assommoir*, and *Nana*,—his literature is simply the literature of the sewer. When he thrusts in his book-learnt details, as in nearly all the books at times, he is merely boring. But in *La Faute de l'Abbé Mouret*, where animal for once becomes human passion, as it does, though less poignantly, again in *La Joie de Vivre;* in *L'Œuvre*, where the artist's monomania for his art is handled amid much inferior and even some foul matter with a true and redeeming pathos; in *La Débâcle*, where the causes of the frightful crash of 1870 are managed with extraordinary power; and not least in all but the latest of the actual series, *Le Docteur Pascal*, where the motive of *L'Abbé Mouret*, in different play, is once more utilised after a fashion which shows the mischief of the author's theory,—what might have been achieved without that theory appears clearly enough. Yet, once more, these escapes and revenges of Art, from time to time overpowering the rebellious artist and forcing him into the right way, do not prove him a failure. They prove, like the accesses of true inspiration which, we are told, sometimes come on the prophets of false gods, that these false gods themselves are, after all, nothing but appearances and wraiths, not entities. For the time M. Zola is not M. Zola as he wished to be, but somebody else. When he is himself as he would be, he writes *Nana* and *La Terre*.

These occasional touches, not of demoniacal but of quasi-angelic possession, had almost *The last books.* from the first, and in increasing measure as they multiplied, partially reconciled catholic critics to him. The general favour was less logically conciliated by the valour (rather divorced from discretion, but not the less reconciling for that) with which he protested, even to incurring unjust persecution, exile, and loss of goods, against the possession, far more demoniacal than any of his own, which came upon France in the Dreyfus case. The later books above referred to show signs of wear and tear; but they show it not so much in the loss of power as in an increasing inability to direct that power. The batch of " Les Trois Villes "—*Lourdes, Paris, Rome*—which immediately followed the completion of *Les Rougon - Macquart*, exhibits this less than the last and incomplete quartette of "Les Quatre Evangiles"—*Fécondité, Travail*, and *Vérité*, the last of which appeared, with a black line on the cover, after the author's tragical if accidental death in 1902. These last enormous rhapsodies, preaching the gospel of their several titles in an almost apocalyptic fashion, brought out what some critics had already noticed as M. Zola's tendency to a kind of inverted fairy tale. The gospel of producing as many children and cultivating as much land as possible, together with the plagues of celibate or sterile and idle vice, occupies *Fécondité ;* that of co-operative semi-socialism as opposed to capitalism, *Travail ;* while *Vérité* is a parable of the Dreyfus case itself. And all are permeated by a strange fanaticism of anti - religiosity, M. Zola being apparently persuaded that if you can only kill God, the Devil will die,—an idea which seems to leave

out of consideration the idiosyncrasy of a third
personage, Man. These books are, from more than
one cause, difficult to read; but a careful reading
of them is indispensable to a clear understanding of their author, and that understanding will as
usual bring not a little pardon with it.

He was partly, though by no means wholly, in
his better mood when he wrote the story serving as
The School   title-piece to a collection which introduced
of Zola.   to the public a novelist of less power but
of much finer genius than his own. Nearly all
Frenchmen write short stories better than they write
long,—with us it is, or has been till lately, just the
other way,—and, as noted above, M. Zola had begun
with some very agreeable efforts in this kind, which
he followed up later, by no means ill, with *Nouveaux
Contes à Ninon*, and with another collection or two—
Le Capitaine Burle and *Naïs Micoulin*. In *L'Attaque
du Moulin* (1880) he gathered round him a band of
younger disciples and fanatics of "naturalism." The
title-piece itself deals with an episode of the war of
ten years earlier, and has been scarcely over-com-
plimented by being set not too far below Mérimée's
magnificent *Enlèvement de la Redoute*. Of M. Zola's
young companions some are still living, and have
experienced vicissitudes.

But by far the greatest of them,[1] Guy de Mau-

---

[1] The next, perhaps, J. K. Huysmans (1848-1907), passed away
when this book was already in the printer's hands. He began as an
extravagant Naturalist and ended as a sort of mystic. His most
notorious book was *Là-bas* (1891).

passant (1850-1893), the Marcellus—or at least the Titus Tarquinius — of Naturalism, stained, indeed, with the faults of the breed but too good for it, was taken away when there were at least some signs that he was working himself clear of his faults.

M. de Maupassant was the son of very intimate friends of Flaubert, acted as usher to his master's correspondence, and showed his influence strongly in many ways. At about the same time with the appearance of *L'Attaque du Moulin* he published a volume of poems simply called *Des Vers*, somewhat lacking in the technical perfection which the Parnassien school (see last chapter) had made almost imperative, but full of a certain kind of quality. His bent, however, towards prose was much stronger. His contribution to *L'Attaque*, entitled "Boule de Suif," is sufficiently audacious in subject to defy argument in books not constructed on Naturalist principles. But it is a story of extraordinary humour, irony, and pathos, told in a fashion for which "supreme" is hardly too extravagant a term. M. de Maupassant wrote many other short stories, and in them chiefly developed the quality in which he differs most from Flaubert himself— that of commanding the purely comic. Especially in his earlier work (*La Maison Tellier*, 1881 ; *Bel Ami*, 1885, &c.) the Naturalist preference of "fie-fie" subjects too often smirches them ; but to those who can exercise discernment it is almost invariably noticeable that Maupassant's fun never comes merely from the presence of naughtiness. The comedy—as

Maupassant.

for instance in *Les Sœurs Rondoli*, 1882—is as genuine and independent as in the case of Aristophanes, though, as in that case also, it may too often be inseparably though accidentally connected with what is not convenient.

Maupassant was more like Flaubert on some other sides of his literary character,—in the tragic, that is to say, and the leaning towards the uncanny, which is noticeable enough in the author of *Salammbô* and the *Tentation*. But Flaubert himself, at least for all his later life, had been irregular in living only by his abnormal devotion to work and his habit of working at night,—things not conducive to health or longevity, perhaps, but not absolutely ruinous. Maupassant, on the other hand, was an extremely reckless liver, and may have invited the approaches of general paralysis or some other form of brain-degeneration. The ghastly story of *Le Horla* (1887), which he produced some time before his death from cerebral disease, might not necessarily—as the work of Sheridan Le Fanu and others, including, perhaps, even Edgar Poe, shows—betoken anything functionally wrong. But, however this might be, the enemy came upon him, and he died.

His genius, but for this vein of morbidness, had been steadily ripening, and his taste had, as has been said above, shown almost unmistakable signs of spurning the naturalist level. The great novel of *Pierre et Jean* (1888), which wants but very little to be one of the greatest of the half century, is not wholly for the young person. But it is nowhere

"grimy" for grime's sake; and the fire and force
of the handling melt and hammer out of its substance all the baser elements. In no case, perhaps,
—for Flaubert, as has been partly explained above,
is not quite a case in point,—has the unhealthy
atmosphere of too large a part of modern life claimed
such a sacrifice as in that of Maupassant.

Beyond Maupassant it seems unnecessary to pursue
the story of the French novel, though the present
writer is fairly well provided with mate-
The rest. rials for doing so. Such breaking off may
seem horrible or contemptible to those who inform
us that "a new school of French literature appears
every fifteen years." But even they might take
into consideration the fact that, on their own hypothesis, each school of French literature becomes old
in fifteen years; and therefore that what may have
come into existence about Maupassant's death is
nearly or quite ready to be cast into the oven, and
had better wait till its residuary ashes—if there are
any — can be scientifically treated. Many writers
who have given the historian pleasure, or boredom,
or "honest journey - work in default of better," as
the case may be, could be strung together with ease
here, and allotted rations more or less unsatisfying,
doses more or less homœopathic, of criticism. But
the plan of gradually curtailing such notices as we
reach the end has almost everything in its favour,
except the risk of disgusting the reader who wants
to hear most about what he knows best already; and
this risk must be risked. Indeed, most of those

G

who have made much name since are still alive,
and therefore are taboo, according to our system,—
pleasant as it would be to dwell on the unequalled
grace and style of M. Anatole France, the admirable
wit and winningness of " Gyp " (Madame de Martel),
and the solid landscape painting of M. André
Theuriet, to mention no others.[1]

In no case, perhaps, throughout the present volume
is it so necessary to disregard the famous and urbane
The English   appeal to " Bélier ! mon ami," and to begin
Novel in 1850.   perforce in the middle, as in reference to
the English novel.   It is true that a remarkable
change of minor and general writing coincided pretty
nearly with the middle of the century.   But in
fiction, as in poetry, though not quite to the same
extent, the greater persons outlived and overlapped
in a way which cannot be neglected.   Of the four
novelists whom Mr Omond selected in *The Romantic
Triumph* for his leading figures after Scott's death,
Thackeray, the shortest lived, passed 1850 by thirteen
years, and in those thirteen accomplished the greater
part of his greatest work ; Dickens passed it by
twenty ; Bulwer by twenty - three, during which he

[1] M. Theuriet, like M. Huysmans, died just as this work was being
printed.   Of those earlier removed, the most noteworthy work wholly
or all but wholly belonging to the time and not yet noticed is that
of M. Victor Cherbuliez (1829-1899), *Le Comte Kostia, Méta Holdenis*,
&c., in which the labour a little overtops the matter and the art,
but where there is still much of both art and matter ; and that of
Ferdinand Fabre (1850-1898), a novelist whose specialty was delinea-
tion, in a "non-naturalist" tone, of country life and especially of the
country clergy.

exhibited again and again his remarkable and almost unique *variety* of power; and Disraeli by more than thirty. Of this last we need not speak, for *Lothair* and *Endymion* have been already referred to, and in all but insignificant respects they are at one with *Tancred* and *Sybil*. But the others could not be passed over; and we may best take them in reverse order to that just dictated by chronology.

At the beginning of our period the sensitive and versatile talent of the author of *The Last Days of Pompeii* seems to have felt and almost anticipated the set of public taste away from Byronism and romance towards the novel of ordinary life; and he at once began in *The Caxtons* (1850) an example of the new kind, which in its day and way has had few superiors in popularity, following it up with *My Novel* (1853) and *What Will He Do with It?* (1859)—books with a touch of Richardsonian quality and more than a touch of Richardsonian length. It might have been supposed that the working of a vein so entirely different from that of most, if not all, his earlier books would have sufficed him; but this was by no means the case. The rather quick reaction from the purely domestic to the "sensational" tale found Bulwer ready with nearly the best of all supernatural short stories in English, *The Haunted and the Haunters* (1859), which he contributed to *Blackwood's Magazine*, and with the longer *Strange Story* (1861), which, though very far from deserving the same rank among its kind, gave the periodical in which it appeared (Dickens's second

Bulwer.

venture of the kind, *All the Year Round*) probably
a greater circulation than any English paper of the
sort had ever had.   Nor even then was the versatility
of Sir Edward (soon to be Lord) Lytton exhausted;
for in the last years of his life, books, hardly any
two of which are exactly alike in class, *The Coming
Race* (1870), *Kenelm Chillingly* (1873), *The Parisians*
(1874),[1] showed absolutely no failure of power.   Indeed, he would be a critic more self-willed than
catholic who should maintain that *Falkland* or *Pelham*
shows anything like the ability of these forty years'
younger products of a forty years' older brain.   Nay,
the Devil's Advocate could only recoup himself by
bringing a charge, applicable likewise as we shall
see to all but one or two of Lord Lytton's younger
contemporaries in the novel, that though there was
no falling off there was at the same time no absolute
attainment of the consummate in any particular
instance,—that, as of *Ernest Maltravers* and the *Last
Days* and the others, so of *My Novel*, so of the *Strange
Story*, so of the latest novels of fantasy and society
it might, nay must, be said that there is something
wanting—some last drop to crystallise the product,
some final elixir to accomplish the full projection.
This is the appropriate and allotted curse of profuse

[1] Of these the second and third are novels of society, drawn with a
wonderfully unjaded eye and hand.   The first is an early example, if
not, as so often happens with Bulwer, an actual anticipation, of a kind
very popular since in most countries,—the imaginary account of
a future state of life, scientifically developed and perfected.   Much
tedium has been bestowed on us by this,—mixed, however, with a
little amusement not always intended by the authors.

novel-writing—and it has been avoided with increasing rarity in our time.   But, on the other hand, few novelists have escaped the just charge of producing *bad* books as Bulwer has.   Faults in almost all there are,—bad faults in many, especially of the earlier; the want of consummateness in all.   But a really bad book is hardly anywhere.

With his friend and editor, Dickens, things were different.   Between 1850 and his death, twenty years

Dickens.

later, Dickens did things which, according to absolute standard, were much greater than anything of Bulwer's; but in relation to his own work, neither his whole production nor any undivided part of it—one singular and outlying example being, and this not by general consent, excepted—will bear comparison with the summits of the chain from *Pickwick* to *Copperfield*.   This was partly due to the fact that neither by disposition nor by training was Dickens one of the persons for whom irresponsible prosperity is no mischief, while both as novelist and as editor he had the public completely at his feet in the last twenty years of his life.   He had read very little, and there are no signs of his having thought very much.   But he had imbibed the crude Liberalism of the mid-nineteenth century, and his intimacy with Carlyle had caused him to imbibe the Carlylian exaggeration without its redeeming atmosphere and halo.   In pure literature, moreover, where he had had no critical inoculation to protect him, he had already betrayed symptoms of infection with two very bad literary diseases—proneness to mannerism and prone-

ness to emphasis. Of his chief substantive productions (his Christmas numbers for *Household Words*
and its successor often contain priceless things),
published during the first seven years of our period,
one only, and that the first, can be said fully to carry
off its defects by its merits. This is *Bleak House*
(1852-53), and even here one would perhaps rather
not be driven to a too arithmetical figuring out of
faults and beauties. In *Little Dorrit* (1855-57),
though it has some capital things, and in the shorter
Manchester, or at least Lancashire, story of *Hard
Times* (1854), the faults outnumber and outweigh the
beauties rather disastrously; while in *The Child's
History of England* (1854)—a book which the author
had, as the popular phrase goes, no earthly "call"
to write—the beauties are simply absent, with the
rarest exception. It is curious that Thackeray and
Dickens should both have tried this singular experiment of attempting, on no better research than a
reading of the ordinary school manuals, and in the
style of a comic partisan leading-article, something
so difficult that nobody, with the fullest knowledge
and in the most serious manner, has done it perfectly yet. It is still more curious that "Miss
Tickletoby's Lectures," written when Thackeray had
not yet found his true way, are by no means
unamusing, while Dickens's book, written in his
maturity, is not even that.

His next two books are evidences that the sense
of unrest which seems to have come upon the novel
generally at the time affected him. *A Tale of Two*

Cities (1859), dealing with Paris and London during the great French Revolution, had a considerable popularity at first, and has generally, I believe, maintained it, while some critics of worship extol it as a masterpiece both of plot and character. But there are those who think it one of the author's greatest failures —melodramatic where it would be tragic, forced and feeble in its comedy, almost destitute (save in the figure of Sydney Carton) of character, wooden, if elaborate, in plot, and positively ridiculous as an attempt in novel to reproduce, much more to vie with, the magnificent presentment of Carlyle, which no doubt inspired it. *Great Expectations* (1860-61), on the other hand, which followed it, was not very generally popular, but it has from the first had warm and faithful admirers. In no book is that imaginative quality, which was especially dwelt upon in the last volume, more prominent; in none is Dickens's almost constant failure to create other than grotesque female character so nearly exchanged for success in a real heroine. Critically, one must not perhaps pronounce the thing entirely happy, but it has gone near (some think) to a greater success than anything that Dickens actually accomplished in the marriage of the fantastic and the real. In his last decade he wrote little, being much occupied with "readings" in England and America; and his final book, *Edwin Drood*, was left unfinished, and, in fact, hardly more than begun. But *Our Mutual Friend* (1864-65), the last complete work, is "true Dickens" in its faults and in its merits,— something of the manner of *Little Dorrit* being redeemed by much extraordinarily vivid description and not a little inimitable character-painting.

The much slower development of Thackeray as a writer almost necessarily brought with it a different *Thackeray—* result. In 1850 he had only just, with *Esmond, &c.* *Pendennis* and the lectures on the *Humourists*, reached his full and characteristic self-representation; for though there may be greater things in *Vanity Fair* than in either of these, it is a more unequal book, and was besides but two or three years old. The astonishing masterpiece of *Esmond*, in 1852, showed the application of the studies of the century in political and literary history to the novel as no book had done before, and, indeed, as none has done since—the adjustment, without falsetto or pastiche, of early eighteenth and mid-nineteenth century language, thought, and feeling being not more wonderful as a *tour de force* than the character-drawing and scene-painting of the book, its humour, its pathos, its infinite criticism of life, were in absolute power and truth without any effort at all. This he followed by a return to the style of *Pendennis* (with somewhat less though still some autobiographic admixture) in *The Newcomes* (1853-55), and *The Newcomes* in turn by a continuation of *Esmond*, *The Virginians* (1857-58), which is perhaps not so far inferior to its predecessor as has been generally thought, though the completion of the history of Beatrix is too ruthlessly realist to please sentimental tastes, and too full of poetic feeling to please the sham anti-sentimentalism of a later time. A (second) journey to America gave lectures on the *Four Georges* —brilliant adjustments of the *Esmond* and *Virginians* style from the novel to the popular address. And in 1860 came his appointment to the editorship of the new *Cornhill Magazine*. Merely as editor Thackeray was not much of a success, being too impatient both of drudgery and of the inevitable duties of that painful position. Of the three novels which he contributed to it during and after his tenure of the post,—for he soon resigned it,—the two first, *Lovel the Widower* and *Philip*, are not of his very best class. The first, which throws into novel form an unsuccessful earlier play, though full of amusing things, is both slight and a little *raw;* while *Philip*, which connects itself with *Pendennis* and *The Newcomes*, and like them has a dose of autobiography, is, though even better in parts, badly constructed, and suffers from the joint burden, too heavy for any novel, of a rather "chuckle-headed" hero and an insignificant heroine. The third, *Denis Duval*, was by a strange coincidence broken off even shorter than Dickens's last attempt seven years later, but it promised exceedingly well.

If Thackeray's contributions to the *Cornhill* had been confined to these, we should have had to thank that periodical for comparatively little. But he had begun in it from the first, and continued till his very last, a series of disconnected essays, entitled *The* Round- *Roundabout Papers,* which contain the very about Papers. essence and quintessence of his genius, setting aside (and even not wholly setting aside) the application of that genius to the creation of character.

The intense humorous appreciation of life, the kindly irony, the myriad - glancing interests, the wonderful power of thumbnail sketches of place and person, above all, the unique style, so unique and so un-conventional that some persons have found fault with it, but supremely adequate, ineffably personal, *l'homme même* as hardly any other style has been,—display themselves here as fully and happily as Addison's do in the *Spectator*, and with (to us at any rate) infinitely more variety, gusto, tantalising and yet satisfying interest.   There is almost everything in these papers —description, criticism of life and literature, remarks on events and persons, little stories (the burlesque of the sensation-novel in *The Notch on the Axe* is one of the very triumphs of the kind), reminiscences, travel-pictures.   Except in his verse—of which he still wrote a few pieces, though very much fewer than earlier—it is nowhere so easy to see the real Thack-eray,—a vision, it is true, which can hardly conceal itself from any not quite purblind reader even in his most immature work, but which in that is partly obscured by simple immaturity, and in the longer books sometimes disjointed and made difficult to seize as a result of the artist's studied desultoriness and of his occasional mistakes in construction [1] and purpose.

A few words may be properly added to the sum-

[1] Thackeray's "inaccuracy" in fictitious history is a curious parallel to Mr Froude's in actual. Cf. (an instance less noticed than others) the way in which the "Sir Thomas de Boots" of an important early scene in *The Newcomes* becomes "Sir George Tufto" in the later reference to it.

maries of the work of these three novelists in the
last volume, in reference to their later
production, and the subsequent fortunes
of their fame. Bulwer did much to vindicate himself from the mere ridicule which the excesses of his Byronic period had brought on him:
it cannot be said that he was ever, during this time,
ridiculous. But that very gift of his, of adjusting
himself to the contemporary, carried with it a share
of the disadvantages of the ephemeral, and has
multiplied them in a manner curious and almost
unique in degree, but in kind contingent to the study
of all the modern literature of the novel. The critic
who is to do justice to the whole of Bulwer must be
acquainted with the idiosyncrasies of three or four
successive literary generations, and at the same time
not sufficiently committed to any one to prevent him
from judging the others impartially. Such a person
has not appeared yet; and however tempting a difficult adventure of the kind may be, it is clear that it
should not be attempted here.

The exercise of Dickens during the period led as
undoubtedly in the other direction. Mr Omond
rightly said that in 1850 he could be placed second
only to Scott among the novelists of the century, and
perhaps in some ways and to some tastes beyond him.
By his death-date in 1870 uncomfortable doubts had
already arisen as to the abiding accuracy of this
calculus—and the succeeding thirty years have confirmed them. The wise person who sets the *enjoyment*
of literature first of all would indeed peremptorily

Some general remarks on these.

refuse any proposition of having Dickens's career cut short at *Copperfield*. We are not going to let ourselves be deprived of Mr Guppy, and the Smallweeds, and Miss Flite; of Mr F.'s Aunt, and Maggie, and Dorrit *père;* of Joe Gargery, and Trabb's Boy, and Mr Wemmick; of the Doll's Dressmaker, and of Silas Wegg, not to mention many other persons (and many things) less relatively, but still idiosyncratically, good. But it would probably be impossible for any Court of Critical Appeal, where the bench is impartially and competently filled, to say that these last twenty years *exalted* Dickens's relative, or even his positive, position, in the sense of making the pedestal higher,—though fresh accretions of good solid boulders may have been rolled up round the older heap. It would be equally impossible for such a court not to pronounce, with whatever sorrow, that the faults which tend to depress that relative position became far more evident—mannerism, bad taste, tedious iteration, mistaken purpose, the persistent habit of attempting to delineate classes with which the artist was not familiar, to deal with questions with which he had no historical or philosophical acquaintance. Even that imaginative power which was justly praised earlier failed him here, except perhaps in *Great Expectations*, or showed itself only in melodramatic fantasies like the death-scene of Krook in *Bleak House*, like the framework of *Hard Times*, like too much in *Little Dorrit*, like almost the whole of *A Tale of Two Cities*, like some things in *Our Mutual Friend* and *Edwin Drood*. Yet this could be said, that never—

in novel at least—did he write anything which did not contain something of the true Dickens, and that he never absolutely and wholly derogated : though he may have failed to maintain his proper place quite as he should, and not have succeeded in exalting it at all.

To Thackeray the Fates, mindful of the short thread of actual days which they had allotted him, were kinder. Even in 1850 he would not have been a *grand peut-être*, but the enemy would undoubtedly have had some ground for questioning the value of the books that he might be going to write. In 1863 the author—taking them alone and with no retrospect, though the retrospect was wholly to their credit—of the books from *Esmond* to *Roundabout Papers* was established securely in one of the highest and foremost places in English literature. That some, who were not themselves fools, in his lifetime gave the cue to others to accuse him of cynicism matters no more and no less than that some, again themselves not fools, have given the other cue since to the others to accuse him of sentimentality. " Cynic, and what for no ? " " Sentimentalist, and what for no ? " These idly flung tickets can be flung back into the waste-paper basket, which is their proper home, and where they may keep due company with each other   Every man who has a brain and a heart is by turns cynic and sentimentalist; and every man of letters of the greater kind underlies the necessity of representing both moods.   Thackeray could not have evaded it without ceasing to " find the whole " as he has, after a fashion which Dickens certainly has not found, which Scott perhaps rather refused to find than could not, which Fielding came too early to find. Thackeray's whole is not indeed the unerring centre and perfect round of Shakespeare. He is weak on religion and politics, and he does not wisely eschew them; his argumentative faculty is not supreme, and he sometimes argues; his criticism, extraordinarily good at times, has a Lamb-like quality of capriciousness and inadequacy without Lamb's almost invariable and instinctive avoidance of awkward places. But in all these points the slips that he makes are human, not asinine: he hardly ever attempts a person or a class of persons whom by want of sympathy or want of actual experience he is incapable of drawing; his character faculty is not phantasmagoric merely, but prose-poetic; and the amber of pure literature that he pours round all his people, all his things, all his very follies, mistakes, questionablenesses, is such as would redeem what has here not to be redeemed at all. The period from 1850 to 1870 will, it is not very rash to predict, be regarded by those critics who can see things from the steady point of distance as one of the greatest in modern English literature for appearances and for confirmations, for introductions and for re-establishments of fame. But surveying its accomplishment from a point already a generation off, one may feel inclined to say that no single thing in it is of equal importance with the establishment and completion of the literary rank of William Makepeace Thackeray.

The time, however, would not deserve the compliment which has just been paid to it if it had merely *The new-comers.* seen work by those who had already distinguished themselves, and it was hardly less fertile of new writers in the present department than in poetry. One of the most remarkable figures, or rather groups,—Charlotte Bronte and her sisters, —has been despatched in the preceding volume with more than merely chronological propriety, because there is undoubtedly a strong tincture of the earlier —even of the Byronic—Romanticism in their work. But there is also much of Realism. And this exhibits itself still more in others to be now mentioned, even where, as in Kingsley's case, the Realism blends itself with a neo-Romanticism as genuine at least—to some it may seem more so—than that of the first half of the century. He himself, George Eliot, Anthony Trollope, Charles Reade, and Miss Yonge must have independent mention, if at no great length. "Other offenders," as the criticism of the older type would have accounted them, "we will pause" less amply "upon."

Charles Kingsley (1819-1875) began to write fairly early, and before 1850 itself, besides sermons, pamphlets in a crude but amiable kind of *Kingsley.* Christian Socialism, &c., he had produced three substantive books, one in verse, two in prose, which, also crude enough in certain ways, were unusually full of life and promise. The verse book, *The Saint's Tragedy* (1848), was a treatment of the story of St Elizabeth of Hungary, intended, no doubt, partly as a counterblast to the "Oxford Movement" (which, though seemingly foiled for the moment in its own line, was really carrying everything before it in art and letters), but itself a testimony to the power of mediæval influence. It is a sort of dramatic novel in verse, and therefore is mentioned here. Its fellows in the more straightforward form of prose, *Alton Locke* and *Yeast* (both of the year 1849), rank much higher. With Carlyle's *Chartism* and *Latter Day Pamphlets* they are the chief literary memorials of the extraordinary measles of unrest and passion which came upon England at the time,—mild diseases compared with the Continental plagues of 1848-49, but connected with and corresponding to them. *Alton Locke*, contributing its picture of a Chartist tailor full of literary aspirations, brought into contact with the university and other life of the classes above him, and half-inspired, half-martyrised by hopeless love, is contrasted in *Yeast* with the pendant sketch of a young man of great abilities but reckless life, who loses his ample means by the misdeeds of others, and his love, Argemone Lavington (a wonderful though half-finished sketch, the vividness of which was apparent long before it was known to be half a portrait), by death, and disappears into the vague. Both are exceedingly "young," and both, especially *Yeast*, are open to the charge of being rather bundles of powerful sketches than satisfactory wholes. But both are full of life, power, imagination, poetic feeling; and both, but again especially *Yeast*, contain lavish description of the kind of which Mr Ruskin had set the example too recently for these attempts in it to be called merely secondhand, while they scarcely yield the mastery to the master's own. Kingsley lived through the whole of the third quarter of the century. But his best work was done by 1863. It consisted (besides sermons of some, and essays of great, merit, with the *Poems* referred to in the last chapter, *Glaucus* (1855), a fascinating introduction to marine zoology, *The Heroes*, and not a few other things of curious and attractive variety) of three novels, two of them containing his very best work, and of a very remarkable fantasy piece, *The Water Babies* (1863), interesting to compare and contrast with Mr Dodgson's later "Alice" pieces which followed it soon. The third novel, *Two Years Ago* (1857), was unequal, and showed perhaps signs of positive declension, though there are very fine things in it. The two earlier, *Hypatia* and *Westward Ho!* (1855), are altogether among the greater company of English fiction. His only later attempt of the kind, *Hereward the Wake* (1866), was something of a failure. He became engaged (1864), half unawares, in a controversy with Cardinal Newman, where he had little chance, and threw that chance away. His work as Professor of History at Cambridge (1860-69) was relentlessly persecuted by unfriendly critics, and gave some handles to its persecutors. As a whole, *Westward Ho!* shows Kingsley at his best, and is a nearly perfect book in its own kind of historical novel—a kind which the retrospective studies of the century have specially fostered, but which, in itself

H

difficult, becomes more so the farther those studies are themselves pursued.

The saturation of the novel with political, religious, fashionable "purpose," which has been signalised to some extent in Bulwer, to much in *"George Eliot."* Dickens and Kingsley, but from which Thackeray fortunately escaped, though he too felt the historic "obsession," seemed at first likely to spare another remarkable novelist who appeared a little later than any of those just mentioned, Mary Ann Evans (1819-1880), by her *nom de guerre* in literature "George Eliot," and by her marriage (very late in life) Mrs Cross. It was not till she had reached middle age that Miss Evans, who had studied much, had gone through a course of freethinking, and had written translations and reviews, produced (1857) in *Blackwood's Magazine* certain short stories, *Scenes of Clerical Life*, which showed a very remarkable power of presenting ordinary experience, especially the remoter and more retired life of the country, with a mixture of pathos and humour. This power was shown on a greater scale, and in a more popular fashion, though still in regard to much the same subjects, in the novel of *Adam Bede* (1858), which at once attained popularity, and was followed by two others in the same general style, *The Mill on the Floss* (1860) and *Silas Marner* (1861). The substance of all these had been provided by long years of patient and unforced observation; the treatment was, as has been said, both pathetic and humorous. If there *was* "purpose" it was not unduly pressed — it "didn't bite," in famous words of another matter. The whole, if not equally attractive to all tastes, was good, and it was fresh. Had the author died or ceased writing then, her position, if not of the highest, would have been at a comparatively undisputed height.

But the "historic obsession" came on her, and she wrote an Italian novel, *Romola* (1863), which, falling in with certain nascent tastes of the day, did much to strengthen her popularity with a coterie and even to make that coterie a large one, but in which she herself acknowledged, and in which others were not slow to detect, the "mark of the collar." Some touch of strain, however, is almost inevitable in the sufficient assimilation of a foreign and distant period: it might have been hoped that return to domestic and contemporary themes would bring relief. This, however, was not quite the case. She only wrote three more novels before her death, though seventeen years passed between the appearance of *Romola* and that event— *Felix Holt the Radical* (1866), *Middlemarch* (1871), and lastly, *Daniel Deronda* (1876). The first of these is the least faulty, but it is also much the least ambitious, and is on the whole rather negative. *Middlemarch* was a great effort, and was hailed by admirers as a great triumph. They named their houses after it; they were never weary of quoting its scenes, its characters, its sayings; it was supposed to mark—and to mark at high-water—a fresh tide in the affairs of the English novel. Yet the fame of its author, where it exists, now rests upon other books;

and this was foreseen by some critics, at least, of the time. For the book, though mightily machined, *is* a piece of machinery; it does not live and grow. It has neither the Classical Unity of Action nor the Romantic Unity of Interest; its various motives rather fade away than come to an artistic close; its figures, strongly as they may seem at times to be projected,—Casaubon, Dorothea, Lydgate, Rosamond, and the rest,—neither transport nor even leave a lasting and poignant impression. But if this was the case with *Middlemarch*, still more was it so with *Daniel Deronda*. In the earlier book the motives and appeals, if not quite happily worked out, were in themselves sufficiently human. The later selected for its mainspring the particularist enthusiasm of the Jew for Judaism, and, not content with this, the supposed delight of a young man who has always believed that he is not a Jew on finding himself to be one. An excellent subject for Comic Opera, this could hardly be satisfactory for a very serious novel; and its inevitable failure carried with it two very strong and almost principal figures, the heroine Gwendolen Harleth and the wicked hero Grandcourt, though they are among the best things the author ever did. They might even have dragged Deronda himself with them to safety if George Eliot had not loaded them with one of the most astounding jargons, gradually accumulated no doubt, but never till now fully poured forth, that novelist has ever attempted — a jargon chiefly drawn from scientific and philosophical phraseology. There was a distinct revolt against the book, and this affected rather injuriously the reception of her last work, *Theophrastus Such*, a nondescript miscellany containing not a few good things.

This anxiety—at least this conscious-unconscious desire to give the novel a "modern" twist or touch— *The temptation of demand and supply.* is as noticeable in three later novelists of the mid-century who are catalogued above; but fortunately in all cases it confines itself within narrower limits. In all three, too, as in others of a still later generation to be noticed later, if at all, there is observable something which differentiates the dangers of the novel from those of most other literary kinds. It is wanted, by those who want it, in quantity; it can be provided in that quantity as hardly (since the Middle Ages) the maddest poets dream of providing verse; yet such provision is almost incompatible with excellence in quality. In every view of this triad the question presents itself: "If these writers had not written [as an old French gibe has it] *à la douzaine*—if for every book of theirs that we have we had a tenth of a book—would they have been nearer to the greatest masters of the art?" To this query no positive answer can be given, even after the widest and most "disengaged" study of literature. The leading cases help us only a little. As a rule, extremely rapid and extremely bulky work is not of the best—is not even good; yet the best work in all literature is to be found in Shakespeare's forty plays, written in all probability during not much more than half as many years. Leisurely and

carefully corrected work ought to be good work; yet
the whole history of literature, in every volume and
every chapter, interposes a quiet but inexorable " No!"
to the assumption that it must be.

Of what is commonly called genius the eldest of
these three, Charles Reade (1814-1884), had perhaps
the most unmistakable signs, and it so
happens that he had by far the best
chances of developing this genius at his ease, while
he so availed himself of them as, at least, to produce
by far the least bulk of work. Born a year before
Waterloo, of a county family, at Ipsden in Oxfordshire,
he was elected, seventeen years later, to a demyship
in Magdalen College, Oxford, which was duly exchanged in the year of his majority (1835) for an
unusually valuable fellowship,—one, too, which did
not, as in most cases, carry with it the necessity of
taking orders. No man of letters could have asked
for more; and no man of letters, with even a rudimentary share of knowledge how to live, could have
failed to find in this lot the opportunity of shaping
his life practically as he would. But Reade abused,
as well as profited by, his opportunities. He was
extremely quarrelsome—pushing his quarrelsomeness
to the fatally extravagant point of indulging in law-
suits; he would write plays which were not good and
brought him no money; and he delayed writing
novels, which were very good and brought him much,
until more than half his life was gone. When he
did begin he was already a little of a *maniaque*, in
the French sense, and one of his manias, modern in

Charles Reade.

the highest degree, was the accumulation of enormous
"documents"—scrap-books full of extracts, authorities, *pièces justificatives* of all kinds. He wrote, in the
rather more than thirty years of his remaining life,
eighteen novels, over which he probably took pains
enough for eight-and-twenty, and which would as
probably have been much better if he had only
written eight and had curtailed by half the pains
spent on each. The opening pair, *Peg Woffington*
(1852) and *Christie Johnstone* (1853), are the slightest
but the freshest; *It is Never too Late to Mend* (1856),
at first an exaggeration of a contemporary story of
prison tyranny and later a wonderfully vivid tran-
script of other current stories about life in the new
gold-fields of Australia, retains much of the freshness, adds body and bulk, but perhaps shows effort.

By almost common consent his masterpiece is taken
to be *The Cloister and the Hearth* (1861), though some
readers are still tormented by a doubt how far the
extremest panegyrists are aware of the enormous
drafts made in it on the *Colloquies* of Erasmus.
Reade lived more than twenty years after the publication of this large and really great book: nor did he
ever do anything which had not the seeds (or the
husks) of greatness in it. But the "document," as
well as his various crazes (one of which was a rather
suspicious suspicion of mad-doctors and mad-houses),
got more and more the better of him, and latterly he
wrote very little. He is, with Mr Meredith, whom
we may not here handle, the chief novelist of the
nineteenth century, an absolute criticism of whom

the judicious critic may without pusillanimity decline. We must leave them to the next age.

The over - hurry of critics who are not judicious has seldom been more quickly demonstrated than *Anthony Trollope.* in the case of our next in order of time, Anthony Trollope (1815-1882). Mr Trollope, whose death had been preceded by a decade of constant writing at a level certainly inferior to that of his best work, was scarcely dead before such critics hastened to draw the moral of him,—to pronounce him an example of the unworthily popular writer who to-day is and to-morrow is cast into the oven, and so forth. Already, in less than a quarter of a century, Trollope is "inquired after," as the Stock Exchange people say, and his works are re-printed as fast as their copyright falls in. And it is no wonder: though whether the inquiry will be steadily maintained is still a point on which some who never joined in the "bear" process might wish to exercise economy. The difficulty is, in the enormous amount of the work, to select individual examples which are sufficiently characteristic; and this is only partially met by specifying the famous "Barsetshire" series (1855-67), though it is perhaps the safest. Trollope, a member of a very literary family, entered the Post Office early, and, without neglecting his duty, contrived to unite the discharge of it with the attainment of a remarkable knowledge of English country sports, and of the life both of the country proper and of country towns. He came just at the right time for this,—the coarseness and roughness of this life in the eighteenth century having worn off, while it had not yet been much sophisticated, as it has been since by the incursion of moneyed *parvenus* from the manufacturing towns, and the vast extension of outlying suburbs. But he did not confine himself to it. His official experiences were utilised with some audacity and great success; and few novelists of any country have had a wider and more accurate knowledge of different classes of society.

His industry was extraordinary, his versatility unquestionable, his grasp of situation and character sometimes but a little, *if* even a little, below the very highest. The vividness of the personages and the quick turns of incident and interest in such books as *Barchester Towers* (1857) and *The Last Chronicle of Barset* (1867) are astonishing and delectable; many others, out of a total of fifty or sixty, deserve almost equal praise in parts, and would have made the fortune of a minor novelist as wholes. Always,—in his early Irish books as much as in his later excursions into romance in *Nina Balatka*, &c.,—his skill to catch the manners as they rose, and his wonderful knack of weaving an interesting story (sometimes, as in *Orley Farm* (1862), out of the most commonplace materials), are things that can hardly receive too willing and liberal critical recognition. But always there is that un- grateful yet damaging "If there were only *less* of it all!" If what is good were more concentrated, we think (perhaps it is only a delusion) that what is not so good must have been squeezed or strained out in the concentration; if the merits of the author, instead of being, as it were, dosed into scores of different books to give them just sufficient body and flavour, had been presented in a few specimens of real "vintage wines," how much better had it been! Very likely an unjust complaint: perhaps as such a mere delusion. But so it occurs.

In the case of Miss Yonge (1823-1901) there is an excuse for this voluminousness which does not apply in the others. Charles Reade was so self-willed a person that he would have probably done almost exactly as he did whatever the circumstances of his life. Anthony Trollope, though by no means a mere money-grubber, would probably have been content to write half the number of novels if he could have got the same money for the half as for the whole. But Miss Yonge wrote to do good; she spent a large part of her not inconsiderable earnings on actual good works; and she probably never wrote a line without a hope, most amply justified, that the *prodesse* as well as the *delectare* would result. Given, therefore, a long life, a great industry, and an unfailing flow of matter, and a huge production must necessarily have followed. She began very early (about 1848), and she wrote, in more than fifty years, more than three times as many books. Coming by time, temperament, and even place (for her abode was close to Keble's parish), under the influence of the Oxford Movement, she attempted at once that task of enforcing its principles in fiction, the example of which had been set

Miss Yonge.

much earlier by the Evangelicals, but which had not
in their case produced work of much literary merit.
Fortunately for herself and her readers, Miss Yonge's
education was excellent and her taste capital. She
was no mean historical student,—even from the point
of view of the serious scholar,—and her acquaintance
with general literature was wide and discerning.

Even in very early works — stories rather than
novels—a fresh and vigorous handling of the domestic,
a winning adaptation of the historic, matter was per-
ceivable; and her first really important attempt, *The
Heir of Redclyffe* (1855), had very great popularity
and influence. It is a sign of the deplorable want
of width of literary and historical knowledge now
prevailing that surprise was expressed by more than
one or two reviewers at the acknowledgment of this
influence which was made in the *Life* of William
Morris. Nothing could be truer, and nothing more
natural: for the Oxford Movement really contained
in itself the germ of pre - Raphaelitism and many
other things, which have since in some cases wan-
dered rather far from their origin. Miss Yonge
wrote almost as long as she lived: she "uttered
nothing base," and it may almost be said that she
never did anything bad. No doubt, after about 1870
the enormous quantity began to show some signs of
slackening power, and more of that attempt, not quite
successful, to "follow the period" without deserting
the writer's own ideas, which is one of the great
notes of these immensely productive writers in recent
days. She seldom troubled herself very much about

plot, and not often much about description: but her study of character was unfailingly genial, as well as always noble and full of gentle life; and her dialogue was "a model of the middle style"—facile without being vapid, natural without being either vulgar or commonplace.[1]

These writers, with Mr Meredith, who lodged his diploma-piece with *The Ordeal of Richard Feverel* in 1859, and Mr Thomas Hardy, also happily a survivor, not merely supply the most remarkable examples in different kinds of English novel-work during the last half century, but almost what may be called its *palette*. That is to say, almost all later novelists either follow them as models more or less directly, or blend their characteristics with such further admixture of individuality as may in each case have been found possible. At different times group-characterisations, such as the novel of muscular Christianity, the sensational novel, and others, have been attempted; but they have seldom corresponded to any real distinction of species, and have so passed

---

[1] It would provoke the wrath of many if we left out from this straitened list of the preferred a lady older than Dickens or Thackeray, Mrs Gaskell (1810 - 1865), who, however, *Mrs Gaskell.* hardly began to write till the eve of our proper period. *Mary Barton* (1848), just before the beginning, has had warm admirers, and *Cranford* (1853), a little after that beginning, has never lacked them. Nor, indeed, have most of her books. But there were not many of them, for she died in 1865, after less than two decades of literary activity. *Cranford* is an attempt in that style of domestic miniature-painting which, after being sketched by Addison before the dawn of the novel proper, was brought to unsurpassable perfection by Miss Austen; and it undoubtedly holds very high rank in the class.

out of use. It is safer to mention individuals, though to none of them can much space be given. R. D. Blackmore (1825-1900), barrister, scholar, gentleman, and market-gardener, did not take to novel-writing till he was nearly forty; then after one or two minor works made a great success, in 1869, with *Lorna Doone*, a quasi-historical novel of the West Country, and continued writing in this and other styles to the end of the century and of his life. It is by no means certain that he does not deserve as high a place as any novelist mentioned here except Dickens and Thackeray; it is almost impossible not to think that, with the process of extraction and compression so often referred to, he must have deserved a higher place still. The variety and the vigour of scene and character-sketching in such books, not only as that just mentioned, but as *Cradock Nowell* (1866), *The Maid of Sker* (1872), *Alice Lorraine* (1875), *Cripps the Carrier* (1876), *Christowell* (1882), *Springhaven* (1887), are both extraordinary. Mrs Oliphant (1828-1897) began to write somewhat sooner, and never did anything better than her early novel, or series of novels, *The Chronicles of Carlingford* (1863-76), but accomplished an immense quantity of work, sometimes pretty full and never quite empty of merit. Three prolific writers somewhat under the influence of Dickens, James Payn (1830-1898), William Black (1841-1898), and Sir Walter Besant (1836-1901), were *amuseurs*, as the French say, of extraordinary talent, each of whom more than once showed capacity for giving something more than amusement.[1]   Another scholar of Dickens, but of more definite type, and the chief author of the " sensational " novel, was Wilkie Collins (1824-1886), whose *Dead Secret* (1857), *Woman in White* (1860), and *No Name* (1862) have had few superiors in at least temporary popularity ; while Henry Kingsley (1836-1876), a younger brother of Charles, surpassed his brother in fertility, and perhaps in equality of merit,—*Ravenshoe* (1861) is his best book,—but wrote on a lower literary level, though not a low one.

[1] By a curious but not quite unique chance, much, if not most, of Besant's best work was done in collaboration with another writer, James Rice (1843-1881), whose independent composition was worthless.   It was a trick with criticasters who do not know, or wish to conceal, the fact that it is the easiest thing in the world to avoid the obvious, and the most difficult thing in the world to do or say the obvious well,—that the doing of the latter, or, in the classic phrase, " making the common uncommon," is indeed the main object of art, —to reproach Besant with obviousness.   This was idle, yet here as elsewhere in this bevy there was undoubtedly something which prevented any one of such books as *Ready-Money Mortiboy* (1871), *The Golden Butterfly* (1876), *The Chaplain of the Fleet* (1881), *All Sorts and Conditions of Men* (1882), *Dorothy Forster* (1884), and (in some ways the most remarkable of all) *Children of Gibeon* (1886) from being a masterpiece.   Comparing Besant with Blackmore, it is perhaps worth while to record that in the latter, though he was a keen observer, the romantic temperament had the clear mastery.   In the former, realism—his studies of the East of London and of "labour" problems set an example which has been oftener followed than acknowledged—and romance are yoked unequally and jar.   Other names of things far off, but not unhappy, nor exactly forgotten, crowd on us, but must be despatched after the precedent of Gyas and Cloanthus,—the fertile and well-reputed activity of Mrs Craik (Dinah Mulock) (1826-1887) ; the brilliant artificialities ("nor quite that neither") of George Alfred Lawrence (1827-1876), the author of *Guy Livingstone* (1857) ; the genial sporting and other novels of Major Whyte Melville (1821-1878).

There are incidents in the later history of the novel—such as the change of its form from the long *The New Romance.* consecrated three volumes to one; and the vogue, after long unpopularity, of the short story; as the sudden enlargement, on French and other foreign patterns, of the gauge of decency in fiction; and others—which are more proper to be referred to here, than to be discussed at any length, because they are too near. A more important and a less dubitably permanent phenomenon—one which has at any rate lasted for a time sufficient to give it permanence in history—is the strong turn of the tide towards the romance, as distinguished from the novel proper, which latter had absorbed most of the attention of the middle quarters of the century, or rather of its third and fourth fifths. *Hypatia* and *Westward Ho!* showed a set in this direction which was not maintained; *Lorna Doone,* another which, though not very rapidly or decidedly pushed on, was. But for the last two decades there has been no doubt about the matter, and there are, as yet, no signs of fresh ebb. Most of the practitioners of the new Romance are alive, and young enough long to live, but two very remarkable figures have passed away, and may be dealt with here.

It may be permitted to think that justice has not yet been done to the prose romances of the poet, *Morris.* William Morris. He practically began with the kind in those contributions to the *Oxford and Cambridge Magazine* (1856) which, long inaccessible, recently came, not fresh, but afresh,

to some readers, with the half-pleasant, h
seasoning of a forty years' memory. They
ceedingly crude—for the most part jumbled
ences of Malory and Fouqué, with followin
newer models as Kingsley, and even Mi
written in an equally jumbled dialect, part
part Ruskin, part pure and rather jarring
But the fragmentary *Hollow Land*, the chief
had, and still has for some, a singular and
charm. Poetry, however, at that time, f
drew the poet to its side, and the exerci
middle period in Scandinavian translatio
no necessary desertion. But these exer
vided him with a language which, still o
by some not hostile critics as artificial, as
Street," is a great improvement on the p
breaking down falsetto of the early work.
the last ten years of his life—influenced co
or unconsciously, no doubt, by the gener
tide—he used this constantly in a long serie
ous romances, from *The House of the Wolfir*
to the posthumous *Sundering Flood* (1898),
once more one feels almost inclined to prop
much more than almost disposed to wish, a
and more enthusiastic audience than they
have yet had. For, while full of beaut
attractive fancy, they are the most absolu
scientific—nay, anti-scientific—things that
had for generations. And it stands to reaso
showing of all history, that the twentieth
must be "science-sick" before very long ; ju

There are incidents in the later history of the novel—such as the change of its form from the long *The New Romance.* consecrated three volumes to one; and the vogue, after long unpopularity, of the short story; as the sudden enlargement, on French and other foreign patterns, of the gauge of decency in fiction; and others—which are more proper to be referred to here, than to be discussed at any length, because they are too near. A more important and a less dubitably permanent phenomenon—one which has at any rate lasted for a time sufficient to give it permanence in history—is the strong turn of the tide towards the romance, as distinguished from the novel proper, which latter had absorbed most of the attention of the middle quarters of the century, or rather of its third and fourth fifths. *Hypatia* and *Westward Ho!* showed a set in this direction which was not maintained; *Lorna Doone,* another which, though not very rapidly or decidedly pushed on, was. But for the last two decades there has been no doubt about the matter, and there are, as yet, no signs of fresh ebb. Most of the practitioners of the new Romance are alive, and young enough long to live, but two very remarkable figures have passed away, and may be dealt with here.

It may be permitted to think that justice has not yet been done to the prose romances of the poet, *Morris.* William Morris. He practically began with the kind in those contributions to the *Oxford and Cambridge Magazine* (1856) which, long inaccessible, recently came, not fresh, but afresh, to some readers, with the half-pleasant, half-painful seasoning of a forty years' memory. They were exceedingly crude—for the most part jumbled reminiscences of Malory and Fouqué, with followings of such newer models as Kingsley, and even Miss Yonge, written in an equally jumbled dialect, part archaism, part Ruskin, part pure and rather jarring modernity. But the fragmentary *Hollow Land*, the chief of them, had, and still has for some, a singular and individual charm.   Poetry, however, at that time, fortunately drew the poet to its side, and the exercises of his middle period in Scandinavian translation showed no necessary desertion.   But these exercises provided him with a language which, still objected to by some not hostile critics as artificial, as "Wardour Street," is a great improvement on the perpetually breaking down falsetto of the early work.   And in the last ten years of his life—influenced consciously or unconsciously, no doubt, by the general set of tide—he used this constantly in a long series of curious romances, from *The House of the Wolfings* (1889) to the posthumous *Sundering Flood* (1898), to which once more one feels almost inclined to prophesy, and much more than almost disposed to wish, a far wider and more enthusiastic audience than they seem to have yet had.   For, while full of beautiful and attractive fancy, they are the most absolutely unscientific—nay, anti-scientific—things that we have had for generations.   And it stands to reason, on the showing of all history, that the twentieth century must be "science-sick" before very long; just as the eighteenth became sick of theology, and the nineteenth of common-sense philosophising.

The other novelist of the New Romance (though a very different new romance), Robert Louis Stevenson (1850-1894), was of a younger generation, *Stevenson.* and followed totally different ideals and methods. His popularity, though not quite immediate, was, when at last obtained by *Treasure Island* (1883), very great, and it has maintained itself, not merely during the short remainder of his life, but, rather curiously, during that difficult decade which follows a man's death. Stevenson relied on two things,—the adoption of a very elaborate style, and that of a very simple—a quite fairy-tale or "boy's book"—variety of adventure. How much of the singular charm with which he treated the latter depends on the former is no question for this book to do more than pose. But the spell shows no sign of being worked out: which thing, like others, is an allegory.

I

CHAPTER III.

ENGLISH AND FRENCH—PERIODICAL LITERATURE—
CRITICISM AND ESSAY-WRITING.

FRENCH CRITICISM FOREMOST—THE PREDECESSORS OF SAINTE-BEUVE—
SAINTE-BEUVE HIMSELF—THE CHARGES AGAINST HIM—EMPTINESS
OF THESE—HIS UNIQUE MERIT—NISARD AND OTHERS—GAUTIER—
JUNIORS : SCHERER — MONTÉGUT — TAINE — FLAUBERT AND THE
SINGLE WORD—THE GONCOURTS AND ZOLA AS CRITICS—HELLO—
ENGLISH : FLOURISHING OF THE PERIODICAL—REVIVAL OF CRITI-
CISM AFTER A SHORT DECADENCE—INDIVIDUALS : BRIMLEY AND
OTHERS — RUSKIN — MATTHEW ARNOLD — HIS TENDENCY AND THAT
OF OTHERS—PATER—MR SYMONDS, ETC.—JEFFERIES AND MISCEL-
LANEOUS ESSAYISTS.

IT is by this time a recognised truism that, next to
the novel, the newspaper, in its widest sense,—ranging from the quarterly periodical, which is as much
a book as most things published in countries where
they do not bind, to the most ephemeral sheet of day
or evening,—is the special production of the nineteenth century ; and, as such, it seems proper that it
should have a place to itself in this History. Yet
one at least of the very secrets of its importance
makes it in itself both difficult to deal with and

unsatisfactory in any possible dealing. Much, very much, of what would in older times have made its appearance at once in volume-form has been attracted to periodicals in at least the first place. But there is one department, itself something of a new - comer, though not quite so new as novel or newspaper, to which, for the most obvious reasons, the newspaper itself has almost invariably given its first access to the public: and that is Criticism. It is difficult to think of a single noteworthy critical book of the century which did not — unless, as has happened in the minority of cases of the best, it was originally delivered as lectures—pass through this stage-door. The Essays of Lamb and Hazlitt and Leigh Hunt, of Carlyle and Macaulay and De Quincey, of Arnold and of Pater, the *Causeries* of Sainte-Beuve, the *Tableaux* and *Portraits* of Théophile Gautier, the papers of many another, from Wilson in England to M. Brunetière in France, have each and all not disdained to make their bow to the public in this fashion. The new facility of access has perhaps multiplied bad criticism: it has certainly multiplied bad reviewing. But it has multiplied the good with the bad, and it has in all probability, if not in all certainty, given a means of existence to not a little which would otherwise have remained in the brain of its author. It is not, therefore, in incongruous or promiscuous society that we yoke criticism with the newspaper in this chapter, though we may say little of the newspaper's other contents.

Here—more than anywhere in this volume, and

almost more than in any chapter of any other since
French Criti- the thirteenth century — France deserves
cism foremost. precedence.   Not only does the work of
Sainte - Beuve begin at the time when the great
English criticism of the first quarter of the century
was falling off, and improve steadily during the second
quarter, which was not a brilliant period of criticism
with us, but this work itself serves as direct and
immediate pattern and manual alike to the renaissance
of English criticism when it appears.   "No Sainte-
Beuve—no Arnold," would be excessive and unjust,
if it were taken to imply any undue subordination or
want of originality in the younger critic ; it would be
unphilosophical, as ignoring that principle of sane
literary determinism, drawn from large induction,
which informs us that—certain exceptional geniuses
apart—people do things because the time has come
to do them.   But it has a great deal more to say for
itself than most such trenchancies in literature.

Sainte-Beuve himself was no Melchisedec.   On the
contrary, as he was never tired of frankly explaining,
he had been preceded, and again in a manner fathered
by, the remarkable group of critics who began their
operations under or before the First Empire, and the
youngest and most popular of whom, Villemain
(1790-1865), did not die till the Second was within
sight of its end.

To these critics we have no school directly corres-
The predecessors pondent in England, though Jeffrey, if he
of Sainte-Beuve. had had a wider literary training and outlook, would have been in some respects like them.

They do not, like their somewhat older contemporaries La Harpe and Suard, represent the unflinching, uncompromising "classical" tradition, or rather reaction, of the later eighteenth century : they show widening and still widening views—stretching backwards in their own country to periods before the consecrated Augustan age, and in the case of Fauriel and Raynouard to Provençal, and so necessarily medieval literature—exploring outwards, so as to take in not merely Italy and Spain, which had always been admitted to the "Latin Union" of Letters, but England and Germany.   Some of them, such as Nepomucène Lemercier, are almost Romantics before Romanticism ; others, such as Fontanes (a little assisted by personal friendship), can welcome such a "Gaul at the gates" as Chateaubriand ; others, such as Cousin, Guizot, Villemain himself, can even recognise English and German *criticism*.   But they all fall under the period of the last volume, and some of them even a little anticipate it ; so that they have had their place.   Even Sainte - Beuve himself had spent more than two - thirds of his life when the period of that volume closed.   But the most brilliant time of his work is ours, and the summary of it, which was there postponed, will find proper place here.

Sainte-Beuve himself thought that he had reached his critical acme, or had at least matured his critical attitude and method, by about 1844.   Some of the articles of that time undoubtedly show him near this point ; but one may not quite

Sainte-Beuve himself.

agree that he actually reached it till the remarkable lecture-essays on *Chateaubriand et son Groupe Littéraire,* which he delivered at Liége during the troubles of 1848-49, and published as a book afterwards; perhaps not till the famous *Causeries du Lundi* themselves, which were begun pretty soon after his return, and which, with some interruptions and avocations, occupied him—they and their successors, the *Nouveaux Lundis,* reaching eight-and-twenty volumes—during the two remaining decades of his life. But his earlier work had not merely "made" him,—it had made his public at home and to some extent abroad. It had spread the idea of a method of criticism rather English than French in original conception,— for it can hardly be traced in anything like full force beyond Dryden, and Johnson's *Lives* are, with some drawbacks here and there, the best examples of its middle stage. To this half biographical, half critical discourse—*causerie*—Sainte-Beuve added a double or stronger dose of inquiry into the subject's antecedents and circumstances; his literary teachers, relations, preferences; the points in his work agreeing or contrasting with that of others and the like. This did not very often, though it did sometimes, lead up to a regular "judgment,"[1] a summary of the qualities, merits, defects, place, of the writer in question; more often the directly critical observations are adroitly scattered about the article, or even left in a state rather of suggestion than of positive

[1] Perhaps the most definite thing of the kind is that on Racine in the last volume of *Port Royal.*

formula.[1] Further, Sainte-Beuve did not confine himself to one period of literature, nor even to several. He did not deal much with the modern languages other than English, on which he has left some admirable essays; but some of his very best are on "classical" subjects, and he left no period of French untouched — not even that mediæval division to which in his time, and even since, Academic critics have been wont to turn so cold a shoulder,—while, though conscious of the special difficulties, he was fairly copious on contemporaries.

Few—and hardly any competent—judges have denied the attraction of this criticism, the genial literary *The charges against him.* atmosphere that it creates, the amount of solid information, so different from the rhetorical emptiness of the usual academic *éloge*, which it conveys, the astonishing skill and versatility with which the conveyance is effected. But there have not been wanting grumblers; and it has even become a fashion with some of the younger school to question Sainte-Beuve's eminence as a critic altogether. The complaints began (to put aside the mere temporary and contemporary *tracasseries* to which all critics are exposed) on the part of the *ultras* of the Romantic party, who not merely alleged (what he did not himself deny) that he had deserted them, but accused him of playing almost the part of Judas to Hugo and, in a less degree, to others of the Romantic leaders. This enlarged itself into a more general charge—for

[1] On criticism in general, on the other hand, he has some very striking articles and passages.

which again there is colour, and something more, though it is not just as a whole—of almost persistently avoiding or belittling the consummate,—of preferring and caressing the second-rate. And the latest adversaries, now for a good many years, have gone on —taking some real advantage of a particular dislike of his to the quaint, the abnormal, the conceited—to represent him as a commonplace and *borné* critic, entirely destitute of those graces of personal style which, as some of them hold, are the first, if not the only, necessary thing in criticism, incapable of new, hardy, striking views and expressions, half academic and half Philistine.[1]

This is merely absurd: the only grain of sense and truth in it has been indicated already,—that is to *Emptiness of these.* say, that Sainte-Beuve—as all but the very rarest critics who are real critics are wont to be, while those who escape the rule are apt to exaggerate their tolerance and welcome the *merely* bizarre, the *merely* eccentric—had a distinct distrust of what *was* eccentric and bizarre. A certain amount of truth has also been admitted in the charge of preference, or at any rate of more frequent selection, of writers who are a little below the great, the magnificent, the sublime. Chateaubriand is the chief exception; and Sainte-Beuve made up for the praise he lavished on Chateaubriand's genius by constant, and at times almost malignant, attacks on his char-

---

[1] The essence of all possible devil's advocacy against Sainte-Beuve —put with the writer's usual *diable au corps* — may be found in Nietzsche's *Götzen-Dämmerung*, pp. 57, 58.

acter. But beyond these drawbacks there are very few: and it is to be observed that they are mainly negative. He, as a rule, abstained from the things that he did not like; he seldom thought it necessary to attack them. It is disappointment at not finding something that we should have liked to find, not resentment at finding something that we do not like, which we experience in reading him. In other words, he very seldom goes wrong, though fairly often he goes not so right as we could wish him to do. It will probably be admitted by all fair-minded persons who have read much criticism that, if this is the worst that can be said against a critic, it will not do him much harm, in a fair comparative estimate with his kind.

Perhaps the adjective which has just been used with another intention, if we prefix to it "historic," *His unique merit.* is, on the whole, the key which best unlocks the treasure - cabinet of Sainte-Beuve as a critic. Before him, except very rarely, in the whole long series of critics from Aristotle downwards, the joint historical and comparative method is that which is most to seek. Aristotle himself could not apply it; the Greeks (except Longinus) after him would not, even to the extent to which they could. The Romans did it too tim-idly, and still with an inevitable limitation; and the moderns, with rare exceptions, refused to avail them-selves of the opportunities which they had. After Diderot, in his hasty and haphazard sallies of genius, had shown the way, the Germans followed it up—but too theoretically, and sometimes, as in the case of the Schlegels, with too little knowledge and too much assumption and *parti pris*.   With Sainte-Beuve it becomes the not often expressed, the perhaps never definitely expressed, but the secret, pervading, invariable spring, and guiding as well as moving spirit of the critical method.   And this method forces itself, as secretly perhaps, but in the case of intelligent persons as inevitably, on his readers.   Amid the vast multitude of critical preparations which are contained in his museum — the result of subjects exposed to all manner of reagents, set in all manner of lights and relations and conditioning circumstances — some readers may lose themselves, and others may simply gain a sort of intellectual pastime.   But some, too, will be able to draw, not conclusions but useful intermediate axioms; and all who care to do so must see the folly of conclusions too limited, too exclusive, too *regulative*.   When you have read Sainte-Beuve, you *know* more, you appreciate more—or at any rate it is your fault, and not his, if you do not.   You are in less danger of being "connoisseured out of your senses," you are in better case to be yourself that better connoisseur who acts up to the derivation of his title, and *knows*.   In Coleridge, the greatest modern critic before Sainte-Beuve, and in certain ways greater than Sainte-Beuve himself, the provision of positive knowledge is rather below the provision of comparative-historic principle and theory; in Sainte-Beuve it is just the other way.

The influence of Sainte-Beuve, helped by and helping the general tendency of which it was itself

the earliest and fullest exponent, made itself very
Nisard and others. quickly felt among his contemporaries—
much more among his juniors and the next
generation. Some of the former were indeed recalcitrant. For instance, Désiré Nisard (1806-1888), a
man only two years younger than Sainte-Beuve himself, but who survived him for nearly twenty, and
whose early protests against the Romanticism which
he had once defended have been noticed in the last
volume, continued till not far off the verge of the
twentieth century to maintain, with narrowness indeed, and at a fatal loss to French literature, but
with dignity, consistency, and in his later years at
any rate a commendable absence of violence, the
"classical" theory of French. literature itself,—that
which constructs, chiefly from the writers of the
Augustan age, an abstract idea of what that literature ought to be in its most perfect form, and allows
or disallows all else by comparison with this standard.

Saint-Marc Girardin and Jules Janin (again see last
volume) learnt little from their great contemporary,
—indeed, Janin, with all his brilliancy, was too super-
Gautier. ficial to learn much from any one. But
Gautier, who, though younger than Sainte-
Beuve, was but a decade younger, and who survived
him but three years, was always, despite his loyalty
to Hugo, loyal also to his "oncle Beuve," as he
used to call him. His own criticism, unequalled
for beauty of expression, celebrated for its perfect
amenity, and far too generally undervalued for the
solid qualities of appreciation which it possesses,

has, with much of originality, a distinct Sainte-Beuvian tinge. Although in his later years "Théo," disgusted at being unable to pursue pure literature itself, rather shirked literary subjects for those of art and the drama, his three critical diploma-pieces all belong to our time. They are the masterly obituary on Balzac (whom he had known well and early), the still more masterly survey of French poetry from 1830 to 1867, which was one of the documents of the Exhibition literature of the last-named year, and the extraordinarily subtle, sympathetic, and just appreciation of Baudelaire, written for the posthumous edition of that poet's works; while the vivid and thoughtful *Histoire du Romantisme* was only interrupted by his death.

The criticism, however, which wholly and solely belongs to us is that, in the first place, of a group *Juniors—* of younger men, some of whom were *Scherer.* glanced at and refused by Mr Omond as not being his sheep; while they in their turn have been succeeded by yet another, of whom most are living, and so debarred from detailed criticism here, but of whose critical results we may be able to take some notice generally. The oldest member of the former group, Edmond Scherer (1815-89), belongs by date almost to the generation of Sainte-Beuve himself, and quite to that of Gautier, having been born in the Waterloo year. But his early manhood and earlier middle life were occupied with theological studies and professional exercise; and it was not till about 1860 that, having given up his pastorate and

his religious beliefs, he devoted himself to literature.
He became a very active literary and philosophical
critic, chiefly in the *Temps*, and published at intervals
ten volumes of collected *Études*, besides some others
on single subjects. His knowledge of English and
German as well as French literature was wide and
exact; his logical powers very considerable; and his
judgment—when not biassed by prejudices, literary
and still more often extra-literary—very strong and
sound, though not very subtle or accommodating.
Not merely on Milton and Goethe, where his lucubrations have been introduced to the English public
by Mr Arnold, but on several other English subjects
(notably Wordsworth), and on not a few French, his
Essays deserve to be ranked among the standard
documents of criticism. Unfortunately, the prejudices just referred to were as strong as the judgment
and stronger, while they were more than one or two.
An insistence on the necessarily *philosophical* character, not only of criticism but of all art that is to
be approved, ought perhaps hardly to be called a
prejudice, but rather a principle; yet principle becomes prejudice when it is used to "blackmark,"
a priori, work based on a different principle. There
can be less question of the applicability of the term
to the censure of literary work, not because it is
bad literature, but because it offends morality or
the critic's idea of it, and to a foregone conclusion
against whatsoever is out of the way or bizarre. M.
Scherer had his favourite authors whom it was
heresy to blaspheme, and his pet aversions whom

it was worse heresy to eulogise—Racine, Madame de
Staël, Lamartine, among the first; Molière, Diderot,
and above all Baudelaire, among the second. So
that, on the whole, some caution and a good deal
of previous knowledge are requisite in reading his
unfavourable articles: where he praises, or where he
examines quite impartially, he is a critic of the very
highest value.

Two somewhat younger men, who were at one time
in much communication of thought, deserve also places
of great prominence in this part of the
Montégut.
story, though the one who has the greatest
reputation was much the worse critic. The elder,
Émile Montégut (*b.* 1826), was a man of letters pure
and simple, who passed his life in translating (chiefly
from English), in writing books of travel and others,
but chiefly in reviewing for the *Revue des Deux
Mondes* and the *Moniteur.* M. Montégut, like the
critic last mentioned, and like him who is to follow,
paid special attention to English literature, and published whole books of collected articles on it; but he
was also an expert in German, Italian, and other
tongues, an admirable reviewer (in the narrow sense)
of new books, and a particularly skilful writer of
obituaries. In all those departments of journalism
that can be made literature, he never failed to effect
the transformation by dint of an excellent style, a
remarkably wide knowledge, unusual patience and
thoroughness of analysis, and, above all, an exceptional and in some ways unique sympathy and
subtlety of comprehension. Some of his work, on

such different subjects as George Eliot and Boccaccio, reaches almost the high-water mark of criticism of foreign literature; and though he was at one time a little affected by the theories or manias of his friend next to be mentioned, he shook this off. If Montégut has a weakness—and it is only one likely to infect brethren themselves weak—it is in the very great length to which his appreciations not unfrequently run. But this has been rather a tendency of later criticism,—even Sainte-Beuve succumbed to it in his latest days,—and whole books on particular modern authors, of which Schubarth's on Goethe was one of the earliest examples, have become quite common.

According to the popular judgment, Hippolyte Taine (1828-1893) occupies a higher position in criticism, as *Taine.* well as in general letters, than either of his friends. In the wider region he deserves this preference : for some of his early books— the books on La Fontaine and Livy, and the interesting *Thomas Graindorge* (a half-satirical, half-photographic side view of the state of thought and literature in the Second Empire)—are things which perhaps neither of them could have done; and the great work of his later days, the *Origines de la France Contemporaine*, in which the myth of the Revolution is shattered once for all, is certainly a greater thing than either of them ever did. But as a *critic*—as a patient, keen-sighted, and fairly enthusiastic appreciator of literature — he was far the inferior of Montégut, though he had more strength ; and I do not know that he was quite the equal of Scherer, though on individual points he had more impartiality. His famous *Histoire de la Littérature Anglaise*, which is not only, as is natural, his best-known book in England, but perhaps his most popular book everywhere, shows real if not exhaustive knowledge, an extraordinary vigour, much brilliant writing, and an almost bewildering profusion of the firm, striking, unhesitating views and generalisations which impress the ordinary person. But it has one capital, pervading, fatal fault as a whole, and in detail others innumerable, some of which are not even necessary consequences and children of the *idée mère*. That mother-idea is itself the daughter of the critical method of Sainte-Beuve,—the investigation, as a preliminary to criticism, and as even the chief process of criticism itself, of all the subject's circumstances as aforesaid. But with Taine this method has been married to a strict and almost fanatical determinism ; and the result is that the literature of a country is, according to him, the mathematical product of the circumstances, and that each man's own literature is as rigidly dependent on his race, his time, his *milieu*. There is no doubt something fascinating in this to the average intelligence, which has not given itself the trouble to make any large or independent study of literature as a whole, or of men of letters as individuals. People may feel comforted and encouraged by clinging to the skirts of a critical Mr Greatheart of this kind, who strides along undoubtingly, and hews at every opponent and every obstacle with the great axe of his unyielding theory. Yet it is, in truth,

"all a cheat"; it does not really explain the phenomena, and it leads ineluctably, and in spite of the
fact that M. Taine was one of the most honest of
men himself, to the suppression and the distortion
of fact.[1]

Not a few other critical representatives of this
period would require notice in more extended space,
Flaubert and and some are too important not to receive
the single word. it on a small scale. The great novelist
Flaubert was not a critic by profession; but he has,
in an informal manner, set forth in his letters, especially those to George Sand (who in the same way
contributed a good deal to criticism herself), an exceedingly important critical theory which he carried
into practice in his own work—the theory, as it may
be called, of the "Single Word."[2] All Romantic
criticism, from Hugo's own downward, had exalted
the *mot propre*—the individual, characteristic expression—as against the generalities and conventionalities,
which had been not merely tolerated, but expressly
championed and recommended as the true way of art
by Classicism. But Flaubert refined on this. According to him there could be only one *mot* that was really
propre—only one phrase that really, fully, adequately
represented the artist's meaning. He would toil to
find this, sitting up whole nights over a single sentence; he would be miserable at not finding it. It

[1] Taine's essay on Balzac (1858) almost started the general modern
conception of that great novelist.

[2] This, of course, is not new. It is Virgilian, Ciceronian, even
Nisardian. But he made it his own.

K

gave us, from him, such masterpieces as the *Tentation de Saint-Antoine* and the *Trois Contes*. But it is manifestly not so much a counsel of perfection as an exaggeration—a heresy of excess. And as imitated by others it became in some cases almost a negation of meaning altogether—the mere treatment of words like spots of colour and high-lights in a picture.[1]

It would not be just to his friends the Goncourts (see the remarks on him and them in the preceding chapter) to accuse them of deliberately diverging from or "improving upon" his views. But their Impressionism, just as much as the Naturalism of M. Zola (who defended and exemplified it in a considerable bulk of critical writing), differed from Flaubert's so-called Realism not merely in retaining a much smaller (though some) share of Romanticism itself, but also in other ways. M. Zola's theory was that all literature ought to hasten to become scientific — that the "document" was to be the base of it, that the novel, for instance, must be "experimental," or rather "experiential." The Goncourts—at least the elder and survivor of them, Edmond—had not "the philosophical head," and formulated their views less systematically. But they came nearer to Flaubert than to Zola in insisting on the importance of style in the literary work of art; nearer to Zola than to Flaubert in preferring (without any very clear or obvious reason) subjects of the "grimy" character, and in an almost total abstin-

The Goncourts and Zola as critics.

[1] The chief example of this was Paul de Saint-Victor (1827-1882), an admirable writer if not a very great literary critic.

ence from idealising touches in dealing both with these and others.   In their own work to some extent, in that of their imitators still more, theory and practice alike incline to the subordination of story, of character, even of incident in some degree, to the reproduction, by a photographic process differentiated only by the temperament of the artist, of more or less connected *impressions*. Maupassant (for all this group was critical almost as much as creative) restored a good deal of his master Flaubert's poetic touch, but in theory inclined a good deal to the impressionist and pseudo-scientific line.   And Emile Hennequin (1859-1888), a younger disciple,—at one time greeted with a flourish of trumpets from certain quarters,—endeavoured to formulate a definite general system of Scientific Criticism, intended wholly to supersede the some-what anarchical "appreciation" which the Romantic movement had brought about.

Quite outside of this school and of the general current of French literature, so much so indeed that *Hello.* his work long remained little known, lay one remarkable writer, Ernest Hello, who was born in 1828 and died in 1885—critic, tale-teller, hagiographer, philosopher. A native of Brittany, Hello is said to have had the ardent Catholicism which still, in part at least, dominates that province, made more ardent by revulsion from the attitude of his countryman Renan. His life, though not ex-tremely short, was one of constant disease and pain, but it was alleviated by the care of a most devoted wife. Coming under the influence of Louis Veuillot, he became a journalist on the same side, though he never imitated Veuillot's violences of style and tone —violences which, it may be remarked, were mainly separable accidents. Moreover, it was not politics that, as in the case of his master, were Hello's chief interest, but literature (to which that master had also paid not a little attention) and social philosophy. In this last respect he has been spoken of as a not free-thinking Emerson; but since Nietzsche " took up " the American thinker, it has been fashionable to see all manner of things in Emerson which were not very noticeable to the sober eye before.

Hello has a style of great charm—admirably clear, quite free from the exaggerated preciousness and attempt to " raise language to a higher power " which has spoilt so much well - intentioned writing for the last quarter of a century, but full of really original, striking, and suggestive phrasing. In his *Contes Extraordinaires*, in his most popular book on Saints, *Physionomies de Saints*,[1] and in his abundant critical and miscellaneous writings (from *Les Plateaux de la Balance* (1880) to *Le Siècle*, with others), this style is applied to a large number of subjects, but always under the domination of a central atti-tude, which is interesting *prima facie* because of its absolute opposition to the usual attitude of the day. It might be defined — if one cared to deal in epigram—as Catholicism at bay, because it will not comprehend. But this refusal to comprehend is not in the least merely stupid or dense; it is

[1] Translated into English as *Studies in Saintship* (London, 1903).

compatible with the most active and imaginative exertion of thought. Hello's position in regard to Shakespeare, for instance, far exceeds in interest that of any critic for the greater part of a century, and is quite original. Whether he was aware of the fact that some have even claimed the poet as of his own ecclesiastical communion may be doubted—it seems, in fact, impossible. But Shakespeare, if he has not produced this effect on him, has also not produced the much more commonly experienced and probably true idea of a man who, from this or that reason, deliberately abstains from pronouncing on religious questions, or touching upon them at all.

To Hello, perhaps merely because Shakespeare is an Englishman, Shakespeare is "l'incarnation du Protestantisme," and so the incarnation of evil. But Hello, unlike Rümelin, was too much of a critic to be able to persuade himself that because he did not like Shakespeare he must not admire him. Hello admires, but trembles and detests. Shakespeare is for him ' l'homme des ténèbres "; he is a kind of demon with a taste for obscenity and despair, but so great a demon that you must be familiar with hell itself to comprehend him. The Breton critic is interesting, too, on Victor Hugo, who is " le vers qui s'est fait homme," " désarmé de la rime il n'existe plus," and so forth. A moment's thought will show that the apparent extravagance of these opinions ought not to veil the truths behind it. To use a fine phrase of Mr Swinburne's many years ago about another matter, Shakespeare has " become diabolic " to Hello " because

he will not accept him as divine," though he sees the
divinity; while the first of the two quoted phrases
about Hugo is curiously happy. And everywhere in
Hello there is the same piquancy, the same interest.
It is of incalculable value to have things thus put
from a new standpoint, even if a false one, for we can
allow for this; and it is of more value still to have
them put so well.

The better kind of criticism, however, had, from the
practice and example of the second and third quarters
of the century, established itself in France so strongly
that it has never yet died out; and the last twenty or
thirty years can boast of critics—MM. Brunetière,[1]
Faguet, France, Lemaître, Doumic, and many others—
scarcely inferior to all but the very best of their predecessors, and numerous as in few other times. Indeed
it is probably not excessive to say that, taking rising
talent only, the critical production of this period has
been very much superior to the creative. That there
is nothing in the least surprising in this after fifty or
sixty years of such creative *and* critical production as
the country had previously seen, is of course a truism;
and any hasty generalisation as to periods of critical
production *succeeding* periods of creative is barred by

---

[1] Just as the writing of this book was finished, M. Brunetière's
career came to an end. Born in 1849, he succeeded after some
struggles in establishing himself on the staff of the *Revue des Deux
Mondes*, of which he died editor in 1906. Although somewhat too
much inclined to restricted and "classical" criticism, he possessed
great learning and excellent acuteness, which he displayed in a large
number of books and collected essays, sometimes too polemical and
positive, sometimes lacking in catholicity and flexibility of appreciation, but always masculine and sane.

the fact that from 1820 to 1870 the two things had gone on together. France indeed has always, since Du Bellay set the fashion more than three hundred years ago—and indeed a little earlier—been a country of criticism, bad or good; but while some of the older French characteristics of literature have hardly maintained themselves of late, this has certainly done so in no ordinary degree.

In England, as has been already admitted or asserted, the torch of criticism, which had been lighted earlier than in France, did not continue to burn so steadily. The periodical, it is true, obtained and held even greater importance, and varieties of it established themselves which have never made a secure lodgment across the Channel. In particular the weekly literary review, which has been such a feature in English literature for the greater part of a century, has again and again failed in Paris; nor has the true monthly or weekly "Magazine" as opposed to the "Review," the *olla podrida* of stories, criticisms, and miscellaneous articles of travel, history, social comment, and things in general, been much more fortunate there. This no doubt has been partly due to the much larger room given to such things in the French daily newspaper than (until quite recently) in the English; but it also connects itself beyond doubt with those mysterious differences of nation and nation which serve to amuse some inquirers, but which rarely admit of any satisfactory explanation. If we had room, a good deal might be

English—Flourishing of the Periodical.

said about periodicals of various kinds and dates which have figured as wholes in the outer provinces of English literature, and have even contributed some of the greatest things, and not few of them, to its central region. Some were weekly magazines, as they might almost be called, like Dickens's *Household Words* and *All the Year Round;* some monthly ones of reduced price and somewhat altered style, like *Macmillan's* and the *Cornhill*, the last named starting, as has been said, under the uneasy editorship of Dickens's great compeer; some weekly reviews like the *Saturday Review;* some evening daily newspapers of a new type like the *Pall Mall Gazette*. But little more than a mention of these is possible, and not even a mention can, though certainly out of no disrespect, be given to others. Many of the contents of most, if not of all, figure elsewhere in the chapters dealing with fiction, with poetry, even with the graver prose. Here we may, as in the French case, confine ourselves in the main to the department for which this periodical literature has supplied facilities never before known, —that of literary and other criticism, and forms of essay-writing pretty closely connected with it.

Once more this did not open with cheerful prospects, though as a matter of fact relief and renaissance were at hand. Not much was said in the last volume on this subject after 1830, and not much could be said; for the general English literary criticism of the second quarter of the century was too often bad—justifying Mr Arnold's soon-to-come censures if those censures had been more

Revival of criticism after a short decadence.

carefully limited to it than they were, justifying even
worse things.   When it had been good it had been, as
in the leading cases of Macaulay and Carlyle, only
"applied" literary criticism, not pure for the most
part; when it tried to be purely literary, it was for
the most part only "*mis*applied," if we may play on the
word—full of personal and other prejudice, ignorant
of the history both of criticism and of literature, ama-
teurish of the bad amateur kind, provincial and popular
in again the worst senses.   It had kept two great poets
—Tennyson and Browning—the one out of his rights
as far as it could, the other out of them almost altogether.   In the hands of a person even of the magnificent genius of Thackeray, it had zigzagged between
truth and error with almost bewildering uncertainty.

All this, however, was now to come right, or at any
rate to turn towards the right.   The most interesting
place in which to watch the process is the
Individuals— *Essays* (1858) of George Brimley, who died
Brimley and too soon to come to full maturity as a
others.
critic, but who is always making for righteousness
across all sorts of mists of ignorance and prejudice
and misconception.   Men like Bagehot and G. H.
Lewes and Kingsley exhibited the same tendencies in
different ways and with different alloys (especially in
the last named) of the shortcomings of the preceding
generation.   But two great writers—one a rare,[1] the
other a constant, contributor to periodicals, but both

---

[1] Yet he put in the strongest claim to appearance here by adopt-
ing, in *Fors Clavigera* and elsewhere, the periodical form for his own
publications.

best treated here—exhibited the revival of criticism
in regard to many subjects besides literature in such
a fashion as to give them the right to the fullest treatment here possible. The first was Mr Ruskin, the
second Mr Matthew Arnold.

The *débuts* of the first named belong to our last
volume, but though in a sense their whole author

Ruskin.   occurs in them, yet they are mainly a precocious anticipation; and Mr Ruskin is, in
fact, the greatest English prose writer, quantity and
quality taken together, of our own period, with which
his later years were exactly contemporary. He
appeared as "A Graduate of Oxford" (a title to
which he had just acquired a right), in 1843, with
the first volume of *Modern Painters,* a book scarcely
less epoch-making than that with which, at an age a
little younger, and thirteen years before, an *under*-
graduate of Cambridge had determined the course
of all later nineteenth-century poetry in England.
Mr Ruskin outlived Tennyson by nearly as many
years as those which made him Tennyson's junior;
and, unlike Tennyson, he did not retain his literary
faculty unimpaired and in full vigour to the last.
But for more than forty years his production had been
incessant, voluminous, multiform in appearance but
really integral in character, as has been the production of few. *Modern Painters* itself extended to five
volumes in bulk, and covered seventeen years in
publication, the *Seven Lamps of Architecture* (1849)
and the *Stones of Venice* (1851-53) reinforcing and
enlarging its lesson as it went.   In the thirty years

following he produced a score of separate volumes (sometimes issued in parts) and a great irregularly periodic series of deliverances called *Fors Clavigera*, which ran for thirteen years (1871-1884). Of these, only the handbook of a semi-socialist political economy (1861), called *Unto this Last*, and a few smaller things, belong strictly to "periodical" literature. But the whole is akin to it in spirit, being always the personal utterance, and in most cases the personal utterance in strong sympathy or *dys*pathy with the current opinions of others, which is the soul of periodical publication, and quite a different soul from the at least professedly abstracted, reflective, generalised *ethos* of the Book. It would be difficult to name any subject at which Mr Ruskin did not sometimes aim; while any subject at which he had ever aimed was certain to present itself to him again, no matter how different the target which might seem to be exposed to his "arrows of the chace" at the moment. But he started from, he chiefly affected, and he was rightly throughout associated by the public with, the criticism, the teaching, the "improvement" in the theological sense, of what is commonly called "Art."

The study of this had hitherto been rare in English literature. Eccentrics like Pepys and Roger North had devoted some attention to it in the latter part of the seventeenth century. Horace Walpole dilettantishly, Sir Joshua Reynolds professionally, Blake prophetically, Gilpin in the manner (not the bad manner) of the gifted amateur, and devoting himself chiefly to "the picturesque" in nature, had occupied

themselves with it in the eighteenth.　Hazlitt and
Lamb in the early nineteenth had combined it remarkably with literary interests.　But on the whole,
the subject had hitherto stood out of the usual curricu-
lum of English education, English literature, English
interests generally.　It had been the butt of eighteenth-
century satirists from Pope to Wolcot; it had had
a sort of stigma of "un-Englishness" on it; and it
had never been brought within the circle of subjects
from which the ordinary man of letters took his
themes, his illustrations, and his seasonings.　All this
had already been sensibly altered by the Romantic
Revolt, and by the intense striving of poetry towards
the accomplishment of the visual effects of pictorial
and other art.　The great Oxford Movement had
awakened a vivid interest in architecture; the opening of the Continent after the war an interest in
painting and sculpture; and the rise of native English artists, especially Turner, of real and commanding power completed the determining forces.

But it was undoubtedly Mr Ruskin himself who gave
at once force and voice to these new interests.　He
had from youth up, in a household which was an
odd mixture of strictness and unconventionality, been
allowed and encouraged to read; he had had early
and extensive experiences of Continental travel; he
possessed not merely abundant originality, but that
energy and self-confidence by which originality is by
no means always accompanied; and above all he had
a wonderful genius for prose style.　Taking up (for in
this point he was but a successor) the general tend-

ency towards ornate prose, in which, for twenty years
before, Wilson, De Quincey, and especially Landor
had been pioneers, combining with it the elaborate
and imaginative description which Keats and Tennyson had reintroduced into English poetry, he hit
practically at once (for some of his best passages are
very early, and perhaps all the best of them date
before 1860) on a style of astonishing fascination,
which has been constantly imitated since, but which
cannot fairly be said to be itself copied from any of
those just referred to. It is a style of enormous
sentences,—sentences of almost Clarendonian length,
but perfectly clear, the clauses being in effect joints—
"members," as the Greeks used to call them—which
serve to compose, not to confuse, the body; of the
most daring rhythm, often distinctly metrical, but
saved from the drawbacks of metre in prose by a
conscious or unconscious avoidance of coincidence in
the rhythmical and syntactical pauses; gorgeous and
varicoloured, but by no means depending, as some of
the clumsier ornate styles depend, on mere clots and
clusters of adjectives. Through these mighty sentences and mightier paragraphs the rhythm of the
parts symphonises itself into a larger and mightier
rhythm of the whole, — so that the effects which
Hooker in a simple and severer form, Browne and
Taylor, Landor and De Quincey in a more elaborate, had produced, are here extended and varied
into amazing amplitude and with not less amazing
sureness.

In this subtle and gorgeous medium the artist

wove or limned endless pictures of natural and artificial beauty, ranging from the minutest details—a
corbel or a tuft of wild flowers—to cartoons of vast
buildings or whole cities, to maps of a continent with
its flora and fauna touched in. But both he himself
and his more special and fanatical admirers would
have been very wroth if his praise had been limited
to that of a consummate artist in words—a consummate describer of Art and Nature. He had, indeed,
nothing of the older English contempt of technique,
and very little of what artists contemptuously call
the merely "literary" spirit in regard to Art; but he
had a double or tenfold dose of moral, and of what
he at least would have considered philosophical and
religious, purpose. He was sharp-sighted enough in
his way; and was one of the first to detect, and the
first to characterise as "the pathetic fallacy," that
identification of external things with the temper and
mood of the spectator which had necessarily resulted
from the spread of nature - poetry after Cowper
through Wordsworth. But he himself was possessed
and permeated by innumerable forms of this fallacy,
ethical chiefly but pathetic also, and not seldom
merely *crotchety*. In his later period and smaller
books especially, no crotchet, no "fad," no prejudice
is too absurd or too flagrant for him to espouse it,
and no fact of history, of logic, of art itself, is stubborn
enough to turn him. So that after he had educated
the English mind as no one in the same way had ever
educated it before,—after he had converted it to many
noble things, from the art of Turner and the pre-

Raphaelites onward,—a sort of revolt came upon the public not merely towards his crotchets but towards his central doctrines, and he lost very much of his influence. These revolts, however, never matter much: they only cancel precedent excesses of wild worship. A noble but rather wayward heart; a very childlike thinker; and a perfectly childish critic when he goes wrong,—there is no doubt that Mr Ruskin will be regarded to all time as one of the very greatest of English prose writers, and as the David who vanquished the Goliath of English Philistinism in matters of Art.

The parallel contrast between Mr Ruskin and Mr Arnold is very curious and complete. Here, *Matthew Arnold.* too, we have a man who is nothing if not critical, and who in one branch of criticism is, if not consummate or infallible, stimulating, reforming, beneficent in a very high, in almost the highest, degree. And here also we have one who attempts to extend his faculties from the field in which they are valid to fields in which they cannot work or cannot work well, coming to some disaster accordingly. Fortunately the scenes and subjects of Mr Arnold's catastrophes or blunders— theology, politics, what may be called the general lighter morals of the nation — do not here at all concern us, and we may dismiss them with little more than an allusion. But the field of his proper activity, and his activity therein itself, concern us very much.

We have said that in the twenty or five-and-

twenty years before he appeared upon this field
it had been ill-tilled. The great critics of the early
nineteenth century had disappeared, and at the
last some of them (if Coleridge's views on Tennyson,
which we have only at second hand, be rightly
reported) had shown an abatement of natural force
No new ones of any high power had appeared.
Moreover, the inevitable weaknesses of the new
Romantic criticism had made themselves fully, and
painfully, apparent. The older critics, however often
they might be led into injustice and insufficiency
by their creed, *had* a creed to fall back upon, and
one which—in the case of Dryden often, of Addison
not never, of Johnson sometimes—had not merely
allowed them but helped them to go right. The
new critic was anarchic, guide-ropeless unless he
could supply rule and clew for himself. For this
he needed wits, reading, power of comparison, power
of clearing the mind not merely of cant but of
prejudice, power of directing it to the proper
objects. He had certainly not shown much of these
good things in the England of 1830-1850.

It was perhaps, in the nature of things human,
inevitable that Mr Arnold, in his character of
reformer, should go a little violently in the direction
opposite to that of the path of anarchic and agnostic
individualism which had led his immediate predecessors astray. In the singularly weighty and well
written *Preface* which he set before his collected
Poems in 1853, he announced recurrence to "the
ancient laws of poetry," he extolled the quality of

Greek poetic art as against modern, and besides combating some special and mushroom crazes of modern criticism, he practically declared war against its main principles, or wants of principle, in denouncing "Caprice" on the one hand, and the attention to treatment rather than to the Subject on the other. To this general attitude he was always true during the thirty-five years of his life after this manifesto,—in the lectures which he delivered on various subjects from the Chair of Poetry at Oxford, but specially as reproduced in book form, on "Translating Homer," and on the "Study of Celtic Literature"; in the extremely interesting, stimulating, and almost epoch-making essays which he collected and issued in 1865 as *Essays in Criticism*, and in all that followed—especially in the important *Introduction* to Mr Humphrey Ward's *The English Poets* (1880). His doctrines often took epigrammatic, sententious, and so distinctly provocative forms,— the extolling of the mysterious "grand style" to be found in Homer, Dante, and Milton, but not continuously or surely in Shakespeare; the definition of poetry as a "criticism of life"; of criticism as the knowledge itself of "the best that had been known and thought in the world"; the adoration of "lucidity," "sweet reasonableness," "ideas," "sweetness and light," &c. He enforced these doctrines with a style which at first (as in the *Preface* above referred to) full of a singular mixture of dignity and in the good old-sense elegance, if a little academic and colourless, afterwards acquired greater ease, flexibility, and colour, but at a certain cost of indulgence in mannerism and even a little foppishness. And he illustrated them in a series of dealings with literary subjects which could not but interest and amuse even when they provoked, and which, when the author can keep his somewhat aggressive and also somewhat artificial playfulness in hand, supply some of the very best specimens of the lighter criticism to be found in all literature. Moreover, they always serve, by precept and example alike, as a protest against and a corrective of the clumsy illiterate "Philistinism" (Carlyle had introduced the word, but Mr Arnold himself was the first to give it general currency and to search out and attack the thing) which had marked English criticism, and too often still continued to mark it for some time. He quite admitted his discipleship to Sainte - Beuve, which indeed was far more thorough and wide - reaching than those who are not intimately acquainted with the works of both may suspect. But it was never slavish.

Like Sainte-Beuve also, Mr Arnold always retained a very much larger leaven of Romanticism in his composition than might appear from his general principles. The qualities, for instance, which—rightly or wrongly, but certainly on no very extensive acquaintance with the originals — he detected and extolled in Celtic literature,— its "vague," its interest in nature, its faint and eery suggestiveness,— are among the most distinctive characteristics of Romance itself, and the most foreign to what are

at least generally thought the notes of the Classic.[1]
But the same double allegiance is notable in a
hundred other places — from his famous and very
beautiful apostrophe to Oxford to his admirably
critical examination of the poetical qualities of
Keats. In other words, he was really a critic—
really, that is to say, a lover of literature who was
prepared not merely to confess but to defend his
love,—not a swallower and disgorger of formulas.

But he at least endeavoured to be very formulative;
and though the best critics since his time have not
allowed themselves to be enslaved by his theories,
they have had their due influence, and his practice
has had more. These theories were at least a sovereign antidote (though, like other antidotes, they
might be somewhat dangerous in themselves) to the
worst faults of English criticism,—not merely that
"facetious and rejoicing ignorance" which Lockhart,
himself a critic with some sins of other kinds
to answer for, had denounced nearly forty years
earlier, but still more the stolid and stupid varieties
of the same ignorance, the insularity, the neglect of
comparison and contrasting observation, the acquiescence in slovenly and undisciplined impression, the
"irresponsible indolence," the Philistine narrowness
and blindness and cant. He was not a physician

[1] It should not be, but perhaps is, necessary to guard this by
observing that the writer does not in the least deny these qualities
to "Classical" literature; but is, on the contrary, prepared to
assert their existence in Homer himself, in Æschylus, in Lucretius,
in Catullus, and elsewhere, with all the knowledge and power at
his command.

who himself required no healing.   His admirations,
as in the case of the Guérins, were sometimes excessive; and his depreciations, as in the much later
case of Shelley, were sometimes defective and unjust
to an amazing extent.   His majors could often be
denied, and his logical processes were the very
reverse of infallible.   But he was almost always—
even at his worst—a real and a valuable corrective;
and when at his best (or even not quite at his best)
his positive value was all but of the very highest.   He
was far from being a critic to trust implicitly,—it
may be doubted whether such a critic has ever
existed; and Mr Arnold was certainly not one of
those who came nearest to the impossible.   But he
was, at a point of time, the restorer of English
criticism, to speak unscientifically,—the first to give
voice to the principles of restoration, as the most
grudging accuracy may be content to define his
position.

And this voice was by no means left long to cry
alone in the wilderness, though some, perhaps most,
of the other voices that joined it hardly
*His tendency
and that of
others.* did so in unison.   The persons and the
papers named above, with others, display,
with much mutual bickering and more lack of any
other than individual creed, a distinct and remarkable dead-lift from the low critical level of 1830-
1850.   The chief thing still lacking — and it was
lacking in Mr Arnold himself, who had a singular
and unlucky impatience of history on almost all
subjects — was a sufficient acquaintance with the

actual history and development of literature and of criticism, and in this respect also progress was made before long. Even Matthew Arnold, suspicious and even contemptuous as he was of the historic estimate, laid valuable stress on the comparative — urging that the diversities of different literatures as well as their consonances *must* be studied. As a set-off to this he had unfortunately adopted, and not seldom inculcated, Goethe's strange, illiberal, and profoundly unphilosophic notion that such and such a writer, period, subject, group, of the past "cannot help us," "is not important," and the like. But this was luckily to some extent neutralised by the strong antiquarian tendency of the age in general. Meanwhile his own work was the most representative, as well as in most ways the most accomplished, of the latter half of the century in English. Moreover, during his time, and not so very late in it, there appeared an interesting further development of criticism, which was in fact a blending, or rather the result of a blending, of his own methods and principles with those of Mr Ruskin. And of this the most remarkable representative, a man a good deal younger than Mr Arnold, though not long his survivor, was Mr Walter Pater (1839-1894).

Like his two predecessors here, Mr Pater was an Oxford man, and was indeed far more closely connected than either of them with his University, where he actually resided for the greater part of his life. And his attitude—with a logical consecutiveness which life does not always

Pater.

observe—was distinctly more academical than theirs.
Both of them—though neither could be said to be
a very practical man, while Mr Ruskin was in some
ways most unpractical in the ordinary sense—had
been intensely interested in the ways and things
of ordinary practical and public life.　Mr Arnold
was for half his days a hard-working official; and
there was no handiwork from that of navigators in
the old sense to that of navigators in the new, no
head-work from theology to politics, upon which
Mr Ruskin did not bestow his erratic energy and
eloquence.　But books, art in the ordinary sense,
and a certain kind of moral philosophy or practical
psychology, between them monopolised Mr Pater's
attention.[1]　That extensive reinforcement of the
appeal to the intellectual faculties by appeals to
the visual and auditory, which has been specified as
the note of nineteenth century poetry, had shown
itself in the *practice* of prose long before; but Mr
Pater carried it even further.　Up to this time no
one has surpassed or equalled, though many have
tried to imitate, the ambitious and successful refinement of his prose, with its extension of the nicest
shades of rhythm and colour from the sentence to
the paragraph, and with the varying and subtilising
of those rhythms and colours themselves, till the
whole becomes a kaleidoscope of *nuances* in the one
direction, and a fugue of tones and semitones in
the other.　Opinions have differed as to whether Mr

[1] With for chief results, *Studies in the History of the Renaissance*, 1873 ; *Marius the Epicurean*, 1885 ; *Appreciations*, 1889.

Pater himself carried this "adultery of art" too far: his imitators certainly have both sinned and failed in it. But its results are, at their best, so extraordinarily beautiful in themselves, and so suitable to the matter conveyed by the medium, that it would not be easy to find an equitable scheme of criticism under which they would not pass muster.

This matter, however, is itself by no means uncontentious. In regard to it also there have not been, and are not ever likely to be, wanting those who declare that it is "confusion," in the Biblical sense of the term, — not merely that the imagery and terminology of painting, sculpture, architecture, music, are carried too lavishly into the domain of literature, but that the whole point of view is *metabolised*, "translated" as Bottom was, though in a more comely fashion, intermingled and travestied in a bewildering and illicit manner. On the other hand, there will always be others to whom this revival, with a nineteenth-century dress, of the metaphysical impressionism of Taylor, and almost of Donne and Browne, will be inexpressibly attractive and caressing. But the antagonism, perhaps, reaches its highest in regard to the third point. The whole of Mr Pater's work is associated with a peculiar ethical-æsthetic or æsthetic-ethic to which he sometimes gave the name of Neo-Cyrenaicism; the installing, that is to say, of the μονόχρονος ἡδονή, the "moment of pleasure," not merely as the criterion of happy life, as Aristippus and his followers had held, but as the criterion of art and literature. This doctrine, though carefully purged of all grossness, could not but be rather horrifying to those accustomed to the, at least in principle, ascetic doctrines of modern religion and even philosophy; and many who would not have taken philosophical or religious objection denounced it as involving an effeminate dilettantism in the estimate of art and letters themselves. But we are approaching subjects which hardly concern us. It is probably enough to say here that to those who could "taste" him at all, Mr Pater provided his own moments of pleasure as few critics or writers of the last half of the nineteenth century in England have done.

Many names call—sometimes rather reproachfully —for discussion here, but perhaps to four only must *Mr Symonds, &c.* it be granted of more or less necessity. All four were contributors to periodicals, and three of them were eminent as critics. These last are John Addington Symonds (1840-1893), a writer in the ornate style, who only needed compression and economy to have come nearly as close to Mr Pater in achievement as he was in attitude,—the author of a wonderfully rich but not well *ordonnanced* book on *The Renaissance in Italy* (1875-86), of one not to be neglected on *The Predecessors of Shakespeare*, and of many others, partly made up of his innumerable Essays; William Minto (1845-1893), a critic of much solidity and fair catholicity, a novelist of some merit, and the author of two very sound and scholarly manuals of English literature; H. D. Traill (1842-1900), who has left the least adequate memorials of all in book form, though even here a volume of dialogues of extraordinary merit, *The New Lucian*, and two notable literary monographs on "Coleridge" and "Sterne," should preserve his name, but who, as a contributor to newspapers and periodicals, was the inferior of no writer of his time for vigour, wit, knowledge, versatility, and that indefinable quality which, as in manners and wine so in literature, can only be called "breeding." The fourth was a remarkable isolation, Richard Jefferies (1848-1887), who, after undistinguished beginnings, contributed to the *Pall Mall Gazette* a wonderful series of country sketches entitled *The Gamekeeper at Home* (1871), and followed it up, during the remainder of his short and not too fortunate life, more copiously than equally, but still with unique power.

From Jefferies we might proceed or return to a very large number of essayists, dealing sometimes *Jefferies and miscellaneous essayists.* only indirectly with literature, whom the extension of periodical literature has inevitably fostered. The immense popularity and influence of the *Spectator* throughout the eighteenth century had firmly established the miscellaneous essay in English, and this popularity was further increased by the fact that some of the chief writers of the Romantic Revolt and of the Romantic Triumph — Coleridge himself, Lamb, Hazlitt, Leigh Hunt, and others—took it up. Nor has it ever lost its hold, but, on the contrary, has strengthened it,— some of the very greatest of nineteenth century authors having touched it more or less. Dickens

began with it in the crude but promising *Boz*
Sketches.   Thackeray ended with it in those perfect
Roundabout Papers which have been noticed.   Mr
Stevenson experimented largely in it, and his desertion of it for his true field was even lamented by
some of his earliest friendly critics.   George Eliot,
in this, and this only, like Thackeray, ended with
it.   Popular varieties of it have at times enjoyed a
very great vogue, the *Friends in Council* of Sir Arthur
Helps having been succeeded by the *Recreations of
a Country Parson* (1859) of the Reverend A. K. H.
Boyd (1825-1899).   And these, after falling into discredit with young and sprightly judges, are, as
usual, themselves succeeded in the present day by
things almost indistinguishable in kind but suited in
externals to the day's fashion.   In fact, the opening
of the twentieth century has seen a greater devotion to this kind than ever; though so far, perhaps,
the particular Muse has not been very kind to her
worshippers.

CHAPTER IV.

ENGLISH AND FRENCH—THE OLDER PROSE KINDS—DRAMA.

DISABILITIES OF THIS CHAPTER—HERBERT SPENCER—BUCKLE—SIDGWICK AND GREEN—HISTORIANS : FROUDE—FREEMAN—GREEN, KINGLAKE, STUBBS, AND OTHERS—THEOLOGY : COMPARATIVE BARRENNESS NOT DUE TO THE OXFORD MOVEMENT—PHYSICAL SCIENCE—CLASSICAL SCHOLARSHIP—FRANCE : THE GENERAL DEPARTMENT—TAINE—RENAN—MERITS OF HIS STYLE—DRAMA.

IN popularity and profit the novel and the newspaper, as we have seen, far outstripped, during the present period, their older and still perhaps more dignified rivals—the history, the theological tractate or discourse, the philosophical disquisition ; and though physical science comes in a manner to the support of these against *belles lettres*,[1] yet she is recognised as but a dangerous auxiliary.

Yet for a time at least, in both the leading literary countries, very remarkable additions were made in all

[1] In some uses of this rather ambiguous term, History would be included ; but it is better to take it as designating Poetry, Fiction, Criticism, and miscellaneous Essay-writing only.

these kinds, and more especially in the historical de-
Disabilities of partments of the others, as well as in His-
this chapter. tory pure and simple. Only of very recent
years has the sorrowful fact been recognised by the
persons themselves concerned that " history has killed
the historian "—that the document has overwhelmed
the art. And there are, perhaps, some faint grounds
for hoping that this recognition is only a passing
spasm of pusillanimity. Theology and, as far as
mere writing goes, philosophy are in a somewhat
worse way; yet they also are not wholly forlorn. Of
all and of others we may contrive to set forth no such
very beggarly array, though it is only by borrowing
from *belles lettres* themselves that the severer Muses
can sustain a competition with their most engaging
sisters. Even with this aid the contrast is rather
against them.

Moreover, the special figures of the past volume
invade our province here even more notably than
elsewhere. Macaulay and Carlyle, Grote and Thirlwall,
Mill and Hamilton, Pusey and Newman, though most
of them lived far into our period, all belonged of right
to Mr Omond. Villemain, Guizot, Cousin, Michelet,
Quinet, Comte, Tocqueville, belonged to him in France;
and though in all these cases, English and French,
more or less important work was added to the tale of
each during our own time, it would skill but little to
examine it minutely here. The prose writer, unlike
the poet, very seldom develops quite important new
gifts late in life; in any case, no one of the writers
named can be said to have made, after 1850, the solid

and important additions to their budgets which were made by Tennyson and Browning and Hugo. Even Darwin, Montalembert, and one or two others, who perhaps may be said on balance to belong rather more to us, have received sufficient treatment in *The Romantic Triumph ;* and though Mr Herbert Spencer's

Herbert Spencer. career and productions were prolonged for more than another half-century, it will not be necessary to say much of him. Eminent among the thinkers of Europe, particularly influential on its rawer and less cultivated nations, and on those non-European peoples who have been anxious to "get" European culture, Mr Spencer was perhaps the least literary of all philosophers. This came not merely from the fact that he had no style—not even a bad one—but from the other fact that his entire spirit and attitude were anti-literary,—that literature is, in short, the most impregnable and annoying Decelea in the territory, the most gruesome skeleton at the feast, of the Spencerian philosophy. To be a Spencerian you must ignore literature, and, therefore, without any undignified resentment, but as charitably as justly, literature may ignore Mr Spencer. Yet there are some gleanings of the old harvest-fields left, and some sheaves from newer ones.

Among these figures a name which, once unduly exalted, has perhaps for some years been rather un-

Buckle. duly ignored. The same generalising mania which was epidemic in the middle of the century, and which found its most distinguished patients in Mr Spencer himself, in Comte, and later in M. Taine, found an exponent of far greater literary power than at least the first of these in Henry Thomas Buckle (1821-1862). It was perhaps fortunate for Buckle that he died rather early, for his system, which nearly caricatured itself in the two actual volumes of his *History of Civilisation* (1857-61), must almost to certainty have completed the effect in any possible continuation. The atheistic, though not necessarily antitheistic, determinism which is so often found in connection with this mania, and which, indeed, is almost logically necessary to allow it full swing and sweep, took in him a rather lower and more Philistine form than in the greater men just mentioned ; and, young as he died, he was even younger than his years in a certain clever crudity, which marked and marred all his work. But he was nearly as clever as he was crude ; and his purely literary faculty, though not of the highest order, and marked, like the rest of his composition, by a certain vulgarity, was extraordinary in its own way. His clearness was free from that "offensive" quality, that exasperating determination to make everything quite plain as to a very little and rather stupid child, which, in the even greater clearness of John Stuart Mill, was gibbeted by Nietzsche's epigram-epithet.[1] And the extreme ingenuity of his complete explanation of all the History of Spain and Scotland, by climate, geography, and religion, atoned to some extent for its manifest futility.

Both Spencer and Buckle represented a mixed class

---

[1] "*Beleidigende* Klarheit." See the *Götzen-Dämmerung*.

of historian - philosopher - politician which has more
and more enlisted men who in former days would
have been philosophers pure and simple ; and Mr
Omond, by arrangement, took into his view not only
Mr Spencer but some names representing work belonging to almost the latest years of our own period.
The chief now to be added are those of Henry
Sidgwick and Green. Sidgwick (1838-1900), a Cambridge moralist and political philosopher of the most
amiable character and the most varied acquisitions,
possessing a power of thought which could meet with
no disparagement, except that it "divided itself this
way and that" almost too swiftly and impartially, so
that the reader was often left in a state of mere
adiaphoria if not in sheer puzzlement ; and of his
Oxford compeer, T. H. Green, who combined a tendency to very abstract philosophy with a considerable
turn for practical affairs.

History proper, despite its affecting and Laocoontic
struggles with the document, has been somewhat
Historians— Froude. more brilliantly and numerously represented. If the epitaph chosen for himself
by one of not the least of its representatives, the
lamented Bishop Creighton (1843-1901), author, among
other things, of a valuable *History of the Popes*—" He
tried to write *true* history "—be the whole motto for
the historian, then we must refuse the highest place of
all to James Anthony Froude (1818-1894). But some
of the Bishop's greatest admirers would prefer, even
in opposition to him, to confirm this primacy to Mr
Froude. He was most certainly not accurate : he was

not even impartial; and though the two qualities ran
perpetual races in his work, inaccuracy had so much
the better of partiality that he could not even be
accurate on his own side. But, paradox as it may
seem, it may be doubted whether the faculty which
he had of making the past alive, of knitting the
historic contact between reader and subject, is not a
more valuable thing—as it is certainly a much rarer
one—than inviolable fidelity to fact or evidence. You
may never call a spirit James whose name was John,
and be ready to die rather than represent an event as
happening on Tuesday when it happened on Thursday;
you may be as judicial as Minos and as scrupulous
as a Quaker, and yet leave your reader in the possession merely of a bundle of dead propositions, packed
into his mind as the books from which they are derived
are packed into their shelves, and having as little
influence on it. Froude never did this; he always
kept the live continuity of human events, human
character, human motives,—always the contact between his own and his reader's historic sense. And
he did this at least partly by means of a style always
good, and at its best admirable, if not almost unique.

It was one of the numerous and rather fatal frank-
nesses of Froude's enemy and predecessor in the
Freeman. Oxford Chair of History, Edward Augustus
Freeman (1823-1892), that he sneered and
stormed at this very phrase of "the historic sense,"
though he was himself by no means wholly devoid of
it. A man of immense energy and industry, of headstrong views and more headstrong confidence in them,

essentially (Matthew Arnold called him " ferociously ")
pedantic, utterly destitute of courtesy or even fairness
to his foes, but respected in a fashion and liked without any restriction by his friends, Mr Freeman early
threw himself with unsurpassed enthusiasm into the
study of English history of the Norman period, and
some other matters connected with it. He was one of
the first to utilise—according to the general tendency
of the century to combine arts and sciences, which we
note so often—the study of architecture in its bearings
upon history; and throughout his life he inculcated,
in practice and theory, the necessity of illustrating his
subject by the most diligent research into all sub-
sidised aids of the kind. Whether he himself was
impeccably accurate is another matter. As usual in
the case of these priests of the Diana Aricina of
accuracy, he had towards the latter end of his life to
stand sharp attacks from his would-be successors. He
was very voluminous, and his style, though not incorrect, was very annoying to some readers by dint of
its mannerisms, its verbosity, and, above all, a certain
trick of allusive paraphrase and periphrase caught
from Gibbon and Macaulay, but used neither with the
judgment of the one nor with the sympathetic *popularity* of the other. These faults, combined as they were
with a large share of the hectoring and snarling habits
which are too common in a certain kind of scholar and
critic, and which latterly directed themselves not
merely to his crafts-fellows but to political adversaries,
were undoubtedly grave. But it is bare justice to Mr
Freeman to say that it is hardly possible to mention a

M

single English historian [1] who has thrown such light
on a given and important period of English history as
he threw on the eleventh and twelfth centuries.

His principal disciple, John Richard Green (1837-
1883), followed the same general lines, and occupied
himself very mainly with the same early
period, though he made wide excursions;
but his bent or his gifts, or both combined,
made him much more popular. Indeed, while Freeman
could hardly be read by anybody who did not take some
special interest in his subject, and certainly could not
be read with advantage by any one who had not more
than "every schoolboy's" knowledge of it, Green
nearly rivalled Macaulay in the popularity of his
Short History of the English People (1874). His style,
though vivid and picturesque, and free from the thorny
aggressiveness and repellent pedantry of Freeman, was
perhaps not much less offensive to a pure taste from
its gaudy colouring and rhetorical emphasis; but it
was for these same reasons thoroughly popular.
Kinglake, mentioned for *Eothen* in the last volume,
belongs to our period by his great work on the *Crimean
War*, another of the popular histories of this time,
immensely voluminous,—almost the whole of a volume
is devoted to the single battle of the Alma,—elaborately documented, written in a style of higher literary
power than Green's, but as inartistic in its violent and

*Green,
Kinglake,
Stubbs, and
others.*

---

[1] Some would except Samuel Rawson Gardiner (1829-1904) for his
extensive and laborious dealings with the Stuart period. In exploration and arrangement of fact he has had few superiors : opinions differ
more as to his power of character-drawing and as to his historic *grasp*
generally. But whatever his merits, they were not primarily literary.

popular effects. Strongly contrasted with all these was the work of Bishop Stubbs (1825-1901), who by some critics is regarded, not without reason, as the master and almost the soul of the school of which Freeman and Green were only *concionatores ad vulgus*. Stubbs, one of the wittiest of men in private life, and even in some published speeches and letters, chose, not quite impossibly in reaction against the flourishings of the one and the fireworks of the other, to write his *Constitutional History* in a style of extraordinarily dryasdust character, but its pith and substance are even less ordinary. Bishop Creighton (1843-1901) (who resembled his master and brother in the contrast of his spoken and written style, though he was never dryasdust) has been mentioned; Skene and Burton, Seeley and Stirling Maxwell can only be so. And this slight sketch of the most recent English historical school may be fitly closed with the name of Lord Acton (1834-1902), who, in his inaugural lecture as Professor of History at Cambridge, himself made the moan above quoted as to "history killing the historian," and who illustrated it by producing next to nothing at all to justify his nevertheless well-founded reputation as one of the deepest and widest students of history in our time.

In theology also the writer of this volume has to submit to a self-denying ordinance, imposed by him *Theology—* as editor of the whole book, and to re- *Comparative* linquish Newman, who lived till 1890, and *barrenness* Pusey, who lived till 1882, with others, to his predecessor's treatment.[1] Undoubtedly, however,

---

[1] See *The Romantic Triumph.*

the subject has not, for the last fifty years, received the tribute of its professional exponents as
it would once have done. In the seventeenth and
even in the eighteenth century, men like Bishops
Stubbs and Creighton would probably have given to
it a larger share of their literary work; while it is
impossible not to recognise the fact that the throwing open by Mr Gladstone of College fellowships has
made it less and less easy for men of talent to devote
themselves, after they are in orders, to subjects
neither popular nor paying, perhaps even to take
orders at all. Even preaching, the most popular and
paying form of ecclesiastical literary exercise, has
shown distinct decline in literary and intellectual
level since the death of the late Dr Liddon (1829-
1890), who could not himself pretend to the highest
intellectual or literary quality. That the wheel will
turn again may be certain enough; but meanwhile
there can be at least as little doubt that the latter
half of the nineteenth century will never count as a
palmy time of theological literature or oratory in
England, and that such illustrations as it did possess
were almost wholly bequeathed to it by earlier days.

In reference to this last point, and as a correction of
considerable importance, one word may be permitted
here on a singular fallacy which has been propagated,

not due to the Oxford movement. —the idea that the Oxford movement interrupted, sterilised, acted as east wind to
the intellectual and literary current, if not
of England, at any rate of a great part thereof. It is
quite true that a certain number of persons stood

aloof or fell away from that movement, and that some of these persons—Arnold or the Arnolds, Pattison, Froude, Clough—were persons of great mark and of more than likelihood. But the current ran otherwise. All the greatest literary achievement of England, till quite late in the nineteenth century, set as the Oxford movement set, not necessarily in the dogmatic channel, but in the channel of recurrence to the past, of admiration of things mediæval, of that blending of arts which the Church had always understood, and which the Tractarians wisely adopted. In persons the very farthest removed from High Church ideals as far as religion is concerned—in Mr Morris, in Mr Swinburne, in Mr Pater,[1]—the influence of the movement is unmistakable. Mr Ruskin is simply a " trace-horse " who sometimes kicks over the traces—a skittish but powerful auxiliary of it. All the revolters, unless they happen to be shallow sciolists, feel it and show it. The combined effects of Mr Gladstone's University legislation of 1870 and of Lord Beaconsfield's Church Discipline Act of a few years later did, no doubt, irreparable harm to it. But it had had already thirty, nay, forty, years of influence on the best intellects of the nation, and thirty or forty years of such influence means something for ever.

If, however, literature in England has not been *Physical science.* quite so well served as she might have been in her graver and severer departments, some departments of conventional gravity and

---

[1] There *was* a very strong High Church element in Mr Pater ; but at times it could be overlooked.

severity, which for some time had not contributed much, have come to her reinforcement. From the days of Bacon and Browne to those of Sir Humphry Davy, not many "physicists" had taken high rank among men of letters; but the growing public interest in the subject from Davy's time onward, and especially from the time of the *Vestiges of Creation* and of Darwin, changed this to no small extent. Among the exponents and defenders of physical science during our time, John Tyndall (1820-1893) was no contemptible man of letters; and Thomas Henry Huxley (1825-1895) had literary power which would have distinguished him in any branch of literature to which he chose to devote himself. This power actually made him an admirable expositor, a luminous and acute critic, and a controversialist who, if his heat and occasional one-sidedness rather too often reminded one of that *odium theologicum* to which he opposed and exposed himself, possessed extraordinary logical (perhaps not seldomest *para*logical) skill and resource, an excellent style, and even in his assaults on literature that literary *ethos* which is as unmistakable as it is indefinable, and which seldom exists, and still seldomer comes to much, unless it is fed by some study of literature itself.

The disuse, too, of Latin as an almost necessary vehicle of classical scholarship, in the strict and *Classical scholarship.* technical sense, opened up a new and, as it has proved, a very fertile and "amene" field to literary exercise in the vernacular. The work of John Conington (1825-1869) at Oxford, of William Young Sellar (1825-1890) at Oxford, St Andrews, and

Edinburgh, of Hugh A. J. Munro (1819 - 1885) at Cambridge, about the middle of the century, set an example of treating the Classics from the combined literary and philological point of view, and in some cases at any rate, in admirable literary form, which has been happily continued and even improved upon. Were it not for the rule of not discussing living persons here, it would be possible to mention more than one or two names of scholars who have contributed to the history and discussion of Greek literature, Greek poetry, classical scholarship generally,—work of which no country and no department of the graver letters need have been ashamed as original contribution at any time and in any tongue. While between the two groups some names, especially that of Henry Nettleship (1839-1893), show that the new kind has been established by no accidental or sporadic appearances. This phenomenon is almost of the highest importance to literature, because the emollient and restraining influence of direct classical study is being yearly exercised on a smaller proportion of those who write and read, and so the transmission of it, even at second - hand, becomes all the more sovereign. But quite independently of this, it has resulted in positive additions to literature which would have been welcome at any time, and are doubly welcome now.

The remarkable sympathy between the processes and phenomena of French and English literature which has distinguished the nineteenth century, perhaps beyond any other period, shows itself also in

France— the general depārtment.

this matter of " re-humanising " as it may almost be called, Humanism itself ; of re-establishing—with the due allowance for the fact that Latin was no longer the language of ordinary speech and writing — the relations of scholarship and literature which had existed in the Renaissance. But in France the example had already been set by one who was less of a technical " scholar " than of a pure man of letters— by Sainte-Beuve himself, whose essays on classical literature are among his most characteristic and delightful; not by men who, though they showed admirable literary gifts, were scholars first of all, like those who have been named or alluded to in the last paragraph. It has been excellently continued by writers from M. Gaston Boissier downwards. But it may here more concern us to consider those representatives of the older departments who have been left us by the concerted depredations of our predecessor. They are not numerous, for the earlier harvest of French literature began to fail rather sooner than that of English; but they include two prose writers who, on by no means unduly liberal principles, will probably always be admitted to the first rank of prosaists in French, and some others. We have already in the last chapter said something of these two, but almost the sole importance of the one, the main importance of the other, there lay beyond us.

Hippolyte Adolphe Taine (1828-1893) and Ernest

Renan (1823-1892) were friends; but frequent and proverbial as is the difference between friends' character, it has seldom been more accentuated than here. Whatever may be said against Taine—and we have said something —his was eminently a masculine mind. He early devoted himself to philosophical and historical studies of by no means a superficial and popular kind, and the greatest work of his life, the *Origines de la France Contemporaine,* was not only a book of immense erudition and research, but one guided, schemed, constructed throughout by the clearest and most vigorous conceptions and master ideas. Even the faults of his style — its hardness, its brassy brilliancy and clang, its uncompromising perspicuity — had nothing feminine or effeminate about them; and his rigid determinism had less of the extravagance of the mere generaliser than of a sufficiently genuine, if mistaken, "scientific" drift. As a philosopher Taine contrasts certainly not ill with the visions of the later Comte, if not with the assumptions of the earlier. As a historian, especially in his last stage, he contrasts yet more favourably with the picturesque but rather invertebrate interpretation of Thierry, the doctrinairism of Guizot, the flagrant partisanship of Thiers and Lanfrey, and the brilliant but too often utterly unhistorical phantasmagoria of Michelet. Both in writing and in thought, whatever faults we may find with him as writer or thinker, Taine emphatically deserves the epithet with which, as I

Taine.

understand, the French family doctor gladdens the hearts of nurses and mothers when he compliments a new - born baby as *bien râblé* — well ribbed and chined — sturdy — with nothing limp or sickly or rickety about him. Nor, though it may sometimes pass into emphasis and even violence, does this strength often degenerate into clumsiness or brutality; nay, it can not seldom invest itself with a certain amount of rather florid and *viraginous* beauty.

The exact opposite is the case with Renan. Everything about him—his gifts and his graces, his failings *Renan.* and his faults alike — is feminine. His unorthodoxy itself is like the infidelity of a girl who has been brought up from her infancy as the betrothed of a man, and who takes a dislike to him for that and no other reason. His literary likes and dislikes; his political indifferentism, which, revealed by the tale-bearing of M. de Goncourt, once brought him into no small trouble; the easy morality, which in the latest days of his life degenerated into that of the nurses of Elizabethan drama, or even of less equivocal characters of the female sex in the same—are all feminine. He disliked Béranger, who was rather too manly for him and was a Bonapartist; but his last word to humanity is extremely like Béranger's famous "Baise-moi, Suzon, et ne damnons personne," except that it is rather the utterance of a complaisant third person than of either of the actors in such a tableau. Further, M. Renan's logic is the most capital example in

existence of what is with by no means universal justice of application called feminine logic: the astonishing eclecticism and assumption as to evidence
of the *Vie de Jésus,* and still more of the *Histoire
d'Israël,* which caused such tribulation to his equally
unorthodox but much more logical and masculine
friend M. Scherer, give an inexhaustible quarry of
every logical fault and fallacy that the books specify,
and of most that imagination can conceive. Anti-
Christian as he is on almost every point,—history,
drama, ethics, politics, ecclesiastics,—he cannot help
loving Christianity for its amiability, for its pity, for
just the qualities, in short, which made Nietzsche
hate it. The German's favourite symbol for his
new man was a roaring lion; the Frenchman's
should have been a purring cat—though with the
usual possibility of scratch not far off.

And here too the style, and not merely the fashion
of writing but the general character, were *l'homme
même.* It is impossible, however far one may be on
the other side in opinion from M. Renan, however
much one may dislike some points in his manner
of expressing the opinions which he holds, to deny
the qualities of his style. With all the clearness
which is supposed to be the inalienable birthright
of the French, he has a "sweet, attractive kind of
grace," which by no means always, or even very
often, accompanies it. Ungallant critics have sometimes assimilated French writings to French women,
and have said that with unsurpassed neatness, skill
in presenting themselves, adroit *savoir faire* in

company, genius for dress, practical shrewdness, and so forth, the more witching charms of feature and expression are not uncommonly common in the whole of Gaul. But the beauty of M. Renan's style *Merits of his style.* is, let it be repeated, undeniable. It is never merely trivial; it is always "about something"; and it never fails to put what it is about with that *indescribableness* of charm which all human beauty, artistic or natural, possesses, whether in high or low degree. Neither can it be justly said that this charm is monotonous. It can bestow itself upon the most varied subjects, and in the vast range of the author's work it exhibits at least two general phases, differing from each other with a difference which few writers have been able to give to their prose. The narrative purple patches of the *Vie* and the *Histoire* require and exhibit by no means the same faculties (though the *Histoire* occupies a sort of middle position, is a sort of "bridge") as the semi-dramatic oratory of the *Drames Philosophiques*. Yet both attain all but the highest excellence, and the *Drames* supply beyond all reasonable question one of the chief prose books as prose books, not merely of French nineteenth century literature, but of the literature of the nineteenth century and of the literature of France.

But the defects of this feminine quality of beauty do not fail to exhibit themselves. M. Renan's style is *ipsa mollities;* but softness, though a very agreeable thing in certain cases and conditions, is not always so, and even when agreeable is not always quite

healthy, quite trustworthy, or quite durable. It is
curious that his most elaborate attempt at grandeur
—the passage on Carmel and Elijah in the *Vie*—is
obviously, and almost consciously, written in a sort of
shrinking distaste for the grandeur and the terror of the
subject itself. On milder themes M. Renan is always
about to convert, and not seldom actually does convert, the feminine into the effeminate. Many of the
most distasteful passages in reference to Christ himself are made so by this *delumbe*, this *in labris natans*
—two epithets of Persius which apply to M. Renan
better than to almost any other writer known to me.
So with the treatment of the *Shepherd* of Hermas,
where, however, the faults of taste are fewer; so
passim. One of the oddest things in his whole work,
the extraordinary romance which he gets out of the
character of Jezebel, by combining the Book of Kings
and the 45th Psalm, is rather like a *Men and Women*
study, excogitated by Mr Browning, but put into
literary expression and prose by his wife. In the
Drames themselves, to say no more of the ugliest
touch in the *Abbesse de Jouarre*, observe how all the
virility is taken out of Prospero, how feminised is the
savage allegory of the Priesthood of Diana Aricina.
Far be it from the present writer to speak evil of
the *Ewigweibliche* as it is in woman; but it is scarcely
necessary to cite Shakespeare and many earlier and
later authorities to justify small liking for the
womanish in man.

From these two great writers the descent to others
is considerable, and the exclusion of the living is

perhaps rather a relief than a loss, as far as individual mentions are concerned. France, however,
has developed schools of historians, philologists, &c.,
in the full modern senses of these terms. Albert Sorel
(1842-1906), who devoted himself especially to the Revolutionary period, and who wrote an excellent book
on Madame de Staël, need fear comparison with few
historians of his day; while Gaston Paris (1839-1904)
had absolutely no superior in Europe for that combination of philological and literary accomplishment which
should be so easy, but which seems to present almost
insurmountable difficulties. Great as had been the
services of his father, Paulin Paris, to French language
and literature, the son surpassed them, and from his
early *Histoire Poétique de Charlemagne* (1866) (which
from a scholarly striving after perfection he kept out
of print all the later years of his life) through many
contributions to the periodical *Romania*, an invaluable
Primer of French Mediæval Literature, an excellent
book on Villon, and other things, he displayed the
rare union just noticed, together with that—not much
less rare—of an appreciation of modern as well as of
old literature. Some notice ought also to be given
to the valuable work, chiefly on eighteenth century
diplomatic history, of the Duc de Broglie (1821-1901),
while France has at present younger writers in history
who may almost vie with those critics to whom we
have paid guarded respects above.

In philosophy, on the other hand, she has not
produced any great name, though many respectable
workers; and in theology and its products that of

the Père Didon is the chief that can be actually added to the list, though we may spare a salute of the exceptional kind to the living M. Paul Sabatier —*le Renan de nos jours.*

On the subject assigned in the heading of this chapter for its close there is here some diffidence in writing. Sparing and infrequent attendants at the theatre are fervently admonished by theatrical critics, that the man who cannot speak as one who knows about "the front of the house," and what is behind the scenes, and the demands of an exacting modern audience, and "problems," and the rest of it, had better hold his tongue. Yet for those who can read Greek Drama from Æschylus to Aristophanes, and English from Peele to Farquhar, and French from Garnier to Musset with delight, there should be some minute *locus standi* in reference to these and other theatres. However this may be, the present writer has found a French play here and there, though by no means frequently, among the productions of the French stage during the last half of the nineteenth century [1] that he can *read;* but an English play that he can read, taking any interest in it as a play, he has not found. All the plays of Tennyson date from this period; but some Tennyson-

Drama.

[1] Their number is, of course, immense; and since the *débuts* of Angier and Dumas *fils*, which were noticed in *The Romantic Triumph*, a large proportion of the men of letters in France who have attempted *belles lettres* have been dramatists, while some like Labiche, Sardou, Halévy, Pailleron, have been dramatists mainly or merely. But for reasons outlined in the text we need not discuss them minutely.

ians would not care if this division of Tennyson's works perished utterly from record and memory. Mr Swinburne's *Atalanta* (one must break the rule of silence here in order to get anything to talk about) is delightful, and his *Erechtheus* respectable in the French sense as well as in the English; but both are *tours de force*, while Mr Arnold's *Merope* is a *tour de faiblesse*. Hardly any of Mr Browning's very undramatic attempts at drama belong to our time. The later work of Horne and Sir Henry Taylor calls for no special notice. Most of the work of writers lately dead is either mere closet drama-book poetry cast into dramatic form, or stuff so utterly unliterary that it simply escapes literary treatment altogether, —that it cannot be condemned because it is out of jurisdiction, belonging to other planes and spheres. The French, helped by a long tradition and by the universal discipline and form of their literature, have done better; but even in their drama the decadence —at least the interval—is perceptible enough. In English there is no such discipline, and the tradition is all the other way. When one hears of the guileless foreigner, misled by his own atmosphere, selecting modern English plays as subjects of literary study, there is nothing for it but to take refuge in shrug or smile or sigh, according to temperament.

That the decadence of the drama is due to the uprising of the novel is an old theory, and one which has a good deal to say for itself. One can only wonder whether it will receive corroboration or confutation from the possible decadence of the novel—

which is asserted by some, and on which, rather than
on any positive renaissance in the other form, they
lay stress. Still, it may be admitted that men of more
literary skill, combined with some practical knowledge
of the stage, *have* recently turned their attention to
it in England. But finding some of these unhappy,
we may pass them by, and the others, as living, are
not within our scope. For France we may be more
particular, although even here the limit of living
persons intrudes itself, and though in both countries
the influence of Ibsen, which will be fully dealt with
in its own place, accounts for a very fair part—
for nearly all the *differentia*—of the production. It
happens, however, that in France the most prominent leader of this new movement, M. Henry Becque
(?-1899), is dead and can be dealt with.

In fact, the two volumes of his plays (for though
he wrote for some thirty years he was not a fertile
producer) may serve as a handbook of that modern
drama, which does not affect either the Ibsenic preposterousness or the mere epigram - and - paradox
douching - process. The reading of them may be
said to be an unfair test, for they are evidently only
meant for the stage; and they have, off it, only an
interest of curiosity which soon palls. Of literary
appeal there is practically nothing. There is next
to no story; the characters are limited simply to
the situation or series of situations, and acquire
none of the old "dramatic" personality to the mind;
the dialogue, if it escapes the reproach of inveri-
similitude, escapes it only by being quite unre-

N

markable; there is hardly any conclusion. No doubt a sufficient previous interest in the theatre as the theatre, in the actors as actors, in dress, scenery, decorations, might give such plays zest; and there is no reason for contesting the proposition that, with no added ornaments, they have the merit of actable situation. But in this case they only supply a further support to the paradox—which is receiving more and more approval, as something better than a paradox, from different and opposed thinkers— that the drama and literature have nothing necessarily to do with each other. Now this is a History of Literature.

CHAPTER V.

GERMAN LITERATURE.

PARADOX OF THIS CHAPTER — THE OTHER HEINE — SCHOPENHAUER —
SCHEFFEL—EPICS : JORDAN—ORIENTAL AND OTHER SCHOOL-WRITING
—FONTANE—GOTTFRIED KELLER—K. F. MEYER—FRAU VON EBNER
ESCHENBACH — HEYSE — PRINCE VON SCHÖNAICH - CAROLATH —
FREIHERR VON LILIENCRON—O. J. BIERBAUM—THE HOLZ SCHOOL
AND OTHER MODERNITIES — ANALYSIS OF TWO ANTHOLOGIES —
NOVELISTS : AUERBACH—FREYTAG—THE HISTORICAL NOVEL : EBERS,
ETC.—OTHER KINDS—DRAMA—FROM FREYTAG TO HAUPTMANN—
NATURALISM, ETC., IN GERMANY — THE PRECINCTS OF DRAMA :
WAGNER — CRITICISM : SCHOLASTIC AND LITERARY — GRILLPARZER
AND OTHERS — HILLEBRAND — BAHR — PHILOSOPHY—LOTZE —HART-
MANN — NIETZSCHE — HIS EARLIER AND MIDDLE WORK — ZARA-
THUSTRA — NIETZSCHE'S MASTERY OF STYLE — HIS ATTITUDE AND
INFLUENCE—THEOLOGY AND SCIENCE—HISTORY—MOMMSEN—NOTE
ON PLATT-DEUTSCH : REUTER AND GROTH.

THERE is no territorial division of European Literature during our period which lends itself so well
Paradox of to separate treatment as does German,
this chapter. though the reason is not altogether com-
plimentary. To deal, in a book of the scale of this
present, separately and inclusively with English, or
separately with French, literature, would be impossible
except at the sacrifice of all proportion in chapter

division, as well as of the best opportunities for that comparative dealing which is of the essence of the whole book. To deal separately with any of the other literatures would be a sin against proportion in the same way, though differently worked out by excess instead of defect. On the other hand, both its bulk and a certain importance—partly traditional and partly a reflection, false or true, from politics—almost demand that German literature shall not be merely lumped with others; while the substance and merit of its contents are by no means such as to make it difficult to deal with them in a single chapter of moderate bulk.

The fact is, that during this period Germany presents us with perhaps the most remarkable instance which we have had in our fifteen hundred years' survey, of a great, a rather sudden, and a nearly universal *drop* in the value of a national literature. The circumstances, the reasons, the probable duration of this dead season, can only be indicated briefly and tentatively here; but the fact is quite beyond all but pseudo-critical denial, and curiously enough it was foreseen and foretold by the greatest of German men of letters, the man who is German literature personified—Goethe. It is not too much to say that since the death of Heine and that of Schopenhauer, nearly fifty years ago, Germany has not produced a single writer of the absolutely first class, with the rule-establishing exception of Friedrich Nietzsche: and very few indeed who approach it. Her literature of erudition is, of course, enormous in bulk, if

perhaps more imposing in appearance than really
solid in value;[1] her literature of power has been,
during the half century, in such strange contrast with
itself for nearly a full century earlier as can hardly
be witnessed in any other case.

The last of the greater gods of pure Teutonic
letters hitherto, belongs to us by the latest years of
The other his painful life to a certain extent, inas-
Heine. much as the decade 1850-1860 is common
ground between this and the last volume; and also
for another reason. It was right and proper for Mr
Omond, dealing with "The Romantic Triumph" as
he had to do, to put that view of Heine's work and
ethos which takes into full account his apparent
Romantic iconoclasm—the invasion of Mephistopheles
into Fairyland. It is, I think, equally right for me to
point out that this is not the only view of Heine that
is held, or the only side of him that may be reasonably brought under consideration. There are persons
who, admitting for themselves the soft impeachment of
being almost *romantiques enragés,* would eagerly assert
that none of the great writers of the past have been
to them such friends and masters in the Romantic

---

[1] If this seem grudging, *v. inf.*, p. 233. Works on German literature are extremely numerous in German. Of general histories available in English, the translation of W. Scherer's *History* (Oxford, 1886)
and Professor J. G. Robertson's later and original work (Edinburgh,
1902) are probably the best. For recent and contemporary work,
among many German treatises I have found Professor Dr C. Beyer-
Boppard's *Einleitung in die Geschichte der Deutschen Literatur, unter
besonderer Berücksichtigung der neuesten Zeit* (Langensalza, 1905)
extremely useful. It is arranged dictionary-fashion for the most
part, but classified and interconnected.

spirit as Heine and Thackeray,—those two dissolvers and destroyers of illusion, as some hold them. And this is more especially the case in regard to Heine. That complication and contradiction which has made it perhaps more difficult to draw up clear cut-and-dried estimates of nineteenth century writers than of any others in the history of the world, displays itself nowhere so much as here. We have all been, for two or three generations, so little of a piece—the absolute *integer vitæ*, the man with one hood and one face only, has been so rare among us—that different pieces of this writer have constantly appealed, and been bound to appeal, to different pieces of different readers. To men of one combination or constitution of temperament and intelligence, what will be most noticeable in Heine will be his sarcastic criticism, his political and theological unorthodoxy, his militant aggressiveness, his gibes and flouts and jeers. To men of another, these things will be but slightly marked, and will serve rather as lemon and cayenne to relish what is to them the substance of Heine. And that substance—*to them* —is mere poetry, pure Romance, " star-fire and tear-dew and rainbow gold," as it was once put, of sheer imagination. The real Heine—*to them*—is the Heine who wrote in his youth,

> " Mein süsses Lieb, wenn du im Grab,"

and

> " Die alten, bösen Lieder,"

and the unrhymed wonders of the *Nordsee;* who followed these up in middle life with that marvellous picture of the moonlight,

" Überflimmernd Gregors Kahlkopf
Und die Brüste der Mathildis,"

and *Die Flucht*, and the meaning of yellow roses, and the night-ride of the Goddess and the Fairy in the midst of the satiric Walpurgis of *Atta Troll;* who has made the histories of the *Romanzero* one unbroken carcanet of gems in romantic workmanship; and who, when the *Matratzengruft* was already closing over him, matched the rarest things he has ever done with the infinite pathos of *Bimini* and the infinite tenderness of the *Lotusblume.* This is *our* Heine; and though we do not in the very least wish that the other Heine (save on very rare occasions) were non-existent, and take, as has been said, that Heine's idiosyncrasy as a very great enhancement and relish to the other, it is the first, or rather both together, who is, who are, *the* Heine—as unique, if not as universal, as Shakespeare; as deep, if not as high and pure, as Dante; as genial, if not as unsophisticated, as Homer himself. Take the negative side of him only, and Heine is not much greater than Voltaire; take the positive, or (better still) both, and he leaves the Frenchman so far behind and below that it is hard to bring them together in one purview. Yet Heine, as a great admirer of his and a great admirer of Germany has said, was " not a German, but a Jew." It is possible, though hardly probable, that Jewry will yet send us his fellow; what is neither possible nor probable, but certain, is that Germany has as yet shown not the very slightest signs of doing or of ever being likely to do so, except in the anti-Semite Nietzsche.

So, too, without any disloyalty to my predecessor, I think a short addition on the other side may be made to what Mr Omond has said[1] about Schopenhauer, who survived our barrier for ten years. In everything that is to be found in *The Romantic Triumph* on Schopenhauer as a philosopher I acquiesce completely. But I think we may here just call additional attention to the extraordinary advance in German *style* shown in *Die Welt als Wille und Vorstellung*, and still more in *Parerga und Paralipomena*. Heine is a poet; and even their successor and thirdsman Nietzsche (who went out of his way to contradict whatever could, and many things that could not, be contradicted) admits that good poets, when they wrote prose at all, have generally been good prose writers. But Schopenhauer was not a poet; and his ascetic-pessimist scheme of thought might be thought likely to numb style—to make a "dreary porcupine" of him, as was said of another famous person in our period—after a fashion of probable operation quite different from that of the Aristophanic quality of Heine or the Dionysiac revelry of Nietzsche. But the actual results contradict this. Even competent judges, to the manner born, admit that Schopenhauer's is about the best German style —that it is, in fact, "perfect." He, of course, does not allow himself the "alarums and excursions" of his pupil and only successor, Nietzsche; but in the grave and caustic way, not without an amount of fire, he seems to me the *ne plus ultra* of German prose.

Schopenhauer.

[1] See again the last volume.

The assets of the past which Germany still enjoyed, after putting these two great names in verse and prose respectively, were of no very important kind, in verse especially. Uhland, Rückert, Freiligrath, Geibel, will be dealt with, as far as we need deal with them, later. Hoffmann von Fallersleben survived for years after 1870, but his best work had been done far earlier, and not so much in the field of poetry as in that of literary history; while his latest was of the school of political verse, which the great triumph over France naturally encouraged, but which was even less fertile in really great work than political verse, out of the satirical department, usually is. His school was itself something of a continuation of the "Young German" school of thirty or forty years earlier. Of its other representatives—Franz von Dingelstedt (1814-1881), who tried the satiric style in *Lieder eines kosmopolitischen Nachtwächters* (1841) and *Nacht und Morgen* ten years later, and who later gave himself up to translation-adaptations of Shakespeare for the German stage; Gottfried Kinkel (1815-1882) (mentioned by Mr Omond, and for a long time a refugee and teacher of German in London); Georg Herwegh, who was also a revolutionist in 1848 and an exile till 1866—little need be said.

Not least satisfactory, perhaps, of the German verse of this period, is that provided by the cheerful but versatile and not frivolous Muse of Joseph *Scheffel.* Victor von Scheffel, poet and Romance-writer (1826-1886), whose poem of *Der Trompeter von Säkkingen* in 1853 and his prose story of *Ekkehard*

in 1857 took, and took deservedly, the taste not only
of his native country but of Europe, the editions of
both running into hundreds. In these, as in his later
works, for more than a quarter of a century, *Frau
Aventiure* (1863), *Juniperus* (1868), *Bergpsalmen* (1870),
Gaudeamus (1877), and *Waldeinsamkeit* (1880), he employed, as some of the titles themselves will show,
a mixture of appeal to the old German motives of
humour, romance, fondness for tradition, and other
right respectable things, with deserved success.
There are no great heights or depths in Scheffel, no
triumphs of art or wonders of harmony and phrase.
But there is that happy marriage of form, such as
it is, and subject, such as it is, which never fails to
satisfy competent judges, and which sometimes, as in
this case, succeeds in satisfying the public.

It was, however, not common at the time for German verse - writers to *indulge* their genius. Even
before, but much more after, 1870 a fell determination
to write great poems seized upon too many of them,
with a result of epics, philosophical and other, which
posterity is pretty safe to neglect.

Philosophical poetry has, as a matter of history, less
promise even than political; but it was almost a necessity in Germany, though we need hardly try to survey the attempts in it from the *Ahasver* and *Lied vom
Ritter Wahn* of Julius Mosen (1803-1867) downwards.
The epical turn, however, which this philosophical
poetry took may be worth indication; and one of its
practitioners—for before the work which we are about
to specify he had written *Demiourgos* (1854) and other

such things—produced a poem which, if not of high literary quality, is of genuine literary appeal.

This is the new *Nibelungen-Lied* (1869-1875) of Wilhelm Jordan (1819-1904) in four volumes, and *Epics— Jordan.* not much short of forty thousand lines. But even the archaic metre in the original (German) poem is not archaic enough for Herr Jordan: he must go back to alliteration and endeavour to supply the admitted poverty of High German as we have it in the oldest metre. The result, as the following specimen will show, is not exactly calculated to make one regret the process which, in the twelfth and thirteenth centuries, substituted rhymed metre for alliterated rhythm in English, and for the matter of that in German too:—

> "Die Sage versiegte, die Sänger verstummten,
> Ihr lautes Leben verlor die Dichtung,
> Und Verse fürs Auge formte die Feder."

It will be observed that the rhythm is much more marked than in most of our genuine old examples of alliteration, and resembles rather the revived English variety of the fourteenth and fifteenth centuries. This was probably unavoidable, from the effect on the language itself of practice in the other kind, and from the set of German towards the trochee. But at the same time it deprives the *pastiche* of the sole merit that it might have had. At any rate, Herr Jordan's work contrasts most signally and most unfortunately with Mr Morris's *Sigurd the Volsung*, which was its pretty near contemporary. But to study this epic school further would be right little joy, nor is the study imposed on us by peremptory duty.

Perhaps one of the most unsatisfactory signs in German poetry during the whole of our period is the tendency — noticeable of course to some extent in all European poetry and litera- ture, but elsewhere not quite so docile and scholastic — to imitate and follow the "printed book." Because Goethe and Rückert and Platen had made Oriental verse-studies, Schefer and Daumer, Stieglitz and Bodenstedt (1819-1892), did the same, and Bodenstedt's *Lieder des Mirza Schaffy* (1851) became very popular. Of the very considerable Austrian school of poets during the middle of the century, the best was probably Robert Hamerling (1830-1889), who again attacked the subject of the Wandering Jew in his *Ahasverus in Rom* (1866), and had earlier written *Venus im Exil* (1858), *Sinnen und Minnen* (1859), *Das Schwanenlied der Romantik* (1862); while Betty Paoli (really Elizabeth Glück, 1815-1894) was a productive and meritorious poetess between 1840 and 1860, and may have set some example to a still better — Frau von Ebner-Eschen- bach (*v. inf.*)

Oriental and other school- writing.

In reading these and others, uncomfortable reflec- tions occur. German is one of the languages in which it is comparatively easy—thanks partly to its natural capacities and partly to the excellent models existing in it—to produce something that is not unpoetical in sound; while practically all human emotion, and most human experience of other kinds, provide possible poetic material in sense. This is no doubt a great convenience and a great temptation for the *mediocris poeta;* but then the *mediocris poeta* is not a person whom the human race gladly encourages, or whom perhaps it ought to encourage.

Take, for instance, such a writer as Theodor Fontane (1819-1898), poet and novelist. In neither capacity is he contemptible, and there is some reason for the alleged pride of the "Mark of Brandenburg" in him as her most remarkable poet. He travelled in England pretty early, and seems to have experienced, afresh and independently, the charm which Percy's *Reliques* had exercised on the German mind nearly a hundred years before. He translated many ballads, venturing even on *Chevy Chase* and *Sir Patrick Spens,* and he wrote a good many new ones on subjects of English and of German history. His novels (to take the prose fiction for convenience' sake together with the verse), written for the most part late in his life, have some power and passion, which is particularly noticeable in one of the last, *Effi Briest* (1895), written when he was nearer to the fourscore than to the threescore and ten. But in prose and verse alike there is something wanting. He is (to use one of those slang expressions which often deserve to make their entrance into literature, and which, when they have done so, are accepted by the very elect who are horrified at them before) never quite "on the spot."

This sense of failure or of incomplete success—of "some want, some coldness"—is perhaps more com-

Fontane.

mon in the reading of modern German literature than in that of any other. Until quite recently (when it has done much to make up the neglect) it had paid less attention to the preposterous and the acrobatic than others, and so its shortcomings were less glaring; but a practised critical habit could hardly miss them. Let us take two others, also poets and novelists (the conjunction has been almost the rule in the Fatherland)—Gottfried Keller and K. F. Meyer.

The first (1819-1890) is one of the most respectable, in the old and better sense of the word, of the modern writers of German - speaking Switzerland.

Gottfried Keller.

Born near Zurich, he gave himself up at first to the study of art, especially landscape-painting, but turned to poetry pretty early (his first published verse dates from 1846), became a scholar in the older forms of the modern languages, and for nearly the last forty years of his life was a famous and popular novelist, his *Leute von Seldwyla* (1856) being an especial favourite, though the earlier (1854) and partly autobiographical *Der grüne Heinrich* was perhaps more popular still. No prejudice against Keller ought to be created by the silly title of "the Shakespeare of German tale-tellers" given him by, it is said, no less a person than Paul Heyse. These sillinesses affect all literatures; though, from the celebrated instance of Klopstock downward, they are perhaps exceptionally common in German. But if Keller, as poet or as novelist, be taken and read simply on his own merits, the sense of disappointment—even of half-puzzled disappointment—which has been referred to above will, in some cases at any rate, be curiously prominent. He is never bad; and as he affects, though not wholly, the short poem in verse and the short story in prose, no absolute struggle is necessary in reading him. But there is too often, though not always, a sense of flatness—of something that has not "come off"—which contrasts strangely not merely with the best contemporary English and French work, but even with much that is far from being of the very best.

Konrad Ferdinand Meyer (1825 - 1898), also a Zuricher, though not a very much younger man, *K. F. Meyer.* belongs to a somewhat younger school, and does not seem to have made much name in literature before 1870. There is more *diable au corps* in his verse than in Keller's; and his stories, *Denkwürdige Tage* (1878), *Die Leiden eines Knaben* (1883), *Die Hochzeit des Mönchs* (1884), have power. But he would hardly rank as more than a second-rate poet or novelist out of Germany.

Of the Austrian Baroness Marie von Ebner-Eschenbach, who was born so long ago as 1830, one can *Frau von Ebner-* speak more cordially. She cannot be *Eschenbach.* missed as among the most undoubted possessors of really poetic spirit who have written in German during the last half century. She also is a novelist as well as a poetess; an author, occasionally very felicitous, of aphorisms, as well as a novelist; and her poetical work is by no means large in bulk. But it has the true, and, what is more, the true German, quality, as, for instance, in this

little piece, which some readers who may not know
it will not be sorry to have at length,—

> "Ein kleines Lied, wie geht's nur an,
> Dass man so lieb es haben kann,
> Was liegt darin? Erzähle!
>
> Es liegt darin ein wenig Klang,
> Ein wenig Wohllaut und Gesang—
> Und eine ganze Seele!"[1]

It will be observed that this has not only the right
German sentiment, but is a most happy exemplifi-
cation of the poetic capacities of the German tongue
itself, in the repeated sighings or breathings of the
final *e* in the last line, with the full vowel sound
of the preceding syllables contrasting, supporting,
and embellishing them. In much reading of modern
German verse, it will not be easy to find an example
of equal scale better in itself, or better illustrating
the unforced and natural character of the best work
of the same kind in the same country.

Paul Heyse, born in 1830, began, before he was of
age, with *Franzeska von Rimini*, a series of poems,
Heyse. novels, and plays, which, with not a few
translations, extends to scores of volumes,
never falls to a low level of merit, and not seldom
reaches a high one, though perhaps it never even
approaches the highest. The early novel *L'Arrabiata*,
and the late play *Maria von Magdala* at an interval of nearly half a century, may be singled out

---

[1] This very perfect little thing is in Bern (*v. inf.*) But the
present writer was not acquainted with that useful collection when
he selected it from the poetess's own *Works* for appearance here.

as characteristic of Heyse in their different ways. But his *forte* lies perhaps in the short story. Of his poems, as of some others, it may be said, in an old *mot*, that they lose a good deal when they cross the frontier.

Perhaps, on the other hand, the most remarkable exponent of the conservative side, in the general and *Prince von Schönaich-Carolath.* not merely the political sense, is Prince Emil von Schönaich - Carolath (*b.* 1852), whose *Lieder an eine Verlorene* made their mark as long ago as 1878, and whose *Gedichte* (1883) have received high commendation from those who do not look first for novelty of aspect in poetry. But he has not, and perhaps does not deserve, so high a reputation as is accorded to a poet of the same generation but a little older, who would also figure in a German Walpole's "Royal and Noble Poets" as a Holsteiner, but who would have been a Dane but for Bismarck; while the Prince, but for Frederick the Great, would, as a Silesian, have been an Austrian.

For when improvement is claimed for the verse of the last twenty or five-and-twenty years, there are *Freiherr von Liliencron.* some who say that the only considerable German poet since Heine is Baron Detlev von Liliencron (*b.* 1845), that he *is* a really considerable poet, and that his *Adjutanten-ritte* in 1884 marked a definite turning-point, and one for the better, in German literary history. It is the uncomfortable duty of the historian to point out that even if this is so, dates are a little awkward, for Baron von Liliencron is now past sixty; and it will be

difficult to find in history a real poetical leader
whose school has not added something very positive and very substantial to his country's poetical
treasures before such a space of years has past.
Now, to read Herr von Liliencron himself is a quite
agreeable task. His *Ausgewählte Gedichte* (1896) is
undoubtedly *the* volume of German verse for the
last fifty years that you can, in De Quincey's phrase,
"recommend to a friend" with a clear conscience,
and, if the friend knows poetry when he sees it,
without much fear of reproaches.[1] He is very good
at descriptive writing, without inflicting on his reader
that sense that here is description for description's
sake, which is so common in nineteenth century
verse. He has come nearer than any one else to
Heine's own idiosyncrasy in the piece called "Seine
Hoheit auf absonderlichen Wegen," which is a longer
and more satiric variant on the theme of Mr Swinburne's "When the game began between them for
a jest," though it is not to be supposed that the
German poet knew the English in the least. It is
an extraordinarily good thing in a peculiar kind.
He experiments in prosody a good deal, and interestingly, though one of his favourite metres, a trochaic dodecasyllable, is rather teasing to an English
ear. He is so satisfactory in himself that one is excessively reluctant to put him into comparative esti-

---

[1] But certainly not without recommending the friend also to
proceed to the *complete* "Poems." They fill four volumes (7, 8, 9,
10) of his *Sämmtliche Werke*, 5th ed., Berlin and Leipzig, *n.d.*, and
are things not only to read but to possess.

mate. But it is certain that the sense of *pastiche*, of
the presence—to put new names in Mr Browning's
line, and give it a twist of meaning — of "Goethe,
Uhland, Heine, and the fifty" in the background, is
rather disquieting.

Round Herr von Liliencron in the last two decades
there has grown up a lively school of semi-anacre-
ontic poets, of whom the chief are, per-
O. J. Bierbaum. haps, Herr Otto Julius Bierbaum (*b*. 1865)
and the novelist and dramatist, Ernest von Wolzogen,
born ten years earlier. Herr Bierbaum's *Erlebte Gedichte* (1892) and *Irrgarten der Liebe* (1901) are also
things not unpleasant to read, and it may be said of
them that the sense of "missing," of not "coming
off," which has been mentioned, is much less prominent. Whether that of sincerity and "inevitable-
ness" is much more present is another question.
One seems to see on the covers of the books ghostly
portraits of Heine and Baudelaire now and then,
while the nonsense-refrain (a capital thing in its way,
and very German as very English) is a little over-
done. But it is curious that this laureate of the
wine-house, besides his anacreontics,—which are very
good in *their* way,—has touches of the real old
German sentiment, the immortal, the all-saving, that
would not disgrace the greatest of his masters. As
for instance—

> "Sonntags Friede liegt
>   Heilig über der Stadt.
> Ach ! wie ist mein Herz
>   Seiner Wochen satt !

> Quälen, Keuchen, Kampf—
> Um ein kärglich Brod—
> Ach ! wann machst du frei
> Lebens-Sonntag, Tod ?"

When commonplaces are once more put with that simplicity and freshness, things are perhaps not so very bad after all. The curse of the epithet has at any rate disappeared.

An echo, probably, of the French inquiry after the *vers libre*, and of the French experiments in *The Holz School* that direction, is to be found in the work and school of Arno Holz (*b*. 1863), who, beginning with easy verse of the Geibel pattern, turned later to complicated unrhymed strophes (exaggerating the drift of Heine[1] in the *Nordsee*) in *Phantasus* (1899) and *Lieder auf einer alten Laute* (1903). Herr Holz, perhaps with a rather naïf ignoring of the fact that he is merely formulating the general drift of the despised nineteenth century, expressly declares for appeal to eye and ear rather than to the intellect. He and his followers seem to resemble their contemporaries elsewhere in affecting an attitude of contempt towards the great poets of the immediate past — an attitude which will certainly not excite so much indignation as amusement from experienced onlookers. We have known more than four-and-twenty leaders of such revolts—we other critics ! At the same time, it is

---

[1] Heine's originality in this has been contested. But in fact it has hardly been absent from any period of German poetry—so naturally does the rhythmical trend of the language incline towards something of the kind.

only fair to say that German, which had already abundant examples of it from mediæval, or almost mediæval, times downwards, is better suited than almost any other European language for the style which, out of regular blank verse, has never been a real success in English, and which in French is frankly impossible unless all but the faintest echo of verse rhythm is abandoned, as in the *Gaspard de la Nuit* of Louis Bertrand and the *Petits Poèmes en Prose* of Baudelaire and his imitators. Whether, however, German or any language naturally inclines toward the sort of thing that follows, readers may judge for themselves. In it, at any rate, poetry loses a great deal of its difficulty. It is the work of Herr Georg Stolzenberg (*b.* 1857) in his *Neues Leben* (1898-1902):

> " Ich singe ihnen meine Lieder vor,
>   den Herzen von Stein.
>
>   Aus dem Klavier
>   Tränen.
>
>   Meine tiefste Seele
>   schluchzt.
>
> Ich dreh' mich nicht um.
>   Ich weiss :
> hinter mir hocken Götzen.
>   Ihre Opalaugen
>   träumen mich an.
>
> Ich spiele stärker.
>   Sie müssen !
>   Ich schreie !
>   Plötzlich
>   Zu ihren Füssen.
> ein rotes, zuckendes Ding . . .
>   Ich lächle verlegen."

In a good deal of contemporary German verse, in fact, there are all the signs that we know so well— *and other* small pamphlets of tolerably large quarto *modernities.* pages, unsized, printed with unusual founts, few stops—anything else to be, as a satirist of the last generation observed, "strange and wild and odd." There is a great deal of colour — "bronze-brown" and "gold - green" will meet you (as old friends to you and each other) in a single line. Identical rhymes are indulged in. Further, there is in Germany as elsewhere (especially in France) the odd phenomenon of foreigners writing German verse, and, as usual in such cases, pretty extravagant verse. But these symptoms are all well known : we need not delay on them. If we have brought this school rather beyond the line, it is because of the interest that attaches to the singular decadence in poetry of a great poetical country and language. No doubt Lazarus will arise at last.

And on the other hand, the "xenomania"—to use an excellent word invented by one of the foremost German writers of our period, Karl Hillebrand —the devotion to foreign modes which has always characterised Germany even more than other nations, has reappeared almost to the fullest extent, if not quite so much as in novel and drama perhaps. French Parnassianism, Naturalism, Symbolism, have exercised almost as much influence as Ronsard exercised centuries ago on Opitz; and a famous jest may now be paid back in kind by the perfectly true statement that bad English paradoxes, when they become malodorous, are eagerly accepted in Germany. The mixed eagerness and solemnity with which new eccentricities are welcomed, and with which the work of writers who have hardly had time to show what they may do, and have done next to nothing, is discussed, are things not peculiar to Germany. But they are perhaps more noticeable there than elsewhere, because the extreme methodicalness of German ways brings out their absurdity.

As it happens, this remarkable combination of industry, method, and business spirit has actually provided hardly surpassed opportunities for those who wish to acquaint themselves, without plunging into the unsifted chaos, with the German poetry of the last half or three-quarters of a century. Constructed on parallel lines in almost all respects, Bern's *Deutsche Lyrik seit Goethe's Tod*[1] and the *Moderne Deutsche Lyrik*[2] of Herr Hans Benzmann supply, in about twelve hundred pages and perhaps forty or fifty thousand lines, specimens, not strictly lyrical only, of a good couple of hundred German poets from 1830 to 1900, and even later,—including almost all the famous names from Uhland downwards,—with some, at least, of their more famous pieces.

[1] Sixteenth edition. Reclam, Leipzig, *n.d.*
[2] Reclam, Leipzig, 1903. With an elaborate introductory dissertation. This book contains in its text nothing, and in its introduction only two specimens of a poet, Stephan George, whom some consider the "new poet" of Germany. I have read a good deal of his work, which is excessively full of deliberate mannerism, by no means shutting *out*, but rather ostentatiously shutting *in*, the poetry. He is to be dealt with respectfully, but would require much room.

One is bound to say that the not particularly cheerful view of German literature which has been *Analysis of two anthologies.* taken in this chapter, though by no means based on the reading of a couple of anthologies (with which, as noted above, the writer was not acquainted till the greater part of it had been written), is confirmed by these anthologies to a disheartening degree. Even the earlier volume, when the selections from Heine himself, from Uhland, and from a few others are left out of the question, though it contains many interesting things, is on the whole what is called in Scots "wersh." But it compares most favourably with the second; and (which is unluckier still) the best things in the second, with a very few exceptions, are by poets who have already figured in the first. Baron von Liliencron plays his part doughtily in both; his friend and pupil, Herr Bierbaum, backs him up well in the second.[1] But though Freiligrath and Geibel, Rückert and "Anastasius Grün," were not exactly great poets, one certainly remembers the old saying, "Seldom comes a better," when one passes from them to the meaningless "aureatenesses" of the modern imitators of the French Parnasse, or the prose-splitting-itself-into-fragments of those about Herr Arno Holz.

When our period began, the four best of these older writers, as well as Heine, were still alive;[2] while Lenau

---

[1] As specimens of this agreeable writer's lighter and sadder veins, "Jeanette" and "Josefine," "Lied in der Nacht" and "Neuwein-lied" will, as some say, "repay perusal."

[2] Even Uhland, who stands far above them all except Heine, lived till 1862.

and Platen (whom, in spite of Heine himself, one must pronounce no such bad poet) were but just dead. Moreover, all the four, except Rückert, lived long enough to see 1870, and two of them, Freiligrath and Geibel, hailed the events thereof on a rather twangling lyre. These six, with Scheffel, probably represent the special favourites (with the eternal exception,[1] so far above them as to be out of sight to some) of the German Muses at this time. No one of them is over strong; not even Rückert, though he could hit, and not seldom, on lines like the famous " Du meine Wonne, Du mein Schmerz," while the same sort of easy sentimental music finds expression, weaker still, in Freiligrath and Geibel. There was something more masculine and more individual in Platen — for instance, in the strangely moved and moving echo-piece of *Reue*, with its refrain (interwoven rather than sewn on) of

" In der Nacht, in der Nacht."

And Count Auersperg (A. Grün) and Lenau have something of the indefinable quality — freshness, freedom from pedantry, " race "—which South Germans, when they have any literary faculty at all, generally show in comparison with North. But all these writers have received more or less attention in the previous volume, and we must not delay on them here. It is enough to say that, though certainly no

---

[1] It is well known that the Germans themselves do not much like this exception of Heine to be made. Dr Brandes, in his *Main Currents*, has interesting remarks on the fact.

one of them rises above the level of poetry of the
second class, all more or less attain that; and that
they attain it, and sometimes something more than
its mere level, by getting what they can out of the
natural poetical tendencies and facilities of the language — its remarkably varied music of consonant
and vowel sound (the old notion that German was a
"harsh" language is incomprehensible, except as to
some dialects),—and by opposing, to say the least, no
resistance to its tendencies in meaning towards sentiment, melancholy, and general agreeable *mist* of the
kind that makes rainbows. Nor were they so badly
backed by the *numerus* of their own period. To take
the useful Anthology just mentioned as a treasury of
object-lessons, the pessimist poetry of Ferdinand von
Schmid (1823-1888) (who called himself "Dranmor")
and Heinrich Landesmann (1821-1902) (who called
himself "Hieronymus Lorm," and had reason enough
for sadness, seeing that he became deaf at fifteen and
blind at thirty - five) retains a certain amount of
musical appeal, though it does somewhat remind one
of Longfellow's satirical criticism of an earlier pair of
German bards,—that they "walked through the world
with pocket-handkerchiefs at their eyes." The melancholy dropping of the trochees in Lorm's "Nach
hundert Jahren"; the curious echo-sobs of Dranmor's "Du verwaistes Haus," are worth reading. And
the same tone (which it is all very well to sneer at,
but which has rather more *vérité vraie* than the
crudest naturalism) sounds in the "Märchen vom
Glück" and "Die Verlassene" of Ernst Eckstein

(1845 - 1900), and the "Warum?" of the novelist
Franzos. The religious poetry of Karl [von] Gerok
(1815-1890), a dignitary of the Church in Stuttgart,
has echoes of the time—a long time ago mostly—
when Germany almost led Europe in that department.
"Ein stiller Ort," by Max Haushofer (b. 1840, and
one of the numerous epic celebrators of the Wandering Jew), is one of those pieces—probably "single-
speech" utterances—which the author never succeeds
in duplicating. The ballads of Mosen (such as an
admirable one on Hofer) are much more acceptable
to weak human nature than his epics; and the verse
of Konrad F. Meyer may seem to some preferable to
his prose. The also previously mentioned "Betty
Paoli" (Elizabeth Glück (1815-1894), whose life as
governess and companion may not have been unconnected, like Lorm's physical troubles, with the melancholy tone of her verse) is principally noted for this,
but, as in the singularly simple and genuine "Rath"—
"Sollst du von einem Ort, In Bälde scheiden"—there
is good criticism of life; while, on the other hand,
there is something more than bravado and convention
in the cheerfuller verses of Oskar von Redwitz (1823-
1891). Theodor Storm (1817-1888), a novelist specially popular for his short tales as well as a poet, had
a genuine if not very deep or individual lyrical touch;
and Julius Sturm (1816-1896) was popular. But it is
very hard to discover the likeness to Heine which
some have seen in Eduard Grisebach (b. 1845), who
perhaps did not mean to describe himself in the
title *Der Neue Tannhäuser*. In Ernst Ziel (b. 1841),

though there is, as in almost all poets of the century, not a little literary echo, there is stuff as well.

Of two of the writers who appear in both volumes, Detlev von Liliencron and Emil von Schönaich-Carolath, we have spoken already. It is one of the least cheerful features of the present examination that, while they are good in themselves, they are not the best contributors to the earlier volume; and that they are, with one exception (also treated), Otto Julius Bierbaum, by far the best contributors to the second. Elsewhere in that second all is not barren, but there is very much less of the cedar great and tall than of the hyssop on the wall. There is plenty of experiment, but it is usually experiment against the grain of the German language and of German poetry; and it has an uncomfortable habit of suggesting a reflection in the experimenters,—" I cannot be great; let me be odd," or, " I cannot be *vornehm;* let me be fashionable." Some general features of this newer or newest poetry have been mentioned already; a few persons and pieces — in the object-lesson kind, as earlier—may be noticed here and now. There are some of Nietzsche's verses—sufficient to prove to those who do not know his work generally what is already known to those who do, that he was entirely sane and right when he made prose his usual vehicle. A new Baron von Münchhausen, who is quite young (*b.* 1874), convinces us that there is still literary talent in the family. He seems about the best of the more direct followers of his brother baron, Liliencron, for Herr Bierbaum has ways of his own. " Marie Stona,"

or Marie Scholz (*b.* 1861),—the German poetesses,
weight for sex and for number accorded, appear to be
quite able to vie with the German poets,—has both
individuality and music in "Meine Lippen brennen
so." The average writer of her school—the school of
highly modern and emancipated naturalism — would
have spoilt these lines by amplification and over-
emphasis, while as it is they are worth quoting, little
as we can quote :—

> " Meine Lippen brennen so
> von den Küssen, die sie nicht geküsst,
> von der Sehnsucht, die mein Herz zerfrisst.
> Nimmer werd' ich meiner Liebe froh,—
> Meine Lippen brennen so.
>
> Und die Augen sind so schwer
> von den Tränen, die kein Blick gesehn,
> die mir finster in der Seele stehn,
> wie ein weites, todtenstilles Meer . . .
> Meine Augen trinken dran sich schwer."

But there is elsewhere little temptation to quote or
cite. A good short study of Midday Glow, by Paul
Barsch (*b.* 1860); and some others of a similar kind
(a kind which gives most of the good things) by Karl
Bienenstein (*b.* 1869); the elaborate and not quite unsuccessful naturalist pessimism of Hermann Conradi (*b.*
1862); imitations of Verlaine and of Baudelaire right
and left; card-houses of unrhymed staves, of the most
different lengths, built up and balanced with the art
of the acrobat; some simpler and better nature-studies
by Franz Evers (*b.* 1871); some attempts in the older
and more natural German manner by Gustav Falke

(b. 1850); more new Tannhäuserisms ("the old was better") of Herr Grisebach's; specimens (interesting chiefly because of the names) of the dramatists Hauptmann and Sudermann; yet others of the card-castle or pagoda type from the master, Herr Arno Holz himself; a "Weisst du—Wo?" of Karl Ernst Knodt (b. 1856), which would be better if it did not inevitably recall Gautier's far superior "Chimère"; some of the less defiant utterances of Mr John Henry Mackay (b. 1864), whom Scotland lent to Germany; some noteworthy pieces of two other poetesses, Klara Müller (b. 1861) and Alberta von Puttkamer (b. 1840),—these are the chief things that an enthusiastic lover of poetry has been able to winnow out of the heap. In the elaborate and deliberate "knappings" of thought, and phrase, and metre which have procured admiration for Alfred Mombert (b. 1872), that lover sees little to love, though there are some possibilities. It may be said, with judicial seriousness, that two similar volumes could be filled either from the English or from the French poetry of the same period (1830-1900), the weakest of the specimens in which could vie with all but the best of these.

As regards fiction, the peculiarity (more than once referred to) of German literature in this respect must *Novelists—Auerbach.* be remembered—the overlapping, namely, of verse and prose.[1] The Germans began our time with no such towering example and pattern in the novel as Heine in poetry. But they had at

---

[1] In fact, the indiscriminate use of the word *Dichtung* is a positive trap for the unwary in German literary history.

least two novelists of much more than ordinary powers. One of these, Auerbach, who continued to live and write till 1882, Mr Omond dealt with; the other, Gustav Freytag (1816-1895), he named, but left for this volume. Of the former, therefore, we need say little more except that the strongly *localised* novel, of which *Barfüssele* is such an agreeable example, though it has been cultivated in most countries during the century, has perhaps nowhere such a congenial and such a varied soil as in Germany, where the greater political unifications—the age-long one of Austria and the more recent addition of the new Empire—have perhaps rather encouraged than stifled the cultivation of particularist styles.

As for Freytag, he had perhaps less genius, in the strict sense, than Auerbach, but he had a very much

Freytag. wider talent. His novel of *Soll und Haben* (1855) speedily attained European reputation, at a time when the English and French schools of novel-writing were, the former at its very best and the latter not far from it. In fact—putting books of philosophy, and others where the literary side is not the chief, out of the question—it is almost the only German book of the last half-century that has done this. It is true that its successor, *Die Verlorene Handschrift* (1864), is not its equal; and that the curious pair of series, *Bilder aus der Deutschen Vergangenheit* (1859), which are historical documents, and *Die Ahnen* (1872 - 1880), downright historical novels, do not escape the fate which waits upon all attempts to enslave *belles lettres* to purpose and system. They are, however, greatly superior to some other German efforts in the historical novel which will be mentioned presently. Nor do Freytag's literary claims rest on the novel alone. Not only was he an industrious and prolific dramatist for many years, but his *Technik des Dramas* (1862) is a very solid work in a certain kind of criticism, and he published a volume of poems as early as 1844. As has been said, one looks for genius somewhat in vain in Freytag; even *Soll und Haben* is rather an intelligent piece of craftsmanship in the new domestic or semi-domestic novel than one of those books which add scenes and characters to the furniture of memory. But he *is* an intelligent craftsman of almost the best kind, and his craftsmanship was rewarded by a popularity only inferior to that of Scheffel's two books already noticed—of which *Ekkehard* was published two years later than *Soll und Haben*, and the *Trompeter von Säkkingen* two years earlier.

But, as we (who invented it, and by the hands of Scott, Thackeray, and some others brought it to its

The historical novel— Ebers, &c.

greatest perfection) know to our cost, the historical novel is a most difficult kind to manage; and the very conscientiousness and thoroughness of German study opens the deeper pits for Germans to fall into. To avoid these pits you need either the general literary tact of the two great English writers just named, or the special theatrical aptitude of a Dumas. Scheffel had the former in at least a sufficient degree: of two most estimable writers, one of whom is still living, hardly

as much can be said. Georg Ebers (1837-1898)
attempted, between 1864 and 1886, a series of
Egyptian romances alternating with novels of actual
German life. The sense of learning something may,
in virtuous minds, communicate a certain pleasure
to the reading of *Uarda* and *Die Nilbraut*, but it may
be feared that some such extrinsic douceur is required
to achieve the effect. And the same is the case
with Herr Felix Dahn's (*b.* 1834) rather celebrated
Ein Kampf um Rom (1876), which was followed by
others. But the style does not appear to have ever
lost its hold upon German taste ; and in greater space
we might mention Ernst Eckstein (*v. sup.*) (1845-
1900), Wilhelm Jensen (*b.* 1837), Friedrich Spielhagen
(*b.* 1829), and others ; while of the writers mentioned
under other heads—such as K. F. Meyer—not a few
have touched this form.

Germany has, however, been much happier in the
other, which was specially mentioned above—the
story or novel of manners, especially of a
Other kinds.
provincial or parochial cast. At one time
F. W. Hackländer (1816-1877) bade fair to obtain
something like the European reputation which was
actually the lot, in greater and lesser degree, of Auerbach and Freytag and Scheffel ; but he wrote too
much, and never achieved real distinction in any
kind. There is much more quality in Wilhelm Raabe
(*b.* 1831), humourist as well as novelist. *Die Leute
aus dem Walde* (1863) seems accepted as his principal work. Of women, Amely Bölte (1817-1891) and
Fanny Lewald (1811-1889) were popular writers in

P

the middle decades of the century, while about the same time (1856), as much else of mark, the stories of Wilhelm Heinrich Riehl (1823-1897) attracted a good deal of attention, not merely in Germany. Very recent novels hardly require mention: one of the most effective for a time—a "purpose story"—was Frau Bertha von Suttner's *Die Waffen nieder!* in 1889. But few divisions of German fiction have recently been more profitably worked than that of the local story, which has been especially a product of the Austrian provinces in the hands of the dramatist Anzengruber, of Leopold von Sacher-Masoch (1836-1895), who, however, availed himself too freely of "naturalist" licence, of Karl Emil Franzos (1848-1904), whose *Die Juden von Barnow* (1877) made his reputation, and of Peter Rosegger (*b.* 1843).

In quite recent times the influence of the French Realist and Naturalist schools, glanced at more than once already, has indeed made itself felt in Germany even more than in other countries; but the effect is said to be passing, and indeed could not be likely to last, the whole genius of the people, and indeed of the language, being unsuited to it. Of German indecency in general it may be said, as Scott said admirably of Dryden's in particular, that it sits as awkwardly as the forced impudence of a bashful man. Indeed it may be doubted whether, except in the case of the *märchen*, where Germans are unapproached, and of some other kinds of short story, the novel is very suitable for German genius. Until Schopenhauer and Nietzsche showed the way to write accomplished prose, the very implement was hardly in the novel-writer's hand; and even the romancer was apt to season his mixtures too heavily with erudition, or not to quicken them enough with character and dialogue. It is really curious how comparatively small a part this last element — almost the most important of all—has generally played in the German novel.

There is no department of German literature on which the hopes and boasts of Germans (who have *Drama.* been, perhaps, a little apt to run the one into the other for the last generation) are more confident than the drama. It would indeed be surprising if something did not come of a devotion to the theatre which has probably exceeded that of any other country in Europe for more than a century. It is notorious that almost all great German men of letters, from Goethe downwards, have felt this devotion, and that many have carried it into actual play-writing. If, as some hold, the subsidising of "national" theatres, and the cultivation of the art of acting in the most assiduous fashion, both from the theoretical and the practical side, are more or less sure means to the attainment and the maintenance of great drama, every state, important or petty, in Germany has long taken these. Nor has it been done without at least some result, —whether with so great a one as the persons just referred to might expect is another question. At any rate, the bulk of dramatic production during the past half century in Germany has been enormous, and a few names of mark emerge from it, especially, some would say, in the last decade or two. But here we shall have once more to put in the warning to allow for foreign influence.

The first important name in drama definitely belonging to our period is probably that of Freytag *From Freytag* himself, whose work has been already *to Hauptmann.* glanced at, but who is likely to live in this particular branch of literary history rather as a critic than as a creator. Like him fertile as a novelist, and like him a dramatic critic in his *Beiträge zur Theorie und Technik der Epik und Dramatik* (1898), Spielhagen produced in 1874 an ambitious drama in *Liebe für Liebe;* while Adolf Wilbrandt (*b.* 1837) has been fertile in tragedy and comedy, his *Jugendliebe* (1872) being much praised. But though perhaps a majority of German poets and novelists have tried the stage more or less in their time, its most remarkable, or at least most remarked, practitioners belong to younger, though not in all cases very young, generations. Ernst von Wildenbruch (*b.* 1845) may be put as the *doyen* of these. He was the author (following with them patriotic epics) of patriotic dramas on German historical subjects, which fall into line with the other *belles lettres* of 1870 already noticed, and perhaps do not, any more than the rest of them, escape Nietzsche's early and withering denunciation of this Philistine chauvinism. On the Austrian side, his somewhat older contemporary Ludwig Anzengruber (1839-1889) practised rather the social and religious drama, shot with a good deal of humour and raciness, while Oskar Blumenthal (*b.* 1852) and Franz Adam Beyerlein (*b.* 1871), also a novelist, have repute for comedy. But pages would not suffice for their companions. The "dioscuri of the dawn" (to borrow an aureate phrase) of modern German drama have, however, been hailed after such Stentor-fashion in two writers—Hermann Sudermann (*b.* 1857) and Gerhart Hauptmann, five years younger—that something must be said of them. Both exhibit the combined influence of at least three of the four presidents of dying nineteenth century literature—Nietzsche, Zola, and Ibsen,—that of the last naturally showing itself most in consequence of the coincidence of form. The agreeable title of Herr Sudermann's work, *Sodoms Ende* (1891), is perhaps somewhat deceptive, but the play should make up expectation in another way. He had displayed no very different temper, but a much more solid talent, earlier in the almost deservedly famous novel of *Frau Sorge* (1887), in the much discussed play *Die Ehre* (1890), and in *Heimat* (1903); while a series of later dramas carries out the same sort of action in the same sort of atmosphere. Herr Hauptmann, with rather less imagination than his compeer, apparently prides himself upon an even closer and minuter observation,—in the manner rather of Ibsen than of Zola. Beginning with *Vor Sonnenaufgang* (1889), an agreeable potpourri of *L'Assommoir* and other things, he has followed it up with *Das Friedensfest*, *College Crampton*, *Die Weber*, and many others, the most Ibsenish of all being *Die versunkene Glocke*

(1896)—a work in which one side of his quality
may perhaps be as well studied as anywhere. It
is Ibsenish on the mystical side, it should be understood, and like that side—like the apocalyptic atmosphere of the later work even of Zola, and like the
dream-character of Nietzsche throughout—exhibits a
reaction which no one possessing the slightest critical
competence or experience can find surprising. The
same tendency is noticeable in some work of Herr
Sudermann likewise, while Hauptmann's elder brother
Carl (*b.* 1858) is claimed as a convert to idealism in
his later work.

No very extended comment is necessary on these
phenomena — all such comment being easy and
Naturalism, obvious enough. The curious resemblance
&c., in of this *fin de siècle* development in Germany
Germany. to that other, exactly a hundred years
earlier, of the *Sturm und Drang* writers, can, of
course, escape no one even rudimentarily acquainted
with literary history. There is, however, the difference—not very encouraging for Germans—that while
in that case, although the general fermentation of
temper may have come from abroad, the *literary*
movement was comparatively original : in this only
Nietzsche, and he at some distance, represents home
industries, while Zolaism and Ibsenism are imported,
nay, positively dumped without payment of duty,
and to the detriment of native German products.
On another disheartening quality, that of mere
"topsy-turviness," we shall presently have more to
say in respect of Nietzsche himself. And as for

the *furore*, the *engouement*, with which these things
have been received, not only in the country of their
birth but on re-exportation, that is a phenomenon
even more familiar than all the rest. Rare—so rare
as to be almost unknown—is it that literary work
of the very highest class achieves any such popularity: what it gains, it gains slowly, but keeps
for ever. The popularity of work which is (to
speak politely of contemporaries) not exactly of the
highest is, on the other hand, constantly of the
prairie-fire order. It blazes — not without much
smoke; it scours the plain and it disappears—sometimes after doing useful manuring work, sometimes
after merely destroying good things and bad.

Busy men of letters of all work like Herr Paul
Lindau (*b.* 1839) have contributed much drama, some-
The precincts times well received, to the total; and very
of drama— unlikely subjects have proved welcome to
Wagner. the combined stage fancy and deliberate
patriotism of the Germans, like that of Hans Herrig's
Martin Luther (1883), or like that of Wolfgang Kirch-
bach's *Gordon Pasha* (1894), — a most curious and
perhaps unique instance of the revival of a very
old kind of dramatisation. On the bridge between
drama and criticism it would be impossible to pass
by the great name of Richard Wagner (1813-1883),
the libretti of whose operas belong to the creative
division of the subject, though to the least literary
side of it, while his famous *Oper und Drama*, early
in our period, belongs to the critical, and is an
important feature therein. It is impossible to ex-

aggerate the literary influence of Wagnerian music.
From Baudelaire downwards it has never been missed ;
and there is little doubt that Nietzsche's hatred for
literature—for, himself all but one of the greatest
of men of letters, he *did* hate it, or would have hated
it if he could, as fatal to his notions—had something
to do with his becoming a "rancorous *renegado*"
from the Wagnerism of which he had once been
an enthusiastic devotee. To dwell on this here
would be to step out of our province, and we have
only too much to do to cover it. But the reknitting
of the connection of Apollo's two arts—poetry and
music,—so long severed from each other by nothing
so much as by the frivolity and mindlessness of the
older opera itself, is a phenomenon in the history
of literature far too important to escape notice here.
Even if it has not given direct impulse to much
literature important in itself, it has coloured and
inspired so large a part thereof that it does not so
much invite as insist upon a moment's attention.

Reference has just been made to the subject of
Criticism, to which, in the tour of the *belles lettres*, we
should naturally come. On one side of
this subject the position of Germany is a
very high one, and must be acknowledged
with gratitude by all who have ever had anything to
do with the study of literature. From the time of
Lessing, and even earlier,—from that of Bodmer and
others,—German (using the term in the wide sense
for the language of all German-speaking countries,
including Switzerland) had been honourably dis-

*Criticism—
Scholastic and
literary.*

tinguished for the attention paid to this matter—
especially, though not exclusively, in regard to the
classical languages of antiquity. With Herder and the
Schlegels (to name no others) this form of scholarship
was extended to the more modern tongues, and to
investigations not merely linguistic and textual, but
literary in the widest sense. And for the last three-
quarters of the nineteenth century the tradition, on
some of its sides at least, has been faithfully kept up
and even extended. During the whole of that time
students, not merely of the classics, not merely of
German, but of English, French, the Peninsular
languages, and, in fact, those of all Europe, have
certainly received more assistance from German
scholarship than (until quite recently) any one of
them could look for in his own language — perhaps
more than could have been obtained by amassing the
results of investigations in all other European tongues
put together. The extent and elaborateness of the
German University system ; the fact that in Germany,
as hardly anywhere else, the pursuit of learning has
been regarded as itself a profession, not a luxury to
be enjoyed at the rash seeker's own cost and risk ;
and the singular blend of method and industry in the
national temper, have brought this about. It would
thus be not merely ungrateful and illiberal, but idle
in the extreme, to attempt to obscure or belittle the
acknowledgment of it.

Whether, however, the really "higher" form of
criticism—which is sometimes called "appreciation"
—has been, during these same three - quarters of a

century, represented with equal completeness in Germany is quite another question. Some fairly competent and unprejudiced students have felt inclined to doubt or deny it; and it is at any rate quite certain that no German critic of the second quarter attained anything like the deserved eminence of Sainte-Beuve; that none of the third could be put in competition with Matthew Arnold; and that, even since the eager attempts made to recover or advance the literary position of Germany to the level of her political and commercial eminence which the last decade or two have seen, there is no critic within her borders who can be ranked, to say nothing of Englishmen, with the best living critics of France. Again, Schopenhauer, in his own peculiar cross-grained fashion, had indeed the elements of a very great critic in him; and Nietzsche, in *his* own fashion of not quite sane or wholly insane perversity, had those of perhaps a greater. But these were, in the main, "might-have-beens," not actualities of criticism. And in the vast and miscellaneous regiment of editors, literary historians, and so forth, as a rule the very last thing that will be found is pure literary criticism at once acute, wide, sensitive, and original. Among students of our older English, Dr Eugen Kölbing occupied something like the position of the late M. Gaston Paris in French, as a critic combining linguistic and literary competence. Gottfried Keller himself, as we noticed, did some scholar's work. But as a rule the German editors, not merely of foreign but of their own texts, have not distinguished themselves by real appreciation of literature; and though German *bel-*

lettrists may have escaped the sciolism too common
in their kind among other nations, they have not as
a rule been deep in criticism itself. Even the enormous German Shakespeare-literature might be rather
roughly handled, if it were worth while; and it is a
most singular thing that the age-long devotion of
Germany to classical scholarship has produced not
very many important works on classical literary criticism. Sometimes, indeed, one is inclined to say here
and elsewhere that, though the German is certainly
intellectual, he is not on the whole intelligent.

Some exceptions, however, may be made to this
ungrateful but necessary judgment. The Austrian
poet and dramatist Grillparzer (1791-1872),
who was noticed in the last volume in his
creative functions, revealed himself, perhaps not till
posthumously, as a very remarkable critic, who had
thrown his energies in this matter, not into the form
of regular essays on general subjects or reviews of
particular works, but into that of jottings or aphorisms—something of the Joubert kind, or (as perhaps
in his case it would be fairer and more accurate to
say) of the kind of Goethe's *Sprüche in Prosa*. The
individual deliverances on authors and subjects which
these aphorisms contain offer, of course, that opportunity for alternate agreement and disagreement with
their special purport which is unavoidable in such
cases. But Grillparzer's general principles are remarkably sound. He looks back on a pervading
weakness of perhaps the larger part of older
criticism, and anticipates the revival of the fallacy

Grillparzer and others.

which we have seen since, by denouncing the "pot-
tering pedantry" of judgment by Kinds. He makes
the all-important but too frequently ignored distinction between admiration and approval; and he affirms
boldly that the appeal of poetry is not primarily,
much less wholly, to the intellect. There are, in fact,
few better critics (though he is something of an
irregular and volunteer in criticism) among German
writers than Grillparzer. He appears to have owed
much to an older Austrian writer, Joseph Schreyvogel
(or West), with whose work the present writer has
not yet been able fully to acquaint himself.

In fuller space it would be agreeable to dwell on
the *Æsthetik* of the Hegelian Moriz Carrière (*b.* 1817);
on the heretical but not unamusing *Shakespeare-
Studien* of Gustav Rümelin (1815-1889); and on not
a few historians of literature, German and other,
the chief of whom is perhaps Wilhelm Scherer. But,
as it is, a few words on one dead and one living critic
must suffice.

There can be little doubt that the chief German
critic, who was mainly a critic, of the third quarter
of the century, and of nearly a decade be-
Hillebrand. yond it, was Karl Hillebrand (1829-1884).
Hillebrand was a very cosmopolitan person, and he
lived a great deal out of Germany, and wrote in other
languages besides German. Indeed, he preached this
quality of cosmopolitanism as well as practised it, and
took upon himself to reprove other nations, including
ourselves (he had some knowledge of England), now
for lacking it, now for cultivating it in an improper

fashion. It may be questioned whether he did not himself lose some grip and force by his theory as well as by his practice. In particular he seems to have been led by it to suspect and dislike all literature that is specially racy, either of a soil or of a personality,— to have wished to reduce all taste under a sort of international *Zollverein*. Now, this is not the way to secure great or delightful literature. And accordingly his own work, though full of knowledge and not destitute of power, now reads thin and stale: it is fashionable in an out-of-date fashion—the worst of all things either in literature or in dress.

The most promising of German living critics (to take the licence once more) appears to be the Austrian Hermann Bahr (*b.* 1863). Herr Bahr is classified by the classifiers (who haunt German literary history and criticism even more than any others) as a writer who has deserted Naturalism for Symbolism. To those who pay no attention to these idle and, as has been more than once pointed out, mainly imaginary tickets, but who read his work, a good specimen of which is *Renaissance* (1897), he may seem to have followed his generation a little too much in overvaluing modernity. But he is a critic of individual things, well furnished with knowledge and not ill-furnished with appreciation and "grip," and he is certainly more able to meet French or English critics at their own weapons than most of his countrymen are, or have been for a long time.

Bahr.

The acknowledgment made above of the gratitude

due to Germans for extending and assisting the extension of the knowledge of languages and literatures will apply likewise to those other and older departments of literature itself,— history, philosophy, theology, and (on its literary side) science, which are themselves literature of knowledge rather than (though sometimes also) literature of power. In philosophy—once almost a German pro- vince—we have spoken of Schopenhauer, and we shall speak of Nietzsche. With these two remarkable exceptions, the German accomplishment during the half century has been again rather scholastic and didactic than original. In *Histories* of Philosophy from Erdmann, Überweg, and Schwegler, through Kuno Fischer to Windelband, Germany has been exemplary and unapproached; in continuing the great succession from Kant or even Leibnitz to Hegel, rather less successful. Rudolf Hermann Lotze, for instance (1817-1881), who began as a student of physical science, but published a *Metaphysik* in 1841, an anti-Hegelian of a kind but by no means a materialist, was much more of an eclectic critic of others than an independent thinker, though his *Microcosmos* (1856-64) and other books had influence in their day. So again, at one time there seemed to be a prospect of Eduard von Hartmann (1842 - 1906) " making school," as the French say, with almost the best of them; and his *Philosophie des Unbewussten* (1869), with a considerable after-train of treatises comple- mentary and subsidiary to it, went through many

Philosophy.

Lotze.

Hartmann.

editions. But whether owing to the sudden appearance of the less strictly philosophical but far more
variously and eccentrically fascinating paradoxes of
Nietzsche, or for some other reason, the vogue of the
"Philosophy of the Unconscious" died away, and its
author's recent death caused very little stir. Hartmann, who frankly avowed that his system was a
sort of eclecticism from Schelling, Hegel, and Schopenhauer, was sometimes spoken of as an apostle of
pessimism. But though in some respects this was
true, he was a believer in the possibility of reconciling
philosophy and science, in progress and development,
in "modernity" generally, and had no idea of turning
things and thoughts upside down, like the far greater
writer who succeeded and obscured him.

This main exception to the disappointingness of
modern German literature is a strange one—in fact,
the figure which constitutes it is one of

Nietzsche. the strangest to be found in literary
history. Friedrich Nietzsche (1844-1900) was born
and bred under no extraordinary pressure of circumstances, seems to have been as a boy only rather
unusually quiet, pious, and well-mannered, was somewhat retiring and unsociable, and therefore not very
popular as a student, but showed distinguished
ability, and was (1869), when very young, appointed
Professor of Classical Philology at Basle. The combined influence of Schopenhauer and Wagner, however, effected, or helped to effect, a great revolution
in him, and he became an entire recreant to religion,
and a fervent devotee of art. To what exact extent

we must add the physical effects of an almost mortal illness brought on by the hardships of the Franco-Prussian War (in which he served as a non-combatant volunteer, his Swiss naturalisation preventing his taking the sword) is a question impertinent here, and probably insoluble anywhere. Soon after the war (1871) he produced an interesting and rather chimerical but quite sober work on the *Birth of Tragedy*, in which he endeavours to represent that form as a half revolt against, half development of, the Epic or "Apollonian" principle of Dream into the "Dionysiac" one of *Rausch* or orgiastic excitement, and as having been sophisticated and brought to an end by the philosophisings of Socrates and their action on Euripides in drama itself. The germ (at least a possible germ) of his farthest and wildest imaginings is perhaps here: he and his extremer partisans maintain that it is. But, for all that, the book contains no very extravagant development or divagation. It is written at the best well, but rather unequally, and does not display the extraordinarily vivid, forcible, and flexible style which is the redeeming point of Nietzsche later. His next work, a collection of Essays under the eccentric but sufficiently German [1] title of *Unzeitgemässe Betrachtungen* ("Unseasonable Considerations," or "Tracts *not* for the Times"), displays (1873-76) a somewhat greater unrest, but is still sober enough, and in parts extremely vigorous

---

[1] How much in Nietzsche is a kind of reversion to the *manner* of writers like Hamann, Lichtenberg, and Jean Paul, must strike every one—at least every one who has read them.

and really "seasonable." The first of the four Essays is an onslaught at a hand-gallop on Strauss as a representative of the "Culture-Philistinism," the ignoble self-satisfaction with German civilisation, education, and all the rest of it, which had been fostered if not created by the victory over France; the second, an examination (slightly paradoxical but acute enough) of the dangers as well as the advantages of the study of History; and the third and fourth, panegyrics on his two favourite masters,—on Schopenhauer as the great "Educator," and on Wagner as the "Alexander Magnus" of modern Art.

This book was finished in 1876; and though the literary side of Nietzsche's genius continued to grow *His earlier and* till his mind utterly gave way, as much *middle work.* could hardly be said of others. His health grew worse and worse; and in 1879 he had to resign his Chair, in which he seems to have done excellent work. But meanwhile he had produced (1878 and later) another book, entitled *Menschliches Allzumensch-liches* (" Humanity-and-a-great-deal-too-much-of-it "), which contains, if not exactly a violent revulsion from his earlier ideas, a violent revulsion against his earlier teachers and idols. This continues all through the subsequent works until Schopenhauer, once the great Educator, is a "debaser of the currency," and Wagner, the "Alexander" of Art, is its seducer, debaser, poisoner, an "old sorcerer," &c. By degrees in (for him) rather cheerfuller books, entitled "Dawn" (*Morgenröthe*, 1881) and "The Gay Science" (*Die Fröhliche Wissenschaft— La Gaya Scienza*, 1882), and a further pair, *Jenseits von Gut und Böse* (1886) and *Zur Genealogie der Moral* (1887), with, side by side with them, his chief work, *Also sprach Zarathustra* (1883-85-91), Nietzsche developed what can hardly be called a system, but a concatenation of elaborate parody-reversals, not merely of Christian or even theistic religion and morality (denial of all this may be said to have been merely his starting-point), but of *all* belief and morality as entertained and championed by negative as well as positive thinkers from Socrates to Schopenhauer. There is no God, *He* is dead long ago ; actual Humanity is effeminate silliness ; what we must strive to produce or develop into is the *Übermensch*, a being with no virtues in the present sense of that word except an infinitely strong will, endurance, and determination to enjoy. Cæsar Borgia and a "fallow wild beast" are the moderate examples tendered ; but they are to be much improved upon.

These lucubrations towards the end—the author became absolutely insane in 1889, though he lived to the close of the century—were diversified by smaller pieces, such as an almost *Zarathustra.* incredibly violent attack on Wagner (*Der Fall Wagner*), a most interesting batch of miscellaneous flings and broadsides at everything and everybody, *Götzen-Dämmerung* (the "Twilight of the Idols"), and some preparations towards a grand "Revaluation of all Values" (*Umwerthung aller Werthen*); while large masses of posthumous works (not, it would seem, of much importance) have been issued. But for us here attention may be concentrated on *Also sprach Zara-*

thustra. [1] This extraordinary work, produced at intervals in four parts (three of which only were published before Nietzsche's unhappy occultation), is in form more like Lamennais' *Paroles d'un Croyant* than any other book, being arranged biblical-fashion in chapters and verses of rhythmical prose, which, however, sometimes passes into verse proper. Its appropriation of the name of Zoroaster does not appear to be warranted by anything actually attributed to the Persian sage, but is probably a symbol of Nietzsche's "Aryanism" against "Semitic" morality and religion. The scheme is vaguely narrative: Zarathustra, usually abiding either on the hills with his eagle and serpent, or in the "Happy Isles" over-sea, occasionally comes down or over to the haunts of men, and walks about, sometimes with disciples, addressing them after the fashion of Jesus. (It should be observed that Nietzsche, though frantically hostile to Christianity, is not often personally disrespectful to its Founder.) He meets with various astonishing and allegorical experiences; preaches constantly against Pity, and the ways of the "good and just" in favour of joy, dancing, self-will, war, "hardness" generally, and the *Übermensch ;* and winds up in the fourth part by a wonderful series of *rencontres* with persons easily identified as Schopenhauer and Wagner, less easily as some other realities, culminating in an assembly of them which is a sort of parody of the Last Supper, a "Drunk-Song of Eternity," and an

[1] Leipzig, 1904 ; when, in its complete form, it had reached its fortieth thousand.

expectation of the Great Noon-day which is to shine upon the *Übermensch*.

To say that a great deal of this is indisputable madness would be merely banal; and to say that it is only this madness which saves a great deal more from being intolerably offensive, is, though perhaps necessary, a little obvious too. But if there were no other characteristics in Nietzsche than these, all his singularity and all his fame would procure him here nothing but silence, or at least a short shrift and a sharp impalement. There is, however, much more. The spilth and wreckage of great powers are everywhere visible, even as regards the thoughts; there is even, as has been well said, a certain Miltonic magnificence in the conception of the *Übermensch-liches*. But what makes the value of the book, to us and here, is the extraordinary quality of it as literature. Nietzsche himself has somewhere defined Art as "the power of reproducing that which you have felt," and few people have ever shown this power more fully than the author of *Zarathustra*. Anybody who is capable of appreciating it at all need not read more than a few pages before he "gets the atmosphere"; and understands that, putting aside all thought of agreement or disagreement with the author's thought, he is going to see it unrolled before him with all the magic of the greatest literary phantasmagoria. For this purpose Nietzsche has forged for himself an instrument of German prose which, even after Heine, even after Schopenhauer, is marvellous and almost inconceivable. All the defects so famous in the medium have gone — its long-windedness, its obscurity, its clumsiness and lack of grace. All the beauties of German verse

Nietzsche's mastery of style. style—its music, its mystery, its haunting suggestiveness—have come to endow the homelier sister; and she has decked herself to boot with the best gift and graces of foreign prose—English, Italian, French. Nietzsche himself—who would have been a great literary critic [1] if his head had been steadier —selected Leopardi, Emerson, Mérimée, and Landor as the four masters of prose in the nineteenth century. Not to dispute about this, there is no question that we may pronounce him of the company. Consecutiveness and sustained architectonic he has not; he is best, if not only good, at the phrase, and the short scriptural "verse." But in that form he has the most astonishing force of hit, the most enchanting grace of melody, and the strangest power of suggestion. The irony of the fact that it took a madman to make German prose thoroughly beautiful may be rather terrible; but the fact of the beauty does not admit of question.

It would, however, hardly, and that for many reasons, be sufficient to dismiss the most remarkable

---

[1] I have given full attention to this side of him in my *History of Criticism*, vol. iii. pp. 581-586, to which I may, I hope without rashness or impropriety, refer the reader. Writing on Nietzsche is infinite : I know nothing better for coolness and fairness than Professor Pringle-Pattison's essay in *Man's Place in the Kosmos*, &c., 2nd ed. Edinburgh, 1902.

writer of Germany, and one of the most remarkable writers of Europe, for a generation, with remarks barely on his form. With that we are here principally concerned, but we are not only concerned with it. And it so happens that the temper which is shown in Nietzsche—variant as it is of the temper which is shown in Ibsen, in Tolstoi, and to no small extent in Zola—has had a very large influence not merely on the matter but on the form of every literature in Europe during this generation. This temper or

His attitude and influence. attitude can be looked at from several sides and points of view, and can be described accordingly in varying formulas. But there is one element in it which is perhaps the dominant, and it shows itself more particularly in Nietzsche and in Ibsen, though the latter has nothing like the genius of the former, nor, it would appear (for the present writer does not pretend to judge of Norse style at all, and has had fifty years' acquaintance with German), anything like the purely literary mastery which, amid much questionable stuff, is unquestionable in *Götzen-Dämmerung* and *Also sprach Zarathustra*. This element was shrewdly enough indicated in her last book by George Eliot, who, whatever different estimates may be held of her position as a novelist, was undoubtedly a person of great mental power, unusually well acquainted with more than one or two literatures, and no friend to orthodoxy or enemy to free thought. "Some says one thing," says a character in *Theophrastus Such*, "and some says another; but if I was to give *my* opinion, it 'ud be different."

It is this determination to be "different"—this topsy-turveying of accepted doctrines and positions—which really underlies most of late nineteenth-century thinking and writing. Ibsen was, his admirers assure us, a man of genius, and it may in part be granted. That Nietzsche was a man of genius there can be no manner of doubt. Yet he has chiefly employed this genius in simple topsy-turvification—in "being different"; different from the teachings of Christianity; different from those of accepted ethics, Christian or not; different from his two first masters; different from himself. Cut away, by an effort of thought hardly more paradoxical than his own, these various subjects of difference, and nothing of him will remain but his expression, which itself is very mainly noticeable as "being different" from that of others. This exaggeration of the Romantic Individualism is, after all, in itself no great intellectual feat. Even a naughty little boy has been known to "take the nots out of the Commandments and put them into the Creed" in a fit of temper; and the Nietzschian formula reduced to its simplest terms comes to very little more. What is not formula—the wide reading and the acute if distorted critical appreciation, the fancy that is not seldom real imagination, and the fantastic flame-like glitter and wave of the expression itself—comes to a very great deal more; but these things are entirely separable from the formula or formulas.

It is difficult to say that they are, save to very poor and shallow apprehensions, even assisted by these formulas—that they owe very much to them in any way. The excessively common trick of reversal by parody, or parody by reversal, is a thing which has been a mere trick or *tic* of the last twenty or thirty years, which was hit off neatly by Tourguenieff earlier in the phrase " reversed platitude," and which, long ago stale in French and given up in most other countries, still, apparently, can make a man accounted clever in England and Germany. It was greatly practised by Nietzsche,—he was, in fact, probably the most gifted man who ever did practise it. But this is less than nothing—a mere variety of negation of the parasitic kind. The wonderful excellence of his form remains, but it remains almost alone. It has as yet hardly had full time to produce its effect on German prose generally. But it has already done something of the kind, and will do more. "Do not say what Zarathustra said, but say what you say *as* he said it," should be the advice to every German prose writer.

The notoriety of the country for destructive criticism in theological matters has continued, though the *Theology and science.* temper of the iconoclasts has varied from the extravagant cobweb-spinnings of Strauss and the bitter fanaticism of Feuerbach at the beginning to the more moderate engineer-work of Adolf Harnack (*b.* 1851) at the close. Recently indeed, in Germany as elsewhere, the sort of eclectic compromise involved in a "reverent undogmatism" has found a good deal

of favour. But the division is too controversial a
one to find convenient place for discussion here, and
indeed could hardly be discussed without dropping
into what are figuratively called "politics" and wisely
excluded from general conversation. Whether the
attitude of those who extol the "Higher Criticism"
as valuable, truly pious, and in all respects beneficial;
of those who denounce it as worthy of fire and faggot,
for the books if not for the writers; or of those (a
small but perhaps not quite a negligible body) who
see in it a strange compound of *petitio principii* and
ignoratio elenchi, and wait for it to pass, as other
not very dissimilar things have passed,—whether any
one of these or none be the wise attitude is not for
us to decide. It is at any rate pretty certain that
few of its fruits will survive as literature, and it
is at least piquant that hardly any critic has been
more severe on Strauss himself than the subversive
and anti-Christian Nietzsche.

What has been said of theology applies with a
difference to physical science, though here also there
have been books and men who have made mark in
a quasi-literary fashion—from the violently materialist
Kraft und Stoff (1855) of *Ludwig* Büchner (not *Georg*,
the poet mentioned in the last volume) to the works
in which Ernst Haeckel (*b.* 1834) and others have
edited, applied, and exaggerated the doctrines of
Charles Darwin. Not only have the subjects of
these books little connection with literature, but it
is almost impossible, until a considerable time has

passed, for even the coolest critic to appraise their literary value. Most similar books in the past have quickly become obsolete — Büchner's is so almost already; the rest may follow this rule, or prove exceptions, but it concerns us little.

History is in a safer position; and for the modern conception of it, which puts examination into documents before literary dealing with the results of that examination, the German mind and its training are specially well suited. Fortunately, too, the avowedly unliterary tendency of this conception has been counteracted during our period, if not indeed in the average German literary historian, in more than one or two individuals of exceptional eminence. The great names of Ranke (1795-1886) and of Von Sybel (1817-1895) dominated its beginning, and their work, as well as their names, has found notice from Mr Omond; but they continued to live and write, the one till full two-thirds of the half-century had passed, the other till nearly its close. Another political historian of great eminence specially devoted to the history of his own country was Heinrich von Treitschke (1834-1896); while the modern study of one of the most absorbing periods of all history—the Renaissance— owes not indeed its origin, for that is due rather to our own Roscoe than to any one else, but immense encouragement and assistance to J. Burckhardt (1818-1897), whose *Kultur der Renaissance* appeared in 1860.

History.

But the name of the period in history, as well as in that other great province of German study, classical scholarship, is undoubtedly that of Theodor Mommsen, a man of letters if ever there was one, though so much else also. Born as early as 1817, he very early began the study of Roman inscriptions, and held to it more or less all his life, his studies taking shape in the great collection, *Corpus Inscriptionum Latinarum*, which was begun in 1863. But no one could possibly be less like the antiquary of tradition and imagination—the collector of and potterer over coins and sculptured stones, with his want of interest in everything else, and his recluse or eccentric habits—than Mommsen, who was an ardent and distinctly excitable politician, active and interested in all the concerns of practical life. His hold on literature proper is chiefly effected by his great *Roman History*, 1854-56, with a further instalment, but not exactly sequel, many years later, which is a fragment, but in a way complete. A perfect history it certainly is not; for it is violently partisan, and its partisanship is directed by the blustering drill-sergeant spirit—the cult of the iron fist, divorced from all chivalry and from all conception of the nature of a gentleman — which has been the curse of modern Germany. But even this makes it representative; and its own intellectual vigour gives it a right to represent. Mommsen cannot indeed approach Schopenhauer as a master of easy and quiet, or Nietzsche as one of coloured

Mommsen.

and rhythmical, prose; but his form is far from contemptible in itself and (if his date be considered) very remarkable indeed.[1]

[1] In this history we cannot take much note of merely dialectic literature. But our period happens to have produced two such noteworthy figures in *Platt-Deutsch*, that they must not be quite passed over. Fritz Reuter, the elder of them, was born as early as 1810, and had a somewhat stormy youth, being imprisoned, and even condemned to death, for his share in the "Young German" excitements of the 'thirties. This imprisonment and its consequences made him a very late-writing author, and he was past forty when, in 1853, having tried the literary language with no great success, he made his mark once for all with the Low German *Läuschen un Rimels*. He continued to write prose and verse, his greatest book being considered to be *Ut mine Stromtid* (1862-64), and died in 1874, having attained the reputation of the greatest writer in dialect of the century. Reuter's strong point is humour, of course not divorced from pathos. Klaus Groth (1819 - 1899) was rather more of a "literary man" than Reuter, whom he just preceded with a volume of poems entitled *Quickborn*, in 1852, following it up with other Platt-Deutsch works in prose and verse, and defending the claims of his dialect (he was a scholar and a professor of German) to a place in the Upper House of literary languages. Groth appears to have less "race" than Reuter, but more definite artistic cultivation. But both have admirers—in Reuter's case, at least, generally very enthusiastic ones.

Note on Platt-Deutsch— Reuter and Groth.

CHAPTER VI.

THE SOUTHERN LITERATURES.

THE two preceding volumes in one case, the
volume immediately preceding in both, will have
shown how Italian first, and then Spanish,
Change in their
general position. shook off, under the double influence of
Indebtedness to political changes and of powerful literary
English
invasion from the North, the comparative
torpor in matters literary which had hung upon them
during the later seventeenth and almost the whole
of the eighteenth century. Even the last found little
to notice in the literature of the Third Peninsula,

though this also received a stimulus greater than
either of those administered to the other outliers
of Europe to the southward in the shape of a formal
enfranchisement and readmission to the European
company and comity. It will be our business here
to take up, in differing degrees, the story of all
three. As far as Italy and Spain are concerned,
—for Portugal is in a rather different position,
and the accomplishment of Greece is altogether, and
could hardly be expected to be other than, minor,
—the literary interest of this revenge of the whirligig
of time is, or may appear at first sight, not easily
surpassable. After two hundred years and more, the
Northern nations are seen repaying the enormous
debt which they had incurred to Italy, and the
smaller one which they owed to Spain. And the
reimbursement, such as it is, is effected with a
reversed directness which adds to the interest. In
the Renaissance times England had received the
new stimulus after, though by no means always
through, France ; and the reverse process of borrowing from France had begun again in Italy
long before any recovery of the old debt was made
from England. The same, exactly, had happened
with Spain. But when the nineteenth century came
these things were for a time altered, and Scott and
Byron exercised over the countries to which the
latter at least owed so much, an influence far
superior to that of any French writer, at any rate
for a time. The Anglomania of the Southrons was,
however, strictly limited, and outside of this great

pair it hardly accepted any but scientific and philosophic writers.[1]

Except in regard to these half non-literary matters, the debt to England ceases for the most part in the *and to French.* second half of the nineteenth century. But that to France increases enormously; and by a curious chance it directs itself, in all the three peninsulas, mainly, if not wholly, into one channel— that of the novel. Both in Spain and in Italy, as in Germany and elsewhere, the third quarter of the century is rather a dead season in literature, but in both the fourth has seen, as in the Northern empires, at least a vigorous, if only a convulsive, attempt to regenerate and resurrect. With one remarkable ex- ception, however, and that of the older generation in Italy, such fruits of these efforts, at any rate as have made their way beyond the confines of their own country, are almost wholly in the kind of prose fiction. Putting specialists in the various tongues out of the question on one hand, and deliberate literary explorers on the other, what, among fairly educated and well-read persons, are the names likely to occur as representing these literatures in recent times? Such, surely, as those of Fernan Caballero and Juan Valera for one part of the westernmost peninsula, and of Eça de Queiroz for the other; of Antonio Fogazzaro,

[1] In this chapter I have been much indebted to Signor Angelo de Gubernatis' *Dictionnaire des Ecrivains du Monde Latin*, 7 parts, Rome and Florence, 1905-7. For the Spanish part, my obligations to Mr James Fitzmaurice Kelly's *History of Spanish Literature*, and his article in the Supplement to the *Encyclopædia Britannica*, are still greater, and extend beyond mere information.

Gabriele d'Annunzio, Matilde Serao, for the middle; of Demetrius Bikelas for the easternmost. Now, these writers are all novelists, and the influences *Prominence* which made them novelists are in most *of the novel.* —not quite in all—cases French influences —in a few those of the older romantic novel of Dumas and Hugo; in most those of the various realist-romantic or realist-naturalist schools, from Balzac and George Sand, through Flaubert and Feuillet, to the Goncourts and Zola, especially that of the last-named. For, regret it or denounce it or welcome it as we may, there is no doubt that Naturalism, in the wide sense, has supplied such a literary ferment as has been seldom offered. If any one says that fermentation and putrefaction are not altogether unconnected, he may : but that is another question.

We should begin with Italy for almost all reasons— her central position, her magnificent literary history *Italy—* in the past, and last, but not quite least, *Carducci.* her possession of the exceptional figure above alluded to. Of the positive value of the work of Giosué Carducci (1835-1907)—whose death followed Ibsen's with a sort of annual stroke of removal of the great ones of the last age—it is perhaps too early to judge with absolute certainty of justice. How great it is Time must decide ; that it is great we are perhaps justified in deciding already. But relatively, and taking the conditions in, it may certainly be said that in no other country of Europe during the half century do we find any one—not even Hugo, not even Tennyson — occupying such a position. Like these two, Carducci has been the hardly-questioned head of the poetry of his country for a generation and more; and, like the first, but unlike the second, he has been an important figure in politics as well. But Tennyson was a poet pure and simple; and Hugo, though a grandiose novelist and dramatist, and on certain occasions no mean critic, was all abroad in any regions but these. Carducci has been critic as well as poet, historian at least of literature as well as critic, and centre, rallying-point, starting-point alike to the literary forces of his country, after a fashion thrown up no doubt by the comparative absence of others— by the very poverty of that country for the time in great men of letters, but real in itself and hardly to be parallelled elsewhere or elsewhen. Through the time when Italy, nominally freed in political matters, was least fruitful in literature,—when Manzoni had long been silent, when d'Azeglio was giving himself to politics, Carducci's poems — *Juvenilia* from 1850, *Levia Gravia* as early as 1861, *Decennalia* in 1870, *Rime Nuove* (1861-87), and the famous *Odi Barbare*, with their adaptations of Latin metres to Italian, starting from 1877—maintained the credit of pure literature in Italy as nothing else did, and as few things could have done better. Whether too much importance has or has not been assigned to the sort of literary *cénacle* which the publisher Sommaruga gathered round him about 1880, and of which Carducci was, as it were, summoned from his tent to become the leader, is again one of the questions that must be kept for Time to answer. But there is

R

no doubt that his leadership did more or less animate many, if not most, of the young men and women of letters who have made their mark since; and no one whose attention has been drawn at all, during the last thirty years, to Continental literature can fail to have been more or less aware of the singular position—not exactly as of a light shining in darkness, but certainly that of a light both burning and shining—which this masterful writer and poet has held.

The great glory which has been assigned to him by his admirers, and which does not seem to be merely a fond imagination, is that of having not only strengthened the always graceful form of Italian poetry, but of having applied to it an austere and astringent influence which has to a great extent removed the facility and (in the original, not the offensive, sense) *lubricity* of its effect. He has really done this to some extent, perhaps to a great one; but it is a question whether the Protean slipperiness of the language has not been too much for him after all. For instance, his most famous, or at least notorious, piece, the *Hymn to Satan* (1865, but written, he says, in 1863), is a glorification of revolt in every form. As such we need not discuss it much, except to point out that, by its date, such a glorification was nothing new or daring, but rather a *pont aux ânes*, as Diderot said to Rousseau in days when it was the other way about. Moreover, Baudelaire had undoubtedly preceded him in his *Litanies de Satan;* and the resemblance of the two is much greater than might be thought from Carducci's rather qualified denial of acquaintance, combined as it is with a rather awkward citation of the part of Baudelaire's verse *least* like his. But this matters little. The question is whether *Satana*, though undoubtedly a fine piece of flowing declamation, does not still run too smoothly,—its little verses almost skipping as they pass. The sonnet, of course, saves him from this danger, and so do many of the longer-lined measures of the *Odi Barbare;* while his Italian Sapphics are things of the greatest interest, the *lubricus vultus* being here quite attractive. Whether the Alcaics do quite as well may be questioned, yet the poem to Queen Margherita is a beautiful thing. It is extremely difficult to know what to cite from a poet so voluminous, but the openings of two things in lighter and graver tone respectively, *Alla Rima* and *In una chiesa Gotica*, may perhaps not utterly dissatisfy his admirers,—

> "Ave, o rima ! Con bell' arte
> Su le carte
> Te persegue il trovadore ;
> Ma tu brilli, tu scintilli,
> Tu zampilli,
> Su del popolo dal cuore.
>
> O scoccata tra due baci
> Ne i rapaci
> Volgimenti de la danza,
> Come accordi ne due giri
> Due sospiri,
> Di memoria e di speranza !"

" Sorgono e in agili file dilungano
Gl' immani ed ardui steli marmorei,
E ne la tenebra sacra somigliano
De giganti un esercito

Che guerra mediti con l' invisibile :
Le arcete salgono chete, si slanciano
Quindi a vol rapide, poi si rabbracciano
Prone per l' alto e pendule.

Ne la discordia cosi de gli uomini
Di fra i barbarici tumulti salgono
A Dio gli aneliti di solinghe anime
Che in lui si ricongiungono."

But I do not find Carducci easy to select on a very small scale.

Carducci's influence was exercised partly through his work in literary history,— in his *Conversazioni Critiche* and the like, directed towards the revival of Italian letters by attention to the glorious and long half-neglected treasures of the Italian past in literature. But on this side it was strongly reinforced, and to some extent widened and extended, by an older writer—Francesco de Sanctis (1817-1883)—who is sometimes spoken of, and not without good reason, as the reviver of Italian criticism. Although as patriotic as Carducci himself, his less original genius perhaps made him rather more receptive to outside influences ; and though he too wrote a *History of Italian Literature*, his *Saggi Critici*, which appeared at Naples towards the end of the 'sixties and at the beginning of the 'seventies, pay great attention to foreign books. The weak point of De Sanctis as

De Sanctis.

a critic is that, in accordance with a very common tendency of modern criticism, he will not let literature keep itself to itself, and is always dragging in extraneous considerations. But to some this seems a virtue, and it is at any rate too characteristic of the period to be regarded as a mere vice, rather as a document and symptom. His example has been widely followed; and Italy at the present day possesses many active students and practitioners of the subject, among whom may be specially mentioned Signor Benedetto Croce (*b.* 1866), founder and editor of the journal *La Critica*.

De Sanctis beyond doubt owed most to France and to Sainte-Beuve; but it is fair to assign, not to France *Other critics, scholars, and historians.* but to Germany, the credit of influencing most of the writers who illustrated this third quarter of the century, and who, as has been hinted, represent "knowledge" rather than "power" in the distribution of their energies. The respected politician Ricardo Bonghi (1826-1895) was a man of letters before he took to politics, and in days when, except revolutionary things, there was not much in politics for an Italian to take to. Signor Pasquale Villari, his junior by one year only, early began to pay attention to the great period of Italian history and literature, and especially to Savonarola and Macchiavelli. 1835 was the birth year of two scholars —Alessandro d'Ancona and Domenico Comparetti— of whom the former perhaps deserves the position of his country's best literary historian, while Signor Comparetti attained the more unique one of being the chief authority on divers interesting sides of mediæval life and letters, folklore, superstitions, and the like. With him should be mentioned the younger Arturo Graf (*b.* 1848), a student of things not dissimilar; Edmondo de Amicis (*b.* 1846), a miscellaneous writer who at one time was perhaps better known out of Italy than almost any other Italian, and who is acknowledged in it as a master of easy prose; and Angelo de Gubernatis (*b.* 1840), who has crowned his critical and miscellaneous work with the *Dictionary* saluted above in a note.

For the last five-and-twenty years, however, in Italy as elsewhere, the more ardent spirits have begun to disdain the " porter's work " (as Christopher North put it in a double-edged gibe) of merely studying others, and have, under the powerful influence indicated above, very mainly resolved to " create for themselves." We have already more than once noticed the strong tendency of the time towards "particularist" litera-ture—the literature of dialect, of province, of the small district and place. Now, few readers need to be told that the opportunities for such literature as this exist in Italy as they hardly exist anywhere else in Europe; and fewer should need to be told that the superficial unification of the kingdom has tended rather to bring out—it may be for a time, it may be not—the attention to these local peculiarities.

The first writer to make mark in this line (which almost necessarily leads to the novel) was, by what must be something more than a coincidence, the author of the most recent Italian book which has made for itself European reputation, Antonio Fogaz-

Novelists—
Fogazzaro
and others.

zaro (*b.* 1842). From the *Malombra* of 1881 to *Il Santo* of 1906 a good many things have apparently happened, but the only really sound symptoms of change in literature are the appearance and the disappearance of masters. Signor Fogazzaro (who had published verse as early as 1863, and has never deserted it), as a native of Vicenza, represents of course Northern Italy originally, and so stands at extremest polarity with Signor Giovanni Verga (born a little before him), who is a Sicilian, and who has had the resources of that strange island, the cradle of Italian literature itself, the meeting-point, as hardly even Spain is, of Eastern and Western culture and character, the nurse (not *arida nutrix* from the literary point of view at all) of Theocritus and of Ciullo d'Alcamo. Younger than these, and adding to the Italian imbroglio of country divided against country a fascinating tincture of the oldest mother of European literature (for she was born in Greece, at Patras, and had Greek blood in her), is Matilde Serao (born 1856). Lombardy, Sicily, Greece —the fanatics of connection between nationality and locality on the one hand, and literary characteristics on the other, certainly have a fair field open to them here.

Younger again, but in the general estimation of the moment the chief of Italian novelists, and perhaps,

D'Annunzio.

Carducci removed, of Italian men of letters, came Gabriele d'Annunzio, born in 1864, and so at once exposed to the earliest influence of the latest Italian literary *risorgimento*, and to that more questionable but at least equally powerful one of French Naturalism at its flood-tide. With this last he has drifted perhaps too far, but he has time to turn. And last of all (" Il est de 1870," as one of "Gyp's" heroes says of himself) may be mentioned Antonio Negri, who completes a certainly interesting quintet.

Rules, however thus stretched, preclude our mentioning other writers and other developments of literature which are numerous in all directions throughout Italy at the moment. We shall only draw notice—partly that it may ease the Conclusion, partly because this is a specially appropriate place for it—to the fact that the undoubtedly active and bustling development of letters in Italy during the last two decades, like that of Germany and of Spain, has a characteristic which, though by no means fatal, —nothing is fatal in the *ondoyant et divers* course of literature,—is not, if we may judge from that which has been, altogether favourable to that which shall be. Prolific seasons of literature have been generally due to two different kinds of influences—the influences of schools and principles, and the influence of great men of letters.[1] The former has seldom given a vintage of the highest class by itself ; the latter often has, not so much because the actual following of the chiefs has been productive, as because the " skiey

---

[1] The application of this principle, if not the principle itself, has not been missed in Italy, and people have there asked, pertinently enough, whether a new Marinism is exactly what is wanted

influences" which worked on those chiefs have worked also on others. Sometimes, and happily, the two have coincided; when they have not, the school without the man has seldom done very much. Now Italy has had a great man of letters in Carducci; but there is scarcely much of Carducci in Gabriele d'Annunzio or Matilde Serao, though there may be a little more in Fogazzaro. In the first named, at any rate, Naturalism has had perhaps something too large a say. You may roast your pig well by burning down your house, though even this is doubtful; you certainly roast him with much pomp and circumstance. But it is expensive, and there comes a time when there are no more houses to burn down. So too, dialect and local manners are a rich seam for the miner to work, but not an inexhaustible one. One is sometimes inclined to think of the modern use of guano in agriculture when one considers the character, and the promise for the future, of modern letters.

In comparing Spain with Italy we find that the Western Peninsula has one disadvantage and one

Spain. great advantage,—the latter suggesting a glance at the half-forbidden political considerations touched on in the Conclusion in reference to France, and existing also in the case of Germany. Spain has had her revolutions during the period,— one, more than thirty years ago, of an apparently very serious kind. But they have as yet resulted in nothing at all resembling the definitive reconstitution of the Republic in France, the unification of Italy, or the sudden elevation of Prussianised Germany from the position of a questionably Great Power to that of one of the greatest. Accordingly, or in spite of this (for either side of the question could be argued), there has been no positive breach in Spanish literary development, and no sudden quickening or blossoming of it. On the whole, there appears to be a decided improvement, but there certainly has been no bursting of the aloe. Nor (here the disadvantage as regards Italy comes in) has the country possessed in the meantime any commanding literary figure like that of Carducci, though it has had at least one of great artistic value.

The influence of France has here also been great; but while not pretending to speak on Spanish literature, or on any of these other literatures, *The Novel.* with so extensive a knowledge as in the case of English, French, or German, one may question whether the peculiar *goût du terroir* which is so characteristic of Spain, and the individuality which has prevailed there in mind as well as in manners, may not be traced here likewise. It has been a mark of Spanish literature, during the four centuries or thereabouts of its very distinct and accomplished existence, that it has either been half torpid, or very vividly alive with a life all its own. It began by imitating Italian; but as there is nothing less like the Italian *novellieri* than Cervantes, so there is nothing less like Italian drama than Lope and Calderon. So, too, Spanish novelists of the last two generations have undoubtedly imitated French for better as for worse, but they have

seldom imitated it with the mere slavishness, passing
into caricature, which is so common elsewhere. The
writer has in mind at the moment a Belgian and
a German novel (never mind their names), in each
of which the Zolaesque aping reaches the level of
quite colossal parody, if only the writers had intended
it. There may be such things in Spanish, but they
certainly are not characteristic. Nor, perhaps, has
the line of particularist observation in manners been
followed less than the line of what is euphemistically
called "frankness" in morals; while that remarkable
command of character in which Spanish literature
excels all others except English appears as well. The
present writer does not, it may be well to repeat,
pretend to anything like an extensive acquaintance
with the modern Spanish novel. But he has, like
other people of late years, read, in the originals or
in translations, novels of every European country, and
a considerable number of them from some countries.

He does not remember a single one, putting the
works of the great English and French novelists of the
last generation out of sight, which can in general character compete with the *Pepita Jimenez* of
Señor Juan Valera. There may be more
"excess" (in the old Aristotelian sense) of this or that
quality in others. Such and such a Russian or Norwegian may be stranger, perverser, if anybody likes
more pathetic and more poignant, as well as more
appealing to the modern fancy for seeing the strings,
and the works, and the processes, as well as the finished
result. Such and such a Hungarian, or such and such

Valera.

an Italian, may be more prodigal of action, more violent in passion, more lavish of local colour. Such and such a Belgian, or Austrian, or Italian again, may be more daring (as they call it) in meddling with the simply inconvenient. But then all these things *are* excess; and as excess always is, they are accompanied, compensated, brought, some may think, to the ground, by defects in other ways. Not thus does Señor Valera go to work. He has a numerous team of quite sufficiently spirited horses to drive, but he keeps them all in hand; he makes them pull at the coach together, and obey bit and whip punctually. In other words, he is an artist; and though there has been, and is, much talk of art in literature for these last few decades, there has perhaps been not so very much of it visible in action. His qualities show to less consummate advantage in his other best-known novel *Doña Luz*, but they are unmistakable there also, while good judges put *Il Comendador Mendoza* and *Juanita la Larga* even higher. Yet it is a little noteworthy—the Diablo Cojuelo who so naturally occurs in connection with the subject might say, in pointing it out, that it is also rather unpleasant—that Juan Valera Alcala y Galiano was born in 1824, when Scott was just meeting his fatal misfortunes and had yet seven years to live; when Hugo was but just appearing; when Dickens and Thackeray, and even Tennyson, were boys; when Goethe had not published the second part of *Faust*. Thus he was a man of all but fourscore at the close of the nineteenth century. He has written immensely; and much of his writing, as in the case of so many other authors of our time, was ephemeral, and at any rate seems to have been allowed by its author to remain so. His masterpieces, moreover, were not early; *Pepita Jimenez* itself is of 1874, *Doña Luz* of 1879. But he exercised himself largely in that criticism which, if not a certain preparation for creative work, is not the worst; and he always took, no matter on what side, an active interest in politics and in life.

His chief rival,—it is odd till perhaps one comes to look into it, when it ceases to be so, that the novel more than any other kind seems to encourage the simultaneous or nearly simultaneous appearance of contrasted pairs, Fielding and Richardson, Balzac and Dumas, Dickens and Thackeray,—José Maria de Pereda, was born also far back, though ten years Valera's junior; and by a quaint coincidence his masterpiece, *Sotileza*, was produced in *his* fiftieth year (1884), even as *Pepita Jimenez* had been. Pereda's temper, if thought and subject,—he is a novelist of the sea, a strong Royalist and Catholic, an anti-modern of the most refreshing kind,—pose him in opposition to Valera's Liberalism. But undoubtedly the pair put Spain in no mean position to speak with her enemies in the novel gate.

Yet they are very far from holding that gate alone for her. Fernán Caballero (1797-1877), who, mentioned in the last volume for her chief *Others.* novel *La Gaviota*, continued to write till her death, was indeed not a Spaniard of the whole blood; for her father was a German, and she was not even born in the Peninsula. But she went there soon, returned there early, married there, and spent almost the whole of her life there, showing in her books not merely a real romantic faculty but an intimate knowledge of Andalusia at least. The prolific Fernandez y Gonzalez, whose death followed hers in 1888, hardly ranks among the company of Cervantes; but the younger Antonio de Trueba, who died in the year after (1889), has determined partisans. The *Sombrero de Tres Picos* (*Three-cornered Hat*) of Pedro Antonio de Alarcón (1833-1891) is the best of not a few good short stories by the same author. In 1845, too, as if each decade of these central ones was to provide Spain with a novelist of merit, came the birth of Benito Pérez Galdòs, a writer of fiction as prolific as Fernandez y Gonzalez, much more popular and much more gifted. Beginning with patriotic stories (*La Fontana de Oro* in 1871), he attempted later (it is usually said in imitation of Erckmann-Chatrian, but this is not necessary) a series of such things in his *Episodios Nacionales*, besides many detached novels and plays. His best known book out of Spain is *Doña Perfecta*. And the 'fifties did not fail to keep up the practice with Emilia Pardo Bazán (Señora Quiroga), *b.* 1852, a fertile writer of criticism (she began with a study of her Galician compatriot, Father Feyjoo), and a still more fertile one of novels. In these the corrupt following of French Naturalism sometimes betrays itself, as in *La Madre Naturaleza* (1887), but they have no small spirit and *verve.* Of younger writers still, may be mentioned Armando Palacio Valdés, Leopoldo Alas (who died in 1901), and Jacinto Octavio Picon, who is spoken of with that mixed approval and shake-of-the-head which is not the worst compliment in letters.

Familiars and even devotees of Spanish literature speak with less confidence of Spanish poetry than of Spanish fiction. Even of the central

Poetry.

poetic figure of the period before ours, Espronceda, admiration has not been universal or whole-hearted; but Espronceda died more than sixty years since, and there is hardly any one in these sixty years who unites suffrages even as he did. The fact appears to be that Spanish, even more perhaps than Italian, is one of those languages the very richness of whose general poetical qualities and capacities stands in the way of special poetical development. Perhaps slightness of acquaintance may increase the attraction of it, but it certainly seems to the present writer that Spanish is the most beautiful of languages next to Greek—with which his acquaintance is not so slight. It is so easy in it to clothe the eternal commonplaces, which are the skeletons of poetry, with a sort of *beauté du diable* of glowing, throbbing word-flesh, that those who cannot do anything more have an apparent excuse for being content with this, and that even those who could do something more are tempted to relax their efforts. The warning of Gautier's great poem, *Sculpte! lime! cisèle!* seems superfluous to them. It is at any rate certain that no general reputation of a very wide or deep kind

has been attained by any one from Ramón de
Campoamor (1817-1901) and Gaspar Nuñez de Arce
(b. 1834) onwards through Perez Ferrari (b. 1853) and
Manuel del Palacio (b. 1832); while in the region of
poetic drama Echegaray (1833) hardly makes an exception to the failure of this kind in modern literature—
a failure to which the name of Hugo himself is but
a partial exception of the kind that proves the rule.
In poetry, however, nothing but somewhat minute
examination of individual examples affords any solid
ground for judgment; and fortunately here, as in
some, but not all, other modern literatures, a refuge
from the almost impossible task of searching at large
through unsifted authors is afforded by a collection,
the *Poesias Castellanas del Siglo xix.*, executed not long
before his death by Don Juan Valera himself.

The value of this book [1] is increased, and indeed
put in an almost unique position, by the fact that the
selector was the undoubted leader of his country's
literature at the time that he made it; that he had
earned an almost equally great reputation as critic
and as creator; and that, though he was approaching
fourscore when he began it, and apparently left it
unfinished at his death, he prefixed to it nearly a
whole volume, and appended to it another, of
biographico-critical notes of extraordinary vivacity,
acuteness, and range. A little patriotic exaggeration
will not detract from the value of this in any really

---

[1] Florilegio de Poesias Castellanas del Siglo xix. Con introducción
y notas biograficas y criticas. Por Juan Valera. De la Real Academía
Española. 5 vols. Madrid: Fernando Fè, 1902-4.

critical estimate. When we are told that even Byron and Goethe do not excel Espronceda in certain points, we may shake heads a little as to Goethe if not as to Byron, and at any rate insinuate the reminder that the Spanish poet undoubtedly "came after" both in more senses than one. But this critical matter is a godsend in itself: and the anthology enables one to enjoy, with a fuller atmosphere of intelligence, the greater godsend of the actual anthology. This extends, in due following of the title, to the whole century, and thus includes poets some of whom have been already dealt with in the last volume. But the best of these, Francisco Martinez de la Rosa, Manuel José Quintana, and Angel de Saavedra, Duque de Rivas, lived well into our time. The stately but rather stiff political pindarics of Quintana may not come home much to foreigners; and with regard to the first poetical Duke of Rivas (there has been another), it may be observed that, while Señor Valera pronounces Don Angel de Saavedra "a thoroughly healthy man," borrowing the phrase from Carlyle on Scott, and even speaks of his *immortal corona*, the extracts from him are not over-stimulating. On the other hand, Martinez de la Rosa is spoken of rather mealy-mouthedly by the elect. But where will you find a more delightful thing, or more characteristic nationally and linguistically, than "La Niña Descolorida"?—

> " Pálida está de amores
> Mi dulce niña :
> Nunca vuelvan las rosas
> A sus mejillas !

S

> Nunca de amapolas
> O adelfas ceñida
> Mostró Citeréa
> Su frente divina ;
> Téjenle guirnaldas
> De jazmin sus ninfas ;
> Y tiernas violas
> Cupido la brinda.
>
> Pálida está," &c.

Pastiche and *rococo* and *schablonenhaft* (as the new German critical slang goes, and certainly they know the thing), as much as you like !—" roses " and " poppies " and " nymphs " and " Cytherea " and " Cupid," in a style highly to be deprecated. But what appetising assonances ! what melting dactyls and trochees ! what a fascinating guitar music and "click of the castanets," as the knowing ones say, over the whole ! Perhaps the charm, such as it is, may illustrate what has been said above of the treacherous character of the language ; but one has known languages in which one would not be sorry to meet a Martinez de la Rosa. The rhetorical style, for which Spanish is at least as well fitted as any European tongue, is less attractive ; and such things as the "A la Muerte de la Duquesa de Frias," not to mention the obligatory "El Dos de Mayo," and the truly appalling "A la Influencia del Entusiasmo Publico en Las Artes" of Don Juan Nicasio Gallego, who also lived into our time, leave one cold. But (as it is in the book before us we may notice it) there is no such result from the famous " Canción del Pirata " of Espronceda the legendary, though it is perhaps not well to think too much as one reads it of *Les Aventuriers de la Mer*.

Of the poets more strictly belonging to our period, José Zorrilla, just mentioned by Mr Omond, Pedro Antonio de Alarcón, Adelardo López de Ayala, Ramón de Campoamor, Gaspar Nuñez de Arce, and Miguel Costa seem to have had the highest reputation at home, and to them we may add the Cuban poetess Doña Gertrudis de Avellaneda, the short-lived Bécquer, and one or two others. Zorrilla was mainly a dramatist (as indeed most of these were), and though his practice in the great national metre of the octosyllable must have been meritorious since it was popular, it does not appeal much to a foreigner. Such a one may find more in such a piece as the "Sueños de Sueños" (though the title is dangerous) of Alarcón, and will almost certainly find more in the sonnets of López de Ayala. But Campoamor, as the admitted leader of Spanish poets for a generation, if not for two, should attract more curiosity. He appears to have been a poet rather "cumbered about serving" his poems, and disputes are frequent as to whether his *doloras* and his *humoradas* are new things or are not. This will not greatly trouble those who know that nothing is new in literature. If "Vanidad de la Hermosura" and "Beneficios de la Ausencia" are "doloras," then the Psalmist and the Preacher and Sappho wrote "doloras." "And what for no?" At the same time, these are very nice poems, if not quite so nice as the Psalmist's and the Preacher's and Sappho's. One gathers, however, that Don Ramón had something of a Browningesque ambition in him, and wished to write "Men and Women." Some would put Nuñez de Arce above him, and certainly this writer's monodramatic "Sursum Corda" is emphatically fine. As for the *rimas* of Bécquer, whose short and somewhat sad life gave him a brief European reputation years ago, *non nostrum est* to settle the dispute between Señor Valera, who denies his indebtedness to Heine, and other critics, who affirm it. But they are certainly poetry, as is, perhaps, but less certainly, the verse of Doña Gertrudis. Few living poets could forge a more splendid *stanza* than that of the Majorcan poet, Don Miguel Costa's "El Pino de Formentor"—

> "Hay en mi tierra un árbol que el corazón venera :
> De cedro es su ramaje, de césped su verdor ;
> Anida entre sus hojas perenne primavera,
> Y arrostra los turbiones que azotan la ribera
> Añoso luchador."

It seems to the present writer, who has for nearly half a century gone about to enjoy everything beautiful in form and sound and expression that he could find in not a few poetries, that this quintet is, in its arrangement both of line-length and rhyme, nothing less than a triumph.[1] It may be retorted, in something like an often

---

[1] The effect of the single and double rhymes is extraordinarily striking, because of the *fulness* of sound in both. Not merely in English and German but in French, rhymes on the penultimate syllable are apt to die away too much in the ultimate for *this* effect; and Italian is too prodigal of them to produce it. But I am told (and can see it in other examples) that Don Miguel is rather an adventurous person in metre. And there is perhaps some impertinence in endeavouring to trace "through a glass darkly"

> "La *impavida* armonía
> De aquella gran poesía"—

to borrow from a yet unnamed poet, Gabriel Garcia Tassara, who died in 1875.

transferred witticism, that "All the little boys play
with gold marbles in this country"; but the objection
is not fatal.[1] Be it so; there can be no better excuse
and no better reason for the declaration that the marbles
are gold. And as a perhaps rather unkind juxtaposition of the *Aventuriers de la Mer* and the *Canción
del Pirata* was made above, let us observe equity by
adding that perhaps never does one understand where
Hugo caught the peculiar splendour of his own verse
till one has read some Spanish poetry. The influence
of the Peninsula over 1830 generally has always
been well known; but in most cases it was an in-

---

[1] Although Señor Costa writes in Spanish, yet, as a Majorcan,
he may be thought to have connection with Catalan; and it has
been suggested to me that it would be fair to give
the following stanza from the chief modern Catalan
poet, Don Jacinto Verdaguer (*b.* 1845). It forms the
Dedication to his poem of *La Atlantida*, crowned at
Barcelona in 1877, and published next year in Catalan and Spanish
(Barcelona: Jaume Jepús. A *French* translation also exists (Paris,
1887)).

*Note on Ver-
daguer and
Catalan Poetry.*

> "Muntat de tos navilis en l' ala benehida,
> Busquí de los Hespérides lo taronger en flor;
>   Mes ay! es ja despulles
> De l' ona que há tants segles se n' es ensenyorida
> Y sols puch oferirte, si 't plauhen, eixes fulles
>   Del arbre del fruyt d'or."

It will be seen that there is the same stately undulation of the
longer lines, and the same extremely effective combination of single
and double rhyme,—things not at all improbably helped by the con-
frontation of Spanish and Provençal. But the stanza seems to me, *as
a stanza*, rather inferior. The Catalans, I believe, have (partly under
Señor Verdaguer's leadership) made something like a school of poets
in the last generation. But I have never had much acquaintance
with any of the forms of the Langue d'oc at first-hand, and I know
nothing of this poetry except *La Atlantida* ("with its translations,
sir! with its translations").

fluence of fashion and of costume only, or at the best (as with a few of the greatest artists like Gautier and Musset) of artistic *tour de force*. With Hugo it was the call of the poetic blood.

Much excellent and serious work appears to have been done during recent years in Spain within the more learned departments of literature. *Learned prose.* In 1897 there came to an end the long and useful life of Don Pasqual de Gayangos (much of it passed in England), who had devoted himself to the older literature of his country with the greatest ardour and success. The new historical political school has also made the old tree of history sprout afresh, and it has been held that the distinguished statesman Canovas del Castillo was only prevented by his diversion to active politics and his premature death from making a great name in this department. But perhaps the most remarkable book in serious literature produced during this generation in Spanish—a book practically unique in European literature as a whole —is the *Historia de las Ideas estéticas en España* of *Menendez y* Don Marcelino Menendez y Pelayo (*b.*1856).[1] *Pelayo.* This History of Criticism and Critical Philosophy, which in parts branches out into a survey of matters not merely Spanish, is acknowledged by the most competent authorities to be a model of the language in which it is written, while the learning displayed in it, the acuteness, and (whether one agrees or disagrees with them) the vigour of its ideas

[1] Before this, Señor Menendez had written a *Historia de los Heterodoxos Españoles*, which has a great reputation.

are indisputable. We have already pointed out on several different occasions how very important a part the literature of criticism plays in the whole literature of Europe during our period. It is no slight honour, not merely to Señor Menendez but to his language and country, that the absolutely best book on the subject—distinguishing the "book" from the mere brilliant "essay" or collection of essays, as a systematic and substantive treatment of a subject possessing importance and extension in a considerable degree— should be in Spanish. As is usual, too, the book seems to have made something of a school.

In the case of the westernmost of Peninsular literatures, a departure will be here made from the rule of first-hand treatment to such an extent as the author could achieve it. Why Portuguese has never made itself widely known it is very difficult to say. It has the distinction of having contributed at least one of the very few gods, *majorum gentium*, of European letters in Camoens; and if the attribution of the original *Amadis* to João Lobeira be correct, as it is still possible that it is, it is one of the most influential books of all European literature. It is very old—probably older in some finished literary forms than Castilian. All who are familiar with it are enthusiastic as to its powers as a literary vehicle; and there is perhaps some justice in the boast, dear to a Portuguese in speaking of his tongue, that it alone of European languages possesses a single word, *saudade*, for the expression of perhaps the most

Portuguese.

poetical of human emotions—the combination of love, remembrance, and regret. There have been and are— the late Sir Richard Burton and the living Mr Edgar Prestage are instances—those among us who appreciated and appreciate it. But on the whole, despite all the intercourse, commercial and political, between the two countries since the Methuen treaty, and all the millions of pipes of Port which have gone to the making of Englishmen, the literature has made little way. Nor does it seem to have made much more with Continental nations more nearly allied in blood. The present writer therefore despaired of doing even second-hand justice to the subject, which was also not treated in the last volume. But Mr Prestage himself has very kindly come to the rescue, and the following brief account of the Portuguese literature of the century is from his pen.

At the beginning of our period, Portugal had an inspired poet in Bocage (1765-1805), but a life of excess and bad companions prevented him from achieving any sustained flights. His talents were chiefly exhibited in improvised lyrical pieces; in sonnets on serious and patriotic subjects, which vie with those of Camoens; and in satire, particularly in a famous apostrophe to his enemy Macedo. This ex-friar (1761-1831), who possessed a vast erudition and high intelligence, conceived the ambition of supplanting Camoens as the national poet; and appropriating the subject of the Lusiads —Gama's discovery of the sea route to India,—he produced a lifeless epic, " Oriente." His letters and

Bocage.

Macedo.

satirical and critical pieces show his versatile genius, but his influence on letters was either reactionary or negative. The work of purifying the language and freeing it from gallicisms, which had been begun by the poets of the Arcadia, was completed by Francisco Manuel do Nascimento (1734-1813) in translations and original works. Notwithstanding his exaggerated love of Horace and lack of inspiration, he rendered very considerable services to the Portuguese tongue, and, sung by Lamartine, he prepared the way for Romanticism.

Filinto Elysio.

The nineteenth century witnessed a striking revival in Portuguese literature, and if Camoens be excepted, the writers of the time eclipse in merit even those of the sixteenth century—the golden age of the country. This revival began with the Romantic Movement, the chief names of which are Garrett and Herculano, and it was inaugurated in the field of poetry. Garrett (1799-1854) became acquainted with the masterpieces of contemporary English and German literature during his exile, and, imbued with the spirit of nationality, he wrote the poem "Camoēs," in which he broke with the established rules of composition in verse, and destroyed the authority of the classical and Arcadian rhymers. He was also the first to recognise the value of folk-poetry, which he gathered into his *Romanceiro*. Perhaps his highest achievement was the re-creation of the drama, for which he wrote a series of prose plays dealing with subjects taken from Portuguese

The Romantic Movement.

Garrett.

history, culminating in *Frei Luiz de Sousa,* a tragedy
of fatality and pity, and one of the notable stage
pieces of the century.   Next in value must be ranked
his deep, ardent, melancholy lyric poetry, collected in
Flores sem Fructo and *Folhas Cahidas;* and it was of
the latter volume that Herculano said, "If Camoens
had written love verses at Garrett's age, he could not
have equalled him."   Garrett also produced in the
elegant prose of *Viagens na minha terra* a unique
miscellany of criticism and romance, and, as one of
his followers, Rebello da Silva, remarked, was "not a
man of letters only, but an entire literature in himself."   The poetry both of Garrett and Herculano is
eminently natural in form and expression; but while
in the case of the former the subjects of the short
lyrics are personal, and those of the longer poems
historical, the verse of Herculano (1810-1877) is almost
entirely subjective with a religious flavour.

Herculano.

It is as an historian, however, that the latter
earned his European reputation, and the romances collected into *Lendas e Narrativas* and *O Monasticon,* which
were conceived under the influence of Walter Scott and
editions of Old Chronicles, prepared him for his *mag-
num opus*—the *History of Portugal to the End of the
Reign of Alfonso III.*   Based on a personal study of
documents, and written with rigorous impartiality in a
simple, sculptural style, it formed the first account of
the beginnings of Portugal to be set out on modern
critical lines.   A *History of the Origins and Establishment of the Inquisition* followed, and confirmed the
position of Herculano as the leading historian of the

Peninsula; and he also initiated the publication of a series, *Portugalliœ Monumenta Historica*. A lack of psychological imagination and of the philosophic spirit prevented him from comprehending men and drawing characters, but his analytical gifts and conscientious toil enabled him to present a reliable record of ascertained facts and a lucid explanation of political and economic events. The movement introduced by Garrett and Herculano lost its virile force, and became ultra-Romantic with Castilho (1800-1875), an emotional *Ultra- Romanticism. Castilho and his followers.* man, who, though numerous works in prose and verse proclaim him a first-rate artist and a master of the language, had few ideas. His most conspicuous followers were the lyric poets João de Lemos (1819-1889) and Soares de Passos (1826-1860); while Thomaz Ribeiro (1831-1901), author of the patriotic poem "D. Jayme," and other compositions equally admired, also belonged to the school. The name of José *J. Simões Dias.* Simões Dias (1844-1899) is as honoured in Spain as it is in Portugal. Breaking with the Romantic tradition in which he had been educated, he sought and found inspiration in popular sources with such success that the peasants have adopted as their own several of the poems in *Peninsulares*, and sing them at their gatherings.

In 1865 there arose a serious strife in the Portuguese Parnassus, which was known as the Coimbra *The Coimbra Question.* Question, from its origin in the university city. Castilho had constituted himself the pontiff of a mutual praise school, and while claiming to direct the rising generation, would not tolerate criticism of his methods, and stifled opinions not his own. Anthero de Quental rebelled against his superannuated leadership in *Bom senso e bom gosto*, and after a fierce war of pamphlets, Castilho was dethroned, to the immense gain of Portuguese literature, which then entered on a period of active and rich production under the joint influence of João de Deus and Anthero de Quental. João de Deus (1830-1895) ranks as one of the chief lyric poets of Portugal, but belongs to no school, and stands alone. A son of the people, few have equalled him in the art of saying true and beautiful things in everyday language, cast in harmonious verse. The *Campo de Flores* contains such exquisite poems as "A Vida" and "Rachel," and a distinguished Italian critic has ventured to call him, to whom God and woman were twin sources of inspiration, "the greatest love poet of the nineteenth century." A veritable survival from the patriarchal age, his leading characteristics are simplicity and spontaneity, and his writings are impregnated with the atmosphere of the Bible and of Camoens lyrics —almost the only books he read. Mainly, though not entirely, an idealist, he is eminently national, alike in the tender melancholy and sympathy of his elegies, and in his reverent, prayerful spirit, as in the sensual mysticism of his paraphrase of the Song of Songs — a piece full of the most opulent oriental imagery.

João de Deus.

A preponderance of reflection and foreign influences distinguish the four poets next to be mentioned. Anthero de Quental (1842-1891), a man of genius, described his metaphysical, neo-Buddhistic ideas, his mental sufferings and his pessimism, in more than one hundred sonnets, divided into five parts, marking the progressive stages in his evolution, which have been translated into the principal languages of Europe. The superiority of his poetry is due to the elevation of thought, sincerity, and moral grandeur of one who was only interested in the great problems of the universe, and it is curious to note the influence of French humanitarian theories and of Germanism on the mind of a Southerner and a descendant of the Catholic navigators of the sixteenth century. His *juvenilia,* collected into *Primaveras Romanticas,* are, as he said, "du Heine de deuxième qualité"; while the destiny of man, and the secular struggle between the Roman Church and the spirit of the age, inspired *Odes Modernas,* a book revolutionary and free - thinking in ideas and combative in tone. Quental's prose, especially that of the *Considerations on the Philosophy of Portuguese Literary History,* is singularly refined and concise.

Guerra Junqueiro made his *début* in verse with *The Death of Don Juan,*—a masterpiece of irony, which *Guerra Junqueiro.* brought him many imitators; and in *Patria* he evoked, in a series of dramatic scenes, the kings of the Braganza dynasty, and penned one of the most terrible satires ever written against a royal house. Finally, in the sonorous stanzas of *Os Simples,* he has proved himself a great poet, partly philosophical, partly naturalistic, and, giving play to his potent fancy and pantheistic tendencies, he treats the everyday episodes of village life in the spirit of a southern Tolstoi. Junqueiro incarnates himself in his personages, whom he selects as types of primitive virtues, moral strength, abnegation, faith, patience, and sweetness, and he gives out through them his particular conception of universal existence. A love of mystery inspires Gomes Leal in the *Claridades do Sul,* which is impregnated with the spirit of Baudelaire; and the same sentiment, in combination with the instinct of revolt, explains the production of *Anti-Christo,* a book as wonderful for its flashes of genius as for its faults of taste.

Gomes Leal.

The lyrics of Antonio Nobre (1867-1900), printed in *Só,* caused a sensation on their first appearance by their freshness and lofty inspiration, no less than by their rhythmic sweetness; while the poetry of the Parnassian, Gonçalves Crespo (1846-1883), by its fine taste and perfection of form recalls Coppèe, but the Portuguese has an added depth and greater feeling. His *Miniaturas* and *Nocturnos* have been edited by his widow, D. Maria Amalia Vaz de Carvalho, a critic and essayist, whose personality and *cercle* make her an unique figure in the literary and social life of the country.

Antonio Nobre.

Gonçalves Crespo.

The historical bent given to the drama by Garrett was exaggerated by Mendes Leal, and it is only recently that dramatists treating historical subjects have been able to free them-

The Drama.

selves from the bombast and other excesses of ultra-Romanticism. But notwithstanding the efforts of Garrett, Portugal has not quite succeeded in evolving a modern national drama, and the theatres still subsist largely on translations and adaptations from the French.

In comedy Fernando Caldeira (1841-1894), also no mean lyric poet, is one of the principal names, and two of his pieces, *A Mantilha da renda* and *A Madrugada*, show a delicacy and vivacity which would have gained their author a reputation in any country. The comedies of Gervasio Lobato (1850-1895) are characterised by an easy dialogue, wit, and humour, and among the most popular may be mentioned *O burro do Sr. Alcaide*, *O Valete de Copas*, and *O testamento da Velha*, produced in collaboration with D. João de Camara, a playwright who has seen his works translated and staged abroad, and is the leading dramatic writer of the present day. To these names must be added that of Antonio Ennes (1848-1901), who, besides achieving notable success as a writer for the theatres, was also the first journalist of his time.

The novel shares with poetry the predominant place in the modern literature of Portugal, and there *The Novel— Camillo Castello Branco.* are at least three novelists worthy to rank beside the masters of French and English fiction—viz., Camillo Castello Branco (1825-1890), Gomes Coelho, better known as *Julio Diniz*, and Eça de Queiróz. The first began his career with purely imaginative works, but he owes his fame to his novels of manners. In these he is partly idealist and partly realist, and he describes to perfection the domestic and social life of Portugal in the early part of the century that has just closed. The most national of recent Portuguese writers, his chief characteristics are fecundity, vigour, and narrative power, and his notable books include *O Romance de um homem rico*, *Amor de Perdição*, and the series entitled *Novellas do Minho*. He hardly attempted character study, and his novels are novels of incident, full of dramatic force, wild passion, tragic happenings, and caustic irony, relieved by flashes of humour, pathos, and almost womanly tenderness. The richness of his vocabulary is extraordinary, and the variety of his subjects recalls Balzac; while some of his writings in the domain of history and literary criticism are scarcely less remarkable than his romances, and *Bohemia do Espirito* may be cited as a case in point.

In *A familia Ingleza* Gomes Coelho (1839-1871) records his experiences of English society in Oporto, and his stories are at times curiously Brit-ish in feeling. Looking no farther than his romantic idealism, Portuguese critics are wont to complain that he saw through English spectacles; but though it may be conceded that *Diniz* had the good-natured sentimentality of Dickens, his sensitive nerves and his very nationality saved him from vulgarity and caricature. Herculano was juster to the young author than most of his countrymen, but certainly went too far when he called *As Pupillas do Sn^r Reitor* the "leading Portuguese romance of the

Gomes Coelho.

century." This book, and *Os Fidalgos da casa Mourisca*
and *A Morgadinha dos Canaviaes,* describe country life
and scenery with loving sympathy and exactness, and
hold the reader by a certain charm which Diniz has
a way of imparting to his characters and their background.   An intensely subjective writer, his tone is
moralising, his touch gentle, but he lacks the gift of
analysis, and is no psychologist.

Eça de Queiroz. Eça de Queiroz (1843-1900), after publishing some
admirable short stories, two of which have recently
appeared in an English dress, and a sensational tale, *The Mystery of the Cintra
Road,* in collaboration with Ramalho Ortigão, suddenly
sprang into the first rank of contemporary fiction by
a powerful though unpleasant book, *The Crime of
Father Amaro* (1875), which founded the Naturalist
school in Portugal.   It is interesting to remember
that his great romances, *Cousin Basil* and *Os Maias,*
were written during his occupancy of consular ap-
pointments in England, though they contain no trace
of English ideas.   *The Relic* conveys the impressions of his journey through Palestine, and suggests
his indebtedness to Flaubert, of whom he was perhaps the most brilliant disciple, but its mysticism
is something entirely new and personal.   Both *The
Relic* and *The Mandarin*—a fantastic variation of the
old theme of a man self-sold to Satan—are imaginative
works of a high order, and Queiroz proved the versatility of his talent by these books and by *The Correspondence of Fradique Mendes.*   This latter consists
of a series of epistles purporting to be addressed by a

T

smart man of the world to his relatives, on all sorts of topics, in some of which, like the letters on the Portuguese priesthood and the statesman Pacheco, acute observation is combined with brilliant satire and rich, delicately expressed humour. The latter portion of *The City and the Mountains* is generally praised for its simplicity, truth, and beautiful descriptions, and extracts from its pages are already quoted as classic examples of Portuguese prose; but to call this last book of Queiroz his best (as is sometimes done) betrays confusion of mind, because like cannot be compared to unlike, and so many-sided a writer defies these summary classifications. Taking his works as a whole, critics are agreed that he displayed an originality, analytical power, and artistic talents unequalled in the contemporary literature of his country, and as a creator of characters he was probably unsurpassed by any European writer of his generation. His supremacy was based on a thorough knowledge of life and the passions, which he derived from experience and not from books; and he was thus able, with his absolute command of the language, to present a complete picture of men and women of the upper, middle, and lower class in the 'seventies and 'eighties. As a novelist, Queiroz is the superior of Castello Branco, because he realised the complexity of the human mind and human emotions; and not being compelled, like that writer, to dash off book after book for newspapers, he could satisfy his artistic craving for perfection by polishing with infinite pains his comparatively few publications.

The historical romance still finds considerable acceptation in Portugal, and though many years have passed since their first appearance, *A mocidade de D. João V.*, by Rebello da Silva, and *Um anno na Corte*, by Andrade Corvo, still have readers.

Ramalho Ortigão, the chief art critic of the day, will be remembered principally for the *Farpas*, a

Ramalho Ortigão— Criticism.

series of satirical and humorous sketches of Portuguese society in all its exterior aspects, which he wrote in conjunction with Queiroz; Julio Cæsar Machado (1835-1890) made his mark by numerous publications of a gay and slightly satirical nature, while in the domain of pure literary criticism mention must be made of Lopes de Mendonça (1826-1865) and of Luciano Cordeiro (1844-1900), whose able monograph, *Soror Marianna*, dispelled the mystery surrounding the famous *Letters of a Portuguese Nun*, and showed the Beja Nun to be their authoress. Perhaps the most penetrating critical work of recent years has been done by a true psychologist and sound judge, Moniz Barreto, in his study on Oliveira Martins, and every student of the novel in Portugal must consult the illuminating essays by J. Pereira de Sampaio (*Bruno*), entitled *A Geração Nova*.

The Visconde de Santarem and J. J. Biker in geographical science and diplomatics edited publica-

History.

tions of permanent value; Luz Soriano produced painstaking histories of the reign of King José and of the Peninsular War; and Silvestre Ribeiro compiled an account of the scientific, literary, and artistic establishments of Portugal in sixteen volumes. Later writers, on similar subjects, like Rebello da Silva, and that versatile pair, Latino Coelho and Pinheiro Chagas, wrote at second-hand, and rank higher as stylists than as historians. Recently, however, Gama Barros and Costa Lobo have proved themselves worthy followers of Herculano— the first by a very learned *History of Public Administration in Portugal from the Twelfth to the Fifteenth Century*, the second by his *History of Society in Portugal during the Fifteenth Century*.

Oliveira Martins (1845-1894) possessed imagination, a rare capacity for general ideas, and a gift of picturesque narration ; and in his philosophic *Historia de Portugal, Portugal Contemporaneo, Vida de Nun' Alvarez*, and *Os filhos de D. João*, painted an admirable series of portraits of the great men of the nation. The interesting volumes of his *Bibliotheca das Sciencias Sociaes*, dealing with ancient and modern history and various sciences, display erudition, novelty of views, and critical independence, and they have contributed greatly to the instruction of his countrymen.

Even a rapid survey of Portuguese letters during the nineteenth century is enough to show the high quality and variety of the literary output in every department—the drama, perhaps, excepted ; and if neither poets nor prose writers have generally compelled the attention and appreciation of foreigners, it is because they had the misfortune to write in a little-known tongue. Moreover, there is hardly a branch of pure learning which lacks a Portuguese name of repute, and this is the more meritorious considering the scanty encouragement offered by a public limited in numbers, the educated portion of which is far more interested in politics than in books.

It would be possible to obtain from some specialist a similar survey of the last fifty years' output in *Modern Greek.* Greece, but the inducement here is not the same. As has been observed above, hardly any modern Greek writer during this period, with the exception of Demetrios Bikelas for his novel *Loukis Laras*, has attained in the rest of Europe anything like the reputation, say, of Trikoupis or Coraes earlier; and mere lists of names are of little use. Further, it really seems, on serious principles of literary criticism, unnecessary, if not worse, to admit to parallelism with genuine literary tongues a language which is, in fact, not a language at all. It is well known that we have on one side, as the vehicle of the greater part of modern Greek prose, a manufactured lingo which attempts, in the most painstaking and laudable manner, to repeat Dante's process of extracting or amalgamating an "Illustrious Literary Vulgar" out of the various dialects, combined with as much of the ancient tongue as will go with them, or sometimes as will not go. On the other, it seems to be admitted— and we need not wonder at it—that this composite *pastiche* is utterly unsuited to the purposes of poetry; and apparently most modern Greek poets now write in dialect. Even as regards the artificial language

itself, rather violent differences of opinion—the true
Greek *staseis*, whatever else in Greece may or may not
be true Greek—seem lately to have broken out. It
is almost impossible that great literature should be
written in such conditions as this, and one does not
gather, even from fanatics of Neo-Hellenism, that any
great literature is being written. On the other hand,
the game of appreciating what *is* written would hardly
seem worth the candle of familiarising oneself with
mere dialects; and though any one familiar with the
ancient language can read the artificial modern without much difficulty, he must be an oddly constructed
person if he can read it with any great pleasure.

CHAPTER VII.

THE NEW CANDIDATES.

EXCEPTION may be at once taken, if anybody pleases
to do so, to the adjective in the above title. No
Explanation of one of the literatures to be noticed in the
chapter title. present chapter was exactly new; one at
least of them is a form of one of the oldest literatures in Europe; more than one or two had been,
at this or that time, worthily presented.

But no one of them had at any time—except that
early time of which we can only speak by conjecture,
and at which European literature only existed in the
making—"possessed the *entrées*" among the greater

literatures of Europe. More than seventy years ago
De Quincey made a happy and very illuminative
definition of certain of the languages of Europe as
"completely equipped," and limited it to English,
French, German, Italian, and Spanish—under which
last he might or might not have included Portuguese. There can be no doubt, except among amiable fanatics, that these five (or six) languages have
held, and still to a great extent hold, the position of
an Upper House. Dutch and the Norse tongues in
a group would probably put forth candidature for
admission; but they can hardly be admitted for various reasons—the tendency of the best old Dutchmen
to use Latin, and the dialectic variations of the North-
men, being the chief. Russian, Polish, Hungarian,
and the others could hardly make any just pretence
till recently. Yet recently we have seen the work
of Ibsen and that of Tolstoi not merely arrest attention, but exercise influence, after a fashion which
cannot be neglected. And other minor literatures
(sometimes "political" only, and not possessing independent dialects), besides exhibiting signs of internal
fermentation, have contributed yeast to the older
literary worts of Europe. With two of those which
are in the curious case just noted we may begin,
afterwards following a rough geographical order.

Debating societies have frequently occupied themselves on more frivolous questions than
Switzerland. that "Whether Switzerland ought to be said
to have four literatures at least, or none?" For the

Swiss Confederation speaks at least four languages—
French, German, Italian, and Romansch (which, according to some, is itself two languages); and though
it writes little in the last, and not very much in
Italian, it writes much in the two others, especially
French, and its writers, if they are of merit, tend
to gravitate towards the headquarters of the languages in which they write. We have already dealt
with Keller and Meyer under German, with Cherbuliez and Scherer under French. But there is one
Swiss of our period who stands the test of "European
reputation," and who was wholly Swiss by birth and
residence, resisting even the maelstrom of Paris. And
this writer not merely attained European reputation,
but exemplified European time-tendencies, in hardly a
less degree than the four so often mentioned, though
with a slightly older and more limited cast. When

Amiel. people flew upon the *Journal Intime* of
Henri François Amiel, they comprehended,
or thought they comprehended, a spirit to which
they were alike—or would have liked to be. This
is scarcely a contradiction, though it may be a trans-
position of the Goethean phrase; and it explains a
great deal in literature. Amiel, who died in 1881,
and whose journal (or rather a selection from it) was
not published till after his death, had been born
sixty years earlier; and he represents, in an interesting fashion, what was called the "discouraged
generation of 1850," as one who did not outgrow
its discouragement, but welcomed, in part at least,
the different pessimism of later years. He was a

student, for some time before he became a professor, at Geneva; and he bestowed the rest of his life on professorial duties, publishing nothing except a few poems and essays, and exhibiting himself as a remarkable example of those who "cannot get ready,"— who have plenty of thought and plenty of phrase to clothe it in, but who cannot prevail upon the two to combine, or, even if they do so, to go forth upon the world and try their fortunes.

Amiel's journal, when it appeared, was vigorously *prôné* — the greatest enemies of French words in English may excuse a polite word instead of a rude one — by the greatest living critic in England, if not in Europe, Mr Matthew Arnold, and by one of the greatest critics in France, M. Scherer. But though it did not perhaps wholly deserve their championship, it did in part, and it moreover deserved some praise that M. Scherer at least did not give, though Mr Arnold's finer literary instinct did. Amiel, like most men, and especially most modern men, of parts, was a complex person; he was at least "three gentlemen at once," if not more. The first, the popular and generally admired Amiel, is a fanatic of "Nirvana," a sort of rehashed neo-Platonist who pants for absorption into "the Nothing which is the All," and who thus far is not despicable, but becomes a little so by endless, aimless, backboneless moping and moaning about his sufferings before he is absorbed. Only the Philistine, no doubt, has no such feelings; but it may be a question whether it is not Philistinism turned inside out to wrap your-

self in the *accidioso fummo* instead of not merely
doing the day's work in the day, but, as the Squire
of Amadis said to his master, " taking the joy as it
comes, and leaving the rest to God." The second
Amiel is a lover and describer of nature who deserves very high praise — higher than Mr Arnold,
who loves his old nature-moper Senancour better
than this new one, will allow, — and adds to the
long list of proofs, from Rousseau downwards, what
an unintelligent error it is to say that the inhabit-
ants of picturesque countries do not see their
picturesqueness. The third is a literary critic of
quite extraordinary acuteness and range, who is prevented by his general paralysis of moping from doing
more than jot down scattered impressions and *aperçus*
of literature. This last capacity is by far his highest
and best; and, as will be seen, it once more brings
a chief illustration of the period in one particular
country under one of the two distinguishing tendencies, those of Fiction and Criticism, which characterise that period generally.

Belgian literature is, again, an obviously difficult
subject. It divides itself into Flemish literature,
Belgium. which may be fought for as a mere off-
shoot of Dutch, and French, which stands
in a relation of the clearest unclearness to French
proper.[1] In the former the one great name of the
nineteenth century, beyond all controversy, is that of

[1] The third dialect, "Walloon," is hardly as literary even as
Romansch.

the novelist Hendrik Conscience (1812-1883), a
Flemish writers Romantic of the best water after the earlier
—Conscience. and simpler kind, and an admirable teller
of stories, not a few of which have found their way
by translation into all the chief literary languages.
His best work, *Phantasy* (1837), *De Leeuw van Vlan-
dren* (next year), and the series of tales beginning
with *Hoe men Schilder Wordt* (1843), belongs to the
period behind us, but, as the dates above will show,
he is still ours. One of the quaintest traits of
Fortune (who is so often quaint) was the passing of the
later days of this healthiest and sanest of writers as
keeper of the Wiertz Museum at Brussels, wherein,
by artistic anticipation, some of the wildest excesses
of recent literature are depicted.

But the literary language of the kingdom of Belgium is French, and in regard to this things more
curious than strange happened. For a
French writers. time—even a long time—it was possible
legally for Belgian publishers to pirate French literature wholesale, and they abode by the law staunchly.
Everybody acquainted with the lives and letters of
the great writers of France during the earlier and
middle part of the century knows their bitter cries
about the brigandage practised on them; and it may
be feared that Belgian editions were pretty freely
current then, and for some time afterwards, in England. The natural result followed—that there was no
market for native talent, even if native talent existed,
which it may or may not have done. The Second
Empire, however—which had not much to thank men

of letters for—relieved them of this tax, and about
1855 accordingly, with a curious unanimity, persons
of literary faculty thought it worth while to be born
in Belgium. From this year date MM. Lemonnier,
Verhaeren, and the late M. Rodenbach, while M.
Eeckhoud was born the year before, though M.
Maeterlinck, who has made himself the greatest
vogue of all, waited till 1862. This unanimity had,
however, one drawback—that it exposed them as they
came to literary age to the full influence of Naturalism, to which some have succumbed.

Still, they and some others have earned for so
small a country a remarkable place in the most recent
European literature, such as it is. The novels of MM.
Lemonnier and Eeckhoud might indeed have been
better—they could not in some respects have been
worse — if M. Zola had not preceded them ; but
though they have been praised absurdly, it would
The younger
novelists and be more absurd to deny them energy and
poets. a certain accomplishment. With the
merits of MM. Verhaeren and Rodenbach
there is no need to deal obliquely. The former, in
a long series of mostly small volumes, from *Les
Flamandes* (1883) to *Les Heures d'après Midi* (1905),
and M. Rodenbach in somewhat fewer, of which
Bruges la Morte (1892) is the chief, have carried
nearly as far as it will go the system of short poems
—word-pictures rather than poems merely—on which
the whole century has been more and more con-
centrating its strength, and to which the famous
sonnets of Bowles (many degrees "under-proof" as

they are) inspirited Coleridge even before its commencement. M. Rodenbach, as everybody who knows the place will admit, could not have had a more admirable *foyer* for his work than Bruges, and the results of his brooding over it are distinctly fascinating. Whether the "larger air" does not sometimes make the want of it felt, is a question which one puts with some reluctance, and not in the least in the way of denigration. It may seem paradoxical or ungracious to say that the same question suggests itself in regard to M. Verhaeren's work, in spite of its greater range of apparent subject. The range of subject *is* greater, but the same can hardly be said of the range of treatment. The tendency of modern times towards division of labour asserts itself unduly, and the poet of these isolated impressions reminds one a little of the cook who is said to be kept in great establishments, exclusively for the accomplishment of *pommes frites ;* yet there are not many better things than really good chip-potatoes, crisp, dry, and bladdery.

The time for judging M. Maeterlinck has not yet come. His unquestionable affectation—though there are worse things than affectation when there is something behind it—and the wild excesses of *engouement* which greeted his earlier work, can affect the judgment of no competent critic unfavourably ; but they might in more ways than one affect the reception of that judgment. And inasmuch as he is still almost a young man, and has already described a rather curious orbit from poetry, through

M. Maeterlinck.

drama of a kind, to prose, it might be desirable to see what future work he produces, and to take it in conjunction with that which he has produced, before attempting to grasp him. On one point, to which we shall return in the Conclusion, there can be no doubt, —that his work, almost the latest of the century in unquestionable distinction, shows what an utter mistake it is to suppose that Romanticism is dead. Everything about M. Maeterlinck, down to his very zoological observation, is coloured, dyed, permeated with Romanticism of the purest and most unmitigated kind. It is not merely in his mediæval nomenclature and costuming that this exists and consists; not in his eccentricity; not in his divergence from established models of any kind of speech; but in the constant effort to suffuse and diffuse Imagination all over the work—no matter what its substance may be. Idealist-Impressionist is perhaps as good a label as can be devised for M. Maeterlinck. Now, Romanticism has always been Idealism; and long before the name was ever hit upon it has always been—as long as it exists it always must be—Impressionist. A parallel between Æschylus and Maeterlinck may remind some too much of a famous examination paper, and perhaps those who admire the Belgian most are not very familiar with the Greek. But let them seek and they will find.

The Naturalist movement appears also to have affected Holland very forcibly; but more forcibly than fruitfully, according to the verdicts of the most

ndulgent judges. Potgieter, mentioned in the last
volume, had survived till a few years before
Holland. the influence was felt, and Hofdijk, the poet-
playwright, Anna Bosboom-Toussaint, the novelist,
and others, still later. But little work of the third
quarter of the century became European, the chief
exception being a ponderous purpose-novel (1876)
attacking Dutch policy in the East, entitled *Max
Havelaar*, and written by an author who called himself "Multatuli," but whose real name was Edward
Douwes Dekker. This book, like most things of the
kind, had a wide circulation, and it has even been
spoken of as showing genius. In so far as it is possible to judge from translation, the present writer
would be disposed to describe it as a well-intentioned
but extremely heavy performance, in which the purpose and the materials have altogether failed to be
brought under artistic transformation and control.
The work of "Maarten Maartens" has been mostly
in foreign languages, but the novels of Marcellus
Emants (*b.* 1848) are very well spoken of, as well
as those of F. van Eeden. But the only fruit of the
new or modern movement who is described, without
hesitation, and with colour of reason, as more than
promising, is Louis Couperus (*b.* 1863), a poet and
novelist who seems to be expressing in Dutch that
"creole" influence which has been powerful in the
Romance languages, but which, curiously enough, has
had much less effect on English. Of other novelists
of newest schools, Querido seems to be most in the
mouths of men.

Of the literatures of Scandinavia, the first place must be given — on the one-man principle, which
Norwegian. literature is bound to observe — to the most modern, in a sense, of the three. Norwegian, by its proper name "Norse," is, of course, heir to the treasures of _Old_ Norse, one of the greatest literary languages of early modern Europe; but here it has competitors in Swedish and Danish, not to mention French, German, and English. After mediæval times Norway had hardly any literature at all, and the best known literary language of modern Norway is a partly artificial tongue—Danish with little difference. But when Norway was separated politically from Denmark and coupled with a partner by no means beloved, — Denmark had not been much so, but these things get forgotten,—much really good work, as has been told in the last volume, was done. Indeed the leeway was partly made up during the first half of the nineteenth century.[1]

At present Ibsen obscures all other Norse writers; but it was not so thirty years ago, when the conten-
Björnson and others. tion for the primacy—among those who knew anything about the two—between Ibsen and Björnson was sharp. To these we shall add the names Kjelland and Lie, and this may suffice. Three of the four must put up with summary handling; Ibsen, in any work dealing with European

[1] There has, however, been a more recent attempt to make spoken Norse into a literary tongue quite different from Danish. The chief writer in it, who is very highly spoken of by some good critics, appears to be Arne Garborg.

literature, must be accorded the place due to one who has exercised European influence, and who is a European "sign." Of the other three, Björnstjerna Björnson (*b.* 1832) has still the highest reputation. He attained it, and has, where it is at all well founded, maintained it, by those studies in pure local colour and manners which have been so popular with the last three generations; which, after Scott had shown their great capabilities, were taken up on a lower level by Auerbach and others; and which have continued, until we shall doubtless shortly have a literature of suburbs and villages, just as we have already one not merely of provinces but of towns and counties. *Synnöve Solbakken* (1857) founded his fame in this respect, and he continued it with *Arne* (1858) and others of the same kind, changing later to extensive and ambitious novels in semi-naturalist manner, of which *In God's Way* (1860), and the book whose grand Norwegian title, "The Flags are Flying in Borough and Bay," has been translated in English to *The Heritage of the Kurts* (1884), are the chief.

The great characteristic of Björnson, who has been also a prolific dramatist and a poet, especially a song-writer, of no little charm, is (outside his poetry) a certain roughness, sometimes degenerating into brutality. This, without much loss of real power, is considerably softened in Jonas Lie (*b.* 1833), whose *The Pilot and his Wife* and *The Family at Gilje* are his most famous books. Whether Lie could be reckoned as more than a second-class novelist in English or French may be doubted; he certainly does not ap-

proach the universalising touch of Tourguenieff in
Russian or of Valera in Spanish. But he has the
root of the matter in him, and in another country
would probably have had the flower. The best
artist of the three appears, to the present writer, to
be Alexander L. Kjelland (*b.* 1849), author of *Garman
and Worsë* (1880), *Arbeidsfolk,* and a large number
of short stories. Instead of endeavouring at a crude
photography, as so many recent writers have done,
or trying merely to translate French ways, Kjelland
seems to have taken the better line of blending the
natural Norse *märchen* of Andersen and others with
French literary accomplishment, and to have in no
small degree succeeded. But this is probably hopeless heresy in the eyes of thorough-going believers
in the remarkable writer to whom we next come.

Henrik Ibsen [1] had lived for nearly sixty years, and
had written for nearly thirty, before he attracted notice
outside his own country ; for he had been
Ibsen. born in 1828, and had published his first
drama, *Catilina,* in 1850. But he did no very remarkable work till the 'sixties; and the series of dramas of
which, in a certain sense and for a certain time, " all
Europe rang from side to side," did not begin till he
was nearly fifty years old. The habit, prevalent on
the Continent generally, of regarding the theatre as
a sort of national necessity, and plays as things that

---

[1] This notice is mainly based on the translations of Ibsen's *Prose
Dramas,* 4 vols., and of *Love's Comedy, Brand, Peer Gynt, Rosmersholm, The Lady from the Sea, Hedda Gabler, The Master Builder,
Little Eyolf, J. G. Borkman,* and *When We Dead Awake,* which have
appeared by various hands, with H. Jaeger's *Life,* also translated.

ought to be supplied like gas or water, gave him early opportunities of playwrights' work. But the earliest section of his drama (1852-64), in so far as it is accessible (it has not all been translated, nor, I believe, all published even in Norse), is not of a very characteristic kind. It consists of historical or quasi-historical romantic dramas, *Fru Inger til Ostrat*, *Haermaendene paa Helgeland*, *Gildet paa Solhaug*,[1] *Kongsemnerne*, &c., in which the influence of Oehlen-schläger has been generally recognised, but which do

His periods—the historical dramas, &c.

not, in translation, reveal any very novel or extraordinary powers. About his thirtieth year, however, more individual developments showed themselves in two different directions. The first was towards dramatic satire of manners and actual life, the second and higher towards mystical drama of the *Faust* kind, imbued with a strongly imaginative or at least fanciful criticism of humanity generally, and of its attitudes towards religion, love, morals, and so forth. The first, after a sort of *coup d'essai* in *Kaerlighedens Komodie* (*The Comedy of Love*, 1862), was for a time staved off by the great developments of the second, *Brand* (1866) and *Peer Gynt* (1867), and then after a fresh experiment in *De Unges Forbund* (1869), claimed the dramatist for the rest of his career (1877-1906) in the series which made so much stir; while *Emperor and Galilean* (1873), dating just before

[1] I do not know this, which is highly praised. There is clever character-drawing in *Kongsemnerne* (*Royal Candidates*), but the character of Hjordis, the degenerate Brynhild of the *Warriors at Helgeland*, is the most notable. Some, however, put *Fru Inger* highest of all.

this later group, exhibits a sort of combination of the mystical, the historical, and the satiric. We may take the experiments in comedy first, then the two romantic mystery-plays, *Emperor and Galilean* by itself, and the "series" last.

The comedies, like the early historical plays, probably lose more than the others by translation : as *The comedies* translated they are certainly not very *of manners.* effective. The manners and situations are *too* local,[1] and whatever literary merit may invest, conceal, or recommend this locality in the original, is of course absent. It is difficult to say much of them, except that here is obviously a clever man, still rather "young," with a good deal of satiric faculty, and a rather turbid and topsy-turvy view of life itself, critical in one sense, uncritical to the last degree in others.

A more particular examination may, however, be given to *The Comedy of Love,* which is spoken of with *The Comedy* much admiration by Ibsenites, and is said *of Love.* by some of them who know the original to be especially well presented in the English version by Professor Herford and Mr Archer.[2] It is not merely in verse, but evidently to some extent in poetry—though not yet the poetry of *Peer Gynt,* or even of *Brand.* In action a story of student and boarding-house life, and, consequently, of middle-class Norwegian society, it has unluckily for motive even more of a *secret de Polichinelle* than most of Ibsen's plays.

[1] " The local situation " is a catchword in *The League of Youth.*
[2] London, 1900.

We have heard for many centuries that "the light, light love has wings to fly At suspicion of a bond," though that particular phrasing may be modern. Such a (to Ibsenites) unexpected person as Dryden once put it in a fashion which would arouse ecstasies of admiration if Mr Smith or Mr Brown said it to-day (especially as there are half a dozen different forms of it in the same passage), "The only way to keep us new to each other is never to enjoy." On this principle the young author Falk and his beloved Svanhild love and part, Svanhild making a prudent marriage with the "wholesale merchant," Guldstad, who is not in the least a dupe, but, on the contrary, spontaneously expounds the philosophy of the whole matter. With this half-passionate, half-cynical central motive are mingled divers merry humours of a long-engaged couple, of Svanhild's more (or less) practical sister, Anna, and her divinity student; of a country clergyman, Strawman, who *has* married for love, and is in consequence the victim of a dull wife and an endless family, &c. The last sentence of the last paragraph, which was as a matter of fact written before the writer had read *Love's Comedy*, fits it exactly, though with some added praise for poetic glimmers and flashes. But to the literary historian the most interesting thing about it is that while its humour and satire are in parts very Dickensish, its poetry is quite extraordinarily "Spasmodic." Falk, both in character and expression, reminds us of the heroes of Alexander Smith and Sydney Dobell almost startlingly; and the date, be it remembered, is 1862. I need not say that I am not insinuating plagiarism: there is no need of that, and there would be no interest in it to me. But as a fact in comparative literature it is very interesting indeed.

It is very different with *Brand* and *Peer Gynt*. They also must lose a very great deal of their *The* literary and poetical beauty in transla- *"Mysteries."* tion, but so much remains that the original must needs be very considerable. They are, especially *Peer Gynt*, aggressively romantic and obscure—so much so that any one who finds "difficulty" in the second part of *Faust* (which, as has been said, must have had a great influence upon them) [1] had better not attempt even *Brand*, and will probably be aghast or indignant at *Peer Gynt*. The former has most of the practical-satiric in it, and is only in parts mystical. Brand is a village parson, full of the undigested mixture of philanthropy, free-thought, and mysticism which has developed itself in many (including almost all non-Catholic) branches of the Christian Church during the nineteenth century; and he fights with the materialism, the officialism, and so forth, of his parish and his mother, sacrificing also the health and happiness of his wife and child. The hero of *Peer Gynt* is said by Norwegians to be a mystical adumbration of the typical Norwegian (of whom it may be very shrewdly suspected that he deserves *ni cet excès d'honneur ni cette indignité*). The piece

---

[1] This influence has been denied, but the denial almost "disables the judgment" in literary criticism of the deniers.

has also been said to be "a ball aimed straight at the heart of Romanticism," of which once more it may be remarked that in that case the modern bullet must have been endowed with some of the virtues of the ancient sword, and be able to cure the wounds it has made. For there hardly exists in literature more essentially Romantic work than *Peer Gynt*. But we have already seen the same state of things in regard to Heine, to Flaubert, and to Thackeray. In both plays the characteristic scenery of Norway is powerfully if phantasmagorically depicted; and in *Peer Gynt* the wandering hero is brought into contact with all sort of persons, human, allegorical, supernatural, and miscellaneous, after a nightmare fashion, which is highly effective when it is taken with due generality, and sufficiently tedious when it is subjected to chapter-and-verse "explanation." These two plays are, according to the purely literary view of literature, and perhaps not according to that only, Ibsen's greatest works by far. In *Peer Gynt*, especially, he is a poet, and one of the few whom translation cannot hide.

The huge *Emperor and Galilean*, really a pair of plays on the Emperor Julian, is one of the least

Emperor and Galilean.

satisfactory of Ibsen's works. This is almost a necessary result of the fact that the historical picture, the satirical sermonising, and the mystical motives jostle in it irreconcilably,—so much so, that two quite different drifts have been detected in it by different persons. One is the establishment of Christianity by the very effect of Julian's efforts against it; the other the adumbration of a third "kingdom," as different from Christianity as from Cæsarism, upon which Ibsen's hopes are fixed.

But there is no doubt that if Ibsen had died after writing this piece—nay, if he had died or left off *The social-ethical series.* writing after *Brand* and *Peer Gynt*—he would never have attained European popularity. People in general do not like the eccentric when it is difficult and poetical; they are very frequently attracted by it when it is comparatively easy, prosaic rather than otherwise, and somewhat scandalous. One may dare the wrath of Ibsenites by warranting this as scarcely too harsh a description of the series of works which Ibsen produced after 1877. The first of these, the *Pillars of Society*, belongs still to much the same class as the *Comedy of Love* and the *Young Men's League*, but with greater infusion of topsy - turvy morality. This last reigns supreme in the plays which followed in rapid succession. In the first and most famous, *The Doll's House*, a frivolous and criminal (though not conjugally criminal) young wife discovers that she does not love her husband (who certainly is one of the poorest of creatures), that she has "duties towards herself," and that she must leave him and her children — which she does. In *Ghosts* the doctrine of heredity is brought on the stage in singularly offensive fashion. An *Enemy of the People* is rather political, and reverts a little to the earlier style. The *Wild Duck*, one of the most

powerful of Ibsen's later plays, has no general drift
that can be easily explained, but is a sort of tragi-
comedy (with the tragedy predominating) of grime,
including two masterly presentments—one of a selfish,
worthless, phrase-making husband, and the other (the
most original thing Ibsen has done) of an unselfish,
affectionate, "notable" wife, whose conscience, however, goes as slipshod as her person and her tongue.
Their luckless child, Hedvig, whose suicide concludes
the play, is really pathetic. *Rosmersholm* reverts to
something like the theme of *Ghosts*, but blends with
it some of the mystical quality of *Peer Gynt*. The
Rosmers have a habit of committing suicide off a
bridge in the family garden when a fatal white horse
appears. The last of them, an unfrocked clergyman, duly drees the family weird with an unduly
beloved housekeeper, who has, by her own confession,
induced his wife to take the same course before.

The Lady from the Sea gives us something of an
escape from what Goethe used to call "Lazaret-litera-
ture," but not from that of something like the lunatic
asylum. It is a sort of contrast - complement to
The Doll's House. A wife has betrothed herself
before her marriage to a mysterious seaman, but
has jilted him and married a doctor. The first lover
turns up and claims her, and she insists that she is
free to go with him *if she likes*. Dr Wangel has the
wit (or the remembrance of old stories) to say "Go,
if you like," so of course she does not like, and re-
jilts the unlucky mariner. There is minor by - play
of some merit, and the whole, though preposterous,

is sometimes amusing, and never quite disagreeable.[1]
As a white companion for the black *Wild Duck*, it
perhaps shows Ibsen's powers best of this batch of
plays. In the two which followed, preposterousness
ran riot, with hardly an alleviation of real pathos
or real comedy. The heroine of *Hedda Gabler* is the
daughter of a certain general (who had a pair of
pistols) and the wife of a man of letters. As a
matter of course she loves another man of letters,
who is unsatisfactory, and who, when she has lent
him one of the pistols to shoot himself with, disgusts
her by doing so in an unpoetical part of his person.
Nor is this her only ill fate, for having destroyed
manuscript which her lover had composed under the
inspiration of another woman, she finds that her rival
and her own husband can reconstruct it from rough
drafts. So there is nothing to do but to use the other
of "General Gabler's pistols" on herself—poetically, it
is to be hoped. As for *The Master Builder*, it defies
abstract criticism and, though it has been parodied,
parody. For sheer *tolles Zeug*, "mad stuff,"—as the
Germans, who know this stuff well, put it,—there
is nothing like it in literature among the works
written by presumably sane writers for presumably
sane readers.[2]

---

[1] Accordingly, the Ibsenites are rather contemptuous of it.

[2] Yet there is one thing in *Hedda Gabler*—the ludicrous-pathetic
attempt to restore an aristocratic ideal in a hopelessly democratic and
vulgarised society,—which, though it was perhaps but dimly present
to the author, and is naturally ignored by most of his admirers, is
noteworthy. And, if we take *The Master Builder* with Zola's
L'Œuvre, it is for thoughts.

The three last plays published in Ibsen's life-
time showed no general differences from the batch
The three last plays. just reviewed; but there was at least in
the last, one of those curious reversions
which are not infrequently seen in the work of men
of genius. For that Ibsen was a man of genius is
a fact which even his idolaters cannot obscure, though
the mists of a certain kind of incense are of all mists
most obscuring, as well as most offensive.

Little Eyolf (1895) has perhaps most of the *irritating* quality of its immediately earlier companions;
though this quality is not, as in *Hedda Gabler* and
The Master Builder, almost unrelieved. The hero,
Alfred Allmers, belongs to the idiot division of Ibsen's
wrong-headed characters. He has a perfectly charming wife, Rita, the most delightful of Ibsen's heroines
(till she also goes mad at the end), who adores him,
idiot as he is, till he, being a cad as well as an
idiot, tells her that he no longer adores her. He
has an attractive though lame child, the name-giver
of the piece, whose lameness has been indirectly
caused after a fashion which Ibsen reveals with
almost more than *Doll's House* delicacy. He has
a "Great Book" about human responsibilities which,
not out of a sense of human responsibilities themselves, but merely because he is too stupid, he does
not write. And he has an interesting, enigmatic
sister, Asta, who is not his sister, and knows it
though he does not; and who would probably give
the piece another characteristic smirch but for its
central incident, or catastrophe, or whatever it is to

be called. This is the drowning of Little Eyolf, in consequence of the sorceries of a "Rat-Wife" (rather agreeable and Peer Gyntish), his lameness, and the unpopularity of the Allmerses with the fisher population, who will not rescue him if they could. Poor Rita would console herself with her husband, but is not allowed. Revelations of unpleasantness are made on all sides; but the ending which some may expect does not happen. Asta goes off with a cheerful[1] "Engineer Borgheim," whom one does not envy much; and Rita, for whom one is extremely sorry, submits to join the offensive idiot, her unloving husband, in an allegorical expedition "to the peaks," and a more commonplace "work of repentance" in improving the lot of the fisher population. This last may seem surprisingly un-Ibsenic, but there is something to match it in the others of this last triad.

John Gabriel Borkman (1897) is said to have caused some anti-Ibsenites up to its date to find salvation. It is certainly more powerful and much less irritating than *Little Eyolf;* and it again contains a heroine— Ella Rentheim—who attracts if she does not charm. Borkman himself belongs to the other division from that which Allmers graces. He is not an idiot, but a criminal lunatic. He has a monomania—the development of the metallic riches (if any) of all his country's mountains. To do this he has made fraudulent use of the funds of the bank of which he was a director, and is a (released) convict. But

---

[1] "What a joy it is to be a roadmaker!"

he has done much worse than this. Loving (if one can so profane the word of words) and being loved by one of two sisters of wealth, Gunhild and Ella Rentheim, he finds that this one, Ella, is also loved and coveted by a man who can, he thinks, make or mar his schemes. He hands, or tries to hand, her over (though she does not at the time know it), and marries Gunhild. This latter is a violent and selfish woman who, when her own fortune is lost by her husband's misdoing (though through Ella's generosity she is still able to live in the family mansion), vows eternal *non* - forgiveness ; and on his release and return practically will have nothing to do with him. On the other hand, she adores their son Erhart, and educates him to live only for her. The end here is again a mixture of the extravagant and the common-place. Mrs Borkman is punished by Erhart's running away with a rich and handsome *divorcée*—one of Ibsen's most offensive female characters,—just as might have happened in the old poetical-justice days. Borkman dies of a "metal hand" (heart-disease the prosaic will probably say), in a wild scene among the snow, with Ella, whom he has already informed of his own mad baseness and madness generally. Except in the point touched on, the play is as "preposterous" as any of them; but the way in which Ella's unpretentious heroism—not in the least goody-goodiness—and hapless case are held up in a sort of succession of background-contrasts to the selfish vile-ness of other characters, is certainly arresting. The piece may rank with *The Wild Duck* as the most *powerful* of the group; and it shows, as most of them do, that the dramatist can draw a woman when he chooses, while in no single one of his plays has he ever drawn a man. This, of course, is most unusual : it would be well if he had cultivated the unusual in no other way.

The very short curtain-piece *When We Dead Awake* (1900), a piece which would shut up into almost nothing if the elaborate stage directions were cut out, has the simplest of situations and the smallest possible list of characters. Professor Rubek, a great sculptor, has married a young wife, Maia, whom he bores, and who no longer amuses him. Irene, a former model and, in a way, love of his, has married one or more Russians, and gone mad or nearly so, but has a Sister of Mercy as keeper. They meet—the rubber being made up, in justice to Maia, by a "Mr Ulfheim," a sportsman-Lothario. Irene and Rubek talk immensely about "Our Child," who is, in fact, a sculptured group. Maia and Ulfheim go bear-hunting — other diversions not excluded. They, in coming down a dangerous mountain, with a storm threatening, meet the others going up. Ulfheim behaves rather well for the vulgar libertine that he has been represented, but cannot stop them. He gets Maia down, and her song of freedom is heard. Rubek and Irene are whelmed in an avalanche. *Voilà tout* — except more Peer Gyntishness (not unwelcome). And so, after a hundred years in one case, and fifty in another, the last word of this Newest Prophet is the "Chop and change ribs *à*

la mode Germanorum" of Canning, crossed with the
Excelsior of Longfellow! [1]

The space given to these works is due to the
often-mentioned fact that Ibsen, with Tolstoi, Zola,
His general position. and Nietzsche, makes up the group of
writers who produced the greatest effect
in the European literature of the last quarter of the
nineteenth century, and who, in effect, gave pretext,
if not actually excuse, for the charge of positive
morbid degeneration brought against the end of that
century generally. A more charitable, and perhaps
even a more philosophical, explanation of their popularity may be found in the fact that all four are
obvious "last stages" (with the irregular and exaggerated flash of the last stage, and something of the
smoke and smell of the stage after) of the burning of
the Romantic candle, which had always burnt somewhat
fitfully and flaringly. But it is difficult to think that
much of Ibsen's work will retain, in the calm judgment of posterity, a very high place in literature.
Of what may be the merits of his form the present
writer cannot judge. But his matter, thought, scheme,
creative and critical attitude, are certainly not of great
value. They, in fact, present, as a kind of second
childhood, a return to something like the first as it
existed in the German *Sturm-und-Drang* school of a

---

[1] Oddly enough, there had apparently been something of this moral
(which is not to be found in *Love's Comedy*), and even a little of the
scenery, but far more sanely and poetically treated, in a very early
piece, *Sancthansnatten* (*St John's Eve*), which was acted in 1853, and has
not, or had not when Jaeger wrote, been printed. It did not succeed,
but, from the biographer's account, I have always wished to read it.

century earlier. Even the elaborate stage-directions show their ancestry; and there are speeches and passages, in *Rosmersholm* more particularly, which, with the slightest possible change of dialect and setting, might come out of *Stella* or *The Robbers*. It may be added that nothing in Canning's *Rovers* itself caricatures *Hedda Gabler* or *The Master Builder* so much as several things in that anticipate the criticism of these. That it is possible to be too commonsense-sane, too merely orderly in thought, too conventional, need certainly not be denied. But it has hardly been left for the twentieth century to discover, and it is not likely that the thirtieth will be able to demolish the counter-proposition, that it is possible to be too unconventional, too preposterous, too *insane*.

It is, one may fear, impossible to deal with Ibsen in a manner which shall not seem to Ibsenites flippant and unworthy. The element of topsy-turviness in him is so all-pervading—the demand that such a thing as humour shall be banished from his world so constant—that those who are not prepared to stand, as the satirist has said, "erect on their passionate heads," and who cannot for the very life of them shut their eyes to the ludicrous, simply cannot take him seriously. Parodies of him are of course tempting and common; there is one well-known set in especial. Yet one may in all seriousness doubt whether, if parts only of even this set, and the corresponding originals, happened to turn up in the fortieth century, without any apparatus but the bare texts, it would be a very foolish mare's-nester

Characteristics of his work and its partisans.

X

of a critic who took the parody for the original and
the original for the parody. Of the larger part of
Hedda Gabler and of *The Master Builder* this is especially true, and of no small parts of many of the
others. As for "morals," we need not trouble ourselves much with them here. Ibsen, it is said, very
vehemently, and no doubt with perfect honesty, dis-
claimed any prophetic, priestly, or preacherly attitude:
he merely observed, he said, and interpreted his observation in the manner required by his art. Further,
critics of his—and not unfavourable critics—have
pointed out that such "message" as he has is nothing
like such a message as his more illiterate admirers
think,—that much of it, for instance, is in such a
very popular writer as George Sand, with "griminess"
substituted for George Sand's rose-pink and sky-blue
sentimentality and sensuality. But the griminess is
certainly there; and the topsy-turviness is there still
more, together with a third thing which is specially
queer in their company,—a quite extraordinary *puer-
ility*. Good or bad, naughty or nice, the characters,
with very few exceptions, are never "grown-ups"
at all.

It would, however, be either pusillanimous or impertinent, or both, to neglect the demurrer. "Then
how is it that so many—and some who seem to be
pillars—uphold Ibsen as one of the greatest of men
of letters?" There is not the slightest disinclination
to face this question here. In the first place, and
without the least intention *cauponari bellum*, to cap-
itulate or compromise or hedge, let it be repeated

that there *is* genius in Ibsen. It is unmistakable in *Brand* and *Peer Gynt*; it is not absent from the nastiest of all the pieces, *Ghosts*; it is certainly present in the *Wild Duck*; it flashes and glimmers amid the crudities and the perversities and the childishnesses of most of the others. And it is not the most damning peculiarity of *die verdammte Race* that, when it does not neglect or ignore genius altogether, it is apt to swallow it blindly with whatsoever adulteration and alloy. The real *critic*, the real separator and discerner, is a very rare person indeed,—*tant pis* or *tant mieux* according to taste and fancy. This is the good side of the matter.

But there are other sides not so good. There is, beyond all doubt, the childish delight in heterodoxy, in unconventionality, in "being naughty," which rises up to meet and greet the corresponding other childishnesses in Ibsen himself. There is the appalling eclipse of humour—"visible at Greenwich" and away from Greenwich — which has been for years past noticed, and which shows no sign of clearing away. There is the touching (if only it were not so ludicrous!) desire for some anti-dogma — for a solemn form of Catechism, and another of Confirmation, in morality and religion turned upside down. And there is something else in some of the teachers of the public which is perhaps more special and more noteworthy than these things, which are of general application.

It will almost (not quite, no doubt) invariably be found that the admirers of Ibsen manifest, or have manifested, either a positive dislike, or an uneasy

jealousy, of the great classical authors of the past.
Of the "classics" in the limited sense they most
commonly (though, of course, not universally or anything like it) know nothing or next to nothing; and
it is no doubt comforting to have something to set
against your Greeks and your Romans. Of the more
modern classics they may know something, but they
(again generally) for the most part regard them as
distressingly *not*-modern. "The Modern Spirit" cried
for its Shakespeare, and the Modern Spirit says that
it has got him. In the choice of sticks wherewith to
beat something or somebody, when the beating is
ardently desired, criticism is proverbially apt to be a
little forgotten. And the state of the case is perhaps
revealed most clearly by those who are intelligent
enough not to make animus or paradox too clearly
evident. One distinguished person, writing in English
on the death of the dramatist, remarked that "what
Shakespeare had done for mediæval, Ibsen had done
for modern mankind," or words to that effect—the
"mediæval" being certainly textual. A slight examination of this remarkable utterance, which probably
crystallises "Ibsenism" as well as anything could do,
may fitly conclude this notice. We are not in a bad
position for making it, since we deal with mediæval as
well as modern life in its literary aspect, not merely
in this series, but in this very volume.

The "virtue" (or vice) of "mediæval" cannot want
much exposition. It is, of course, inaccurately
enough used, for Shakespeare had and could have
no knowledge of things or persons mediæval, except

in virtue of his semi-divine knowledge of man in general. But it is meant, of course, to convey the idea that Shakespeare's man is obsolete, while Ibsen's is not. To the persons who think so, this may be the case. But they have this little difficulty before them. Ten generations, themselves changing at least as much as generations usually do, have each agreed that Shakespeare's man is *not* obsolete. In the present generation, very numerous representatives, of whom it may be said with the strictest ἐπιείκεια that they possess brains quite as good as any Ibsenite's, find him, if it be possible, less obsolete than ever. But the Ibsenites have not given themselves time to find out whether even a single generation accepts their man as genuine and adequate. It certainly does not—yet.

Moreover, there is this further *aporia* for them. Their man can be perfectly well equated in terms of our—that is, Shakespeare's—man. He is, as a rule, an exceedingly poor specimen, weak in morals, weaker in mind, quite astonishingly weak in speech. But Shakespeare would have known all about him—would have "put you in," as the old phrase went, a regiment of the article at a few months' notice. Will anybody say that Shakespeare's men—and women—are expressible in Ibsenite symbols? that Ibsen could even have conceived them? Take Hamlet, perhaps the most Ibsenitish of them all. Could all the Four Winds of the Spirit, searching the ends of the earth and bringing their results together, construct us an Ibsenite Hamlet of any serious substance?

No! the result of the examination is fatal. Ibsen may be of an age—it does not say much for the age, but let it be so. He is not for all time. He is parochial, and not of a very large or a very distinguished parish. He is, in that parish, a frequenter chiefly of the hospital and the asylum. Stagecraft he may have. A certain poetical gift he certainly has, though he throws it from him for the most part. Given his types—if you can call them types—of character, he knows how to manage them: *sibi constant*, though the results of their consistency are truly wonderful. He has certain stabs or twinges of truth to nature now and then. But the age has certainly done better with even Nietzsche for its Bacon than with Ibsen for its Shakespeare.

Sweden, which immediately before, and for half a century after, the union with Norway had been far ahead in literature of her unwilling yoke-fellow, has recently fallen back somewhat in the European reputation of her men and women of letters. No one in this respect has succeeded Runeberg and Frederika Bremer, or even Emilie Carlen, who lived till 1892. The poets Rydberg and Snoilsky, King Oscar himself, and others scarcely took the vacant places; and though, about twenty or five-and-twenty years ago, the wave of Naturalism reached this extremity of Europe as it reached others, it does not seem to have had any immediately following results of remarkable quality. The oldest, and to all appearance the most noteworthy, representative of

Swedish.

this new school, August Strindberg, was born as far back as 1849. He is, it seems, a Naturalist-misogynist, a Nietzschean after a sort, a convert to all the madder 'isms which have pullulated during the period, and a rover through all the fields of literature. His driving power seems to be pretty generally admitted; but whether it is under the command of any helm, or simply hurries the ship anywhither, seems to be more doubtful. It would appear, on the whole, that the country is going through a very natural transition-period after the blossoming-time from Bellman to Runeberg, and that the present or recent literary activity is mainly on the surface, and of no particular importance. Perhaps this might be said of the parallel movements in more countries than one, or two, or three. Even the literary poly-pragmatism of Strindberg, as of other contemporary writers, is a "sign."

Strindberg.

In the literature of the third of the Scandinavian kingdoms,[1] there is at least one point of remarkable interest from the point of view of our period and purpose. Nobody seems to put the actual creative turn-out of Danish very high since the great writers of the earlier century died off—Kirkegaard, the Danish Joseph de Maistre, in 1855; the inimitable Hans Christian Andersen in

Denmark.

[1] It may be well to repeat that linguistically there is little or no difference between Danish of Denmark and the literary Danish of Norway. Iceland, moreover, has bestirred itself, and produced not a little literature in modern days and ways.

1876; and F. Paludan - Müller in the same year. Respectable position is, however, claimed for J. P. Jacobsen (see below) (1847-1885), Holger Drachmann (*b.* 1846), and Sophus Schandorff (1836-1901), as well as for others still younger. But, for the first time almost in history, and in a manner illustrating the general point, predominance in the history of our time of criticism next to the novel, the accepted European representative of Danish literature is a critic, and (after some early verse, &c.) nothing but

Brandes. a critic — Georg Morris Cohen Brandes (*b.* 1842). Dr Brandes, who, as his third name shows, is of Jewish extraction, has, rather after the fashion of these Scandinavian writers, lived much out of Denmark, and is said to write German indifferently with Danish. But nobody disputes his representative nationality, or the immense influence which he has exercised on the literature of his native country. He has written a large number of critical monographs, of which those on Shakespeare, Ibsen, and Björnson are perhaps the best known.

But his most extensive and most ambitious work, which, though of comparatively old date in composition (the early 'seventies), has only recently (1901-1905) been translated into English, is a vast study, in so - called Comparative Literature, of what the author calls the *Head Streams* [or Main Currents] *of Nineteenth - century Literature.* In this an entire volume is assigned to each of the following subjects: *Emigrant Literature* (Chateaubriand, Madame de Staël, and some others); *The German Romantic*

School; The Reaction in France (Chateaubriand again, Maistre, Bonald, and the beginnings of Lamartine and Hugo); *Naturalism in England* (this means the great English Romantic School); *The Romantic School in France* (1830); and *Young Germany*. As something in the arrangement and titles may have forewarned the wary and not ignorant reader, Dr Brandes' point of view is almost entirely political and theological. The literary Ormuzd for him is Liberalism; the literary Ahriman, Reaction. Every one is judged according to this classification; and it thus follows that Byron is very nearly Ormuzd incarnated from the critic's point of view, with other degrees of literary divinity and diabolism adjusted accordingly. For here, as elsewhere, we find that while the strongest Tory critics can admire Liberalism that is literature, it is almost impossible for a Liberal critic to admire literature that is Tory. To Dr Brandes, Scott is an author "whom no grown-up person reads"—a generalisation perhaps the rashest, except Tolstoi's that "all prostitutes and madmen smoke," which, in the course of a large experience of books, the present writer has registered. Perhaps it is not wholly unfortunate that Dr Brandes indulges in detailed criticism but rarely. It would be difficult to find two more remarkable instances of the pedant-meticulous turned loose than two of his strictures on *The Heart of Mid-Lothian*—that Scott has suggested the lights and shades of Rembrandt in connection with the outline of Michael Angelo, and that he has mixed historical and fictitious utterances of the Duke of Argyll's in the same scene.

But he writes more commonly in such a vein as this—that the German Romanticists are unforgivable, because they took from the women they associated with "their noble liberal-minded enthusiasm, and made them first Romantic and literary, then remorseful, and then Catholic." That other persons may use his blame exactly as stated, and turn it into the highest praise, does not seem to have occurred to the critic. Yet it would be quite a mistake to belittle the value of this—perhaps the most extensive and not the least well-informed of single and substantive critical efforts in our time. It contains a great deal of the actual utterances of the authors dealt with, either translated or aptly digested; it includes vividly and interestingly written accounts of such things as the fate of Robert Emmett, the various French and German coteries, and the like. It has a very great deal about men of letters; and if it contained a little more about literature one might vary the old joke, and say that it contained a good deal about everything. Actually, it is a most remarkable contrast-counterpart to Señor Menendez' book noticed above, and deserves to rank with it.

One original writer in modern Danish, however, is spoken of with such confident enthusiasm by students of the literature that, especially *Jacobsen.* as his work is done, he should perhaps be put into companionship with Dr Brandes, who was his fervent admirer. This is Jons Peter Jacobsen,

who was born in 1847, and died, after long illness
and great suffering from pulmonary disease, in 1885.
Jacobsen's largest work in literature (he was also
devoted to natural science, and was a botanist of
distinction) was the historical romance of *Marie
Grubbe* (1876), and six years later he published a
volume of short stories entitled *Mogens*. But his
central, and apparently his most characteristic, work
was the novel of *Niels Lyhne* (1880), which has been
translated into English under the title of *Siren Voices*.
Jacobsen's great glory is said to be that of style,
which, of course, is all but invisible in translation; we see the frames of the pictures, and can
read the descriptions underneath, but the picture
itself is veiled. Otherwise the book, which is
actually said to have been written under the influence of Flaubert, betrays that influence unmis-
takably, though not slavishly. It is, indeed, itself
a sort of *Education Sentimentale* complicated with
a study of pessimistic atheism. The tone given by
this last is pathetically explained by the author's
physical sufferings, and we can easily accept the
vouchers for abundance of beautiful writing in the
original. There is, however, little real character, save
in flashes, though there is a good deal of realist
analysis; and the whole has the note (which Flaubert,
though he too has been accused of it, saves by his
art) of a disconnected phantasmagoria of the uncomfortable. Power Jacobsen must certainly have had;
but there is in him, as in most of the writers of the
minor literatures and some of the major since the

"Naturalist" movement, a curious *childishness*,—the eagerness, partly of a good child at a new study, and partly of a bad child at a new mischief,—and not the criticism and the control of self, with the criticism if not the control of external things, which belongs to a man.

The literature of Russia during our period, though admittedly of great interest and importance in the general European survey, and exercising an influence which it has never exercised before, is in a very curious position. By consent of those who are competent to criticise it at first hand, it is inferior, in the premier department of poetry, and also in most of what we may call the applied departments of history, &c., to the period that precedes it. There is no Pushkin, no Lermontoff, no Krilof, no Karamsin. But, on the other hand, the Russian novel, following the general bent of the century, has far transcended even the relatively high point which it reached with Gogol and with Lermontoff's prose; and has begun to pay back with interest its debt to other countries. More than this, Russian literature has, in the person of Count Tolstoi, completed the quartette of revolutionary agents who have acted on the literature of the last twenty or thirty years, to such an extent that the twentieth century may be said to have made its *début* with them for sponsors. On the chief representatives of this novel, therefore, we may concentrate attention, with a few previous words on the two poets who seem to require most notice—Nikolas Alexeivitch Nekrasof (1821-1877) and F. J. Tutchef.

Russian.

Some years ago a critic spoke of the mixture of "crudity and rottenness" in the Russian nature, and *Nekrasof.* was sharply taken to task for doing so. The phrase was no doubt injudicious, considering the hardness of men's heads and the softness of their hearts; for "unripeness" and "over-ripeness" would have done just as well, and have been less provocative. In that form, at any rate, the truth of the description may be maintained, and is well seen in most of the figures that we are about to discuss.[1] It is certainly not least seen in that of Nekrasof, who seems to be recognised as the greatest poet of the middle of the century; and who does not seem, even in the judgment of Russophile specialists, to have been succeeded by any one of much importance. It is, indeed, impossible to judge poetry as poetry from a translation,—the growing impression to the contrary is one of the most unfortunate delusions of the day. But what is claimed for Nekrasof does not seem to be the strictly poetical merit of form, so much as that of original and forcible thought and illustration of thought,—things which, if only as through a glass darkly, can be detected in another language. As far as this goes, the force (or at least the violence) may be granted at once; and the originality need not be denied. But these good qualities seem to have been put merely at the

[1] It is certainly not contradicted by a phrase in the latest and most enthusiastic book on Russian poetry in English—*Poetry and Progress in Russia*, by Rosa Newmarch (London, 1907). Mrs Newmarch (to whom I owe my knowledge of Nadson (*v. inf.*)) speaks of "the rapidity of florescence and decay" in Russian literature.

service of ill conditions and bad blood of the extremest kind. The political state of Russia may not have been, and may not be, of the most gracious; but it does not appear that Nekrasof had much reason personally to complain of it. He had severe sufferings in youth, and represents his father as a brutal tyrant; but one would like to hear the father's version of the matter, and it is quite clear that "the wolf-cub," as the poet dubs himself, would have snarled and bitten at any hand which touched him. A worse nature than Nekrasof's does not occur to us in the long and sometimes unhappy roll of poets; and he seems to have poured forth his "ill conditions" in scores of thousands of lines of poetical envy, hatred, malice, and all uncharitableness. Nor does the saving grace of absolutely first-rate poetical expression seem to be claimed for him by any one. A certain excellent saying in Scots irresistibly suggests itself respecting him, " Ye're a clever chiel, man ; but ye wad be nane the waur o' a hanging."

Tutchef, on the other hand, presents a dreamy idealism scarcely cheerful—Cheerfulness would seem *Tutchef.* to be a nymph who has never visited Russia — but peaceful enough, with an agreeable mysticism and a philosophical touch, without the stiffness and pretension of many philosophic poets. He certainly translates admirably;[1] but how

---

[1] Pieces of him will be found in M. de Vogüé's *Regards Historiques et Litteraires* (Paris, 1892), where also is a good study of Nekrasof. I endeavour to read my Russians as much as possible in French translation rather than English, for in the latter language Russian never seems to "go" well.

much of his merit is due to translation, alas! once more, one cannot say.[1]

Some, though of course not by any means all, of the difficulty is removed when we come to the novelists. The dark side—that of style and strictly literary form—is a heavy loss, but it is not here the most important side: we can judge the plot and the characters, if not quite the description and the dialogue, almost as well as if we read them in Russ. Three great names, Tourguenieff (without prejudice to the innumerable other forms of the name down to "Turgenjew"), Dostoieffsky, and Tolstoi, must receive more or less detailed notice; the later and actually contemporary Maxim Gorky need only be referred to as an advance in grime.

Ivan Sergitch Tourguenieff, who, though a younger man and writer than Gogol, practically founded the

Tourguenieff. repute of the Russian novel in Europe, was born in 1818 and died at Paris, where and at Baden he had for the most part latterly lived, in 1883. A man of birth and property, he held a government appointment for a short time, but gave it up, and for nearly half a century lived on his means. He

---

[1] An additional illustration of the union of "Sorrow and Song" appears to have been given, wholly during our period, by the young poet, Simon Yakovlevitch Nadson, Jew on the father's side, Russian on the mother's, who was born in 1862, and died after much ill-health, but at the end, it seems, really " snuffed out by an article " in January 1886. Nadson's career was pathetic throughout, and he seems to have been really amiable : nor are these qualities absent from his poetry ; but the translations of it do not suggest much originality or vigour.

began, as Mr Omond noted within the period of the last volume, with the *Sketches* or, as they are sometimes called, *Annals of a Sportsman* (1846), and got into some trouble for a *Letter to Gogol* six years later. For Tourguenieff, while entirely free from the crank anarchism which has obtained such a sway over the Russian mind, was a rational reformer and an enemy of serfdom. His most brilliant work came later—the three greatest books, *Fathers and Sons, Smoke,* and *Virgin Soil,* in 1861, 1867, and 1876 respectively. But all his work, earlier and later, displays the same literary characteristics, and no very great difference of outlook, though, naturally enough, he is more sympathetic with the movement of his time in the earlier work, and more critical of it in the later. For the said "crank anarchism," indeed, he never had any sympathy at all, and was extremely unpopular with its votaries. Even Tolstoi, a personal friend, fell violently foul of him, but was forgiven: for Tourguenieff's temper and disposition seem to have been nearly as amiable as Nekrasof's were diabolic. He was a great favourite in European, and especially in Parisian, society, and was a sort of honorary member of the coterie of the Goncourts, from whom we have glimpses of him rather pleasanter than those which they generally give of their friends. He was, moreover, a man of brilliant wit and wits. He is credited with the invention of one of the happiest of words for one of the unhappiest of things, "Nihilism"; and, as noted above, he first seems to have formulated and stigmatised, in the phrase "reversed platitude," the barren, childish paradox-mongering which has made fortune in the last generation.

So far as it is possible to judge under the disadvantages confessed,—disadvantages, however, which seem to apply, here as elsewhere, at least equally to most of those who have come to an opposite conclusion,—the present writer has no hesitation in ranking Tourguenieff as the greatest novelist of Russia, and almost her only one fit to take a seat in the cabinet council of European novelists of the nineteenth century. That he has been eclipsed by Dostoieffsky and Tolstoi, even by the mere grime-novel of Maxim Gorky, does not matter at all. The passion for strange local colour, for topsy-turvy sentiment, for extravagant Naturalism,—together with some even less respectable forms of the sheer silliness which seems, in the late nineteenth century, to have succeeded the somewhat narrow wisdom of the eighteenth and the extensive wiseacreishness of the earlier nineteenth itself,—sufficiently account for this. But he has the qualities of the artist in all but the very highest degree; and he applies them to matter of quite sufficient interest. Take, for instance, what is perhaps his capital work *Nov* (*Terres Vierges* or *Virgin Soil*). The amateur of local colour, of local manners, must be a glutton indeed if he is not satisfied with the amount of it here, or in *Smoke*. But instead of this local stuff remaining crude and undigested, as it does in so many books of the last half century, it has undergone the universalising touch—the touch which, if not quite Shakespearian, is of the family of Shakespeare.

Y

Mark how completely Negdanoff, the Russian Hamlet, is "succeeded," as wine-merchants say of a vintage; how the artist has exactly hit off the mean between too little and too much. Characters like Machourina and Marianne are much more really explanatory of that singular Russian specialty, the revolutionary girl, than, say, Mary Paulovna in Tolstoi's *Resurrection*, precisely because they are less photographic. And so of the minor characters, among whom "Fomouschka and Fimouschka" are simply triumphs. The way they turn the tables on their modern visitors is humorous to the sublime; in fact, enough in itself to disgust all those in whom the sense of humour is dead or dormant,—a sad but numerous band. In certain points—humour, perfect projection of character, and perhaps also a certain neglect of plot as plot—Tourguenieff reminds one of Thackeray, of course with numerous accompanying differences. His style is highly praised by those who can judge. Even Mérimée, a most competent and a very severe critic, could find no fault with Tourguenieff's writing, except that it occasionally abused the abundant but rather disorderly resources of the language. And the same infrequent but accomplished censor notes, as a specially Shakespearian touch in Tourguenieff, his extraction of "the soul of goodness in things evil," which is all the more remarkable that Mérimée was not exactly a belauder of the sentimental. "Le soin que ces messieurs mettent à signaler les vilains côtés du monde où nous vivons" is most undoubtedly the main fault of Russian literature. Certainly Tourguenieff does not sin by undue optimism, but from this un-hallowed *soin* he is free.

That the two remarkable writers to whom we now come are not free from it is clear enough to all; that their slavery is a cause of their popularity is clear enough to some. It is fair to say that neither of the two appears to have taken the least pleasure in these studies of the repulsive, but to have been driven to them by some curious overmastery of impulse. The lesser of them—Feodor Mikailovitch Dostoieffsky—was born, like Tourguenieff, in 1818, and, like him, published his first work (*Poor People*) in 1846. The very title speaks the tone and subject; but the author brought upon himself opportunities for even closer study of human misery. He engaged in some of the plots of the stormy period of '48, was arrested, tried, and condemned to twelve years' labour in the Siberian mines—seven of which he actually served, though he was released in 1856. He wrote a definite account of his experiences as prisoner soon afterwards; but the chief fruit of them was his famous masterpiece of *Crime and Punishment* (1868). He did a good many other things, and died in 1881, having latterly turned to a sort of Old-Russian patriotism, very excusably intolerant of the introduction of those Western ideas which have certainly done Russia very little good hitherto, and which in at least many cases appear to be totally unsuited to her. Dostoieffsky's general characteristics are somewhat

Dostoieffsky.

narrow strength and depth, occupying themselves by preference on subjects unhappy, squalid, and altogether unbeautiful, but by no means rejoicing in moral grime. It will, therefore, necessarily appeal very differently to different temperaments. Those who follow the fashion will like it (or think, or say, that they like it), because it is eccentric from the older kinds of art; some may like it sympathetically, or dislike it from want of sympathy; while yet others may regard it as a curious "sport" of nature affected by time and circumstance, interesting in a way, certainly not horrible or disgusting, but unattractive, and "such as one could have done without."

The foremost instance of the necessity of dealing here with living persons is undoubtedly Count Leo

Tolstoi.

Tolstoi. Actively as he is of the present in some ways, his age makes him a writer of the last generation; and he is also, as we have had to say more than once or twice, the fourth of the quartette who have dominated European literature for the last quarter of a century. About his biography we shall say little or nothing here, only noting that most of those who write about him (including himself) say a very great deal, and that there is something tell-tale in the fact. Hardly anybody can require to be told that Count Tolstoi, who was born in 1828, belongs to a family of unusual distinction in many ways. He was himself heir to large estates; fought in the Crimean war; wrote tales and sketches (partly autobiographical) very early; became a prominent novelist on a larger scale; went through (about 1878) a process of "conversion" to undogmatic and revolutionary religion, but to revolutionary politics of a non-resistance kind; and has since written freely in support of his convictions, both in and out of the novel form. The singularity of his career, the eccentricity of his principles, and the qualities of the works in which, first more or less covertly, then openly and deliberately, he has set them forth, have obtained him European—indeed, world-wide—notoriety; and he has, through his writings, probably influenced more writers and more readers than any other author except the three so often referred to in his company.

In the case of these (except as far as regards Nietzsche's unhappy affliction) it was not necessary to say anything about the men. It is one of the first important points about Count Tolstoi that, in his case, the man is much more prominent than the writer. One cannot say that his personality "obtrudes itself," because there is something offensive and ungentlemanly in the idea of obtrusion. Now, except on religious questions (where everybody except the very elect loses his balance, and where nobody is the elect to anybody but himself) it would be impossible for Count Tolstoi to be offensive. It is curious that he, leveller and, as it were, New Fifth Monarchy man as he is, is one of the finest and most absolute gentlemen in literature. This comes out in the most curious fashion when one

compares him with his companions. For it would
be impossible to perceive from the works of Ibsen
and of Zola that they even knew what the word
gentleman means; while, though Nietzsche certainly
did, or could have done so, he chose to select for
his admiration the Renaissance or Cæsar - Borgian
variety of gentleman — a variety which, on the
whole, one prefers to leave in museums. It is
needless to say that this gentlemanhood, though
birth and breeding may have assisted its development, has nothing necessarily or exclusively to do
with them. The Count is a gentleman as Lamb
was and as Byron was not; just as he is a
gentleman as Shelley was and as Hazlitt was not.

But he is a gentleman of most eccentric differences,
and these differences show themselves in all his
work. On the less strictly literary part of it we
must not dwell long, but must say a little — the
chief texts being *What is Art?* and still more the
invaluable collection of *Essays and Letters*, presenting comments on all sorts of things, contemporary
and otherwise, during the last twenty years.[1] Here
you may find explained with almost invariable
epieikeia — the exceptions are, as just hinted, in
religious parts, where the Count exposes himself a
little to Lamb's rapier-question to Southey, "You
never spoke disrespectfully of what *you* thought
sacred, but how about what others think?"— how

---

[1] Translated by Aylmer Maude (London, 1903). Not much need
be said as to his recent lucubrations on Shakespeare. They contain
much to amuse, and nothing to surprise or shock.

Count Tolstoi is of those who forbid to marry[1] and command to abstain from meats; how he mentions with ingenuous wonder that "many English men and women, *for some reason or other*, are specially proud of using a great deal of soap and pouring a large quantity of water over themselves"; how he ejaculates in derisive horror, "Christianity [or virtue in general] *and beefsteaks!*"; how he is certain that all bad things occur because people will imagine [*et toi - même, M. le Comte?*] that "they know what is necessary for mankind and the world"; how angry he is with Nietzsche (who, you see, thought different things necessary for the world); how prostitutes and madmen *all* smoke; what hard things (in both senses hard, for they are hard to answer) he has to say of science; how horrified he is at corporal punishment (one of the infallible marks of the crank); how, in the original strict Godwinian, and therefore amiable, sense he is an anarchist—quite certain that everything will go on charmingly without any government, law, police at all. It is perhaps not ill to read these things and so "focus" the author — find his range—before reading the novels. For, though what are generally taken as the greatest of these were written before the conversion, the drift of them is quite clear. And the most remarkable thing in the volume — the "Afterword to *The Kreutzer Sonata*" —contains, like most afterwords and postscripts, the gist of the matter.

[1] The contrary has sometimes been said—*e.g.*, by Mr Arnold. But see below.

Count Tolstoi's work is extensive. As he says in his peculiar way, "I write books, and therefore know all the evil they produce"; and the present writer is not acquainted with the whole of it, even so far as it has been translated. But the early Cossack stories, the two great novels of *War and Peace* and *Anna Karenina, Ivan Ilyitch* and some other short stories, *The Kreutzer Sonata* itself and the long recent novel of *Resurrection,* should give fair texts for judgment on those points that can be judged from translation. One thing strikes us in all, as it struck even a critic so favourably disposed as the late Mr Matthew Arnold,—that the novels are hardly works of art at all. It is, however, pleaded for them that they are "pieces of life"; and so perhaps they are, but in a strangely unlicked and unfinished condition. One constantly finds touches, not of talent so much as of genius. But these touches are hardly ever worked even into complete studies; while the studies, complete or incomplete, are still less often worked into pictures. It is almost startlingly exemplary and symptomatic, for instance, to find, in the early, vivid, but emphatically local studies of the Cossacks, that the best of all Olyenin's moods and manners is a study of Incompleteness itself. The greatest and most powerful thing, in the writer's humble judgment, that Tolstoi has ever done,—*Ivan Ilyitch,* that terrible and wonderful picture of the *affres* of death and the preliminary gloom of hopeless disease,—however marvellously observed and imagined, *has* to be

incomplete, and so escapes the fault found elsewhere.

Again, Count Tolstoi owes nothing to deliberate
Impressionism, yet he is the head malefactor of the
Impression itself. Even Mr Arnold himself gently
complained of the irrelevances of *Anna Karenina*,
and these are multipled ten times in *Resurrection*.
Yet more, there is in him, and in fact in most of the
authors of these younger literatures,—the absence of
it was the reason of the special praise given to Señor
Valera in the last chapter,—a singular particularist
parochialism. They are so constantly absorbed in
special things that they cannot bring them *sub specie
æternitatis*. They do not see, as their literary elders,
by no merit of their own, have been brought to see,
that things are merely parts of life,—that you must
rise and "find the whole"; while of course in books
like *Resurrection*, the purpose, the *tendenz*, entirely
blinds them to proportion, art, and everything else.
They seem—at least this greatest of them seems—to
be constantly duped by single observations or sets of
observations, just as they are by individual writers:
not merely, in Tolstoi's case, serious if faulty thinkers
like Herbert Spencer and Karl Marx, but mere blatant
quacks like Henry George. So that the great war
scenes of *War and Peace*, the sketches of society
and the autobiographical study of Levine in *Anna
Karenina*, the "crimes and punishments" of *Resurrection*, leave us—all of them, if not all of us—with
a sense of the half-digested, the crude.

This crudity comes no doubt from more causes than

one; but one of the causes from which it comes is very noteworthy. Soon after *The Kreutzer Sonata* became known among us, an English critic admiringly observed that when you compared *Tom Jones* with it you saw "what a simple, toy-like structure had served Fielding for a human world." It was rather unlucky for this critic that Count Tolstoi very shortly afterwards explained, in the remarkable paper referred to above, to what the complexity of *The Kreutzer Sonata* was due. It was due (*habemus confitentem*) to the existence of a large number of crotchets and fads, most, if not all, of which Fielding undoubtedly would not have admitted to his simple, toy-like structure.[1] And these crotchets group themselves round a central one—the doctrine that marriage, and love itself, are bad things *per se.* There is no need, if there were room, to discuss this crotchet here. But it cannot be improper to say, at the end of a survey of European literature, that almost all the greatest things in that,

[1] More recently another victim of that innocent delusion, the worship of "our noble selves," declared that the great novelists of the middle of the nineteenth century in England "could do anything but think," contrasting with this the thoughtfulness of Tolstoi and others. The fact, of course, is that it was exactly because Thackeray and others *could* think — think unerringly and intuitively,—and because their readers could follow the suggested thought, that they did not abound in so-called "analysis." They did not need to cover the alternate pages of their books, like those of a schoolboy's examination-paper in mathematics, with by-work and subsidiary calculations; their readers knew how to take the time of day, so infallibly told them, without requiring endless chatter about the machinery of the watch. And those readers did not demand the rather clumsy flattery, and the more than rather coarse stimulation, of alternate obscurity and fireworks.

and in all literature most probably,—that an enormous proportion of these things to a mathematical certainty,—have been dictated, directly or indirectly, by the inspiration of Love—physical Love in the end, though sublimated more or less now and then. The man who denies himself this inspiration is in effect a member of the sect, in Russia itself, of whom most tolerably well-informed people must think when they read some of Count Tolstoi's writings. He condemns himself to sterility and impotence.

This particular craze, though it had not developed itself explicitly at the time of the writing of *Anna Karenina*, explains why the heroine of that book and the book itself, interesting as they seem to be to some people, are almost absolutely uninteresting to others. Anna has no more real love for Wronsky than for her husband; and her false love is infinitely less interesting than that of Emma Bovary, with whom Mr Arnold very rashly compares her, to her and her creator's advantage. But we must not digress into particulars. The point is that a man who sets his face, as Tolstoi does, against both Love and War (though he had really utilised the latter in *War and Peace*, and had tried to utilise the former in *Anna Karenina*), deprives himself of the two great reagents, solvents, harmonising and unifying *catholica* of his art. There remains Death, and he has, as we saw, got a wonderful success out of that; but even in days that like to deal with gloom and grime, Death is not a card that you can play very often. He may by sheer *tours de force* — and again in a time

which likes *tours de force*—utilise exceptional and
minor motives to some extent. But he cuts himself
off from the real and principal things. Add to this
that Tolstoi, though not exactly destitute of humour,
—he has not a few quaint and interesting touches
of it,—possesses it in nothing like the abounding and
universal supply which makes it almost a sufficient
solvent or *menstruum* of itself. Add once more
that in him — as in all his three compeers — we
never get rid of the passing hour: and it will be
of little need or use to say more. Ladies who are not
prepared to wear their garments for a day and then
to cast them to the winds or the waiting-maids, have
a well-grounded objection to things that "date themselves"—that are *merely* fashionable. In literature
nothing that is merely fit to be cast to the winds,
and the readers in circulating libraries, is of any
value at all; and here too the fact of "dating itself"
too much is a serious drawback to any work. That
there is much in Count Tolstoi which is not merely
fashionable may be and has been freely granted. But
there is a great deal too much that is. "What does
it matter to me," Prince Posterity will say, "that
this was the way they crotcheted then? Art is
long, and the crotchet, thank Heaven! is short. Give
me Art and give me Nature, which is long likewise."
Now, the Prince will not find very much art in the
Count, and the nature which he *will* find is too often
unnatural.

Of some other Russian writers said to be of note,
such as the novelist Pisemsky, the present writer

cannot speak at first hand; and there is no need here *Marie Bashkirtseff.* to discuss the very respectable contributions which Russia has made to applied literature in law, science, scholarship, &c. But there is one remarkable book which, though not written in Russian, throws the strongest possible light on the Russian character in its literary aspect, and that is the *Journal* of Marie Bashkirtseff.[1]

This young lady, besides the attractions of youth, birth, and station, with a certain *beauté du diable*, it would appear, both of body and mind, in her lifetime, had those of early death. There remains, on the most rigid and unsentimental calculus, something pathetic about her. But her main interest is different. In the first place, she illustrates the prophetic omniscience of genius: because she *is* Thackeray's Blanche Amory, better born and bred and coming into the world more than a generation later. In the second, she illustrates in quite a different way that "halfripe-overripe" character of the Russian mind and emotions which was referred to before. As of her great prototype, it may be said of her that "in this young lady there was nothing real" (or *si peu que rien*) except vanity. She could take the colour— chamæleon fashion —of all the fashionable facts and fancies; she could simulate the fashionable sentiment; she could be artistic, passionate, and so forth by turns. Because

---

[1] I am well aware that questions have arisen as to the amount of editing in the original editions of this journal, and that additions have been made since. But neither point affects the remarks in the text.

Bettina had written to Goethe and " L'Etrangère " to
Balzac, she must have a correspondence with (*faute
de mieux*) Guy de Maupassant. Take her, take
Tolstoi, and take Nekrasof or Gorky, and you have
the elements of what seems unluckily to be the
prevailing national spirit. Fortunately there is
Tourguenieff not too far behind as a consoler.

In Polish no writer seems recently to have taken
up the mantle of Nickiewicz, or even that of Kasinski
Poland. or Slovacki; but the novelists Kraszewski
and Sinkewicz, especially the latter, have
represented Poland not ill in the popular department
of the time; and the latter at least made all Europe,
not to mention America, ring from side to side with
Quo Vadis? in 1896.

The position occupied in European reputation by
Petöfi during the earlier years of the century has not
Hungarian— been quite lost for Hungary. But, according
Jokai. to the general tendency of the century, the
poet has been succeeded by a novelist, Maurice Jokai,
who was born in 1825. Not that Jokai is only a
novelist, but that his novels have given him his chief
fame at home and his whole reputation abroad. They
are very numerous,—indeed Jokai is the Dumas of
Hungary in more ways than one,—and not a few of
them, from *The New Landlord* (1862) to *Timar's Two
Worlds*, have been translated into English. His style
is the older romance of adventure, not the newer novel
of manners, though he is by no means without com-

mand of the latter; and as a politician and journalist
he has given a very practical side to his status as the
first man of letters of his country. But it does not
seem necessary to dwell on any of his compatriots.

We must be even less complaisant to the other
great non - German language of the Emperor of
Austria's subjects—Czech,—no writer in that tongue
having recently attained to European rank; and to
Roumanian, though Queen " Carmen Sylva " (whose
own work in German deserves mention), her lady of
honour, Helène Vacaresco, and others, have taken
trouble with it, It, with Basque and one or two
more, must be silence, because, as far as our general
subject is concerned, they have themselves been
almost silent.

CONCLUSION.

I.

OF THE PRESENT VOLUME.

THE DIFFICULTIES AT THE THRESHOLD — SURVEY OF LITERATURES : ENGLISH—THE CONTINUITY OF ROMANTIC INFLUENCE HERE AND ELSEWHERE—THE DEVELOPMENT OF THE NOVEL : ITS DOMESTICA- TION—EXAMPLES FROM SMEDLEY, TROLLOPE, AND BULWER—AND OF THE NEWSPAPER — FRENCH — GERMAN — THE PENINSULAR LITERATURES—THE MINORITIES—THE NEW COMPETITORS : RUSSIAN AND NORSE—ALWAYS ROMANCE !

OF the various literary fallacies which so easily beset opinion, and which, though the student of comparative *The difficulties* literature should be well guarded against *at the threshold.* them by their constant recurrence in his studies, too often deceive himself, none is more com- mon than the tendency to mistake, and so to misjudge, periods just behind the present. Prophecy is usually idle ; retrospect from a great distance is sometimes quite purblind, sometimes illusively fond ; the view of the present is almost always out of focus. But the estimate of what is a little, and only a little, way off is hindered and tricked by a whole host of disturbing

influences. And none of these—not even the confidence, obtruded or concealed, that we are wiser,
better, greater than our fathers—is more treacherous
and more persistent than the other belief that we are
at any rate *different*. As a rule, Youth would rather
admit its inferiority to Age than the fact that it is
la même chose,—an innocent independence, perhaps,
but a very disturbing influence on literary judgment,
to all but certainty.

Even the disinterested and fairly distant student
does not always recognise the fact of the extreme
rarity of sharp breaks in literary continuity: the
average man of the day and hour, as soon as he
begins to take any interest in the matter, almost
invariably believes—or at any rate would like to
believe—that his day is a new day, and his hour
a new hour. This tendency, always more or less
present, has a curious and historically certain, though
apparently absurd, habit of reinforcing and concen-
trating itself at the ends of centuries, and would sometimes seem to have made the deed follow—to some
extent—the idea.

Whether any such process of compulsion is actually
going on at the present moment is luckily a question
quite out of our province. It is possible, however, to
accept, and perhaps to answer, the previous questions
as to the general characteristics of Later Nineteenth
Century literature, and as to their connection with
the phenomena already observed. Indeed the acceptance of these questions, and the endeavour to provide
at least some answer to them, are necessary justifica-

z

tions of this book and its companions—things without which it has no business to present itself.

We must, however, distinguish between the characteristics of individual literatures, or groups of litera- *Survey of literatures.* tures, and those which display themselves more or less all over Europe ; and the natural way to ascertain what distinction is necessary is to survey the former class of results first.

In English—though the contrary opinion is very commonly expressed, for reasons just given—it is not *English.* obvious, to persons accustomed to the comparative study of literature, that any process of change save that of the usual " blossom-flourish-fade" order has taken place in the history of Victorian Letters. The extraordinary vitality of Tennyson and Browning in poetry is, historically speaking, a symptom, unmistakable and undelusive, of persistence. And if this seem too rash and metaphysical an argument, an examination of English poetry at the beginning of the last decade of the century, when one of these two poets was dead and the other soon to die, will give evidence, not to be weakened by repeating the examination a decade later. We shall see many interesting *attempts* to be different—" Celtic renascences," recourse to rhymelessness and irregular line-composition, recourse to this, to that, to the other — sometimes even valiant efforts to effect that dethronement of "visible" and "audible," that restoration of "intelligible" poetry, for which no less a person than Gustave Planche sighed at the very beginning of our period. But these are all what we have called them — "recourses"; they are nothing new, and they are scarcely great. On the whole, the poetry of the period has, since the appearance of the pre - Raphaelite school more than forty years ago, made no striking or definite advance upon the movement of 1830, while the movement of 1830 was itself but a striking and definite advance upon Keats and Shelley, as Keats and Shelley were scarcely more than an advance upon Coleridge.

Compare any of our best and newest utterances in poetry of late years with "The Ancient Mariner" and "Kubla Khan"; compare "The Ancient Mariner" and "Kubla Khan" with any typical eighteenth-century verse, even pretty late, and the difference of the differ ences must surely strike. In the one case it is a difference, not even of family, but of the older and younger members of the same family. In the other it is very nearly, if not quite, a difference of species. The appeal to visual and audible effect, the eclecticism of subject, the very differences of versification and diction, are all but essential — perhaps they are essential. From the higher and less quibbling stand-points of classification the English poetry of 1898 is *The continuity* not less "Romantic" than that which—for *of Romantic* us—is the poetry of 1798. Free to any *influence here* *and elsewhere.* one who likes to say that as the *Lyrical Ballads* were not to these contemporaries, or most of them, "the poetry of 1798" at all, so something of 1898, which we have neglected or ignored in 1907, will seem to be its real poetry to 1998! We do not deal here with prophecy. Indeed, the retort would miss its mark in any case. The *ruling* poetry of 1798 was still that of a century earlier. And the object of the present contention is merely to vindicate for English nineteenth century poetry at least as great a solidarity as that of eighteenth. To the present writer it seems very much greater: there are no such ancestral voices prophesying war as those of Collins and Gray, at a greater distance behind the *Lyrical Ballads* than the beginning of our period is behind the end of it. But here difference of individual opinion may come in: in the other and general respect the facts—though they may be ignored—are very nearly out of reach of debate when known.

Passing from the supreme and architypal form of literature to its juniors and inferiors, we find that the English novel pursues, and very largely extends, that process of development which has been traced in the three preceding volumes of this book. Indeed, as we have noticed, the middle of the nineteenth century is a most important stage-point in this development. The kinds of Fiction, which, after the death of Scott, had somewhat languished, save for the exceptional and fantastic genius of Dickens, received, about that period, extraordinary reinforcements in variety and strength from Thackeray as first and greatest, through the Brontës, George Eliot, Kingsley, Trollope, and others, down to the youngest but not least notable, Mr George Meredith. On the one hand, the purely domestic novel — of which Miss Austen had first shown the possibilities in a form wholly independent of romantic incident—displays the most various re-

sults in hands so capable and so various themselves
as those not merely of Thackeray and Miss Evans and
Trollope, but of Miss Yonge, Mrs Oliphant, Mrs
Gaskell, and scores of others.   On the other, the
more or less historical romance, which, after its long-
delayed birth, sprang forth almost full-grown at the
wave of Scott's wand, but had been rather unworthily
put to nurse under James and Ainsworth and Bulwer,
was thoroughly renewed in youth by Thackeray and
Kingsley, and towards the end of the century came in
for a fresh burst of popularity and practice.

It is not too much to say that the novel-crop
of this half-century in English excels in combined
The development volume and goodness that of all previous
of the Novel.   time in English itself and all other
languages to boot, though it can show perhaps only
Thackeray as master, and only *Esmond* as masterpiece, to match the masterpieces of Cervantes and
Fielding, Miss Austen and Scott.   And here, as in other
countries, and even more than in other countries, the
novel imposes itself as *the* dominant form of what
is at least popularly considered literature, succeeding,
and in a way ousting, drama and sermon, pamphlet
and poem.   It is written by those who write for
fame, and by those who write for money, and by
those who write to enforce some principle or some
prejudice.   It is read by those who read nothing else,
and by those who read everything else, and by
specialists in every study and science and profession.   It preaches virtue and it panders to vice; it is
the vehicle of the propaganda of faith and of free-

thought, of politics and of philosophy, of science and of sport. It is the very *satura* of the Roman poet and more; it deals with everything that men do, and everything that men think; with everything that they feel and desire, and with everything that they love and hate.

It is almost impossible to attach too much importance to the part of this change which concerns the *Its domestica-* *domestication* of the novel. One may *tion.* choose this word, though it is not one of those generally used, and though it is susceptible of misunderstanding, because the common coins or catchwords have been clipped and battered out of all respectable currency. "Realism," in particular, has come to mean anything or nothing. When we find such a critic as M. Brunetière apparently holding that there was no realism before Balzac, and even that nobody before Balzac made furniture or costume play an important part in the novel, some new terminology seems to be imperatively necessary. "Naturalism," on the other hand, can hardly be touched except with a pair of tongs. What is meant here by the "domestication" of the novel is the discovery that no unusual incidents, language, or "properties" are necessary to fiction. Fielding had seen this perfectly; Defoe, in what are called his "minor" novels, had seen it too. But what were usual incidents in the days of Fielding, still more in those of Defoe, had ceased to be usual, without the novelists allowing for it. Both had perfectly kept the language of their day, but that language had later become obsolete; and here also, but still more strangely, novelists had been unequal to the occasion. In fact they had, as had their still feebler fellows of the stage, been much worse than unequal. They had allowed fiction to be invaded by that extraordinary jargon of the stage itself which was built up (it would be interesting and by no means difficult to show how) in the eclipse of the drama from 1700 onwards. In this jargon no live human being ever talked as in his natural form of utterance: we know that from the indisputable testimony of private letters, diaries, and the like. But it was *de rigueur* on the stage, and from the stage it passed into the novel. Even Miss Austen, who almost entirely freed herself from the unreal incident, did not invariably, though she generally did, free herself from the unreal lingo. Dickens simply wallowed in it in the serious parts of his early books: it is the glory of Thackeray that he did *not*. But he, if the greatest, was also almost the first to emancipate himself, and the emancipation was by no means general even so late as the 'fifties.

This may be seen very interestingly in a parallel, which has not, one thinks, been drawn, between the novels of Frank Smedley and Anthony Trollope, in the 'fifties themselves. And let nobody pooh-pooh the author of *Frank Fairlegh* as a mere author of obsolete boys' books. They are nothing of the kind. *Frank Fairlegh* itself, and the more unequal and ponderous *Lewis Arundel*, are full of excellent humour, fancy, and " differences " generally; while *Harry Coverdale's Courtship*, inferior

Examples from Smedley, Trollope,

as a whole, contains a study of matrimonial jangles —really quite causeless, but nearly shipwrecking happiness—which is little less than a masterpiece, and not, so far as I remember, even suggested by anything earlier. Now this book was published in 1855— the very year of *The Warden*, and but a little earlier than *Barchester Towers*. Smedley was not an older man than Trollope; on the contrary, he was three years younger; and though as a lifelong cripple he had not had Trollope's varied experiences, he had seen plenty of life, and, as anybody may learn from Edmund Yates and others, had plenty of shrewdness to divine what he might not have been able to observe.

Yet the two batches of books read almost as if they belonged to different centuries. Trollope's people may wear crinolines and whiskers and so forth, but, mere slang and catch-phrases of the moment apart, they talk pretty much as we talk now, and at any rate always like live people. Smedley's, whenever they get excited or serious, talk the above-mentioned dateless, lifeless, *fushionless* jargon. Trollope will give you a broken bone out hunting now and then, even as you may get it for yourself at this very day; and he does not disdain the Bull—that Golden Bull of fiction—who has saved more situations, made more marriages, and generally helped things along for novelists more than anything else, except the upset boat and the broken ice. Smedley is not content with the bull and the boat and the breaking of the ice,—he must have duels and elopements and all the rest of the obsolete *tremblement*. Trollope can steer

very close to farce if not into and through it; he can
and does give "low" or "lowish" life—the Norah
Geraghty scenes of the *Three Clerks*, Johnny Eames's
boarding - house, the bagmen in *Orley Farm*. But
he gives it without the ultra-Dickensian, the still
Theodore - Hookish exaggeration of the farce of
Smedley. In fact, without any unfair depreciation
—the present writer reads his *Frank Fairlegh* still,
and hopes to read more than once more how they
rang the chimes at Hillingdon, and so forth — the
two may almost be contrasted as an author who holds
the mirror up to ordinary domestic life, and an author
who is not content to do so without preparing that
mirror itself with stock garnishings to the reflection.
Some one may say, "Oh! but Trollope worked in
so much autobiography"; the answer is, "So did
Smedley." The very incident of the ringing just
referred to is said to be historical; and the facetious
"Freddy Coleman" used to be pretty confidently
identified with an eccentric lawyer and politician
in one of the home counties.

If this seem not merely a digression, but a digression
out of keeping with the character of its context, the
excuse must be that this transformation of the novel
—which is quite a different thing from the separation
of the novel from the romance—is one of the most
important of the larger literary facts of the time, and
that it is with these facts that we have to deal.
Fielding, Defoe, and perhaps even Le Sage, were
the original suggestors of the kind; Miss Burney
did something to carry it on; Scott to a great

extent,[1] though with a good many relapses, and Miss
Austen to a much greater but with some, established it.
But the next generation—until Thackeray—fell away,
Bulwer and Dickens being in their different ways the
arch-heretics. Even, about 1850, the Brontës hindered
it nearly as much as they helped; Kingsley (not by
his romances but by some of the talk in *Alton Locke*
and even *Yeast*) jibbed against it for a time, and so did
Charles Reade almost in every book, though not in
every page or chapter. But Thackeray had seen it
and worked for it almost from the first, and George
Eliot and Trollope made it nearly, if not quite,
triumphant.

It is extremely noteworthy that Bulwer himself,
whose faculty of discerning, and in fact forecasting,
changes in public taste was extraordinary,
and Bulwer.
drew the scheme of a "domestic novel" as
early as 1849, when he wrote the Preface to *The
Caxtons*—that is to say, when nobody of importance
but Thackeray had yet dared it. He did not indeed
carry it out in its purity. For, in the first place, he

[1] He himself, in the Introduction to *St Ronan's Well*, comments—
in that curious, careless, sovereign way of his, which, from its utter
absence both of pretentiousness and of mock-humility, escapes the
notice of the non-elect—on the new duty of the novel *celebrare
domestica facta*. The fact is that, as Balzac and others of the elect
have seen, Scott knew everything about the novel. In one short
passage of this very book—the description of the mixture of Lady
Binks's feelings as she sits next Tyrrel—he has given the *scenario* of
a novel *à la Bourget* in twenty lines ; and in a rather longer one in
perhaps the least popular of his early books, *The Monastery*, where
Edward Glendinning confesses to the Sub-Prior, there is a still more
complex and masterly pendant to it in another kind.

adulterated it with more than a dash of Shandian *fatrasie*—to such an extent, indeed, that the Caxton family are simply the four Shandys, with Mr Shandy made less eccentric, Mrs Shandy and Tristram called out of their rather bodiless condition, my Uncle Toby's Quixotry relieved of its perilous simplicity in Roland, while even Dr Slop forces his way in, much improved in manners and wits to be sure. And in the second, he could not help relapsing into melodrama, into the "silver fork" and the fashionable, &c. But his intention is quite plain; and it is by no means certain that it was not rather distrust of his public than positive inability on his own part to keep the path he had traced out that made the book the compromise it is. At any rate, as a tell-tale of the set of the current it is as early and as important as anything not of Thackeray's own.[1]

There is a parallel development and a parallel

---

[1] While speaking of *The Caxtons*, an interesting caution may be drawn from it as to "moral" denunciations of fiction. Readers may remember the horror of Pisistratus Caxton when he found certain French novels in his good-for-nothing cousin's room, before he knew him to be his cousin. Now, Pisistratus certainly was a prig; but his creator, with some foibles, was not that—*was* the author of *Ernest Maltravers*, &c., and had very considerable experience of life and literature. And these terrible books — these "Typhons," as the classical imagination of the novelist describes them—could have been nothing more terrible than the novels of Balzac and George Sand, for the description of them is not applicable to mere Paul de Kockeries (not that there is anything so very dreadful in Paul de Kock), nor to anything lower still. Nobody—or hardly anybody— is frightened of George Sand or of Balzac now. The fable does not, or should not, require a great deal of interpretation, though of course it may be stretched too far. The fault of Naturalism, Ibsenism, and other such things is not that they are immoral, but that their immorality is inartistic.

universality in the companion product—in this case
And of the
Newspaper. a distinct literary vehicle, but not a distinct
literary kind,—the rise of which has been
similarly traced in the same volumes. The Newspaper or Periodical helps very largely in the dis-
crimination, and so in the production, of the novel
itself ; it does the same service, directly or indirectly,
for other kinds of literature ; and it does perhaps a
greater service still, to almost all kinds, by providing
the man of letters with a means of livelihood, independent alike of patrons and of pension-givers, of publishers and of play-house managers. The " hack-jour-
nalist " of popular ideas, though still not an unknown,
has become, or at any rate became not so long ago,
whether there has been a relapse or not, an increasingly rare person ; while the man who, without selling
his conscience, or having the least temptation to sell
it, derives useful guineas, regularly or occasionally,
from periodicals of all kinds has enormously increased.
" To write articles for money and books for love " (as
somebody once put it) is an arrangement which has
nothing that is dishonourable and much that is
convenient. That journalism debases style, fritters
energy, encourages bad work, and endangers the
survival of good—these things are often said, and are
not wholly untrue. But they are not the whole truth ;
and there remains to be set against them not merely
the services just enumerated, but one which is much
more rarely formulated, and perhaps indeed very
rarely recognised at all. This is the *askesis*—the
literary practice and exercise—which journalism of

all but the lowest kind gives to any man of competent culture and freedom from merely vulgar aims. It is M. Anatole France, I believe,—himself no hack or Philistine,—who is credited with the opinion that the great genius of Flaubert would have worked more satisfactorily if he had had to write " articles de commande." And we have all known cases where admirable talents, eximious culture, great designs, and competent allowance of leisure and means have come to nothing (or next to nothing) because their possessor, as Carlyle was fond of saying, " could never be ready,"— because he spent his time on *getting ready*, and could never make the dash—the plunge. To this dash and plunge the journalist is accustomed as to that in his daily bath: it has no terrors and no difficulties for him. He may, indeed, be almost too *autoschediastic*— too apt to compress the nine years of traditional incubation into months or less. But at any rate he attempts, and he does something: if it is ill done, why even then it will probably help some one else to do it again and better; if well, the world is the better for it. But the world is never the better —it is, if only by one more bad example, sensibly the worse—for the spectacle of wasted preparation, of impotent fumbling, of expenditure of time and trouble and self-torture to no purpose except the torture itself, or to the more degrading result of acquiescence in sterility.

One department of journalism calls perhaps for special mention, because it has more than any other (putting the novel itself out of question) shared and evidenced the general development. And this is Literary Criticism. The multiplication of mere reviewing—of the actual "account given" of books as they appear, though responsible for the greatest bulk of critical production and for the greatest determination of energy to the special function—is not the sole noteworthy point. Criticism of a more important, permanent, and disinterested kind has more and more tended to make at any rate its first appearance in periodicals. The book and the pamphlet, in which such criticism still usually appeared in the eighteenth century, have been less and less usually its first vehicles in the nineteenth. If any one will run over in his mind the list of the most remarkable critical books of the last fifty years, he will find that scarcely one in ten, perhaps not one in twenty, has had an original appearance wholly independent of the periodical.

This multiplication and facilitation of critical writing would by no means necessarily increase its goodness in quality or even in quantity, though it almost necessarily must increase the quantity of its badness. But, as a matter of fact, the goodness *has* been increased. The second quarter of the nineteenth century had seen a distinct falling off from the critical Golden Age of Coleridge and Lamb and Hazlitt. The third saw a remarkable revival, of which the most prominent apostle, if not exactly the original and individual prophet, was Matthew Arnold. With the special excellencies of him and of others we are not here concerned, nor (fortunately!)

with the special defects of yet others or of the same. But certain general points of improvement are noticeable; and most of all, the wide application of that comparative study of literature which even Coleridge might have used more largely, though it was one of the strengths of his critical method, and in which both Hazlitt and Lamb were extremely deficient. This comparative study of literature, so late reached in a certain sense so lately even possible, is not only the sole adequate source of just critical judgment in itself, but can be historically shown to be in its absence the cause, in its presence the cure, of the defects both of classic or neo-classic, and of romantic or modern criticism. The neglect of it in the former case leads to the rash construction of rules, and the recourse to it shows at once that these rules have been rashly constructed. The neglect of it in the latter aggravates the dangers of mere lawless impressionism, and the recourse to it obviates those dangers.[1]

The other English departments require much less notice; for though at the beginning there was still a very notable literary school of History, wherein the greatness of Carlyle and Macaulay was worthily continued by Froude, the " document " employed so admirably by the two first, and with such dangerous uncertainty, though with no lack of pains, by the

---

[1] It would be unjust not to mention in this place the name of Joseph Texte (1865-1900), who devoted great part of his too short life to the subject, and even to a certain extent *christened* it in his *La Littérature Comparée* (1900). But the process is much older: and M. Texte's own contributions to it, interesting as they are, take not quite the most excellent way.

third, was proving itself an auxiliary only safe in the management of the greatest masters. It has since, by the almost exulting admission of experts, "killed the historian" from the literary point of view, and the said experts appear to regard themselves as relieved from disagreeable responsibilities by the fact. The phase, of course, like all phases, will be only passing; but until it passes the literary historian must regretfully neglect a department which once gave him all but his choicest specimens.

Of another great, and once far greater, department of literature the glory had gone—in England —much earlier, and there was no return with us. From 1850 to about 1890 not a single English play can be cited which is at once great literature and great drama, while the attempts that have been made since to unite the two have hardly been *great*. Tennyson's theatre adds nothing to—it is well if the best places of his best pieces detract nothing from—his literary position. Browning during this time more and more gave up the attempt at the uncongenial and obsolete form, and devoted the great but incomplete dramatic faculty which he undoubtedly possessed more and more to dramatic or *dramatoeidic* narrative. The lesser men followed suit; and it still remains in great part true that our playwrights who deserve the name are not men of letters—at least as playwrights,—and that our men of letters who are men of letters are very rarely and not eminently playwrights. At any rate, the exceptions are so recent, so doubtful, and so few, that they may well remain undiscussed here. There is no explanation of this curious but, to all competent and disinterested persons, undeniable phenomenon, except the rather metaphysical and easily disputable one that the novel has *ousted* the drama — blocked its way, diverted its feeding streams, accaparated the intelligence and the capacity which should have been dramatic. Perhaps the wheel is turning again, perhaps not.

There is much less mystery about the decline of the literary quality in philosophical and scientific writing, which is akin to, if not absolutely identical with, that undergone by History. In the first place, the *specialising* of all those studies has had its inevitable result in lowering the standard of artistic presentation. When the philosopher was "second best" at least "in everything," he had to be at least second best in literature; his freedom from the larger and general requirement brought with it emancipation in the smaller and special. When the man of science had to appear before a comparatively small body of humanely and critically educated persons, of whom he himself formed part, it was necessary that he should conform to the requirements of the critical Humanities. We have changed all that. Manners of no sort now make man; and this manner has gone with the rest — to return in the case of philosophy, perhaps, in the case of physical science, hardly.

It can, however, be surprising only to very superficial observers that this decline in the general literary character of great literary departments has been accompanied by a distinct and very noteworthy reaction and refinement in the standard of literary Prose as such. This standard, in general English, had never been high, or, to speak more accurately, rigid. Great men, in their different great ways,—Hooker, Bacon, Jonson, Hobbes, Browne, Taylor, Dryden, Addison, Swift, Johnson, Gibbon, Burke,—had written great prose ; and about the second decade of the nineteenth century an elaborate and something like an organised attempt had been made by others — Wilson, De Quincey, Landor, and (as his late-published but most interesting and important pocket-book entries show) Coleridge before any of them—to write distinctly ornate prose. This attempt had itself been not indistinctly connected with the subsidence of the great poetical movement just before it, and— "carried over" in the interval by Mr Ruskin — it was renewed just as the second great poetical movement of the century was beginning to show signs of subsidence. About the 'seventies of the century, when that movement had already produced its best work, efforts—in some cases, as in Mr Meredith's, begun earlier, and in not a few developing somewhat distinct tendencies and setting before them by no means identical aims—were made to " raise," as it has been put, " English style to a higher power." Sometimes these efforts were directed—very specially by Mr Pater — towards the obtaining in prose of something of the additional visible and audible appeal which has been noted as the great gift of

contemporary poetry. Sometimes, as in the case of
Mr Meredith himself, an intellectual instrument—
hardly earned—was especially aimed at. And sometimes—the chief mentionable example is, of course,
Mr Stevenson—these aims were combined and extended in what may be called the experimental
direction, the writer almost or quite avowedly endeavouring, by imitation and by original tentative,
to perfect his instrument, rather in order to see
what new results the perfected instrument would
give him, than to accomplish results previously defined, or conceived without exact definition.

The results themselves have been very much what
might be anticipated. Not a little work, of a quality
seldom exceeded and not often equalled, has been
added to English literature ; and the reproach—a
reproach exaggerated but with some foundation in
fact—of "Early Victorian slovenliness" has been in
a sense removed, though only to be replaced by a
much better founded one of Late Victorian affectation. The consequence, indeed, must have seemed
inevitable to all careful students of literature, and
might have been seen to be such by all careful
students of human nature. What happened with
Greek, with Latin, with fifteenth - century French
and sixteenth - century Spanish, with Elizabethan
English and seventeenth - century Italian, happened
again. The great writers were more "gallantly
great," but the small writers were more bedizenedly
conspicuous in their smallness. The consummateness was more engaging—the failure to engage was

more consummate. For in prose, though not in poetry, a very great deal does depend upon the subject; and the realisation of an occasional "prosaic moment" will not, as the realisation of an occasional poetic moment will, atone for pretty constant failures to attain. To which has to be added the also old and expected endeavours to make up by *more* extravagance, *more* unconventionality, *more* defiance of previously respected canon, for the absence of universal and irresistible appeal. These things must come, and they will go. But the end of the nineteenth century was one of the times at which they have come, and we cannot say that the beginning of the twentieth has yet proved to be one at which they have gone.[1]

The literary history of France during the period presents in some—though of course not in all—ways

French.

a remarkable resemblance to that of England. There is the same domination of "visible and audible" poetry, represented in the same way by brilliant writers, not in their first youth, at the very beginning, taken up by successive generations of *diadochi*, and only towards the end dwindling into a state of what we perhaps must not call decadence, but may certainly call interval or fallow.

---

[1] For the effects of "Naturalism," &c., on English, *v. inf.* They have not been of sufficient importance for separate treatment. On the other hand, the thoroughness which has been used in dealing with other general phenomena in our literature should be permitted to economise space in the dealings with others. Almost all that has been said applies, with the proper allowance.

There is the same abundance of novel and newspaper, and the same remarkable prevalence of Criticism,— here anticipating English, and giving the lead to it, though perhaps not maintaining that lead by any means so decidedly as it has been the fashion to represent. There is again the same diminished literary character in the applied departments of literature — history, philosophy, and the rest; and there is the same remarkable coincidence of a sort of exaggerated *literariness* in *belles lettres*—of "precious" and non-natural theory and practice in prose (and still more in verse) style,—the same quest for the exotic and the bizarre.

The differences, however, are also noteworthy, and certain important general phenomena accentuate themselves in France after a fashion far less obvious with us. The literary drama has never lost its hold on French as it has on English : during the sixth, seventh, and eighth decades of the century writers of high rank, from Musset and Dumas *fils* to Augier and Feuillet, continued or began their dramatic practice; and if at the present moment the drama has no representative of the very highest class, that is merely because French literature has not at the moment any such representative. Specialisation also has not killed literature, nor even *tranced* it,— M. Gaston Boissier in the department of antiquity, and the late M. Gaston Paris in that of the mediæval period, being worthy to rank with the best literary scholars of the past.

The "school" influence, however, has always been

more powerful south than north of the Channel; and
France offers us the central and best opportunity
for discussing that alleged procession and succession
of schools—Romanticism, Realism, Naturalism, with
'isms of sorts of minor or different extensions and
directions, Impressionism, Symbolism, "Naturism,"
"Simplism," what not—which has been more than
once referred to in the foregoing pages, and which
is almost an accepted doctrine with the majority of
literary critics. Not a little of what we shall say
will "throw back" to matters English, and nearly
all of it will throw forward to the other literatures,
on most of which the influence of French has exercised itself with even more than its old authority,
though with more reciprocity than of old.

Some expression was duly given in the last volume
to the doctrine just referred to—the doctrine that
Romanticism, if not exactly dead by 1850, had passed
its meridian by a long way; that the agencies of
"scientific" physical study, of sceptical criticism in
religion, philosophy, history, politics, sociology, had
begun to undermine, and almost succeeded in under-
mining, the walls of the Castle of Romance; and that
the succeeding generations have seen it further if
not finally mined. The justification of this idea in
the present period would probably be found, by those
who entertain it, to some extent in the undoubted
prevalence of the scientific and (in a limited sense)
critical spirit itself. But they would doubtless
point—at least in the sphere of *belles lettres*, and to
confine ourselves to this for the present in French

belles lettres more particularly—to the growth, first, of
the *Parnassien* or "Impassible" school of poetry, with
its devotion to metre and subject and so forth; and
then of the Symbolist or Material-Mystical school,
with its metrical heresies and its experiments in
"atmosphere." They would point still more to the
Realism of Flaubert, and the intrigue-manners
tragi-comedy of Feuillet,—most of all to the Naturalist movement and all its eccentricities, down to
Là-Bas and *Les Morticoles* and *Vérité*, in the novel.
These things have indeed been actually pointed out
so often that they have, as was hinted above, assumed the appearance of a kind of "matter of
breviary." Astonishment or resentment or contempt
would seem to be occasionally provoked by a different
interpretation of them. Yet such an interpretation
can perhaps be put forward not in mere paradox,
and can certainly be supported by something very
different from mere ignorance.

The mistake—apologising for the assumption contained in that word—may seem to be one of failure
to take a sufficiently distant and a sufficiently panor-
amic view. Looked at near, Leconte de Lisle may
seem very different from Hugo,[1] and Mallarmé, not to
say M. Moréas or M. Vielé-Griffin, from Leconte de
Lisle,—Flaubert, a wholly other sectary, from Gautier,
and Zola from Flaubert, and others from all. But

---

[1] A curious error on the part of a severe and usually accurate
critic has been pointed out by M. Catulle Mendès. M. Brunetière
once stated that *Poésies Barbares* preceded *La Légende des Siècles*.
Unluckily the *Légende* is three years their senior.

this is not the more perfect way of literary or of any
natural history. A black Shetland pony is a very
different beast in appearance from a bay Arab, but
they are both horses, and you see it when you compare them with another beast even so nearly allied as
a white ass. So, if you take *Vérité* and, say, *L'Âne
Mort* at seventy years' distance, and the latter from a
time far antecedent to the beginning of our period,—
nay, *Là-Bas* and *Melmoth the Wanderer* at about the
same interval, but in different countries,—the resemblance, as contrasted with the work, say, of Fielding
or of Marivaux, will "leap to the eyes." And the
Romantic quality in the novel, which is itself historically and essentially anti-classical, is less eminently
and essentially *divisible* and extractable than it is in
the poem.

Here the real identity, in apparent diversity, of the
different products is even more easily, triumphantly,
and universally demonstrable. Take *Les Orientales*
and any piece of the late M. Verlaine's latest, or of
the youngest living French contributor to *Vers et
Prose* who is not merely trying to *embêter* or *épater* his
reader,—take instances at any reasonable stage-dis-
tance between,—and just as in the case of *Claribel*
and the latest English verse (with the same proviso),
the common agreement will emerge at once, when
you compare the one set with a piece of Delille's or
even of J. B. Rousseau's, the other with a piece of any
eighteenth-century English poet—even Thomson, even
Gray—except Blake. It is the "way" that is different, and the spirit of the nineteenth-century way is

always the same spirit, remarkably different as are
its administrations. It is, one may venture again to
think, a mistake to regard Romanticism as a question
of faith against unbelief, of sentiment against satire
or criticism, of optimism against pessimism, of fancy
against science. You can be a Classical believer,
sentimentalist, optimist, fantast (this most difficultly
but possibly), a Romantic infidel, cynic, pessimist,
and (this most difficultly but possibly) scientific person. It is "the riding that does it."

When the eyes have been duly purged by this only
euphrasy and rue of literary study — the comparative method—there will be no difficulty in seeing
that the groups and individuals which before seemed
separate, or even opposed, are in reality staged
merely — *échelonned* on a road which is nowhere
abruptly broken, or sharply turned, or held in part by
the enemy. In no case is this more easily demonstrable than in that case of the French novel, which
has often been thought, and is apparently still thought
by many, to give the strongest evidence in the other
direction. Even some of these many have been
brought to acknowledge that Flaubert, the apostle
and prophet and coryphæus of Realism, is not only,
as he himself said, an "unfrocked Romantic," but a
Romantic with hardly his coat turned inside out. But
these, or some of them, would make a fresh stand at
Zola, or at least at the Goncourts. They have this of
plausible in their attitude, that in Zola there is little,
and in the Goncourts and the followers of both less,
of the *poetry* that distinguishes the earlier stages of

Romanticism. But this, though hardly an accident, is what we may, in the teeth rather of logical phraseology than of logic, call a "separable property." The other and inseparable properties of Romanticism—its individualism, its eccentricity, its colour, its vagueness even—all these reappear and assert their quality; for the endless facts and documents of Zola float and fringe off into a haze of gigantesque phantasmagoria, and the much boasted "vérité vérissime" of Edmond de Goncourt has the loom and the distortion of a spoon-reflection. Nothing is more curious than the way in which the "scientificisation" of literature turns, with a kind of sardonic rebellion, to the exaggeration of the most anti-scientific peculiarities. Perhaps, if a reason must be given, we had better seek it in the effects of specialising. When all departments of science and philosophy were literary, and when at least many men of letters were contemporaneously men of science and philosophers, the pooling of faculties and methods restrained the predominance of men as individuals, and established a classical *modus*. Dissolution of partnership may have produced, as it tends to do in private circumstances, an actual and mutual repulsion,—a bent towards extreme polarity and isolation.

However this may be, the present writer is entirely disinclined to allow that the Romantic succession has yet failed,—that a different, at least a hostile, dynasty has come into existence either in England or in France. It is more difficult to deny that in both countries to some extent—but in France more par-

ticularly and decidedly—it is a case of *nos nequiores*.
It would be hard to name a date at which French
literature, while full of practice, was so weak (putting
criticism aside) in great individual practitioners; it
would certainly be very easy to name many at which
English was stronger in this respect. No prognosti-
cation can be drawn from this as to the future, for
similar phenomena in the past have sometimes been
succeeded by continued decadence, and have sometimes changed suddenly into the most brilliant flourishing. It is the fact that we note; and the main
caution which the fact suggests is this—to beware of
seeing revolution where there is only evolution in the
story. The history of Nineteenth Century Literature
is still, and throughout, the history of a dominant
Romanticism, showing beneath it, as all dominations
do, the struggles—which may be birth-struggles and
may not—of more or less antagonistic principles.

One special point—rather a dangerous one to touch,
perhaps—presents itself in reference to this period of
French literature. The judgment which would allow,
much more that which would insist on, very large
influences by political conditions on literary productions is but a rash one. It is, however, rather less
rash in regard to France than to most other countries,
because of the gregarious and imitative character of
the nation, of its dependence upon state arrangements,
and of the comparative absence of overmastering
individuality. At any rate, if not certainly correct,
it is very tempting to see something corresponding to
the Second Empire in the French literature of 1850-

1870, and very much corresponding to the Third Republic in that of 1870-1900. The Restoration and the July Monarchy had not been glorious times for France historically: the two reigns constituting the former period had been well-meant failures, and the third a sordid and pretentious sham. But they had done little either to check, to direct, or to express the spirit of the people; and that spirit was not, for literary purposes, unfavourably affected by certain things connected with them. Excitement is probably all that politics can do for literature; and during the thirty-seven years from Waterloo to the Second of December, France had been very strongly excited by the working of the dregs of the Republican fermentation, the glories of the Napoleonic conquests, and the not dishonourable sting of the Napoleonic defeat, by the romantic mediæval phantasies that assisted and defended the Restoration, by the rebellious zeal that attacked it, by the dreams of perfectibility that rewarded the first attempt at Constitutionalism, and beguiled for a time the sense of its sordid breakdown. All this produced that "glow of"—perhaps in this case rather hectic—"life" which critics of the most diverse schools acknowledge to be favourable to the production of great literature. And accordingly great literature was produced in body and quantity perhaps surpassing that shown during any other single generation in French literary history. Most—Balzac is perhaps the only pre-eminent exception—of the great men of this period survived it, some for a very considerable time; and they served to maintain the

apparent splendour of the literature during the whole
of the Second Empire, and even in some cases far into
the Third Republic.   But a strict critical accuracy
would refuse to credit their production to the actual
dates of its later appearance; and the newer generation, in some ways very far from contemptible, has
been of a very different character—a character again
reflecting, with allowance, the political surroundings.

The chief of such allowances is, of course, the simple
impossibility of a great literary period continuing indefinitely.   " O king ! live for ever," may be a dutiful
sentiment and a compliment not ungraceful ; but it is
not to be taken seriously in literature any more than
in life.

Only partisan blindness or more partisan impudence
can deny that the government of Napoleon III. was
accepted, and almost to the last continued to be accepted, by the French people with something much
nearer unanimity than any other since the delusive
calm of the *ancien régime*.   It really divided a people,
governed much by crazes and little by facts, less than
any other ; for even the extremest Republican could
console himself by the reflection that it theoretically
rested on the popular will from first to last ; and even
the extremest Royalist could not but prefer it either to
the detested Republic itself, or to the sham monarchy
of the Orleans line.   But its acceptance was an acceptance of acquiescence, not of enthusiasm,— even the
borrowed aureole of Napoleonic glory shone faintly
and but for few, and it really meant much rather that
fatal belief in mere material progress, and that more

fatal content with it, which found expression in the London Exhibition of 1851 and its continental followers, and which gangrened half Europe till the cautery of the *Année Terrible* checked it to some extent. On the other hand, the Third Republic has notoriously been, for a longer period than can be paralleled anywhere in history, a reign of political agnosticism, if not actually atheism, a sequence of insignificant governments following each other to the dustbin, developing no great or even respectable statesman, acquiring neither enthusiasm nor even esteem, jobbing and intriguing their way till some cleverer or even merely newer jobber or intriguer shoulders them off it.

For neither of these *régimes*, we say, was enthusiasm even possible: it is more curious that, with one magnificent exception of the older times, neither was able to rouse literature producing enthusiasm against it. And that exception most certainly proves the rule. It may seem almost literary blasphemy to make any proviso in praise of the "Chasseur Noir" or the *Contemplations*. But Victor Hugo, like another king of literary men, "could write beautifully about a broomstick," and he could hardly help writing beautifully about any of his own particular broomsticks. It was, one may fear, much more personal resentment than patriotic wrath that gave us these great things: he was quite as serious when he wrote the ineffable absurdities in the *Année Terrible*, and elsewhere, about the handful of Brussels gamins who threw another handful of pebbles at his windows and woke the baby.

But, outside this, politics have done nothing for French men of letters. They have carried on, according to their age-long habit, an unceasing *fronde* against all governments,—a *fronde* often very clever, sometimes very amusing, but scarcely ever anything better than a *fronde*. In their immense novel-production the revival of historical romance, which has been notice-able elsewhere in the latest years of the nineteenth century, has had hardly any place. In history the fanciful literature of Michelet and the fanciful journalism of Thiers have given way to dull and de-corous document-classing. They have had no great poet since Hugo, and no failure of a great poet even since Verlaine; no philosopher of literary eminence since Comte—even the doctored and blended wine of Renan has been succeeded by vintages not, perhaps, much purer, and certainly far thinner and more flavourless. The torch of criticism still burns with them, and brightly enough; but criticism, as a critic may admit, does at the best but borrow and cunningly engineer the light it gives,—it adds but little of its own to the illumination of the world. The moral who will may draw.

As our survey of the period in England curtailed the necessary length of that dealing with France, so *German.* further curtailment is possible in regard to the other nations. The most remarkable of this group of phenomena is to be found in the literature of Germany. After the immense develop-ment of German literature between Lessing and

Goethe—after the worthy second stage of it between Goethe and Heine—a superficial, and even not so very superficial, opinion might feel justified in calculating upon later stages more brilliant still. Cases, however, so different as those of Greek and Spanish, yet so generally uniform in their lessons, might " cast a cold " upon the trained historical judgment. The shadow would have proved itself to correspond to a real substance. It may be questioned whether, since the death of Heine, the roll of German men of letters has contained one single name of the absolutely first class in pure literature. At first we have indeed interesting survivors, like Auerbach and Freytag, Grillparzer and Scheffel, in *belles lettres*, like Schopenhauer in philosophy. Later we have violent examples of the *extravagance* which has been noted as rising with the set of the century, ranging from the sheer lunacy—lunacy with more than streaks of genius in it, but lunacy unquestioned— of Nietzsche downwards. Eminent men of science have abounded, and men half-scientific, half-literary, with Mommsen at their head, have not been rare. But what German poet since the *Matratzengruft* yielded its prey to another grave, more silent if less cruel, has even made his notes heard to a European audience ? What German novelist has taken up the mantle even of Freytag ? What German critic —in the proper and liberal sense—has sent in his proofs for admission to the company of Arnold and Sainte - Beuve ? Versifiers, respectable or not, and a few fair poets ; novelists, especially novelists of pro-

vincial peculiarities, interesting more or less; some
good playwrights (on this more later); some fair
miscellanists, Germany has to show. She has gone
through the usual stages of the Romantic movement
—indeed, as having begun it almost the earliest, she
may be said to have "got through with it" to the
farthest. But less than anywhere else is there any
sign with her of a really new movement: more than
anywhere does literature really live on the bits and
scraps of the past.

In what relation this condition stands to the world-
famous and world-affecting events of 1866 and 1870
is a question which, to the annoyance or contempt,
no doubt, of a once prevailing school of literary criticism and history, we shall merely state and leave to
other inquirers, as less ripe for even cursory treatment than the contemporary situation in France.
Those who insist on a "movement of national life"
as necessarily connected with a great literary development must, one would suppose, be a little puzzled by
it. Even those who would have the intervals between
such movements to be the literary crop-time will find
the facts awkward. Only those who maintain a philosophic scepticism as to there being *any* traceably
uniform connection between periods of political or
social and periods of literary development can be quite
happy with the phenomenon. *Cantent vacui:* they
need not trouble even to avail themselves of it as an
argument in defence of their own position, acquiescing
in the sounder attitude of *acatalepsy*—of declining to
meddle with the matter altogether.

Some greater comfort might perhaps be derived by the sectaries just referred to from the literary history *The Peninsular* of the two great Peninsulas—Italy and *Literatures.* Spain. The literary revival which might seem to them to have coincided in the first with the struggle for independence and reunion during the first half of the century, has been, at least to some extent, continued during the second, in which that independence and that reunion have been at last, in a manner, achieved. It is true that no individual authors of United Italy, with the exception of Carducci, can pretend to surpass or even to vie with Leopardi and Manzoni, or even, perhaps, D'Azeglio; but there has been a larger and wider crop of literature, and, especially in the more serious departments, where Italy had almost since Vico ceased to count, she has recovered a considerable position, with Rosmini as well as with Carducci. To the worse side of the account has to be set the renewed and not altogether healthy influence of French *belles lettres*, which has shown itself more and more throughout the century. A country like Italy, with such a literary past, should have no need of *xenomania*, except in a measure of healthy stimulation and alterative. The Italians study the great writers of their past with an energy and a minuteness which no nation can surpass; they publish them with a cheapness hardly paralleled, and therefore, as men rarely pursue business on merely charitable principles, it is to be supposed that they buy and read them. But they do not seem to be able—they hardly seem even to attempt—to take real and improving possession of their heritage.

The literary state of Spain has been very similar in almost all respects, except that her general level of production has been somewhat lower; while in no very distant years she has produced in the late Juan Valera an artist in the favourite form of the novel, who has given not merely the local colour so common not merely in national but in provincial examples, but even that transcendent touch—that touch of universality—which is so rare during the century out of France and England, and which has been almost entirely lacked by Italy since *I Promessi Sposi* at least. But, as a rule, French influence has again weighed too much in the western peninsula, as in the central.

The literary state of the easternmost peninsula of all is more a curiosity than a subject for serious critical historical study. Modern Greek had, as a literary language, to be created by Tricoupis and his companions and successors; and from some recent disputes it would appear that the creation has not gone on as smoothly as was at one time thought. However this may be, the modernised Xenophonese which the literati of the Independence elaborated has never seemed to dispassionate outsiders a very inspiring or inspired language; and the old half-barbarous and less than half-Hellenic dialects were incapable of anything more than folk-song or folk-tale. The political and other disappointments which Greece has experienced (and caused) seem to have reflected them-

selves in her literary experiments.   Yet one can have
nothing but cordial admiration for the fashion in
which Bikelas and others have tried to keep the ring
against Fate.

The present writer has, as stated, but little direct
knowledge of the three literatures which serve as
The Minorities. something more than satellites and less
than full companions to Spanish, German,
and French — Portuguese, Dutch, and " Belgian " —
except in so far as French - writing Belgians like
M. Maeterlinck have contributed to French literature, as French-writing Swiss and others did of old.
But it is believed that (with the part-exception of
Portuguese) they have not made any very independent or very considerable contribution, respectable and interesting as their contributions may be.
Isolated examples, though the words just used may
fully apply to them, do not disprove this.   And it
is further believed that in these literatures the immense and even unhealthy influence of English and
French, and especially of the latter, which has been
noted, is increasingly noticeable.   The good-natured
or partisan pleas which have sometimes been made
for the Smaller Literatures—the hopes of new literary
developments from them, of new literary worlds or
worldlets called into existence to redress the balance
of the old—do not seem to have any great justification in fact.   They are, indeed, probably little more
than hasty generalisations from some really remarkable but not too hastily to be interpreted phenomena
in the last group of literatures which remains for us

to notice, and which there, as here, come mainly from the ferment of individual eccentricity.

These, as the reader will have long anticipated, are the literatures of the North, or at least two of them, *The new com-* Norwegian and Russian; for Swedish and *petitors—* *Russian and* Danish proper have hardly maintained the *Norse.* promise which they gave in the first half of the century. At first sight, and not merely at first sight, the position of these literatures is very remarkable indeed. In Norwegian, Ibsen and Björnson have made themselves European reputations of the first class by common, and of a high class by critical, consent. In Russian the slow but unresting progress of centuries has culminated in an extraordinary group of novelists from Tourguenieff to Tolstoi, who have forced themselves upon readers, quite unable to read them in the original, after a fashion which recalls the older invasions of Richardson and of Scott. And these Viking or Tartar conquests have not been due to mere novelty, strangeness of scene, and colour: a great originality of thought and feeling has been claimed for them by at least some critics, and allowed by at least a considerable body of readers. Something like a new literary departure has seemed to be promised.

It is too early to decide this question; but some reasons for not deciding it too peremptorily in the affirmative may be given, or at least some considerations for taking it, as Scotch judges say, to *avizandum*. One of these is derived from the very peculiar characteristics of the nationalities concerned — one

representing the long unstirred bones of a mighty
ancient life in literature and war and travel, the
other a practically savage, and at any rate quite
un-European race-substance, superinoculated with a
civilisation which has no root inside, and has not
even penetrated deeply as yet from outwards. Another is the fact of that contemporary outbreak of
the abnormal, the anti-normal and antinomian, the
bizarre and the eccentric, which we have noted in
every literature during the last decades of the nineteenth century. When we look at these, and look
also at the intensely *imitative* character, the domination of the printed book, which likewise marks the
time, we shall perhaps, while quite acknowledging
the interest and even the magnitude of the phenomenon, be a little inclined to doubt whether it is
a phenomenon of beginning or of end—a promise or
a warning.

Widening the view again, so as to take in the whole
half century, though not the whole century, which is
Always for a still further sweep of the telescope,
Romance! the symptom which has been accentuated
in the remarks immediately foregoing, and indicated
again and again in the earlier portions of the retrospect, points for us to the mediate-general conclusion
at which we have to arrive. There has been much
nonsense, and still more excess, in the talk of late
years about "Degeneration." Physical, and especially
medical-physical metaphors, though tempting, and to
some guarded extent useful, in literary study, are
exceedingly dangerous unless the guard is steadily
kept. Many of the examples selected are merely

examples of a peculiar and eccentric, not of a morbid
or malignant, growth.   It is, for instance, purely
absurd to talk of mortification, of putrescence, of
necrosis, of ptomaines, in connection with such work
as Rossetti's, or even as Baudelaire's.   But in these to
some extent—and still more in such still later work
of the century as, in ascending order of production,
Tolstoi's, Zola's, Ibsen's, Nietzsche's—the excuses of
the exaggeration become magnified.   And in almost
the whole of this later work absence and presence
of character alike give evidence of a process of finish-
ing rather than of a process of beginning of sunset
rather than of sunrise.   It would be more than absurd
to speak of sunset as the degeneration of the sun; yet
there are characteristics of the phenomenon—partly, it
may be, the creations of association and the "pathetic
fallacy," partly, it is pretty certain, not so—which
always seem to us to partake, not of disease but, so to
speak, of *moriturience*—of the sense, if not the desire,
of approaching departure.   And so it is with the con-
cluding hours and minutes of each literary day.   The
emblem-books will dispense us from all enumeration
of the well-known analogies—the leaping, flickering
flame, the colours of the dying fish, the swan-song,
and the rest.   You may find them all engraven in the
seventeenth century on very excellent plate-paper,
and legended in very choice Dutch and other languages; not to mention that even this discovery is
rendered unnecessary by the slightest knowledge of
the literature of all ages, or of that unaltering and
unalterable source of the literature of all ages which
delights to conceal its invariableness of essence under

the most fantastic changes of outward show—that is
to say, the nature of Man.

The day of which we are witnessing the setting
certainly—whether any other has yet dawned few wise
men will attempt to say [1]—is, as the present writer has

[1] If there is one thing which should have been made more clear
than another by this *History*, it is the incalculableness of literary
progress and the consequent folly of literary prophecy. "Who shall
so forecast the years?" is nowhere truer than here. But it may not
be idle to note what others have forecasted, if only as a matter of
curiosity. One thing has for the moment a certain colour of plausi-
bility, and that is the comparative decadence of the novel and the
comparative revival of the drama as the popular form of literature,
or at least of that which presents itself in literary semblance. This
has certainly been visible, and is visible increasingly, in all countries.
Another is a coincident decadence in poetry ; and a third—the most
disquieting of all—a decadence of humour. One of the shrewdest
observers as well as one of the most powerful satirists of the last
days of the nineteenth century (the late Mr Traill in *Number Twenty*)
made this decadence the main feature in his fancy forecast of the
twentieth ; and it must be admitted that the signs are not encouraging. For here it is not as in the other cases. A great poet may
come at any time, and is as independent of an existing audience as
he is certain to create one. A great humourist is powerless unless
his audience can appreciate humour ; and it is doubtful whether he
can educate them. And there is perhaps no side of literature on
which one may be more thankful for the rule of " Present Company "
than that of humour at the present moment. Again, increasing
specialisation in art, science, and learning is not favourable to literature ; nor is the spread of a miscellaneous and sciolist education ;
nor the multiplication of certain kinds of periodical literature : while
the demands made for the larger and larger estatement of Science
itself, in place of Arts, if granted must, though they may not destroy,
seriously hamper the very possibilities of the true letters. But though
these things are not cheerful to contemplate, the cautions at the
beginning of this paragraph hold good, and *Sursum Corda* is a motto
as essentially literary as it is essentially religious. Moreover, whatever may be the morrow, "what has been has been, and [we] have
had [our] day."

already mentioned several times, the day of Romanticism. This much discussed and much defined thing—a disease of literature with some, an alliance between strangeness and beauty with others, a resurrection of wonder with a third set—has been often thought, and has sometimes thought itself, to be dying or—for it is immortal, and is seen in the *Odyssey* at the beginning as in *The Earthly Paradise* at the end of existing literature—approaching a trance. But it has never died or even fainted yet. At a hundred years' distance Fouqué and Maeterlinck join hands as brothers; and their non-fraternity with such work of the preceding century, not merely as *Babouc* but as even *Vathek*, is displayed indifferently through all delusive difference in *Undine* and in *Joyzelle*. Easy for the meticulous and the literal to point out the differences! easier still for those who have ears to hear and eyes to see to perceive the radical indifference! *Le vent qui vient de la montagne* has not yet quite ceased to blow.

If, however, it must be maintained that Romanticism has been the note of all the best literature,—is, with whatever touch of knell, still the note of our period as of the last, the note, that is, of the whole nineteenth century,— no competent interpreter of literary history will deny that the Romanticism of the whole time exhibits variations and developments. If in a certain sense the Romantic quality of such later work as the English poetry of the pre-Raphaelite school is more concentrated, more learned, more conscious of itself, and more " of malice prepense " than that of the earlier half-century, it must be admitted that it has in this very fact less of the "wild freshness of morning," less genuineness of a kind, more deliberation, if anybody pleases more affectation. Yet we must look on all sides. Its *excentricité voulue,* its declared war with science, and even its attempts to wrest from science scientific arms, its *literariness,*— whatever their defects and drawbacks,—have saved it from the rather puerile attempts at a *concordat* at which we still smile in such earlier work as "Locksley Hall," and which could be paralleled even from work so different in appearance as Hugo's. It has the disadvantages, but also the advantages, of a deliberate, of a militant orthodoxy. It has never subsided—and perhaps of its nature can never subside — into the soul-destroying self-complacency which beset the neoclassicism of the eighteenth century.

And in pure literature it has continued to do great things—has made up the tale and set the seal of one of the greatest of secular contributions to the sum of letters. The poetry of the nineteenth century need hardly vail its bonnet to the poetry of the greatest period, whatever that may be, of the world's literature. The prose fiction of the nineteenth century stands hitherto alone: it will be to all time the standard of comparison — to be excelled perhaps, though not probably, but, until excelled, always to stand as measure. In other departments — except, maybe, in drama—it can at this time or at that show worthily enough ; and it has contrived in the periodical a means whereby, if the utterance of bad literature is very deplorably facilitated, the stifling, or rather the abortion, of good is made at least extremely unlikely, if still not quite impossible.

Yet it is ill to end—even in a half-ending—with a boast; and without trenching too much on that summary of summaries which is to come, we may indicate — " for thoughts " — one curious difference between the juncture of the eighteenth and the nineteenth centuries and the juncture of the nineteenth and the twentieth. The eighteenth century was probably, in a certain peculiar and limited sense, the *wisest* century in the history of the world; but its limitations were most peculiar, and in particular it pruned its poetry and its imaginative literature generally with pitiless severity — refused to enjoy them with a miser's self-denial. It was punished by an outbreak of practical insanity at its close, and rewarded by an outbreak of that great imaginative literature which has been described. The nineteenth, while recovering the finer madness, was probably in more than one sense the fussiest and most "wise-acreish" century in the same history; but it gave the reins to its imagination, and spent the heritage of its parsimonious predecessor royally in literature. The completion of the parallel—in bankruptcy or not as to possessions, in mere silliness or not as to wits—may be left to the reader, as well as its application to life and politics.

II.

OF THE WHOLE MATTER.

It may seem presumptuous to attempt, but it would be entirely destructive of the scheme of this book to omit, a survey of the whole history *The retrospect.* which has been covered by these volumes. Up to the present time such a survey, for ordinary readers, has been made nearly impossible by the absence of co-ordinated text-books, and by the extreme self-centredness of most literary histories of their particular tongues. Until quite recently the French —the most acceptable and enterprising of text-book writers—have been beset in this respect by a wilful and wonderful want of knowledge. The Germans, with erudition enough and to spare, have never, save in the case of the Schlegels,[1] attempted com-

---

[1] For the claims of Lessing and Herder on this point and their limitations, see *The Romantic Revolt.*

parative literary criticism from the purely literary
side with much sweep or success—and in that case
were hampered by a certain rather un-Teutonic
rashness, if not even levity, of hypothesis and generalisation. The more than estimable attempt of Hallam
in our own tongue was made a little too early, confined itself within limits even then excessive in restriction and arbitrariness, and was directed by tastes
and prepossessions somewhat narrow and rigid.

We have here—by co-operation in individual parts,
but on a scheme identical and singly conceived —
attempted to enlarge, complete, supple, and vary
Hallam's conception and execution of a History of
the Literature of Europe from the very beginning
of its modern developments. The exclusion of what
is known as Ancient Literature is due to no undervaluation thereof : the present writer and editor
could never have formed, and would never have
taken part in, any project implying that. The
ancient literatures are left out, simply because their
influence is not so much antecedent as accompanying and omnipresent,—because it has to be reckoned
with in the twentieth century as in the seventh, and
in every one between, after a manner varying slightly
in degree and fashion, but always prominent and
dominant. At the times when this influence has
assumed special importance, we have specially noticed
it ; but as a whole, and as implying the history of
the actual literatures by which it is conveyed, we
have taken it for granted. We begin with it as
constituted, accomplished, complete, and — whether

in all cases completely known or not—determining
not the less powerfully, because to some extent in-
sensibly, the characteristics of its successors and
pupils.

In the so - called Dark Ages,[1] the literature of
Europe consists of two parts, connected or discon-
The Dark Ages nected on principles probably now im-
—what they possible to trace certainly as fact, and
found, brought,
and neglected. not worth attempting to trace very labori-
ously as conjecture. The one part was the "classical"
literature of Greece and Rome itself; the other the
vernacular literature gradually emerging from its
unknown antecedents. The imitation or continuation of classical letters in the same tongues, or corrup-
tions of them, constitutes or contains the main known
link of the connection above referred to, in such a
manner that it might not be improper to describe
it as a third part, a centre uniting the wings.

The first part, or Classical Literature itself, consisted of what we have—the smaller part—and of
a great deal that we have not. It has been sufficiently shown that the ideas which used to prevail
as to the extreme ignorance of this classical literature
in the later "Dark" and earlier "Middle" Ages had
no warranty of fact. But that a great deal was
actually destroyed during the anarchy of the period
from the fifth to the tenth century, and a great
deal more lost through neglect and misuse during
the same time and later, is of course certain. In

---

[1] See the volume of that name.

what has survived, however, we have probably, it
is admitted, a remarkably fair "general average"
of classical accomplishment, deplorable as are some
of the individual losses; and this "average," this
"sample," had at least its opportunity of influencing
further composition in the same tongues directly, and
indirectly in the newer languages. From examination of this composition in Greek and Latin, but
especially in Latin, we perceive, however, that even
where there was abundant knowledge of antiquity, no
indisposition to follow it, and perfect *facundity*, such
as it was, in the contemporary forms of diction,—
something makes it impossible for the writers to
write classically. To some extent this is no doubt
due to the very great predominance of theological and
ecclesiastical subject,—the very Renaissance itself,
when it came to air its Ciceronianism on these
matters, slipped into worse than the absurd. But
the insensible leavening of the tongues — more
especially of Latin, for Greek recedes more and more
—with barbarian characteristics must have affected
all subjects. "The Dorian *must*," as well as may,
"speak Doric"; the Teuton, and the Goth, and the
Frank-blended Latin are forced—in spite of themselves, had themselves cared to resist—to speak and
write "Romanced" or "Teutonised" Latin, not Latin
pure. And the language, as always, leads the literature its own way. In the work of Byzantine Greece
little occurs — putting "sports" of Anthology and
Romance aside—but fossil work, or at best galvan-
isation. Latin, from Sidonius to Hilary and onwards,

betrays more inspiring changes,—its disorganisation
has a promise, and not simply a regret. Not merely
the all-important birth-struggles of modern prosody
—the influences of *rhythmus* on *metrum ;* not merely
the quaint barbaric tinsel- and feather-trimmings of
style, but something more general and more inward,
if less definable, shows this promise in ways as mani-
fold as they are mysterious.

There would be less mystery about them if we
were only more certain about the chronology of
our documents. The Romans, inheriting and "passing on," like all schoolboys, the contempt which
they had themselves experienced from the Greeks,
disdained to take more than casual notice of the
original folk-songs with which they came in contact.
We can pardon Tacitus for not having been more
particular about this : it is harder—though his fault
was even more human and natural—to pardon Julian.
As it is, we have nothing from the earliest stages of
Spanish and Italian at all, and less than nothing
from the vernaculars which conditioned at least
Spanish in its birth from Latin. The famous, and
apparently indisputable, early documents of French
leave us almost as much in the dark [1] as to the
"father" tongue or tongues in that case. Of really
early, really "dark" Old High German we have
next to nothing; and while we hope that our oldest
Anglo-Saxon may be of the fifth century, and can

[1] Even after the invaluable *Histoire de la Langue Française* of
M. F. Brunot (Paris, 1905)—the best book of literary philology issued
for years.

hardly push the *possible* origin of our oldest Old
Norse too far back, the chilling logic of literary
history reminds us that we have no certain docu-
mentary evidence. We do not *know* that, in any
case but Cædmon's song, what we have took anything at all like its present form very much before
the millenary, or, at any rate, the eighth century,
of the Christian era.

But as one may easily be too credulous, so one
may, without great difficulty, be too sceptical; and
there is at any rate an extremely strong probability
that in these two last cases we *have* documents representing, with no very great change, what con-
fronted the literature and the language of Rome
at their first invasion, and what influenced them
in producing the hybrids with which we are really
acquainted. And we may at least say that, whether
this be so or not, the conclusions which we should
draw from it are certainly not irreconcilable with
the undoubted and corroborated phenomena later.
We meet, in these possibly and probably aboriginal
literatures, the presence of a new and suggestive
mythology, of different forms and attitudes of feeling, of a narrative faculty quite distinct from the
admirably plastic but somewhat imperfectly *story-
telling* gifts of the classic writers, and, above all, of
a fringe, an atmosphere, a *je ne sais quoi* of Imagination which promises a new plasticity, less orderly,
less finished, less satisfactory to the Understanding
but more satisfying to the Fancy; more passionate;
if vaguer, so much the more infinite; if less like

2 C

Truth, so much the more like Dream. In short, in *Beowulf* as in the Edda-stories, in the Anglo-Saxon religious and non-religious poetry as in the Sagas, we meet—Romance.

The Romantic characteristics have been just outlined with as much precision as is at all safe, and
Mediæval Literature— Poetry and Romance.
with far more precision, as well as with far more safety, than is compatible with caricature - epigrams such as Goethe's "Classicism is Health, Romanticism Disease," or even with sympathetic and in measure not incorrect descriptions such as Mr Pater's "Strangeness *plus* beauty, or beauty *plus* strangeness." But they are visible "confusedly" in these earliest periods, where also the entire uncertainty (for the most part) of authorship, and the far from considerable certainty (in many cases) of the homogeneity of the works themselves, constantly hamper and condition critical judgment. The confusion becomes clearness on the whole, though the individual uncertainties to some extent remain, in the next period, or group of periods, which give us what is called Mediæval literature proper, in its growth, in its perfection, and in at least the beginning of its decay. By combining with the subjects of our second and third volumes[1] that of our fourth,[2] we might include nearly if not quite the whole of this decay itself; but the reasons which dictated the separation in

[1] *The Flourishing of Romance* and *The Fourteenth Century.*
[2] *The Transition Period.*

volume are still potent against the combination in summary.

By the end of the eleventh century, as a central point,—anticipated by the precocious French genius, procrastinated in some other countries, Southern as well as Northern, till French influence itself lightened their darkness and quickened their inertia,— the new languages had taken, or were taking, independent substance and literary capacity, and the new literary forms were being filled up with ever-increasing variety and volume. In most cases these forms owed very little, if anything, to classical models as a matter of origin; though they very soon began to owe something as a matter of influence and modification. The obscurest, if also the most interesting, point in the study of mediæval literary origins is the question of the connection of the narrative Romance with the Saints' Life, and of the lyrical Romance with the Hymn. But this can be neglected by all save those who have an inextinguishable thirst for the conjectural. We are on firmer and less "facultative" ground when we come to the rise and modelling of the modern prosodies, and to the less obvious and important, but equally certain, influence of the Latin sentence on vernacular prose.

Legitimate, interesting, and important subjects of study are to be found in the forms and in the examples of the literature itself. First of all, we have the great form of the adventure - Romance,— prose or verse, or both in different countries at different times,—beginning, apparently, with the verse *Chanson de Geste* in France and the prose Saga in Iceland, absorbing the older native stories of every country, and reproducing the exuberant inventions of France itself, gathering its strength in the twelfth century into the sovereign and all-attracting legend of Arthur, and thence ravelling out again into the myriad details of the *roman d'aventures* in the lesser and special sense. If in comparatively few individual results of this enormous productiveness—perhaps in none, for the supposed primacy of the *Chanson de Roland* is mainly a delusion, and those best acquainted with the original *Arthuriana* would be most puzzled to single out a particular representative — we find the individual qualities of the greatest books, we do find a *diffused* greatness which can vie, when rightly understood, with the greatness of any other—even the greatest. The interest of war and vicissitude of event is given in the *chansons* as vividly as in the *Iliad*, and far more vividly than in the *Æneid*,—though with less concentration of poetic genius than in the first, and with less consummate accomplishment of poetic art than in the second. The interests of mystery and of passion are given in the Arthurian legend after a fashion simply not approached in ancient times.

Side by side with these things, but apparently a little later, there grows up—in all countries more or less, but especially in France, Southern and Northern, and in Germany—a Lyric which, whether profane or sacred, is strikingly different from most

of the ancient lyric which has been preserved to us.
These ancient poems—of course there are brilliant
exceptions, from the great pair of Sappho's odes
down to the pseudo-Anacreon—are either frankly
objective, or as objective as the constant *nisus* of
the lyric form towards subjectivity will permit. In
the mediæval lyric — though the objective is not
wanting, and as the epic breaks down, collects its
fragments and scenes into the charming form of the
Ballad—subjectivity mainly triumphs, and we have
the marvellous passion and majesty of the great Latin
hymns on the one side, the exquisite grace and sentiment of the Romance, and the *Alba*, and the *Lied*, and
the English nondescript lyric, on the other.

Less dignified and intense, but more various and
with even more *future* in it (seeing that the things
just mentioned are eternal), is the profusion of
short Story, sacred and profane, verse and prose,
sentimental and satiric, which manifests itself in a
range of subject and setting extending from the
short Saints' Life to the exceedingly unsaintly
fabliau, not seldom sanctified by clerical use. The
possibly germinal character of the Saints' Life in this
and even wider aspects has been glanced at,—and,
in any case, its mere mention suggests an influence
not so much classical—at least directly classical—as
Oriental,—while the variety of incident and treatment in the Saints' Lives themselves is so great
that they would serve as patterns to almost anything in the whole range of fiction. But however
this may be, the contrast of this enormous volume

and variety of "story" with the meagreness—putting mythology and mythological history aside—of anything of the same kind in the classics, is equally unmistakable and striking.

On the other hand, Drama, though it arises, arises slowly, and is retarded almost more than any other form of literature by the ecclesiastical and theological possession or obsession which, in many ways by no means mischievously, so long keeps its hold on literature. During the strictly mediæval period, or up to 1400, it is almost wholly liturgical, or at least "sacred"—purely secular dramas being of the latest and rarest. But purely, or almost purely, secular incidents and scenes are by no means rare; and they carry in them the germ of the great form of Comedy, while the continuous display of scenes, but partly connected, from the same Life, or of long separated passages from the same Sacred History, leads, with a directness which it is surprising that any one should mistake, to the purely modern drama of character and life-unity, and to the specially interesting development of the Chronicle Play.

If we quit the Belles Lettres, mediæval literature, inestimable to the historian in general, becomes

History. somewhat less interesting to the literary historian, save in the case of History itself, especially in what is called the Chronicle. It reverts—certainly without deliberation—to something like the manner of Herodotus, the ancient who has most of the story-telling gift; but it carries out the reversion with the unconquerable originality and αὐτάρκεια which is the true mediæval note. The theory—actually based on fact in some cases, not impossibly so in others—according to which the older forms, *Chanson* and Saga, of the Romance itself are family histories, derives fair analogic support from the very close connection of the Romance and the Chronicle. Even the more dignified and regular Latin histories, composed, directly or through following of the transition abstract-writers like Orosius, in imitation of the classics, assume the story-form; and not a few of the vernacular chronicles, from the supreme and typical performances of Villehardouin and Froissart downwards, are indistinguishable in arrangement and manner from the *chansons* and romances to which they correspond. But when we leave History the prose literature of knowledge loses interest as literature, much as it has in other ways. Most of it is in Latin; hardly any of it, Latin or vernacular, is of great quality.

But the quality of the rest is so striking, so individual, and so delightful that even the widest *Qualities and* tolerance of information, disciplined by *defects of the* the study of literature in the most *division—* *traditional* diverse countries, periods, and languages, *and real.* can hardly preserve its impartiality in face of the stupid ignorings and misunderstandings common from the early sixteenth century to the late eighteenth, and by no means extinct in the twentieth. Mediæval literature *has* faults; and some of them account for, though they never fully justify, the sciolist railings at "monkish ignorance" and "siècles grossiers" and the rest. Its mere information, though much more considerable than used to be supposed, was defective; and defective in a manner specially provoking to sciolism, because of the apparent absence of any method in the deficiency. Its real independence—more remarkable the more one studies it—is masked (let us allow this) almost to unrecognisableness, from all but very patient and instructed eyes, by a concomitant appearance of slavish deference to authority, and by the curious habit of writing in school and to pattern. Above all,—and here there need be no proviso or qualification,—the *critical* habit as we feel and understand it, and as it had been to some extent, if not fully, understood and felt by the ancients, was all but entirely dormant in the Middle Ages proper. Its two main functions—the distinguishing of the true from the false, and the distinguishing of the beautiful from the not beautiful — were not exercised at all. Men jumbled history and fiction, sober fact and impossible marvel, time and space, character and personality, with a really infantine unconcern. They put on a level the greatest writers of antiquity and the smallest of the Dark Ages. From all these facts, as well as from the further and greater fact that the sense of their special beauty—the beauty of Romance—after gradually waning was "hid in a vacant interlunar cave" for generations, came the misjudgment. From the facts themselves came a peculiarity which still makes just judgment, it would seem, in some cases hard. This peculiarity is not so much to be called inequality as *inconsummateness.* *The* chanson is greater than any particular chanson; *the* romance than *Percival le Gallois* or even *Lancelot*, and so in other cases. Putting the *Divina Commedia* and Dante aside, the single consummate thing is very hard to find in the Middle Ages, and the single consummate known writer harder.[1] And, unfortunately, it is not, it would seem, everybody whose mind is furnished with an alembic in which to distil the essence of acres of flowers not unmixed with weeds, with an apparatus in which to seize and condense the atmosphere floating thinly and vaguely over a distant and unfamiliar world.

To those who are more fortunate, and who have caught this essence, it is, as should hardly now be necessary to say at any length, as delightful, as important, as necessary as anything in literature. No one is now excusable—even such a man as Goethe was hardly excusable early in the nineteenth century —for regarding the account of mediæval literature as a discharged account—a curiosity, something fit, indeed, to be put in a museum, but negligible as a living and working force. As such it is as little to be neglected as Ancient, as Renaissance, as Modern; its

---

[1] Some may interject "Chaucer?" There will certainly be no belittling of Chaucer here. But not to make the rather *nisi prius* reply that a man who usually leaves his best things unfinished can hardly be called consummate, Chaucer is almost as much of the Transition as of the strict Mediæval period.

energy is equally conserved; the neglect of it is as
certain to lead to mistakes, shortcomings, blunders
like those of the eighteenth century, as the neglect of
any of the others. It is behind us, but it works on
us for that very reason; the fibres in our nature
which it has contributed will not suffer us to leave
them out of account with impunity. What has been,
in this case as in others, not only has been, but is.

Putting, however, this philosophical point of view
quite aside, there is as much—there is far more—
to be said for Mediæval Literature from the other
point of view which regards literature as a source of
delight. As origin it has given us the most charming
part of modern poetry, the most characteristic part of
modern drama, the germs, if no more, of that most
epoch-making modern creation, the novel. And it
has given also, to those who care not for origins and
are ingrates to ancestry, an amount of direct, immediate, unallowanced, and unconditioned enjoyment
which is only unrecognised because men will not
take the very slight trouble necessary to surmount
linguistic difficulties, in every case more apparent
than real, and in some hardly real at all. It is at
least a curious coincidence that it ranks, by consent
of many who know little else about it, on equal
terms with Ancient and with Modern Literature in
providing Dante as a companion for Homer and
Shakespeare, as one of the three masters of the
literature of the world.

Above all, it has, in little and in great, in individual and special and general—*quality*. It frees and

exercises the Imagination; it sets the Romantic Unity
or Unities of Design, of Character, of Concatenation,
of Interest, in equal franchise with the Classical Unity
of Fable and Action. It helps—all ignorantly perhaps—to enfranchise, magnify, complicate Character
itself. It holds up unflinchingly the banner of
Variety. It is not so much rebellious as serenely
indifferent to a too much specialised and regularised
æsthetic. It exalts Love, Adventure, Mystery. It
multiplies Form. It effects a complete concordat—in
far more equality than is sometimes thought—with
Religion. It enlists the sister Arts in its service. It
disdains neither Philosophy nor Science, as it understands them. In fact, it emancipates and develops
Literature itself, leaving, it may be, some provinces
uncultivated which had been cultivated before, but
annexing new, and allowing, whensoever time and
opportunity shall serve, the reoccupation of the
old, and so the establishment at once, or in time,
of a complete and universal Kingdom.

Whether, and how, the possibilities thus provided
might have been better taken, are matters of rather
problematical discussion. What actually happened
is matter of history. An abrupter transition, such as
those which happened about the middle of the seventeenth century and at or about the junction of the
eighteenth and nineteenth, might have had some
advantages; but the not too ardent optimist may
acquiesce in a Panglossian contentment with the
actual. That actual in literature (as the fifteenth

century[1] has shown it to us) is somewhat difficult to
realise, and has been not very commonly realised. It
is usual enough to find two literary periods, or movements rather, *spliced*, as it were—set side by side, the
one thickening and strengthening, the other thinning
and weakening, as it goes. But there is something
curiously disconnected in this present juxtaposition:
the usual half-way houses or men, the usual links of
communication, are wanting. On one side especially,
the growing Humanist movement stands mainly apart
from the established vernacular literatures. It is not
so much opposed to them—it becomes that later—as
entirely neglectful of them, something abstracted and
aloof. And this aloofness leads not merely to the
subsequent opposition, but to the exaggerated and
disastrous ignoring and contempt which followed,
which continued, and which, even at the present
day and after a century of Romantic reaction, has
by no means wholly, or even very generally, come
to an end. A feeling grows up that the modern literatures and languages are puerile or vulgar, that they
are for tinkers and tailors; even—most strange of all
—that they have no future, that they will "play the
bankrupt" with the thought and the art entrusted to
them and spent upon them. And this scorn — as
perhaps all scorn does — recoils upon the scorners,
sears and maims their faculty of literary appreciation, impoverishes their conception of philology and
criticism.

It would, however, be mere blind partisanship to

---

[1] See *The Transition Period.*

deny that the vernaculars were themselves partly to
The fifteenth blame for the contempt, or at least the
century. neglect, which they experienced.   There
came on them, in the most important and attractive
departments of literature, something which, if it is
not to be called decadence, must be regarded as a
sort of moulting-time,—a physiological change ana-
logous to this or some other similar phenomenon in
animal life.   Everywhere, except in Italy (and to a
small extent in Scotland), poetry decayed — most
surprisingly in England, where it fell from almost
the highest level attained by any country except
Italy, in Chaucer, to a doleful condition of stammering
platitude, compared to which its mere lispings of two
centuries earlier are inspiriting and attractive.   In
prose it derived a little good from the increased attention to the classics proper as regards style and
adaptation to different subjects ; but even in prose,
and much more in verse, this same attention helped
to load it with trumpery and awkward " rhetorical "
diction,—all the more inappropriate because of the
general lack of thought and imagination in the
matter of composition.   The result of all which was
that the last stage of mediæval literature, if we can
dignify the general fifteenth century literature of
Europe with that name, almost invited the *outre-
cuidance* of the sixteenth century humanists, and
went some little way towards justifying it.   The very
forms, charming once, grew slipshod, and lost outline ;
and where they resisted, the matter, save in quite
isolated cases such as that of Villon, failed to come to

the rescue. Yet there were compensations. In one great department—the drama—though the absence of precise dates makes the due staging of the history difficult or impossible, it is demonstrable that the progress effected during this abused century was very great. In fact, its work, and its work alone, made the true modern drama possible. The renewed study of the classical theatre could never have given us Shakespeare and Calderon, or Shakespeare and Molière, if it had been pursued till the present day. It could have given us Racine—but that is a wholly different matter. All, or almost all, the characteristics of modern comedy are traceable directly to the mediæval drama — most of the characteristics of Shakespearian tragedy are at least clearly favoured by that drama, properly developed and crossed with classical—while they are frowned upon by the classical Poetic and the classical Theatre alike to such an extent that, except by sheer reaction and rebellion, they could never have arisen from either. And when we remember how great the work of the drama itself was in the two following centuries, we cannot but do honour to the humble and obscure beginnings which alone made it possible.

The second great merit of the fifteenth century was to break up and crumble the ruins of mediæval literature into a form which was easily retainable by the popular mind, and which kept its virtue—ready for manuring use in future times. The ballad, as much as anything else, refreshed and recreated European literature three centuries after 1500, and it was, to all probable certainty, just before, during, and for some time after this century that it arose and was mainly cultivated.

The third was that reinforcement of literary means and powers of the languages which has been already described; the fourth, the beautiful literature of Italy, to the best period of which it contributes at least a half; and the fifth, the Humanist proceedings themselves. But these last can only be considered properly in connection with the all-important movement which they constitute, and in which they are merged. In other words, we must now take stock of European literature at the time, and as it experienced the changes and influences, of the Renaissance itself.

The aspects of the literature of the Renaissance from the point of view which the literary historian *The Renaissance.* should endeavour to take are threefold: he must turn himself from one to the other, but not forget each as he changes his position. In the first place, there is the state of vernacular literature actually reached by what we may call 1500 —*i.e.*, a date floating in various countries from 1450 to 1550. In the second, the direct and positive results of the revival of classical study itself. And the third, the literary crop—in the vernaculars of the period succeeding the floating starting-point above indicated, and covering, *as a whole*, though not in any one country, the period from 1450 to about 1620. We may take them in order, premising that the first balance - sheet, so to say, has been very seldom accurately drawn up or audited; that the second, once altogether overrated on the asset or credit side, is still regarded from the same point by a very few, and otherwise mostly neglected; that the third, supposed to be part of the documental furniture of every cultivated mind, is not perhaps entirely beyond need of restating and of reauditing as critically as may be.

The remarks made above will have shown already that no undervaluation of mediæval literature is here to be expected; but it can be guaranteed that no estimate of it has been or shall be given which cannot be supported by a voucher of direct and critical examination. The progress made in some three hundred or four hundred years in most cases (though the time might be extended to a thousand in some) is simply astonishing. Languages which, so far as we know, had started without any provision of literature except folk - song and folk - tale had, partly by simple evolution, but partly, of course, also under the tutelage and mastership of Latin, arrived at such a state that in hardly any department of literature were they quite unpractised, that in many they had accomplished charming work, and that much of that work was absolutely novel in quality and characteristic. They had introduced and nearly consummated Romance; they had refreshed and almost revolutionised Lyric; in this and in other departments of Poetry they had refashioned entirely the main instrument—Prosody ; they had laid the foundations of a new Drama; they had made their own path

Its inheritance.

along nearly all the old roads.   In the case of a few writers — Dante, Petrarch, Boccaccio, Froissart, Chaucer — they had made substantive, individual, lasting contributions to the great works and workers of the world's literature ; in a vast number of other cases, known and unknown, they had added to the delight and the instruction of the world.   Above all, they had made a *place d'armes* and a magazine, the value—the very existence—of which might for a time be ignored, but which was sure to be rediscovered and utilised as time went on.   They had, in the hackneyed phrase, "builded better than they knew"—after a fashion unparalleled in the literary history of any other age.   Their very weakness, their very shortcomings, had virtue in them ; their diseases had prophylactic force for future inoculation ; their ignorances were preservative.   Fate, the kind ancestor, laid down their vintages for us — and bricked them up.   It is really a question, as we look back, whether the bricking - up, which the succeeding generations so sedulously respected in their disrespect, was not even a greater blessing than the original laying down.   It certainly was not a smaller one.

Yet we must not ignore the weaknesses which did exist.   Their education—admirable so far as it went— had been always rather narrow, and was now in-adequate to their new opportunities.   Very much wider exercise was necessary for them.   In certain respects, as has been said, they had been passing through a phase positively morbid.   Their diction wanted much enriching ; their prosody, admirable

2 D

as it was, a process of disciplining and training;
fresh thought had to be instilled into them; and,
above all, Style—in prose most, in verse to some extent
—had to be gained. The obvious metaphor of *status
pupillaris* (and in fact *puerilis*) did really apply to
them. They had to put away childish things; and it
has been observed at all times that those who are
under this obligation are apt to discharge it with
somewhat too exuberant a contempt, with far too
ready a relinquishment, of the childish things they
put away. But there was nothing really to regret or
to complain of in their state : its past was gracious,
its present promising, its future illimitable.

It is more difficult still to appraise, in a manner
likely to commend itself to many readers, the achievements of the Renaissance in and in regard to the
classical languages themselves. For here knowledge,
actually in the possession of many, and supposed by
courtesy to be in that of all, blends or contends with
a multiform if discontinuous absence of knowledge,
while prejudices of various kinds make the confusion
worse confounded. One way of safety is, however,
pretty clear, and that is to keep the accomplishment
of the period in regard to older classical literature,
and its experiments in classical language for new
literature-making, duly apart. In the first respect,
though there is room for large difference of opinion in
detail, there can be, from the point of view of catholic
literary criticism, room for very little on the main
point. The debt which is owed to the Renaissance
for exploring, preserving, and to a great extent in-

terpreting, the treasures of Antiquity, is not only enormous but practically not to be liquidated. Every age inherits it afresh ; no exertions of any can get rid of it. The Humanists of the fifteenth and early sixteenth centuries, in the first place, saved Ancient Literature as we possess it ; and though Humanism is, in a certain sense, responsible for the excesses of the Reformation, this latter might have come without it, and would in all probability have made further havoc with the treasures of the past had it done so. In the second place, the invention of printing, with which they were closely connected, made the recovered treasure safe. In the third, if their study of this treasure was not always conducted on the wisest principles, it was intense, devoted, energetic, almost beyond parallel. They got much, if not all, the rough-hewing, and not a little of the shaping done to our hands. The critical work (in the proper sense), which they based on their classical investigations, reacted on the modern literatures in ways not always immediately, but always in the long-run, profitable. In short, they re-estated literature in its old patrimony, improved and cultivated anew. That, as so often happens, the fresh acquisition for a time diverted attention unduly from that which had been long familiar, was indeed a misfortune, but an inevitable one ; and one which, in the long process of time, was sure to be, and has been, converted into a blessing. The loss could be changed into a gain : the gain, once made, was incapable of ever turning into a loss.

Not so cheerfully can we speak of the actual Latin composition—the Greek is a curiosity merely, and here negligible—of these ages. As we have taken pains to show in the volume devoted to the subject,[1] this composition is itself interesting enough in quite a large part of it, and in a smaller but not inconsiderable part positively delightful. It exercised, in forms already disciplined, the talent of the European world, and enabled it to impart similar discipline to the vernaculars. It had the great, the very great, the almost incalculable advantage of being open to all Europe, and of keeping up the communication between the different countries at the very time when that communication was being endangered by the growth of the new national monarchies. Much of it, especially the verse, has an elegance and an accomplishment which are still attractive to all who are fortunate enough to have been put in the way of feeling them The prose, familiar if in less polished forms, for generations, centuries, almost millennia, provided a vehicle for the copious new thought which could hardly have been provided by any of the vernaculars—even Italian, even French—in quite the same condition.

But here praise must stop. Far too large a proportion of this Latin composition was idle school-work, having no originality or "race." Far too large a proportion of it, on the other hand, failed to play its own game with sufficient strictness, and so deprived itself of its one great justification; while some ran into the opposite extreme, and, as in the case of Ciceronianism,

[1] *The Earlier Renaissance.*

made itself a laughing-stock. But the main fault—
we may almost say crime—of it was that it diverted
genius, talent, even useful industry, from the vernaculars themselves; that it set up a false and tinsel aristocracy of letters; that it hindered, at least as much as
it helped, that magnificent development of the true,
the vernacular, literatures to which we are now coming,
and which is the real glory of the period. Humanism,
especially in its productive phase, did something for
this literature—nay, much. Yet it played the mother
in stepmotherly, the nurse and governess in barbarous
and tyrannic, fashion — grudging the food it gave,
enforcing its discipline with slaps and sneers—nay,
doing its best to give no food and no discipline, save
the crumbs under the table and the mere sight of the
training given to the favoured children.

But the fairies favoured the ill-treated child as
usual; or, if anybody prefers it, the discipline of
Humanism itself was so admirable that, however un-
willingly applied, it could not but be effective. Or
if yet a third way seem better—the mere fatalism of
accepting the hours and the men as having come and
saying no more about it,—that way also shall be left
open to readers of this book. Anyhow, the period—
shifting as usual slightly for different countries and
races—declared itself to be, and has been more and
more recognised as being, one of the few great literary
periods of the world,—admitting as a period only the
blossoming times of Greek and of Roman literature
as its rivals beforehand. In Italy earliest, most
dynamically as far as immediate influence goes, and

with greatest perfection of form; in France considerably later and in somewhat less perfection, yet there also producing in Rabelais and Montaigne two of the Peers or Paladins of the world's literature; in England later still, reaching the highest level of all in Shakespeare and one equal to the highest elsewhere in Spenser, with a vast volume of matter not much less in merit, though more unequal and less disciplined; in Spain contemporaneously with England, and not wholly dissimilar in character, less various, but in Lope and Cervantes again providing summits; in Germany and the minor countries inferior, and even far inferior, but there also showing all the signs of fermentation and new birth,—the spirit works everywhere, and everywhere shows its working.[1]

Perhaps the most curious general feature of this working is the all but invariable blending of the ancient and the mediæval spirit. This shows itself, despite the flouting and scouting of the latter, in which not mere pedants and classicasters, but some of the men whose real title to fame is derived from this element itself, are wont to indulge. Those who delight in nothing so much as in the discovery and exaltation of a "modern" spirit—different alike from that of ancient times and from that of the Middle Ages — may· ignore or dispute this. Those who, excused perhaps to some extent by ignorance of the full facts of mediæval literature, attribute almost the whole merit of Elizabethan as of Italian Renaissance accomplishment to classical influences,

[1] See *The Later Renaissance.*

will no doubt pooh-pooh and deny it. But the facts
are the facts, and they have been sufficiently set forth
in these twelve volumes to enable any one who chooses
to get at the truth. The purposes of our book are
much less controversial than expository, and it is not
necessary or desirable here to argue out the question
whether there is anything in the "modern" spirit
which is not to be accounted for by the blend aforesaid. It is probably sufficient—and it will seem to
some persons more than sufficiently shocking—to say
that such a position as the negative answer to this
question is quite susceptible of argumentative defence.
At any rate, in the Literature of the Renaissance, both
matter and form, whether they exhibit anything else
or not, do exhibit most vividly and most interestingly
what may be regarded from one side as the disciplining
of mediæval luxuriance by classical agencies, and from
the other as the engrafting upon the classic stock of
artistic form and philosophic, nay, scientific, thought
of the vigorous scions of mediæval fancy, religion,
curiosity, and so forth. In Italy, where the mediæval
character had always been weakest, it is weakest still ;
it is strongest in England. But in both and everywhere the Renaissance is Classical *plus* Mediæval or
Mediæval *plus* Classical.

Some have held that the blend — the cross — is
always necessary to the highest excellence, and certainly the present phenomenon, taken as we have
presented it, does not discredit their doctrine. In
a certain sense, Shakespeare is an accident, as genius
always is—but it is only an accidency of transcend-

ence. The property, or rather the wonderful group
of properties, is shown with this or that modification,
in this or that degree, by all the men of the time
from Ariosto and Rabelais, from Cervantes and Montaigne, through the numerous authors of second- or
third-rate genius and talent to the infinite crowds
of " single-speech " writers, or writers of but few things
of excellence, which the time affords.   On the one
hand the immense and sometimes apparently or
really childish nescience, and acquiescence in nescience, of the Middle Ages has been replaced by an
eager appetite for knowledge, and an almost pathetic
belief in it; their almost incredible lack of the
critical faculty by an incessant activity of criticism and exploration; their limitations (exquisite
in a way) of form, and their formlessness when
these limitations are outstepped, by an extensive
and yet disciplined multiplication of kind and treatment; their conservatism by a restless spirit of
innovation.   On the other, the corresponding, and
in a way complementary, limitations of the classics
are removed by the working of the exuberant mediæval imagination in the first place; by the necessity of supplying the demands which that imagination had already prompted in the second; and
by the inevitable effect of the multiplication of
languages, literatures, countries visited, commerces,
sciences, arts, which was produced by the great
world - events of the late fifteenth and early sixteenth centuries.   When Goethe said that Classicism was Health and Romanticism Disease, he said

a rather silly thing:[1] if he had said (what he probably meant) that Classicism expresses Repose, Romanticism Restlessness, he would have said the truth, if not the whole truth. And Restlessness, as we all know, has two great categories. There is the Restlessness of disease itself or of idle fidget; and there is the Restlessness of healthy activity, unable to refrain from self-exercise, from production, from productive labour. This is the restlessness of the Renaissance; and everybody knows more or less the splendour, and the variety, and the value of the results which it attained.

Taking its earlier and later periods together, it created, as the most eminent example of that blending of classical and mediæval lessons which has been noticed, the greatest drama that the world has seen; greater — at least vaster — than the Greek in bulk and range, and equal at least in intensity; hardly inferior, if inferior at all at its best, in form well understood. It saw the beginnings, uncertain and tentative but real, of two great literary kinds which the ancients had hardly known—the Novel and the Essay. It perfected the diction, the prosody, almost the grammar, of the vernaculars. It laid the foundation of the literary treatment of the sciences in them. It revived philosophy and re-created criticism. It gave a new birth to oratory — the least disputable result of its religious convulsions. It essayed almost all the forms of prose. And above all — partly in

[1] For the saving (but not all-saving) respect with which he said it, see *The Romantic Revolt.*

connection with drama itself, but partly also in the purer and less adulterated kinds — it poured forth floods, oceans of poetry, as varied, as potent in intoxicating power, as exquisite in art, and poignant in delight-giving property as the poetry of any period that the world has seen.

The double aspect which we have noticed so often —which belongs, indeed, more or less to all periods of literature—appertains very decidedly to the next period,—to the First Half of the Seventeenth Century.[1] It might almost be—and sometimes has been—taken with the Renaissance, making one long period of two full centuries, from 1450, or even earlier in Italy, to 1650, or even later in England. But this is somewhat too sweeping, and there is distinction enough to justify the erection of the earlier seventeenth into a separate division, with the usual provision of cautions and escapements.

Generally speaking, the characteristics of this period are those not exactly of Decadence—it is only *Between Renaissance and Augustanism.* of Italy that this dangerous word can be used with some justification—but of something like Autumn. The wild freshness of the Renaissance morning has almost or quite disappeared, and in the character of thought which distinguishes the literature there is a prevailing *gravity*. It is a more learned period than ever,—it is perhaps the most learned period of the world's literary history; but except in such places as Eng-

[1] See the volume of that title.

land and such persons as Bacon (who very largely
represents the earlier time—the Renaissance itself),
it has quite lost the eager and towering aspirations,
the limitless belief, of that time.   Even in Montaigne,
who anticipated in France, as Bacon lagged in England, there is nothing like the melancholy which
characterises our great Jacobean and Caroline
writers, and which is observable in different forms
abroad.   But this gravity and melancholy — this
discouraged learning — are balanced, as so often
happens, by a straining (in the other direction, though
often by the same persons) after the fantastic.   There
is a battle—which need not be other than a good-
natured one, if critics could only forget the pedantic
acrimony too common with them—between those who
regard Euphuism, Marinism, Gongorism, the extrav-
agances of the Louis XIIIth men in France, the
"metaphysical" flights of English poetry, even the
falling-leaf magnificence of Taylor and Browne and
others, as a reaction, a decadence from a supposed
Golden Age earlier, and those who think these things
to be the last stage of the Romantic development,
which had gone on side by side with the classical
element in the Renaissance.   But the phenomena
themselves admit, as usual, of no real or reasonable
dispute; and they contribute the greatest literary
interest and charm of the period itself.   The appearance and prevalence, however, of " Marinism," " Metaphysical Poetry," or whatever else any one may
please to call it, seems to be one of those major
literary phenomena which demand some notice here,

as well as in the volumes more specially devoted to
their periods. Few such phenomena have attracted
more conjectural explanations of their origin and
nature,—none perhaps more divers critical opinions
as to their character. The whole thing (in England,
where it is perhaps most remarkable, and where it is
a great mistake to separate the prose part of the
matter from the poetical) may be, and has been,
described as the decadence of Elizabethanism, as
the survival of mediævalism, as the•last gasp (before its trance) of Romanticism, as the bastard
result of a blending of Classicism itself, as many
other things.

The most curious theory, and one which, like others
of its authors, one must feel inclined to take as "only
his f-f-f-fun," was Coleridge's, which *connected* Browne
with Addison and Johnson, Crashaw with Pope and
Darwin, as attempting refinement on the sturdy plain-
ness of the great Elizabethan age. But this, if not
mere paradox, was system run mad, and availing itself
of a rather inaccurate knowledge of literary history.
There is no more probable explanation—if explanation there must be—than that of Elizabethan conceit
and *word*-play changing itself into *thought*-play, under
the influence of increasing learning on the one hand
and of the disillusionment of reaction from the wild,
vague hopes of the Renaissance on the other. But
critical observation of the phenomenon has better stuff
for us than this. We shall hardly now, if we are
wise, wish that "metaphysicalism" in prose and verse
had continued longer ; we shall still less, with the

same proviso, be anything but profoundly grateful for its existence and for what it gave us. For the best things of Browne, Taylor, Glanville even, in prose, of the Caroline poets as a group in verse, are things that we could not spare,—things never to be replaced without loss by others, just as double numbers of rubies and emeralds would never console the true lover of gems for the loss of spinels and jacinths. These things were good in their perfection directly: they were good in their imperfection, indirectly perhaps but as certainly. For that imperfection undoubtedly hastened—perhaps even did directly cause—the growth of that prose style-of-all-work which English at least had never had, and which itself, though a little inferior at its best, could attain no small perfection; and in verse brought about a reaction, not indeed favourable to the very best and purest poetry, but healthy in its effect on the very worst, and directly helpful in applied styles like Satire. The good products of Marinism abroad were less good; but the reaction from it was equally useful in the one case where there was vigour enough in the literature to carry it out. Italy and Spain, unluckily, were not in this case: they could not even make their own reaction for themselves, and had to borrow it from France, which had, in a manner, borrowed from them the original tendency. But France herself, though this tendency produced in her literature no such delightful fruits as it did in England, laid up for herself no small store of them for recourse when the right time came. And in the reaction itself she found her way, as she could hardly have found it otherwise, to achievements peculiarly suitable to her genius, and such as, in the same kind, no other modern literature can boast. Undoubtedly, however, it is England that is best off in this particular time, and that in two respects, each of which is sufficiently important to call for some individual attention even in a space so confined as ours.

There is a point connected with this period which can hardly have escaped any careful observer, which has been dwelt on more or less by some of the best critics, but which (some authorities seem to think) has not been quite sufficiently elaborated by any. The task of giving it this elaboration would not be much over-parted with a volume; it certainly would give very sufficient occupation for a full chapter or a substantial essay; but it can, and perhaps should, be treated, at least summarily, here. This is the extraordinary fortune of England in the possession of Shakespeare, and to a less degree of Milton, not merely as great writers, but as writers popularly great, who came sufficiently early to provide a standard unaffected by Time, by the salt or acid gusts of the popular breeze, and by the caprices and diseases of criticism. Not, of course, that Shakespeare (for we may in our scanty plot confine ourselves to him) has not had his vicissitudes. Even Dryden denied the master (to whom he elsewhere bore such magnificent confession) once or twice: the eighteenth century had its superior provisos and allowances: there are persons at this very moment who tell us that Beatrice is a "barmaid" (one would like to be called to that bar!) or that her creator is "mediæval."

But the point is that for nearly three hundred years this tower of strength has stood four-square and unshaken—not merely in reality, but by admission and confession even of those who would rather like it demolished,—who would prefer it as a picturesque ruin. Did the couplet threaten to tyrannise over English poetry, Shakespeare was there with his unapproached lyrics and his unapproachable blank verse. Was a false and limited "poetic diction," an impoverished and colourless prose vocabulary, the danger? The Shakespeare - lexicon refused to be antiquated, and was there for any sensible rebel to fashion, to employ. No evil beast—Unity, Good Sense, proscription of fancy and imagination, no matter what—could prowl, but the tower was an arsenal of weapons, defensive and offensive, against him. The interesting and acute, if one-sided, Breton critic[1] with whom we dealt elsewhere might, if he had known enough of the history of English literature, have derived from this dæmonic all-sufficiency some support for his theory that Shakespeare was a great Evil Principle—a Throne and Domination escaped for some mysterious purpose from Hell. *We* may see in it just the opposite suggestion, as of the presence of an archangel from the Heaven of Literature. For no other language has anything quite like it. In French, Rabelais is too early and too *eccentric* (in both the true and the vulgar sense), while

[1] M. Ernest Hello,—*v. sup.*, p. 147 *sq.*

even Montaigne, besides the drawback of being a prose writer only, is limited as such.   Dante came too early for Italy and Goethe too late for Germany, while the Spaniards do not seem to have been able to make full use (though they have made some, and are perhaps nearest to us in this way as in others) of Lope and Cervantes and Calderon, who after all do not quite together make a Shakespeare.   Yet, as was said above, it is not so much the greatness as the *admitted* greatness that is the point.   You lay down a bad rule, positive or negative (the negative bad rules are always the worst), to a larger or smaller audience. The audience may or may not accept the rule itself. But it has already been taught that Shakespeare, if not impeccable, is the greatest name in literature, or one of the greatest names.   It goes away and finds that Shakespeare does not care a rush for your positive rules, and breaks your negative whenever he puts pen to paper.   There is not much doubt what will be the result with the wiser part of that audience; the middle part will at least have an equal chance of going right or wrong; and as for the foolisher part, it does not matter what happens to them.   Indeed they are quite likely to go right too.

These considerations chiefly affect what may be called the retrospective or Romantic side of the First Half of the Seventeenth Century.   It cannot, however, be denied, though the order and causal connection of the process admit of endless argument, that in this period another process of development is noticeable—the triumph, namely, of the " classical " element.

What this means exactly, it would be difficult to find two authorities who themselves exactly agree. Some perceive in it the action and gradual triumph of principles of order, reason, science, over the anarchic, the erratic, the irrational, the unscientific. The difficulty in this view is that on principles of literary criticism, generally if not universally accepted by these persons themselves, the triumph of order, reason, science means the deterioration of literature. So long as men really thought, not merely that the age of Louis XIV. was an enormous advance on its predecessors,—a view for which there was some if not complete justification,—but that the age of Anne had quite antiquated the whole Elizabethan period from Spenser to Shirley, it was possible to hold this view consistently. It is now impossible—unless (which those who hold it are, as a rule, equally indisposed to do) you admit that Order, Reason, Science are *not* good things for literature, or that literature is quite disconnected with, and independent of, any such thing at all; that Order and Anarchy, Reason and Childishness, Science and Ignorance or Unmethod, are equally unimportant to it; that things literary move in an orbit of their own, the laws of which, if not actually incalculable, cannot be calculated in any terms such as those just used.

And the other view is at least open to less of this difficulty, though it may have difficulties of its own. According to this, the dwindling of Romantic and imaginative literary faculty let in the already exercised classical prejudice in a new form. The tendency, visible in Jonson and Malherbe, but of which Boileau is the great example, is no longer that of the earlier Humanists, who pooh-poohed vernacular composition altogether and as such. Some distrust of them indeed persists; and the international use of Latin as a vehicle of serious and even of lighter literature almost dominates the seventeenth century, and perseveres into the eighteenth. But actual contempt of vernacular literature is a mere, and a rare, survival; and the very greatest of men who are still guilty of it, or something like it, such as Bacon and Hobbes, are themselves by far at their greatest when they write in their own language.[1] But though the adoration of the Classics thus loses something of its exclusive and arrogant attitude,—though the knowledge perhaps to some extent declines, or at least tends to become the practised possession of the technical scholar,—their influence, well or ill understood, is more powerful than ever on the vernacular literatures themselves. The very appearance of the "Modern" heresy—in Italy at or even before the beginning of the period, in France and England not till towards and even after its close—is in a way a testimony to this. And as a matter of fact this heresy is not taken up in the right spirit or (with the rarest exceptions) by the right men. It is really more a "sport" than an evolution: paradox, mere scepticism, even mere ignorance, have much more to do with it than any better things; and its partisans rarely if ever show

---

[1] For this reason our volume on the period has taken little notice of Latin writing.

any sense of the value of mediæval literature (recurrence to and admission of which is necessary before
the real evolutionary progress can be made), or any
real sense of the value of the best modern. They are
chiefly moved, either as in the cases of Tassoni earlier
and Fontenelle later, by the sceptical reaction from the
Renaissance, taking this special line, or by the mere
vulgar preference of the " up-to-date," which is as old
as its most appropriate and disgusting formula is new.

But Classicism—Neo-Classicism—made advances
entirely unaffected by this. The critical doctrines
of the necessity of Rule and of the exclusive orthodoxy of rules drawn from the ancients had been
formulated—with a mistaken positiveness ot restriction on the whole, but not unintelligently and on a
preliminary foundation of real learning—by some
three generations of scholars during the sixteenth
century in Italy. Later in that century and throughout the seventeenth they were taken up in France
with more zeal and peremptoriness than real knowledge or real critical spirit, but in a fashion to some
extent excused by the peculiar disorganisation into
which French literature had fallen, owing to the
character of the Pléiade movement. Italian itself
had sunk into a sort of stationary state, and was not
for a long time to count for very much in European
literature. But in French first, and in English later,
the altered and to some extent popularised classical
influence more and more affected the literatures of
the respective countries. The greatest writers of
France in the earlier half of the century—Malherbe,

Balzac, Descartes, Pascal, Corneille — expressed it directly in different degrees ; in England, though from Jonson onwards it is very noticeable, the core of Romantic resistance was stouter.   By the latter half, however, this had, even in England, dwindled or was broken down; and from 1660 onwards the so-called Augustan tendency held the field.   The bolt of Spain, like that of Italy, was shot; the Thirty Years' War (and perhaps not the Thirty Years' War only) prevented Germany from doing anything of importance; the minor nations could do—or did—but little. French and English—the first resuming its ancient prerogative, the second acquiring what it had never yet exercised, and both by degrees entering into close relations with each other — became the recognised centres of the literature of Europe.

This hegemony was used in the interests of Classicism ; and it would probably be unfair not to recognise that Classicism furnished by far the greater part of the forces by which it was first brought about and afterwards maintained.[1]   The genius of the French tongue, of the French nature, for "order, regularity, precision," had not been so noticeable in the long and glorious procession of literary work by which, from the eleventh century onwards, France had set patterns and given discipline to Europe, as originality, *élan*, and fecundity; but it was now to declare itself.   The literary accomplishment of England had become vaster and mightier

The Augustan Ages.

[1] See *The Augustan Ages* and *The Mid-Eighteenth Century.*

than that of France itself as a whole; but it was
distinctly in need of more discipline and stricter
patterns.   And the need was emphasised, as has
been shown, by a certain dying-down of the choicer
growths of fancy, and by the appearance in their
place of extravagant and sometimes tasteless eccentricity.   In particular it was time for prose, and for
the more prosaic forms and departments of poetry, to
be organised, polished, brought to such perfection as
was compatible with, and as would facilitate, their
employment for the accomplishment of the average
purpose — philosophical, political, scientific, miscellaneous — for the delight and instruction of the
average man.   It was to this task—by no means
with whole consciousness, for they were profoundly
of opinion that they were improving matters in
pure poetry as well—that the " Augustan Ages "
set themselves.   And they accomplished it with a
thoroughness which must always deserve admiration
—if not quite of the kind and to the degree which
they thought their due.   The French, with Boileau as
their chief tutor, and Corneille and Racine as their
great examples, 'brought the peculiar, limited, but
exquisitely artistic form of drama, which they had
already selected in the very fervour of their Renaissance itself, to a marvellous completeness.[1]   They

---

[1] Of late years ingenious efforts, an account of which will be found
in the proper place, have been made to discover motives—especially
the " conflict of will "—in the French drama, which are to compensate
for the variety of character and plot-interest in the English.   And
there are those who hold that the accusation formerly brought
against this drama, more especially in Racine, that it is "declama-

practically perfected French prose within certain
limits. They fashioned the lighter poetry and some
kinds of the more serious with the most distinguished
ingenuity, deftness, and taste. They led the criticism
of Europe—in a wrong path perhaps, but they led it
—for generations. And they made advances—to be
carried much farther by England—in the direction of
one of the greatest achievements of modern literature,—the Novel.

England herself imitated them a good deal for a
time, and thought she was imitating them a good deal
more. But, as has been said, the towering genius of
Shakespeare had already arrested the English attention in literature—as the cone of Fusiyama did with
the Japanese in art—to such an extent that it was
constantly called away and lifted up from mere rule
and detail. That of Milton—rising a little later and
in a different quarter of the literary landscape—did
the same. And it most fortunately happened that

---

tory," is thus to a great extent removed. Perhaps some may still
remember *The Rehearsal*, and wonder whether its satire on these
explanations beforehand is quite ineffective. In any case, the matter
is not one for settlement here ; but it is not improper to suggest
that this "conflict of will" has not only a suspicious air of after-
thought, but also supplies a rather thin and monotonous mainspring
for dramatic action, as compared, either with the conflict of destiny
and human character of the Greeks, or the unfolding of character *in
itself*, in contact rather than in conflict with circumstance, of Shakespeare. "Pray make up your mind and have done with it" is a
damaging repartee to *it*. You cannot "have done" with destiny, or
with your own nature in its development. Shakespeare himself, it
is true, took this conflict of will, and made of it the stuff of one
masterpiece, and the part-stuff of another. But he had room for
dozens more on motives entirely different.

Dryden—so much the greatest representative man of English literature in the later seventeenth century that there is no second to him—was not only an ardent, if critical, admirer of these two, but also had in his own nature far more than a touch of the old leaven. He intended to some extent to Gallicise, but he naturalised what he introduced by Anglicising it. And the third example which he provided, side by side with those of Shakespeare and Milton themselves, for the coming generation had nearly as much in it of indocility as of docility to foreign, to French, and even to strictly classical influence.

Nevertheless, in both countries and in both sections of "Augustanism," the prevailing, the orthodox opinion tended to the classical side. We need not here recur to, or enter afresh upon, the old, the never-concluded, the never-to-be-concluded dispute as to the exact meaning of the terms "Classic" and "Romantic." Exact definition of either is probably impossible ; sufficient understanding of both and of their difference is quite easy, and by this time probably common enough. That the classic turns by preference to order, reason, definiteness ; the romantic to liberty, imagination, the vague ; that the classic thinks of what ought to please, the romantic of what does ; that the latter is less sedulous to instruct, and when it does convey instruction prefers the allegorical form, —all these things are true enough, and could be truly enlarged and varied. And the accentuation of them on the classic side, with a certain narrowness almost necessarily consequent upon such accentuation, supplies the main note of the Augustan Ages and the partly stationary state which succeeded them in the eighteenth century. It formulates itself in the work of the great Frenchmen of the latest years of Louis XIII. and the earlier of his son; it animates the successors of Dryden much more exclusively than it had animated Dryden himself; it distinguishes the sort of partial revival of Italian literature which marks the latest seventeenth and early eighteenth centuries in Italy; it finally stifles, for a time, the indocile and intensely characteristic genius of Spain; and it is almost ludicrously reflected in one side of the earnest, rather touching, and before long to be successful attempt of Germany to re-create her letters.

It does great things; and that practically final achievement as to prose, which has been and will be referred to, can never be too much acknowledged. It cures some evils in the literary constitution, and supplies much admirable gymnastic thereto. But it has some grave faults and some graver deficiencies. The most offensive and, as it happened, also the most mischievous of the former was its intolerable and pernicious self - complacency. "A good conceit of oneself" is by no means necessarily a bad thing; but as soon as it involves or produces—as it almost always does—an ill conceit of others, it becomes bad, and worse, and the worst. The Augustans had much upon which they might legitimately pride themselves, on the condition that they appreciated things that were different. This was what they would not do. They invented, or at least took from the foolisher

thought of the Renaissance, and depraved further,
the false, ridiculous, mischievous, and even yet not by
any means extinct estimate of the Middle Ages,
their religion, their politics, their literature—as of a
period of mixed first and second childhood, of bar-
barism, of ignorance, and of folly.   Still less excusably, they extended this contempt, with some modifi-
cations and allays of mild patronage, to the period
of literature — infinitely greater than their own—
which intervened between the Middle Ages and
themselves.   Boileau said, and no doubt seriously
thought, that French poetry before Malherbe was
chaos, and after him very imperfectly cosmical.
Even Dryden imagined that the true sweetness of
English numbers had been first discovered by Mr
Waller; and Addison in his salad days called Chaucer
a jack-pudding and Spenser a tedious moralist, while
in his riper years he excepted against Shakespeare's
mixture of tragedy and comedy, and rested the body
of his Miltonic eulogy on the capital parallels to
Homer and Virgil that you could get out of *Paradise
Lost*.   Most of Europe thought Dante a gloomy
mystic, and Ariosto himself a formless and "promiscuous" taker of literary liberties ; esteemed Cervantes
mainly as a burlesquer of romance, and forgot Lope
and Calderon altogether, or regarded them as almost
as barbarous as Shakespeare, with a rather more
civilised language.   Johnson and Voltaire, agreeing
in hardly anything else, carried into the last quarter
of the eighteenth century the curious spectacle of two
men, each in a way the dictator of literature in his

own country, who held a hopelessly wrong estimate of literary history.

The Nemesis of all this was certain and swift. Augustan literature, as we have said, did great things, —drama, excellent in its less excellent kind; satire, equal to the best in the history of literature; admirable history; and, in its latest days (or by its heirs), admirable prose fiction; capital philosophical and scientific exposition; much else that was good. Hardly the maddest Romantic, one supposes, would consent to impoverish the literature of the world by depriving it of Racine and La Bruyère and those who follow them, of Dryden and the Queen Anne men and their successors to Johnson. But in cutting itself off from its root and ancestry in the past, the school which they mainly represented had doomed itself, according to the unalterable law of nature, to dwindling, starvation, sterility. If the classical or Augustan principle had had universal as it had general sway, literature might, were such a thing possible in the Providence of God, have come to an end altogether—would certainly have come to a state of real decrepitude and impotence far worse than what was imagined to exist in mediæval times. As it was, there are few weaker periods of pure literature, in the literary histories of most countries of Europe except Germany, than the latest decades of the eighteenth century.

But for one thing that it did,[1] we must not leave

---

[1] And perhaps for another — that we may observe the utmost equity to it. Not merely does the "Augustan" character *make* such men as Pope and Voltaire, but it may fairly claim a great part

it thus. After what was said previously about the excellences of the more gorgeous prose, it would hardly be fair to leave the classical variety, which is the outcome of this period or these two periods, without its due meed. It has been said that the more magnificent prose-writing was rather unequally distributed in Europe—that, indeed, it is doubtful whether any other country can rival England in it. This was not the case with its own rival and supplanter. England, indeed, again heads the race, for (the Italians excepted, who have always in prose, from the time of Boccaccio, maintained a level of merit broken by feebler heights and depths than their verse, and than the prose of any other country) it would be difficult to find any one at his own time, but not in his own country, to match Hooker. But, for a time, the other style, though not exclusively cultivated, was preferred with us. It was in France, with Balzac and Descartes, with Pascal and Malebranche, with Molière and Bossuet, that "classical" prose made its real modern start, though our men, from Dryden onwards, quickly took up the running.

As in so many things, it is impossible to decide between the two in the offhand and unhesitating manner in which uneducated or half-educated people love. If we take pleasure—the *delectare*—as the cri-

in the making of such very different men as, for instance, Molière in the first period and Fielding in the second, who are less exclusively its children. It is difficult to say how much their genius owes to its discipline and gymnastic. In particular the comedy of manners and the novel, as distinguished from the romance, would have been almost impossible without its creation of simple but flexible prose.

terion,—which it certainly is of poetry, but not quite so certainly of prose,—gorgeous prose will certainly give us nobler gusts, more poignant ecstasies—*when it does give them*. But when it is a failure, it will give us shocks—*dis*gusts—which are very unpleasant things indeed; while the quality of pleasure given by polished classical prose is not contemptible, the quantity of it is great, and its liability to failure is not of a shocking description. But when we turn to usefulness — to the *prodesse*, which probably is the criterion of prose as it is not of poetry—plain prose has, it is clear, an immense advantage. Merely to convey matter of any kind—except those appeals to the emotions, the imagination, which poetry does better still,—it is a question whether very gorgeous prose is a good vehicle at all. And undoubtedly the vehicular business of prose, for the most part, *is* to convey matter. At any rate,—inglorious or even immoral as the compromise may seem,—it is better to be happy with both. If (which is luckily not the case) monogamy were imperative, the plainer beauty should no doubt be preferred. For poetry will come to the rescue here, and there is nothing to do the other work except plain prose.

Fortunately, to recur to what was said above, no principle ever has universal and tyrannic sway,— *The Romantic rally.* there is always a literary Asturias in which the forces of the past, however hard driven and hard bested, are recuperating themselves, and mustering into an army of the future.

In England, as we have seen and said, these forces were in a very peculiar condition. The principles of Romanticism were decried; but Shakespeare, the greatest Romantic writer in the world, and Milton, the greatest combiner of Romantic and Classic, held secure positions. Moreover, the chain, if not of pure Romantic writers, of writers who, in this and that way, act on Romantic principles, is absolutely unbroken. Lady Winchelsea herself spans the whole Augustan period in a life lasting from the time when Milton had more than a decade to live, to the time when Gray was a young man. *The Seasons* appear, in part at least, before some of the most characteristic parts of Pope. And the historical and antiquarian tendencies of the eighteenth century bring the old to support, refresh, strengthen the new. Attention is turned earliest in Scotland, a very little later in England, and a little later still in Germany, to the ballad,—that "lifebuoy of poetry," as it has been termed. The great old writers in almost all countries begin to be critically edited, often by pedants and dryasdusts, but still with the result of attracting attention to them, and of substituting at least knowledge of a kind for mere and utter ignorance. And with this knowledge comes, slowly or not slowly, but surely, first the suggestion that perhaps—and then the conviction that certainly— Mr Waller was *not* quite the inventor of sweetness in English numbers, that many people came before Malherbe, that even Villon "disembroiled" very little, while he inherited much, that Spenser was an exquisite poet and Chaucer a wonderful "critic of life," that Italian and German and French and English and Spanish romance had infinite stores of power and of charm—that, in short, literature is *continuous*, and that no period has a right to say, "I am the time of perfection: everything else is immature or decadent."

The work went on[1] somewhat slowly and irregularly, as so often happens — with apparent reactions and hesitations, with mistakes that look odd now, but were more or less inevitable, with charlataneries and mystifications and caricatures. Yet almost everything contributed—the reactions and delays by preventing too hurried growth, the mistakes by the discovery that they *were* mistakes, the charlataneries and caricatures by attracting immature and weak tastes, which educated themselves later to better things. And in one country—Germany, the most backward of all hitherto — the new growth of literature, after a slight period of hesitation, turned almost wholly in the Romantic direction, even when it gave itself airs of Classicism.

It is not, in such a summary as this, desirable to dwell as a rule, or even as a frequent exception, on individuals. But, in connection with this particular period, there is a phenomenon — remarkable in its very individual aspect, but more remarkable still as illustrating a characteristic—which was to distinguish, not by any means wholly for good, the whole of the

---

[1] See *The Romantic Revolt.*

Nineteenth Century.   This is the Influence of Goethe on the individual side — the Literary Influence on the general.

We have nothing here to do with *estimating* Goethe: that has been done, and done excellently, in the proper place, with results which anybody may accept, reject, or qualify as he chooses and feels competent. But it is scarcely matter of controversy [1] that he exercised an influence hardly to be paralleled before or since.   There have, perhaps, been greater men of letters: some, at least, would grant that very cheerfully.   But these have, in the most undisputed cases, had far longer time in which to exercise influence, and, moreover, they have exercised it in a very different way.   People have imitated Homer, Dante, Shakespeare ; they have imitated Virgil, Ariosto, Tasso, Racine, Milton, Pope, even Addison, enormously.   But they have not made them — in fact, they could not make them—prophets and teachers in life and literature, patterns of attitude, masters, as Goethe was made by some great men and many small in all countries of Europe during the second quarter of the nineteenth century, and perhaps not a few years earlier and later.   We need not here characterise this phenomenon: we were bound to state it.   And it ought to be added that though no second example of equal magnitude has occurred,

---

[1] Even those who may think it so may excuse this passage when they come to its latter part.   It is impossible to exaggerate the exaggeration of "literary" influence in recent times.

this following—in the sense of the old Imitation as well as of this new Discipleship—has been a constant and an increasing feature of the age. Schools and "'isms" have seldom been absent in literature: but they have hardly ever been so numerously and obtrusively present as in our time. "The obsession of the printed book" has positively caricatured itself. Not only have reviewers—at least those who are also critics—come to recognise the different "taps" that come before them as simply drawn off from certain stock casks, but it apparently takes no time to establish a stock cask. In Germany, as one would expect, most of all, but in other countries also, you may find solemn treatises, or tracts, or tractatules on "The Art of A." or "B. as Thinker and Writer," when A. and B. have scarcely run up a decade of years, or a half dozen of not extensive volumes, as poets, or novelists, or playwrights.

To return to the main current, the Romantic ferment of Germany, though set up by yeast mainly imported from England, was there so violent and unmistakable that it exercised a strong reflex influence on English literature itself, and had not a little to do— in connection with the political and mental stimulus of the French Revolution—in bringing about the vast and various developments of the early Nineteenth Century in our country. First Goethe, Schiller, and their compatriots for Germany itself, and then for the greater part of Europe; next Scott and Byron for almost the world, as well as for England, with Coleridge, Wordsworth, Shelley, and Keats exercising

less cosmopolitan but more intensely local influence
—brought about the last great change that has been
seen in European literature.

That France should have lagged behind may seem
at first sight strange. But France had been more
straitly joined to the idols of Neo-Classicism than
any other country in Europe ; and by a chance, less
chanceful and curious than it may seem, the great
dissolving and innovating influence of her eighteenth
century, that of Voltaire, was, in literature, conservative and even reactionary. The tremendous ex-
plosion of Revolutionary sentiment did not at first,
nor for a long time, take any literary turn as it did
in England and Germany. On the contrary, literary
education and literary effort were at their lowest
points from the destruction of the old *régime* to the
Napoleonic attempt to put something in its place.
The two persons of literary genius, however (perhaps
the only two, with the exception of the bright but
slender and soon quenched light of André Chénier),
whom France could boast between the deaths of
Voltaire and Diderot and the rise of Lamartine, or
rather Hugo, Chateaubriand and Madame de Staël,
though neither was quite a pure-blooded Romantic,
worked with great power in the Romantic direction.
They were reinforced by the influence of the Germans,
whom Madame de Staël herself introduced to France,
and, later, by that of Scott and Byron ; and in the reign
of the last legitimate Bourbon the forces of revolt
gathered head, overthrew neo-classic orthodoxy, and
for more than seventy years have, in various forms,

2 F

kept the domination. The successive waves of German, English, and French Romanticism rolled by degrees into all the other countries of Europe, reviving the older literatures, and encouraging the appearance of new, in nations which had hitherto done little, and which had exercised influence not even in proportion to what they had actually done.

Here also it seems permissible, if not even positively necessary, to say something on the men and the things which distinguished this great period of literature.[1] In the right comparison—the comparison of quality, not of rank — it is scarcely second to any; and though it may be idle to attempt to add any special representative of it to the trinity of Homer, Dante, and Shakespeare, it is certain that neither Antiquity nor the Renaissance can excel, and that the warmest rational lover of the Middle Ages cannot pretend that they equalled, the production in the various European countries of the period (a little longer than a century) between the literary appearance of Goethe and the deaths of Tennyson and Hugo. It is elsewhere argued that this period is practically *solid*, and that its dominant characteristic throughout, with whatever variation of phase, is Romantic. But what we have to do with is not so much this spirit in the abstract— that also is dealt with elsewhere—as its manifestations in the concrete. It is difficult to say from

The Nineteenth Century as a whole.

[1] See *The Romantic Triumph* and the earlier part of the present volume.

which point of view the accomplishment of the period
is the more striking—that which considers the Evolution of Kinds, or that which, refusing to crib and
cabin within the Kind the infinity of literature and
of life, concerns itself with individual performance.

From the former it is so remarkable that one understands—in looking back upon it—why criticism by
Kinds has again become popular. The nineteenth
century in the wide sense, though it did not originate
the Novel, saw the growth of it from a sort of "sport"
of the Romance into an organism of such importance
and complication that some, letting the true historic
clew slip from them, have sometimes been half
tempted to regard the Romance as merely a variety
of *it*. It has almost attained—it would be arbitrary
to say "usurped"—the pride of place which in other
times has been held by the Epic and the Drama. It
has combined their attractions and appeals. It has
—whether for good or ill is another and an unnecessary question — ousted the Sermon as the regular
reading material of the unliterary. It has shown
itself capable of adaptation to almost every variety
of purpose, of developing the best style as well as of
admitting the worst, of almost supplanting Poetry,
of pushing History from its seat, of antiquating
Philosophy herself, of supplying a trusty ally or
a formidable foe to Religion, of assuming almost
every literary colour, borrowing almost every literary
weapon, offering opportunity for the display of almost
every literary quality—as well as of some qualities
very unliterary.

Of far more interest, at any rate to some tastes, are the individual results of this development. The work of Godwin and his contemporaries in England, of Pigault - Lebrun in France, requires the historic estimate to give it much charm for us now. But it is very different even with the work in fiction (exceedingly moderate as is its pure *novel* - interest) of Chateaubriand and of Madame de Staël; more different still with that of Miss Austen; most different with that of Scott. Here are once more masterpieces, and masterpieces in a new kind. Here are additions to the stories, the places, the personages, which are more real than reality, more true than truth. And here, in a new fashion, is that which is most interesting of all to human nature—the power of that nature in Art, increased, renewed, exemplified afresh. It is difficult to imagine the House of Literature without the gallery of pictures and portraits which stretches from *Udolpho* and *Atala* and *Pride and Prejudice* to *Esmond* and *Saint-Julien l'Hospitalier*. It is easier to conceive the loss it would be if we knew that we had had this great collection, and yet knew not what the collection actually contained.

There can be little doubt that in this department the representative figure for World Literature is Scott. It is not merely that he created a kind—the Historical Novel — which people had been trying and failing to create for some two thousand years; nor that he led up to that creation by an only less surprising revival of the older art of interesting narration in verse. These things are of chief value, perhaps, to the special students of literary history. To the rest of us the things that he did in doing this are the points of attraction—the "lands of clear colours and stories" that he opened up for us, the troops of personages whom he made our familiar friends, the "interiors" that through his pages we have entered and lived in as though they were our own houses, the conversation that we have heard, the feats and fights that we have seen, through his magical agency. Of his marvellous influence abroad as well as at home, of the range—far greater than is allowed by purblind and conventional criticism—of his literary aptitudes, we cannot speak here. But the whole is such a whole as again it is difficult to parallel, and once more the "aggregate score"—the total achievement—challenges something little short of primacy.

One is not able to single out in the same way any single representative or product of the other great characteristic development of this period—the Periodical itself. But as a Kind, and for number and variety of authors and works to be subsumed under it, this will equal, if it does not even excel, the novel. And even more than in the case of the novel, there is a direct connection between this kind and the Romantic Triumph itself. The variety, the catholicity, the indiscriminateness indeed, of the newspaper adjust themselves much better to Romantic than to Classical principles. This is especially the case in regard to the kinds of literature which the newspaper more especially assists, and which may be said to be, with political writing, the chief of its really literary constituents—the Novel itself, and the critical and miscellaneous Essay. We need hardly say more of the former; but it is not superfluous to remark that serial — even piecemeal — publication certainly encourages the repeated and not very closely connected incident and the variety of character and underplot which are characteristic of Romantic fiction, while it is essentially, and not merely accidentally, unfavourable to the more Classical Unities.

Of the critical and miscellaneous Essay, on the other hand, we must speak a little more fully. It, like the novel, is mainly an English product—in fact, as regards its main developments, it is almost wholly so. Montaigne may be the nominal *atavus*, and in manner at least he may be something more. But it is not till Dryden — for the alleged priority of Corneille in the critical *Essay* as opposed to the critical *Dissertation* may be modestly but firmly questioned—that one kind of the modern "article" appears; not till Addison (with a doubtful, but still English, forerunner in Cowley) that other kinds definitely crystallise themselves. The force of this crystallisation (communicated through Marivaux and others to the Continent) was so great that the eighteenth century hardly saw another. It was not till the very close thereof that fresh shootings of the liquid took place: and these, irregularly and rather formlessly but early in Germany, a little later but with much more variety and vigour in England (for here France was again much later), came—through the agency of the newspaper itself in its various forms from daily to quarterly—to constitute and substantiate, in the most unmistakable fashion, a new and important kind of literature.

At first sight this Kind, in its various representatives and representations from Cobbett to Sainte-Beuve, may seem "a shape that shape has none," or at least one too Protean and bewildering to characterise. But by degrees certain communities of character emerge. On the one hand there is the general feature of the Essay that it *is* an "essay"—a "try" at the subject—rather than a professedly complete handling of it. But, on the other, there is something which vindicates the kind from Ben Jonson's scornful but (save as regards Montaigne himself) not entirely unjust fling at its early examples, to the effect that they were "flashy" and unoriginal, mere bundles of borrowings and citations, with the last read author uppermost. Undoubtedly a vast number of inferior essays and articles do still underlie this answer: you may still find papers and volumes of papers where, if the old image of stripping stolen matter were applied, there would be not only, in the contemporary phrase, "not a rag to cover——," but there would be nothing for the rag *to* cover—no nakedness even, no flesh, no bones, nothing. But in every good essay—even in every good article — there is something which connects itself, not merely accidentally but essentially and logically, with one of the acknowledged characteristics of Romanticism itself—the prominence of Individuality. An essayist—and even a journalist— who cannot give to his work what Goldsmith's Mrs

Tibbs called " a little of my own sauce," is merely a more or less expert précis-writer. It is in this quality of personality that the greatness of the great Essay writers—Coleridge, who, however, concentrated it too little; his pupils, Lamb and Hazlitt; De Quincey, Sainte-Beuve, Arnold, Pater—consists. Even in the lighter vein—the new Essay of the *Spectator* kind, which started with Leigh Hunt—the same quality is the *sine qua non*. The writer ought to have something of his own—imagined or observed—to say: he must have something of his own in his way of saying it, if he is to be of any real value.

Few words are needed on the immense *diffusion* of literary treatment that the development of the periodical involves. As compared with the book, and even with the pamphlet, the periodical has the action of a rose or a spray in contrast with that of a spout or a tap. But this peculiarity is of a double kind: it affects the author as well as the subject. Where the book or the pamphlet is single-sourced, the periodical is *polypidax:* it draws from a hundred fountains to disperse in a thousand streamlets. That there are dangers and drawbacks as well as advantages in this is, of course, clear enough. Any subject whatever is probably capable of satisfactory literary treatment by the right person: that again is a proposition in direct connection with the head-ideas of the Romantic school, and so constitutes a fresh grace of congruity between this kind and its period. But it may be very profoundly doubted whether every person is the right person — even to treat some one subject. In fact, without being a hopeless pessimist and cynic, one may push the doubt to the extent of questioning whether any but a very small minority of mankind have any real qualifications for literary treatment of *any* subject. But this is a different matter. There is—let us grant—in the periodical system the certainty of much bad and more indifferent production. Its saving point is the possibility—which without it would be greatly lessened—of the production of a little good.

The influence of the movement, or if that seem too question-begging, the influences which made the movement and others, showed themselves hardly less in departments which were not so novel as the novel or so new as the newspaper. Only in Theology (with a certain exception, and that not much, for Germany) the accomplishment is not great from the literary side. Newman and Renan have to be waited for—the first for a generation, the second for two. History, following Gibbon in England, and, at a greater distance, Montesquieu in France, not merely in the matter of substance, contributes a vast deal to the spread of Romanticism, and is stimulated by the Romantic curiosity, but in the matter of form contributes a mighty contingent of writers and works to its own literary variety—a variety which, as a department, itself takes form under Herder and the Schlegels and Coleridge. The Sciences also—political and natural—already feeling the impulse of development on their own lines, and not yet parting company with those of literature, enrich the latter not a little; and a variety of book - writing, hardly less multifarious than that of the periodical, comes to increase the enrichment.

The most remarkable, however, without doubt, of the refreshments of the older departments of European *prose* was seen in the case of Philosophy. Here the process was, indeed, more continuous—if only with the continuity of reaction and revolt—than in most others; for the procession of Descartes, Locke (whose literary side was by far his weakest, but who, after all, was a man of letters in his way), Leibnitz, Hume, and Kant is practically unbroken. But the great German trio — Fichte - Schelling - Hegel — connects itself with the Romantic outbreak in the most remarkable fashion, as has been amply shown in the volume devoted to the subject. And the inbreak of partly German thought, through Coleridge, into England, and through various (in the first place mainly Goethean) channels into France, counts, especially in the former case, among the most remarkable impressions that Philosophy has made upon Literature.

And in all these cases the minor literary nations followed their leaders, — in a fashion of following sometimes less direct, sometimes more, and often varying very much in the order of the links of the chain, but always obeying the main direction of sequence, and illustrating its characteristics with an invaluable permutation of atmosphere and point of view.

Yet, after all, when one comes to reckon up the real achievements of a period in literature, it is to its Poetry that one must turn. Prose is but applied literature—it is Poetry, almost alone, that is literature pure and simple. Prose is sometimes wholly—perhaps it should always be mainly—occupied with the matter, with the mere conveyance of fact or thought, of information or argument, or whatever it may be.   Only in Poetry as a matter of essence does the form, the expression, the art, command and maintain the highest place. And it will follow, as a practically unavoidable consequence, that since fact and thought, information and argument, remain fundamentally the same (for there *is* "nothing new under the sun" in these ways), the real differences of periods and movements and phases must be sought in that division of literature which abides by the essentials of form, which can change while matter cannot.   The human intellect and the human temper reduce themselves to few varieties: the human face, gesture, speech, "ways" (as we call them), are as infinite as infinity lets itself be conceived.   And literature proper is the face, the gesture, the "ways," of the mind in written speech, —above all, in Poetry.

Here there can be, in competent judgments, little difference of opinion as to the positive greatness of the earlier Romantic period, however much individual judgments, equally competent perhaps, may differ as to its relative greatness, and as to the relative value of its contrasted constituents.   A period which produced Wordsworth, Coleridge, Scott, Byron, Shelley, and Keats; which saw the beginnings of least of the great French Romantic School and of Heine, the mighty autumn of Goethe, the shadowed genius of Leopardi; which had in England more especially, but also elsewhere, "second strings" of poets who in most other periods would have been worthy protagonists; which—in a manner of itself serving as a note of primacy—adopted and mastered, as it thought fit, every department of its kind—epic, lyric, satire, even the poetical (if not exactly the theatric-poetical) drama,—such a period can have no gainsayers outside the ranks of the incompetent and the crotcheteers. Indeed, if we take it with its natural complement in the middle and later nineteenth century, it will constitute a Major Period such as there are only two others in literary history—the blossoming and fruiting time of Greek from Æschylus to Bion, and that of the Renaissance from Boiardo to Milton. But of its general characteristics we must still say a little more.

The most important, perhaps, of these characteristics from the point of view of literary history is one which is not apparent on the surface, and which has consequently been often missed by superficial, though not by thorough, students. This is the fact that, as was *not* the case with the Renaissance to any great extent (whether it was the case in Greece or not we have no means of judging), there is a very large element of transition — a considerable lingering and looking back to the past. Only in the youngest members—in Keats, who almost belongs to the next stage, and in Heine, who actually does so— is this invisible or almost invisible. The Classicism of the Romantics has been less written about than the

Romanticism of the Classics, but as far as the earlier stage is concerned, it exists altogether beyond doubt. In Goethe it is undeniable and undenied—in fact, if we had not the second part of *Faust* to prove his real faith by almost his latest work, we might take him for a renegade and a lapsed one altogether, as he certainly was a blasphemer occasionally. In Scott the mixture is more a question of streaks — he is sometimes almost pure eighteenth century. The same is the case with Wordsworth, who indeed, as Mr Vaughan has justly pointed out, is a sort of Romantic free-lance, and in some ways not a Romantic at all. As for Byron, his rather blatant Classicism was most certainly not mere pose, but genuine conviction; while his Romanticism is mainly of the cloak-and-sword and local-colour kind, not the pure Romance of *The Ancient Mariner* or *Proud Maisie.* Shelley, here as elsewhere, stands alone. That his inspiration was notoriously classical, not mediæval, is quite indecisive. But it is not mere paradox or mere *galimatias* to say that his poetry is rather Romantic because it is the essence of poetry, and so contains all possible poetic qualities in perfection, than because it has the special Romantic differences in a highly developed degree. It is Romantic as Æschylus and Sappho are Romantic. No doubt this is to be so in the best sense of the term, but it is hardly to be so in the fullest, or the most characteristic.

Still in all these, and in others,[1] an advance is made

[1] The thesis could be worked out in striking examples from Schiller to Lamartine.

much greater than the retrogression—if such it is to
be termed. This advance is on different lines—lines
which, indefinitely in length but definitely in scope,
converge towards the inaccessible but ever-tempting
goal of Romance. There is besides the great compass-
given line of imagination, the line of vagueness, the
line of personality, the line of recourse to the mediæval—others too many to label. But the most important, perhaps, to poetry and in poetry is a double
line—the line of increased and combined appeal to eye
and ear. This has continued to the present day, and
is dealt with in the earlier part of this Conclusion and
also in the body of the present volume. But it is in
the period of the Romantic Triumph that it first makes
a definite and distinct appearance.

The still later and latest phases have been touched
in the earlier part of this Conclusion, of which the
latest of them form the actual subject, and it would
be inartistic as well as tautologous to rediscuss them
here. It is enough to say that German, which led the
movement, ceased first to contribute to it importantly;
that English after some ninety, and French after at
least seventy, years of production, almost incredible in
volume, variety, and vigour, have for some two decades been distinctly less distinguished; and that the
younger or young-old literatures, however interesting
and fertile, have scarcely yet developed either kinds
of practice, or individual practitioners, on a level with
the great older kinds from the Greek epic and tragedy
to the English drama and novel, or with the great
writers from Homer downwards. On the other hand,

no literary movement has ever worked itself out with more fulness or under more favourable conditions than the Romantic, which, as we have endeavoured to show, is not in one sense "worked out" even yet. And certainly no century has ever contributed a *quota* of literature more lavish in volume, more instinct with power, more free from monotony and limitation, or more abounding in delight.

Nothing, therefore, is here for complaint or dissatisfaction, even if it be impossible to pronounce the opening of the twentieth century one of the palmy times of European literature. But the lesson of the whole history is, in a sober and philosophic fashion, quite as cheering. Those who study it with the faculty of learning will draw from it as little of the hot-headed delusion called belief in progress as of the cold fit of despair, which holds that everything *ruit in pejus*. They will probably — though this is very much a matter of taste and temperament —draw from it a very profound *dis*belief in any easily calculable ratio of connection between national and literary idiosyncrasy, between political and literary events, between criticism and creation, between a dozen other pairs of causes and effects which the "philosophic" writer loves to couple together, however hard they strain at the leash. They will perhaps come to the conclusion that while much mediate and average calculation is possible, while nothing is more unwise than to "like grossly" and to neglect the examination of the causes of pleasure, the wind of the spirit blows where it lists, and mocks all attempts to foretell the times and the seasons of its blowing or to discover the causes why it has blown.   But they may, and it is hoped they will, find in the history of the actual accomplishment—in the wind-chart of the past—not a little that must instruct them, and perhaps something that they may enjoy.

INDEX.

2 G

THE END.

PRINTED BY WILLIAM BLACKWOOD AND SONS.